7

AF770369

Table of Contents

Table of Contents

Program Installation

Course Introduction

Chapter 1
Anatomy & Physiology Overview

Chapter 2
Body Chemistry

Chapter 3
Cells and Tissues

Chapter 4
The Integumentary System

Chapter 5
The Skeletal System

Chapter 7
The Nervous System Organization

Chapter 8
The Central Nervous System

Chapter 9
The Peripheral Nervous System

Chapter 10
The Somatic and Autonomic Nervous System

Chapter 11
Sensory Organs

Chapter 12
The Endocrine System

Chapter 13
Cardiovascular System: The Blood

Chapter 16
The Respiratory System

Chapter 17
The Digestive System

Chapter 18
The Urinary System

Chapter 19
The Reproductive System

Chapter 20
Inheritance

Credits and Acknowledgments

MedWorks(TM) - Anatomy & Physiology

Published by: Victory Technology, Inc.

Project Directors: John Stalcup, Ph.D. and Peter J. McAliney, B.S.

Editors: John Stalcup, Ph.D., Robert Meckler, Ph.D., Sandra Sephton, M.S., and Karen Zabel, M.S.

Authors: John Stalcup, Ph.D., Sandra Sephton, M.S., Rajneesh Nath, M.D., Elizabeth Quinn, M.D., Robert Meckler, Ph.D., Karen Zabel, M.S., Lisa Harper M.S., Lisa Temple, B.S., Rachel Hartshorn, MS II, and Jill Abramson, MS IV

Curriculum Design: John Stalcup, Ph.D. and Peter J. McAliney, B.S.

Program Software: Matthew Gordon, P.E., B.S., Dand, Inc.

Medical Illustrators: Thomas Sephton, A.B. and Lainie Nunn

Product Testing: Peter J. McAliney, B.S. and Gabrielle Lewis

Technical Editors: Mark Higuera, M.B.A. and Barton George, M.B.A.

Package Design and Copy: Paul Hammond, M.A., Susan Wood, B.S., and Thomas Sephton, A.B.

Product Production: Terry Chew, TC, Inc.

Administration: Julia McCarthy, B.S. and Gabrielle Lewis

Special Thanks to: Thomas and Charlotte Phillips, Pete and Zeta McAliney, Toby Burgelin, Frank Floyd, Joel Koerschen, Patrick Pangan, Arthur E. Newman, Fred Fusting, Joan Caldwell, Elizabeth Randolph, Helen Beirne, John Leckenby, and Daniel McCarthy.

User Information: The curriculum, illustrations, and software course in *Med-Works(TM) - Anatomy & Physiology* are subject to change and updates. The user is asked to report any omissions or errors in the present edition to the Publisher.

Dedications

This work is dedicated to my wife, Julia, and my children, Olivia and Michael, for their unconditional love, support, and patience.

John Stalcup

June, 1995

My effort in this work is dedicated to my family, for their never ending support and encouragement and their commitment to the future of education.

Peter J. McAliney

June, 1995

Program Installation

Course Components

Check your *MedWorks* courseware package for the following items. Software and Workbooks will correspond to your license agreement.

- *MedWorks* Program Installation Diskettes or CD-ROM
- *MedWorks Student Workbook*

System Requirements

- IBM PC 386 or greater
- Windows 3.1 or greater (with mouse)
- 256 color SVGA monitor and video card
- 4 MB RAM (8 MB RAM recommended for animations) *
- CD-ROM reader and 12 MB hard disk space *
- Printer and sound board are optional but recommended

* For increased video performance, you can copy the videos from the CD-ROM in the subdirectory D:\VIDEO to the subdirectory C:\MEDWRKAP\VIDEO on your hard drive. This will require an additional 18 MB of hard disk space.

Software Installation

The setup program will direct you through the installation of *MedWorks(TM)*. To install the software, follow the steps below:

- Boot up your computer with Windows(TM) 3.1 or greater
- Place *MedWorks - Anatomy & Physiology (TM)* CD ROM into your computer
- From Windows, select **File, Run** and then type: **a:\setup**

Follow the installation instructions provided on-screen. During the installation, some files will be placed on your hard drive while others will remain on the CD- ROM.

If you have any questions as you proceed, check to see that your computer meets the system requirements and that it is configured properly. If you are still experiencing difficulty, call Victory Technology at (415) 431-0225.

Important Note For Institutional Users

In the Institutional version of *MedWorks - A & P* the instructor has special access to the **Grading Tools** and components of the **MedWorks Setup**. Instructor access to these course components is established at installation time.

The password corresponding to the first registrant of the *MedWorks - A & P* course will have the only access to the **Grading Tools** and all components of the **Medworks Setup**. It is important to remember the password you used in order to gain access to all of the customizable components of *MedWorks - A & P.*

Software Operations

Starting *MedWorks - A & P* 

When you've finished with the *MedWorks* software installation, you can start the program from Windows by double-clicking on the program icon in the Victory Courseware program group that is automatically created when you install *MedWorks* under Windows(TM) .

The first time you enter *MedWorks - A & P*, the Registration Form screen will appear, whereby you will register for *MedWorks - A & P* and set your system configuration. (Subsequent entry into the course will present only the *MedWorks - A & P* start up screen.) Enter your first name, last name, Company/School/Association, and password (optional). Note, if you do not specify a password, you will have to call Victory Technology to obtain access to the Grading Tools and MedWorks Setup. You can also configure *MedWorks - A & P* for color configuration (256 or 65K/16.8M) and color shifts (Is "The Thinker" Blue or Brown?). Check your computer's documentation or use the Windows Setup to see what color configuration options you have available. If "The Thinker" first appears Brown, indicate that by clicking on the Brown button, and when you exit the registration screen, *MedWorks - A & P* will properly adjust the colors to display the image. Use the **Tab** key or mouse to move between fields on the registration screen.

After you enter your name and color information, click on the Register button or tab to the Register button and press the **Enter** key. By registering for the course, *MedWorks - A & P* will create a transcript file that will record your progress through the course. More specifically, it will record your results for the Knowledge Survey, Final Exam, Chapter Exams, and Lesson Exam scores.

To begin *MedWorks - A & P*, click on the **Start Medworks** icon which will bring you to the Table of Contents. (If you had entered a password you will have to type it in before you proceed to the Table of Contents.) Begin the *MedWorks - A & P* course by clicking on the *MedWorks - A & P Overview.* Important information about the course, navigation through the course, and other general information about the course is presented in this section. Upon completion of the

MedWorks - A & P Overview, proceed directly to the Knowledge Survey. After you complete the Knowledge Survey, proceed through the course. Upon completion of the Final Exam, you will have completed the *MedWorks - A & P* course.

Program Commands

Program Icons for operation the *MedWorks - A & P* software are listed below:

Course Table of Contents

- **Bookshelf Icon**

Click to enter the main dictionary.

- **Closed Book Icon**

Click to return to the *MedWorks - A & P* Start Up screen.

Chapter Table of Contents

- **Left Arrow/Right Arrow Button(s)**

Click to turn to the previous chapter or next chapter.

- **Table of Contents Icon**

Click to return to the Table of Contents.

- **Bookshelf Icon**

Click to enter the chapter dictionary.

• **Pen and Paper Icon**

Click to go directly to the chapter exam.

• **Closed Book Icon**

Click to return to the Start Up screen.

Lesson Window

Hyperlinked terms are those terms that are defined or pronounced in the *Med-Works - A & P* dictionary. They appear **bolded** in the lesson. Clicking on a hyperlinked term will present its definition and clicking on the **Speaker** icon in the definition box will pronounce the term for you. Terms that have previously appeared as hyperlinks, or are to be emphasized, appear in *italics*.

• **Hide/Show Button**

Above the text on the left, click to toggle display of **hyperlinked** or *emphasized* terms on/off.

• **Left Arrow/Right Arrow Button(s)**

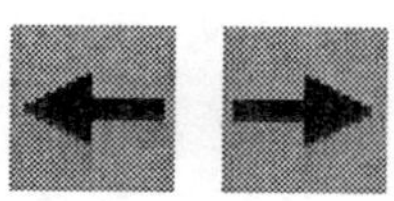

Click to turn to the previous page or next page.

• **Balloon Icons**

Click the black-and-white balloon to cycle through the balloons one at a time. Click the colored balloon to autocycle through the balloons.

- **Video Strip Icon** — Click to launch animation.

- **Bookshelf Icon** — Click to enter the chapter dictionary.

- **Pen and Paper Icon** — Click to go directly to the lesson exam.

- **Open Book Icon** — Click to go to the Chapter Table of Contents.

Exam Window

- **Right Arrow Button** — Click to turn to the next question.

- **Open Book Icon** — Click to Exit to the Chapter Table of Contents.

Dictionary Window

- **Search Window**
  (Located under the list of terms in the dictionary)

  Click in the blank box under the listed terms and type in the requested term for look up.

- **Ear Icon**

  Click to hear the term pronounced.

- **Open Book Icon**

  Click to go to the Chapter Table of Contents.

Grading Tools

To see a graphical representation of your progress through the course, click the **Grading Tools** icon. If you have chosen a password, you will need to enter this password to view your personal results. *MedWorks - A & P* will graphically present your results for the Knowledge Survey, Final Exam, and Chapter Exams. You can view the results of your Chapter Exams by average score, highest score, lowest score, first score, and last score.

Program Icons for the Grading Tools are listed below:

- **Printer Icon**

  Click to print a report of all of your scores (including Lesson Exam scores).

- **Open Book Icon**

Click to return to the *MedWorks - A & P* Start Up screen.

For a printed report of all of your scores (including Lesson Exam scores), click the **Printer** icon which is located in the lower right hand corner.

MedWorks Setup

MedWorks - A & P is shipped with defaults for System Configuration, File Locations, Lesson/Chapter Setup, and Exam Setup. However, you have the capability to set your preferences for these different features within *MedWorks - A & P.*

System Configuration

Click in **Display HyperText** to have the hyperlinked terms in the lessons (i.e., those terms that you can click on to see their definition and hear their pronunciation) appear in bold and those terms that are emphasized or have previously been presented as a hyperlinked term appear in italics. Clicking this option in the **MedWorks Setup** will set the default each time you enter *MedWorks - A & P.* Additionally, within a session, you can toggle this feature on and off in the lesson window by clicking on the **Hide/Show Button** appearing on the top right of the lesson text.

Click **Display Image Hotspots** to show the outline of underlying area of detail for the balloons appearing on the illustrations.

Click **24 Bit Color Shift** on or off if "The Thinker" appears Brown when moving from section to section. You may have to reset the color shift if the graphics display has been changed in the Windows System Setup. Please refer to your Windows manual for more information on graphics display and Windows System Setup.

Enter the display time (in milliseconds, e.g., 3500 is 3.5 seconds) in **Balloon Autocycle Time** for balloons when you select the **Autocycle Balloons** icon in the lessons.

You can also exclude chapters in the generation of the Knowledge Survey and Final Exam if you will not be taking the entire course. Click those chapters that are to be excluded so that they appear gray.

File Locations

The Program Path, Course Path, Image Path, Sound Path, Video Path, and Dictionary Path are all set at installation. Each of the components of the course has both a Primary File Location and Secondary File Location to accommodate curriculum updates. If you want to change any of the paths, highlight the appropriate path and click the **Modify** button. Use the browser to redirect the path and then click the **OK** button.

Note, that if you move the videos to your hard drive to enhance system performance, you will have to modify the **Video Path** to indicate this path change.

Lesson/Chapter Setup

You can indicate your preference to Allow Answer Retry, Allow To Retake Test, Show Correct Answer, number of questions and passing percentage for Lesson Quick Check Questions and Chapter Exams. You can also indicate a chapter exam time for Chapter Exams.

Note, to access all of the Quick Check Questions, leave the number of questions at the default value of **99**. Chapter Exams will randomly select the specified number of questions from the Quick Check Questions in the Lessons.

Additionally, you may change the time period for the Chapter Exam in the Chapter Exam Time field.

Exam Setup

You can change the title that appears on the Table of Contents for the Pre Test and Post Test.

You can indicate your preference to Allow Answer Retry, Allow To Retake Exam, Show Correct Answer, number of questions and passing percentage for the Pre Test and Post Test. You can also indicate a Final Exam time for the Post Test.

The Pre-Test and Final Exam will randomly select the specified number of questions from those chapters that are to be included in exam generation.

Additionally, you may change the time period for the Final Exam in the Final Exam Time field.

Exit

To exit the *MedWorks - A & P* course and return to Windows, click the **Stop** icon.

Sources

Agur, Anne M.R., and Ming J. Lee, Grant's Atlas of Anatomy, 9th ed., Williams & Wilkins, Baltimore, 1991.

Berkow, Robert, et al. (eds.), The Merck Manual of Diagnosis and Therapy, 15th ed., Merck & Co., Rahway, N.J., 1987.

Bullock, John, et al., Physiology, 2d ed., Harwal Publishing, Philadelphia, 1991.

Burkitt, H. George, et al., Wheater's Functional Histology: A Text and Colour Atlas, 3d ed., Churchill Livingstone, Edinburgh, 1993.

Chabner, Davi-Ellen, The Language of Medicine, 4th ed., W.B. Saunders Company, Philadelphia, 1991.

Clemente, Carmine D., Anatomy: A Regional Atlas of the Human Body, 3d ed., Urban & Schwartzenberg, Baltimore, 1987.

Edlin, Gordon, Human Gentics: A Modern Synthesis, Jones and Bartlett, Boston, 1990.

Gartner, Leslie P., and James L. Hiatt, Color Atlas of Histology, 2d ed., Williams & Wilkins, Baltimore, 1994.

Gray, Henry, Gray's Anatomy, 30th American ed., Lea & Febiger, Philadelphia, 1985.

Hall-Craggs, E.C.B., Anatomy as a Basis for Clinical Medicine, 2d ed., Williams & Wilkins, Baltimore, 1990.

Hensyl, William R. (ed.), Stedman's Medical Dictionary, 25th ed., Williams & Wilkins, Baltimore, 1990.

Hole, John W., Jr., Human Anatomy & Physiology, 6th ed., Wm. C. Brown Publishers, Dubuque, 1993.

McCance, Kathryn L., and Sue E. Huether, Pathopysiology: The Biologic Basis for Disease in Adults and Children, C.V. Mosby, St. Louis, 1990.

Moore, Keith L., Clinically Oriented Anatomy, 3d ed., Williams & Wilkins, Baltimore, 1992.

Netter, Frank H., Atlas of Human Anatomy, Ciba-Geigy Corp., Summit, N.J., 1989.

Sieg, Kay W., and Sandra P. Adams, Illustrated Essentials of Musculoskeletal Anatomy, 2d ed., Megabooks, Gainsville, 1985.

Slaby, Frank J., et al., Gross Anatomy in the Practice of Medicine, Lea & Febiger, Philadelphia, 1994.

Stent, Gunther S., and Richard Calendar, Molecular Genetics: An Introductory Narrative, 2d ed., W.H. Freeman and Company, San Francisco, 1978.

Streitwieser, Andrew Jr., and Clayton H. Heathcock, Introduction to Organic Chemistry, Macmillan, New York, 1976.

Thibodeau, Gary A., and Kevin T. Patton, Anatomy & Physiology, 2d ed., C.V. Mosby, St. Louis, 1993.

Tortora, Gerard J., and Sandra Reynolds Grabowski, Principles of Anatomy and Physiology, 7th ed., Harper Collins, New York, 1993.

Van De Graaff, Kent M., Human Anatomy, 4th ed., Wm. C. Brown Publishers, Dubuque, Iowa, 1995.

Van De Graaff, Kent M. and Stuart Ira Fox, Concepts of Human Anatomy and Physiology, 4th ed., Wm. C. Brown Publishers, Dubuque, Iowa, 1995.

Van De Graaff, Kent M. and Stuart Ira Fox, Concepts of Human Anatomy and Physiology, 3d ed., Wm. C. Brown Publishers, Dubuque, Iowa, 1992.
Watson, James D., Molecular Biology of the Gene, 3d ed., W.A. Benjamin, Inc., Menlo Park, 1977.

West, John B. (ed.), Best and Taylor's Physiological Basis of Medical Practice, 12th ed., Williams & Wilkins, Baltimore, 1990.

Wheater, Paul R., George H. Burkitt, and Victor G. Daniels, Wheater's Functional Histology: A Text and Colour Atlas, 2d ed., Churchill Livingstone, Edinburgh, 1987.

The World's Best Anatomical Charts, The Anatomical Chart Co., Skokie, Illinois, 1993.

Course Introduction

- Welcome to *MedWorks - Anatomy and Physiology*

MedWorks - Anatomy & Physiology (A & P) is a self-instructional multimedia course designed to teach college-level concepts in human anatomy and physiology. This interactive 50-hour course presents each system of the body via beautifully rendered, 3D color illustrations. Each illustration is accompanied by basic text as well as pop-up text "balloons" which provide greater detail and actively involve the student in the learning process. Human voice pronunciations are also available to the student for over 2,500 selected terms.

As you make your way through MedWorks - *A & P,* you will quickly see the added dimension that this course brings to the instruction of anatomy and physiology. *MedWorks - A & P's* self-paced, multimedia approach helps to unlock and reinforce the sometimes difficult and complex concepts of anatomy and physiology.

MedWorks - Anatomy & Physiology was created by Victory Technology, a leading publisher of multimedia courses in the medical area. Victory courses are used by colleges, hospitals, and health care providers and services across the country.

- Instructional Philosophy of *MedWorks - A&P*

Overview

MedWorks - A & P was created by PhD.'s and M.D.'s to teach anatomy and physiology at the college level. It can serve as a fun and stimulating way to supplement classroom education or as a stand-alone, self-study course.

Course Goal

After completing the course, you'll be able to:

- Recognize and describe the anatomical structures of the human body
- Understand the physiology of the major body systems
- Understand, pronounce and spell anatomical and physiological terms

- Who will benefit from using *MedWorks - A & P*?

MedWorks - A & P provides an introduction to anatomy and physiology for college students (or advanced high school students) and for adults entering, or currently employed in, the allied health professions.

More specifically, any of the following groups will benefit from *MedWorks - A & P* training:

- Students of allied health, nursing, and other health care professions
- Professional trade schools
- Continuing education organizations
- Claims examiners in health and workers' compensation insurance companies
- Artists and art students
- Court reporters
- Medical Transcriptionists
- Anyone seeking a greater understanding of the human body's structures and functions

- Course Features

MedWorks - A & P is a complete resource for serious study acting as a powerful reference source, a language tutor, an evaluation tool and an interactive, self-study curriculum.

A Powerful Reference Source

MedWorks - A & P includes an on-line dictionary with over 2,500 terms and definitions, covering all body systems. Each word is broken down by component for easy comprehension.

A Language Tutor

At a touch of a key any term in the Dictionary is pronounced by a human voice, quickly building your vocabulary of anatomical and physiological terms.

An Evaluation Tool

MedWorks - A & P tracks your progress and automatically stores the results of your Pre-, Post, and Re-Tests, as well as chapter quizzes, for on-line review and hardcopy printout. Instant feedback on your progress is readily accessible, so you can see at a glance how your knowledge of anatomy and physiology has improved.

An Interactive, Self-study Curriculum

You can learn at your own speed from a multimedia curriculum consisting of text, color illustrations, pronunciations, quizzes and tests, which quickly enhance your understanding of anatomy and physiology.

- MedWorks - A & P Course Organization

MedWorks - A & P is divided into twenty chapters: one chapter for each major body system (i.e., the skeletal system, the central nervous system, etc.), an overview chapter, and chapters on body chemistry, cells and tissues, and inheritance. These chapters are then broken down into several lessons each. Each lesson presents information one screen at a time.

Each screen in each lesson includes:

- text which describes the current concept
- a color illustration associated with the text

Most screens also include:

- text "balloons" which further describe or point out part of the illustration
- key terms in quotation marks which can be pronounced by the computer or further researched in the on-line *MedWorks - A & P* Dictionary

Each lesson also includes quiz questions in multiple choice, true/false, and fill-in formats. In order to accurately gauge your progress, a pre-test is administered before you begin the course, and a post-test is taken upon completion.

- Educational Philosophy Behind MedWorks A & P

MedWorks - A & P is based upon a reflective educational approach that employs three levels of reinforcement using fill-in, true/false, and multiple choice questions. At the end of each lesson within each chapter, there are *Quick Check Questions* that reinforce understanding of the material presented in the lesson. At the end of each chapter, there are chapter review questions that reinforce understanding of the material presented in all of the lessons in the chapter. Finally, Pre-, Post-, and Re-Tests measure your knowledge of all subjects presented in the chapters of *MedWorks - A & P*.

- The Instructor's Role

Take the Course

When teaching any course, the instructor is best equipped by having an in-depth knowledge of the material being taught. Hence, the first step for the instructor is to take the *MedWorks - A & P* course. Taking the course will provide the instructor with a working knowledge of the learning process and familiarize her/him with the specific content of *MedWorks - A & P*.

How to Administer the Course

Once you have taken the course, you have two options for course instruction:

- *Independent Study - Computer Managed Instruction*
- *Classroom Study - Facilitator-Assisted Instruction*

- Independent Study - Computer Managed Instruction

MedWorks - A & P is designed to be self-instructional and its audio function is a valuable aid in learning the course terminology. Therefore, it is highly recommended that *MedWorks - A & P* with the sound option be used when learning via the *Independent Study* method.

- When using the *Independent Study* method, ask each participant to read the *MedWorks - A & P Workbook* and complete the Course Introduction in the software, which includes the purpose of the course, training instructions, and how to operate the *MedWorks - A & P* software.
- Make sure that the participant is familiar with starting the *MedWorks - A & P* software and has the appropriate computer equipment.
- Ask each participant to return a copy of their *Student Results Worksheet* from the *MedWorks - A & P Workbook* after completing the course. You may also wish to obtain a copy of their results file which is stored automatically by *MedWorks - A & P* under the name of the participant.
- **(Optional, but recommended)** Demonstrate the course by starting *MedWorks - A & P* software and by completing the following operations:
    - Start the *MedWorks - A & P* program.
    - Select *Course Introduction* on the *Chapter Guide* and go through the lesson with the participant.

Instructor Note: It is recommended that you provide participants with a distinct name/code so you may easily retrieve their results file. The procedures for retrieving the results files are given in the Results section of this Workbook.

- Classroom Study - Facilitator-Assisted Instruction

When using the *Classroom Study* method for *MedWorks - A & P* training, follow the steps listed below:

- Schedule a course introduction session. Allow a minimum of 20 minutes for course introduction, instruction, and participant questions. Before this introductory session, ask each participant to read Chapters 1 through 3 of the *MedWorks - A & P Workbook*, which include the purpose of the course, training instructions, how to operate the *MedWorks - A & P* software, and hard copy versions of the text for each lesson in the course.
- Identify the training location and the computer workstation(s) to be used. Ideally, select a quiet training room or any workstation(s) with little outside distraction. For the best results, it is important that participants have an environment conducive to learning.

- Review the *MedWorks - A & P Course Introduction* in the participant Workbook. Ask if there are any questions.
- **(Optional, but recommended)** Demonstrate the course by starting *MedWorks - A & P* software and by completing the following operations:
    - Start the *MedWorks - A & P* program.
    - Select *Course Introduction* on the *Chapter Guide* and complete the lesson.
    - Select the *Pre-Test* from the *Chapter Guide* and answer the first three questions and then exit the *Pre-Test.*
- Conclude the course introduction session with the following instructions, which are also in the *MedWorks - A & P Workbook*:
    - The *MedWorks - A & P* courseware is divided into 20 separate training *Chapters*. Complete each *Lesson* exercise in each chapter successively in the order presented in the *Chapter Guide* (*Chapter 1* through *Chapter 20)*.
    - Please note that you should only take the *Post-Test* upon completion. The *Re-Test* can be taken at a later date.

Instructor Note: Schedule the Re-Test for 60 to 90 days after the Post-Test. Also, some people are sharp early in the morning, while others concentrate better in the afternoon or evening. Within the practicalities of your working environment, try to offer the course during the part of the day when participants feel the most alert.

DO NOT CONDUCT TRAINING IN LESS THAN FOUR WEEKS. TESTING HAS SHOWN THAT LONG-TERM IMPROVEMENT IN LEARNING ANATOMY AND PHYSIOLOGY IS BEST ACHIEVED OVER FOUR TO TEN WEEKS.

- The Student's Role

How to Use the Course

As you proceed through the *Lessons* in the *MedWorks - A & P* course, the software will record the responses to the questions. The score for each *Lesson* exercise is automatically presented at the end of the exercise. You can use the *Dictionary* and *Pronounce* option to study and pronounce each term that is new to your vocabulary.

How to Use the *MedWorks - A & P Workbook*

The *MedWorks - A & P Workbook* is designed to be used in conjunction with the *MedWorks - A & P* training software. In fact, the text and questions presented in the *MedWorks - A & P* training software are also listed in the *Workbook* so that you may preview the questions prior to beginning each *Lesson*. As you proceed through the *Lesson* exercises in the course:

- You will type in or select the correct answer when presented with a question in the *MedWorks - A & P* course. You are given two chances to answer with the correct response in the *Lessons* and chapter *Review Questions*.

- You should write in the correct response to each question in the *MedWorks - A & P Workbook.*

- You can use the *Dictionary* and *Pronounce* option to review the definition and pronunciation of terms new to your vocabulary.

Following this procedure will speed your learning, and when you complete the course, the *Workbook* will serve as a reference source which you can keep for future use.

Completing Chapters and Lessons

MedWorks - A & P consists of 20 *Chapters*, and each *Chapter* has several separate learning exercises. For example, the first chapter of *MedWorks - A & P* includes the *Course Introduction*, the *Pre-Test*, and the *Anatomy & Physiology - Overview* sub-chapters. You should proceed through each exercise in each chapter sequentially, completing the first chapter first and the last chapter last.

It is recommended that you complete one-half to one chapter per training session (that is, about two to three hours per training session), spacing the training sessions at least one day apart. It is also recommended that you begin each new training session by first reviewing the last chapter (or portion) you have completed in the previous training session to refresh your memory of concepts previously learned.

You should use this *MedWorks - A & P Workbook* and software to review chapters before beginning a new one.

Pre- and Post-Tests

MedWorks - A & P begins and ends with a test. The Pre- and Post-Tests will aid in determining how well you have learned the material presented in the course. Make sure that you complete the Pre-Test prior to completing any of the chapters in *MedWorks - A & P* (with the exception of the *Course Introduction* exercise). Also, you should complete the Post-Test only after you have completed all of the preceding chapters in *MedWorks - A & P.*

- Final Learning Tips

As you go through the *MedWorks - A & P* course, remember to:

- Take your time.
- Master each chapter before going on to the next. Each chapter builds on previous chapters. If you go too fast, you will quickly feel lost.
- Use the *Dictionary* to study the definitions of terms. The *Dictionary* may be called up from any *MedWorks - A & P Lesson.*
- Use the *Pronounce* option in the *Dictionary* to pronounce unfamiliar terms.
- Use the *MedWorks - A & P Workbook* to review each lesson prior to computer learning. The *Workbook* includes the questions for each lesson within each chapter. Also, write down the answer to each question in this *Workbook* as you proceed through the course.

Enjoy the satisfaction of unlocking the mystery of anatomy and physiology!

Chapter 1
Anatomy & Physiology Overview

1.1.1 Body Organization

15 minutes

Definitions

Anatomy and physiology are two branches of science which, collectively, describe how the human body is organized and maintained. **Anatomy** refers to the structures of the body and how they physically relate to one another. **Physiology** deals with the normal function of the body: that is, how different body parts cooperate with one another in the face of varying conditions in order to maintain life and health. One way to conceptualize the structural organization of the human body is to realize that it exists in several levels: from lowest, the chemical level, to highest, the entire human body.

CHEMICALS (atoms and molecules) > ORGANELLES (functional components of cells) > CELLS > TISSUES > ORGANS > SYSTEMS > ORGANISM

Chemical Level

Atoms and molecules are organized to form the structures of the body, and to carry out processes (such as digestion and reproduction) that are essential to the maintenance of human life. **Organic** compounds are molecules that are associated with all life processes. These chemical compounds always contain **carbon**, and can be manufactured by living systems. Examples of organic molecules include **carbohydrates** (sugar), **lipids** (fat), **proteins** (muscle), and **nucleic acids** (DNA).

Cells

The most basic structural and functional unit of any organism is the **cell**. Cells contain specialized structures called **organelles**, which perform specific functions. The **nucleus**, **ribosomes**, and **mitochondria** are just a few of the many organelles which facilitate cellular functions. In this close-up of a cell's nucleus (in software), part of the nuclear envelope has been cut away to show the structure of the **nucleolus**, which is formed by a cluster of smaller bodies. The nuceolus is active in the cell's production of certain organic molecules (proteins). Molecules can pass in and out of the nucleus through **pores** in the nuclear envelope.

In the course of embryonic development, cells grow, divide, and **differentiate**, or gain the capacity to perform specialized functions. By the time humans are born, they have cells which are equipped to perform many distinct functions. For example, **cardiac** (heart) cells, and **sensory** (nerve) cells can conduct electrical impulses. **Erythrocytes** (red blood cells) carry oxygen in the blood to tissues where it is needed. Other cells are specialized to absorb nutrients from food, or to form the body's structures.

Tissues

A **tissue** is a collection cells which work together to perform a certain function. The cells in a tissue may be of various specialized types, each type performing its own specific "sub-function." For example, **keratinocytes** are the cells which give skin tissue its tough, protective quality, while **melanocytes** give skin its color. The cells which comprise a tissue are surrounded by a substance called **extracellular matrix** (ECM) or **ground substance**.

There are four basic types of tissue in the human body: 1) **epithelial** tissue, 2) **muscle** tissue, 3) **nervous** tissue, and 4) **connective** tissue.

Organs

Organs are the next highest level of functional organization in the human body. Consisting of two or more different types of tissues, organs have specific functions and typically have recognizable shapes. The heart, brain, kidneys, and stomach are examples of organs.

Body Systems

A **body system** is a group of organs which perform a specific function. For example, the organs of the female reproductive system include the vagina, the uterus, the fallopian tubes, and the ovaries. Each organ in a system contributes to the overall function of the system in a different way. In the process of digestion, for example, the teeth, tongue and stomach break up food particles mechanically, while the pancreas and intestine contribute to the chemical breakdown of nutrients. Note that a single organ can be part of more than one body system. For example, the penis is part of both the male reproductive system and the urinary system.

Quick Check Questions

1. Anatomy is the study of the _________ of the human body.

2. Physiology is the study of the ________ of the human body.

3. The most basic structural and functional unit which is present in all organisms is the:
   A. atom
   B. organ
   C. cell
   D. connective tissue

4. An example of an organelle is the:
   A. mitochondrion
   B. heart
   C. urinary system
   D. red blood cell

5. The levels of body organization are: chemicals, organelles, cells, _______, organs, systems, and organism.

6. Lipids, proteins, and carbohydrates are inorganic chemicals important to life processes. *True or False*

7. A single organ can be part of more than one system. *True or False*

8. The specialized structures in cells are called _________.

1.1.2 Terminology - Directional Terms

10 minutes

When discussing human anatomy, descriptions of any region or part of the human body assume that the body is in the **anatomical position**. In the anatomical position the body stands upright, facing the observer, with feet flat on the floor, arms hanging at the sides, and palms facing forward. Other orientations include the **supine** position, in which the body is lying on its back, and the **prone** position, in which the body is lying face down.

Directional Terms

Anatomists use precise words to describe how various regions and structures relate to one another. One must become fluent in these directional terms to clearly understand human anatomy. Take some time to study the following list of directional terms. Note that many of these terms can be paired with opposite meanings. Remember directional terms always assume that the body is in the anatomical position.

- **Superior / Cephalic / Cranial** - Toward the head or the upperpart of a structure.
- **Inferior / Caudal** - Away from the head or toward the lower part of a structure.
- **Anterior / Ventral** - Nearer to or at the front of the body.
- **Posterior / Dorsal** - Nearer to or at the back of the body.
- **Medial** - Nearer to the midline of the body or a structure.
- **Lateral** - Farther away from the midline of the body or a structure.
- **Midline** - Imaginary vertical line that divides the body into right and left sides.
- **Intermediate** - Between two structures.
- **Ipsilateral** - On the same lateral (left or right) side of the body.
- **Contralateral** - On the opposite, lateral side of the body.
- **Proximal** - Nearer to the attachment of a limb to the trunk.
- **Distal** - Farther from the attachment of a limb to the trunk.
- **Superficial** - Toward or on the surface of the body.

- **Deep** - Toward the internal aspect (or organs), away from the surface of the body.

Quick Check Questions

1. The heart is _______ or anterior to the spinal column.

2. The following term best describes the relationship of the left kidney to the right kidney.
   A. intermediate
   B. ipsilateral
   C. contralateral
   D. superior

3. The ribs are __________ to the lungs.

1.2.1 Planes and Sections of Reference

15 minutes

Planes refer to imaginary flat surfaces which slice through the body at different angles, and divide certain parts. A view of the inner surface of the body, where it is divided by a plane, is called a **section** (section means "to cut"). Please take some time to study the diagrams and definitions of the major planes of the human body.

This illustration (in software) shows a section through the female pelvis. Sections allow us to view anatomical structures from the inside as well as the outside. (Note the corrugated appearance of the inner walls of these pelvic organs.)

Sagittal refers to a vertical plane that divides a body or an organ into right and left sides. **Midsagittal** is a sagittal plane that passes through the midline of the body or an organ, dividing it into equal right and left sides. **Parasagittal** is a sagittal plane which divides the body or an organ into unequal right and left sides.

The **frontal / coronal** plane divides the body or an organ into anterior and posterior portions. The **transverse / cross-sectional / horizontal** plane divides the body or an organ into superior and inferior portions. An **oblique** plane passes through the body or an organ at some angle other than 90 degrees to the transverse plane, the sagittal plane and the frontal plane.

Body Regions

It is important for anatomists and physicians to know the location of organs in reference to landmarks on the body surface. The surface of the human body is divided into **body regions**. Each region is characterized by specific underlying structures. Take time to learn the terminology used to reference these areas, and be able to match each major organ to its respective body region.

The major body regions are the: head, neck, trunk, **upper extremity** (arms and hands), and **lower extremity** (thighs, legs and feet). The trunk is further subdivided into the: **thorax** (or the **pectoral** region), **abdomen**, and **pelvis**. The abdomen, pelvis, and upper and lower extremities are described in the next two sections.

The head is divided into: 1) the **cranium** encasing and supporting the brain, and 2) the **facial region** that includes the eyes, nose, and mouth. The neck, technically termed the **cervical region**, contains the bones, cartilage, and muscles that structurally support the head and permit it to move. The cervical region also contains vital nerve and vessel structures (such as the spinal cord, the carotid arteries, and the jugular veins). These structures provide the means of communication between organs in the head and in the body. Explore the balloons on this illustration (in software) which identify regions of the head and neck.

The **thorax** or the **thoracic region** refers to the chest or the upper region of the trunk. The thorax may be divided into the following regions: 1) the **mammary regions** surrounds each nipple and defines the breast, 2) the **sternal region** is intermediate between the two mammary regions, and 3) the **axillary region** is the region of each armpit. The **vertebral region** is also considered part of the thoracic region. The vertebral region is the surface of the body at the dorsal midline exterior to the spinal column (the back).

Quick Check Questions

1. The head and the chest are also known as the:
   A. cranium and the buccal
   B. pelvis and the abdomen
   C. cervix and vertebral column
   D. cranium and the thorax

2. The sternum, the axilla, and the vertebral column are all a part of the ________ region.

3. The buccinator muscle, named for the **buccal region** from which it originates, is located in the:
   A. cervix
   B. cheek
   C. chin
   D. brain

4. The abdominal region lies ________ to the pelvic region.

1.2.2 Abdomen and Pelvis

15 minutes

The **abdomen** is the region of the trunk located inferior to the thorax. Many of the visceral organs shown here (in software) lie below the abdominal surface. The **navel** (the **umbilicus** or **belly button**) defines the anterior center of the abdomen. The abdomen is conventionally subdivided in two ways: 1) into nine regions, or 2) into four quadrants.

Clinical Note:
The simpler method of subdividing the abdomen into four quadrants is commonly used in clinical settings for locating and describing various pains and conditions.

Subregions of the Abdomen and Pelvis

The nine-region method of dividing of the abdomen is commonly used by anatomists to describe the location of the viscera in relation to the body surface. The **right hypochondriac** region contains the gallbladder, portions of the liver, and the right kidney.

The **epigastric** region contains the stomach, the pancreas, and parts of the liver and the small intestine. The **left hypochondriac** region contains the spleen, the left kidney and parts of the large intestine and small intestine. The **right lateral** or **right lumbar** region contains the cecum (the first part of the colon), the ascending colon and the hepatic flexure of the colon, as well as parts of the right kidney and small intestine.

The **umbilical** region contains parts of the small intestine, the transverse colon, the kidneys, and the major abdominal blood vessels. The **left lateral** region contains the descending colon and parts of the left kidney and small intestine. The **right inguinal** or **right iliac** region contains the appendix and parts of the cecum and small intestine. The **pubic** or **hypogastric** region contains the urinary bladder, parts of the small intestine, and the sigmoid (S-shaped) colon. The **left inguinal** region contains parts of the small intestine and the descending and sigmoid colons.

The Pelvis

The **pelvis** or the **pelvic region** is the most posterior region of the trunk, below the abdomen. The hypogastric and inguinal subregions span the abdominal and pelvic regions. The inguinal regions, also called the groin, contain **lymph nodes** (the lymph nodes can become swollen glands in response to infections of the pelvis or the lower extremity).

The **perineum,** the lowest part of the pelvis, contains the anal opening and the external sex organs. Dorsal to the pelvis are the **lumbar region**, or the small of the back, and the **sacral region**, which ends at the **coccyx** where the vertebral column terminates. The **gluteal region**, or the buttock, includes the large hip muscles which move the lower extremities (thighs and legs) in relation to the trunk.

Quick Check Questions

1. The urinary bladder is an organ within the:
   A. pelvis
   B. epigastric region
   C. thorax
   D. head

2. The coccyx is ________ to the cervical region of the spinal cord.

3. The region of the pelvis pierced by the anus and the external sex organs is the:
   A. lumbar region
   B. perineum
   C. gluteal region
   D. inguinal region

4. A general surgeon is most likely to find a ruptured appendix in the:
   A. umbilical region
   B. left lateral region
   C. right inguinal region
   D. left inguinal region

1.2.3 The Upper and Lower Extremities

10 minutes

The upper extremity includes the **omos** or the **deltoid region** (the shoulder), the arm, and the **manus** (the hand). The arm is divided into the **brachium** (upper arm) and the **antebrachium** (forearm) by a flexible joint called the **elbow.**

Clinical Note:
The **cubital fossa**, the area on the anterior surface of the elbow, is a common site for the withdrawal of blood or for intravenous (IV) injection into the cubital vein.

The **wrist**, or the **carpal joint**, is the flexible joint which separates the antebrachium from the manus. The anterior side of the hand (in the anatomic position) is called the **palm** or the **palmar surface**, while the posterior surface is referred to as the **dorsum** of the hand. Each hand has five fingers (**digits**, or **phalanges**).

The thigh, knee joint, lower leg, ankle joint, and foot comprise **the lower extremity**. The thigh is referred to as the **femoral region,** or the upper leg. The knee joint has an anterior surface called the **patellar region** which is distinct from the posterior surface, called the **popliteal fossa**. The **shin**, a prominent bony ridge, and the **calf**, a thickened muscular mass, describe the anterior and posterior leg, respectively. The ankle is the junction between the leg and the foot.

Please note that the term leg is commonly used to describe the entire lower extremity. However, to the anatomist, the leg specifically refers to that portion of the lower extremity below the knee joint and above the ankle joint. The heel, or **calcaneus**, is the back of the foot. The dorsal surface of the foot refers to the entire upper surface of the foot including the surface on which toenails are imbedded. The **plantar** surface of the foot refers to the sole or the bottom of the foot.

Quick Check Questions

1. The thigh is ________ to the leg.

2. **Carpal tunnel syndrome** describes compression of nerve structure in the:
   A. hand
   B. wrist
   C. ankle
   D. calcaneus

3. One would fingerprint the ______ surface of the hand.

4. A common location for a phlebotomist to draw blood from a vein in the arm is the:
   A. deltoid fossa
   B. dorsum of the hand
   C. cubital fossa
   D. popliteal fossa

5. The cubital fossa is located on the ________ surface of the arm.

1.3.1 Body Cavities

10 minutes

Body cavities are confined, membrane-lined spaces within the body. They contain the **viscera** (organs) and their associated membranes. The two principal body cavities are the **dorsal body cavity** and the **ventral body cavity**.

The dorsal body cavity contains the brain and the spinal cord. The ventral body cavity is divided by the muscular **diaphragm** into the upper chest, or **thoracic cavity**, and the lower **abdominopelvic cavity**. The thoracic cavity is further divided into two **pleural cavities**, each contain a lung, and the **pericardial cavity** located intermediate to the pleural cavities, which contains the heart. The area between the two lungs is referred to as the **mediastinum**.

The abdominopelvic cavity is divided into the upper **abdominal cavity** and the lower **pelvic cavity**. Organs found within the abdominal cavity include the stomach, colon, liver, pancreas, gallbladder, kidneys, small intestines, spleen, and duodenum.

The pelvic cavity contains the terminal portion of the colon, the rectum, part of the small intestine, and the urinary bladder. In addition, the pelvic contents include certain reproductive organs. In the male, these include the seminal vesicles and the prostate gland. The pelvic cavity of the female containing the uterus, fallopian tubes, and ovaries.

Note that in addition to the larger dorsal and ventral cavities, there are also many small cavities within the head. One example is the nasal sinuses.

Quick Check Questions

1. The liver lies in the abdominal cavity:
   A. in the lower left region above the left leg
   B. in the uppermost right region below the right lung
   C. ipsilateral to the stomach
   D. inferior to the umbilicus

2. The fallopian tubes in a non-pregnant female are in the ______ cavity.

3. The thorax is divided from the abdomen by a muscular organ called the:
   A. diaphragm
   B. heart
   C. uterus
   D. stomach

1.4.1 Body Membranes

8 minutes

Body **membranes** are thin layers of **connective** and **epithelial** tissue. They function to compartmentalize, protect, and support the viscera. The two basic types of body membranes are **mucous membranes** and **serous membranes**. Mucous membranes typically line those cavities and tubes which enter and exit from the body. For example, mucous membranes line the nasal and oral cavities, and the tubes of the digestive, respiratory, urinary, and reproductive systems.

Mucous membranes secrete a thick, viscous substance called mucus, which is chemically composed mainly of **glycoproteins**. Mucus lubricates and protects the underlying membrane and traps foreign particles and debris. Particulate matter trapped by mucous membranes is pushed towards the body's external orifices by the action of hair-like **cilia** that are attached to some cells of the membrane. (Note: **Mucus** is a noun describing the viscous secretion of certain membranes. **Mucous** is an adjective which describes this type of membrane.)

Serous membranes are smooth transparent membranes that line the internal body cavities and their viscera. They have two parts: 1) the **parietal portion** defines the outer lining of a cavity, and 2) the **visceral portion** covers the surfaces of organs within the cavity. Serous membranes secrete a thin, watery lubricant called **serous fluid**. The two **pleurae** of the thorax, the **pericardium** of the heart, and the **peritoneum** of the abdomen are all serous membranes.

Quick Check Questions

1. _____ membranes function to lubricate and protect the viscera.

2. Serous fluid is best described as more ______ than mucous fluid.

3. The pleurae, the pericardium, and the peritoneum are serous membranes that line the:
   A. stomach, lungs, and cartilage
   B. brain, spinal cord, and heart
   C. lungs, heart, and abdomen
   D. ligaments, liver, and reproductive system

Chapter 2
Body Chemistry

2.1.1 Body Chemistry - Overview

10 minutes

You might have heard the phrase, "You are what you eat." A good understanding of what is meant by this popular phrase is rooted in the fundamental ideas of body chemistry. The common substances that we consume in our diet (that is, water, sugar, salt, oil) enter into chemical reactions in the human body which can build and compose it, or which provide the energy for body activities.

All life's processes involve **chemical reactions**, defined simply as the making and breaking of bonds between atoms. **Metabolism** specifically refers to those chemical reactions which occur within a living organism. There are four main types of chemical reactions common to the human body which provide an essential conceptual framework for understanding the specific metabolic reactions which drive life's processes.

Four Main Types of Chemical Reactions

1) **Anabolic reactions** are the synthesis reactions which involve the forming of new bonds. These reactions require energy input into the system. The following equation represents an anabolic reaction: A (atom, ion, or molecule) + B (atom, ion, or molecule) => AB (new molecule).

2) **Catabolic reactions** are decomposition reactions in which the bonds of larger molecules are broken and smaller molecules, ions, or atoms are formed, usually with the release of energy: AB => A + B .

3) **Exchange reactions** combine anabolic and catabolic processes. They may either consume or release energy. The following equation describes an exchange reaction: AB + CD => AD + BC .

4) **Reversible reactions**, indicated by two arrows, describe those reactions in which the product can be converted back into the original reactant. The direction of reaction is usually determined by energy considerations. The following equation is an example of a reversible reaction: $A + B \Leftrightarrow AB$.

Quick Check Questions

1. A huge explosion which gives off a lot of heat is most likely a(n):
   A. anabolic reaction
   B. catabolic reaction

2. $N_2 + 3H_2 \Rightarrow 2NH_3$ is an example of a(n):
   A. anabolic reaction
   B. catabolic reaction
   C. exchange reaction
   D. reversible reaction

3. When a strong acid like hydrochloric acid is added to a buffer solution of sodium bicarbonate (baking soda), the following reaction occurs:
   $HCl + NaHCO_3 \Rightarrow NaCl$ (salt) + H_2CO_3 (carbonic acid) This is a(n):
   A. anabolic reaction
   B. catabolic reaction
   C. exchange reaction
   D. reversible reaction

2.2.1 Enzymes

10 minutes

A **catalyst** accelerates a chemical reaction, but is not consumed or changed by the process. **Enzymes** are specialized proteins that function as catalysts in living cells. Enzymes have specific binding sites for the **substrates** upon which they act. Enzymes speed up chemical reactions by lowering the amount of energy required for the reaction to proceed (called **activation energy**). For instance, when a substrate is bound to an enzyme, the chemical bonds that hold it together may be weakened. Also, the frequency of collisions between two molecules is increased when they both bind to the same enzyme. In the process of increasing the reaction rate, enzymes themselves are not altered. In summary, enzymes catalyze reactions and are not modified in the process.

Substrates are converted to products by the reaction. The names of enzymes almost always end in the suffix "-ase." Enzymes are grouped according to the types of reactions that they catalyze: **Oxidases** - add oxygen; **Kinases** - add phosphate; **Hydrolases** - add water; **Isomerases** - rearrange atoms within a molecule; **Dehydrogenases** - remove hydrogen; **Tranferases** - transfer groups of atoms; **Proteases** - break down proteins; **Lipases** - break down **lipids** (fats).

Quick Check Questions

1. An enzyme which breaks down a molecule of ATP is called a(n) ________.
   A. carbohydrate
   B. protein
   C. ATPase
   D. steroid hormone

2. People who are **lactose intolerant** cannot digest milk very well because their digestive systems lack the enzyme called _______.

3. Enzymes are:
   A. carbohydrates
   B. proteins
   C. fats
   D. steroid hormones

2.3.1 Elements

8 minutes

The chemical elements are substances which cannot be split into simpler substances by ordinary chemical reactions. All forms of matter (solids, liquids, and gases) are made up of a limited number of elements. Twenty-six of the 92 naturally occurring elements exist in the human body.

Though it is not critical to memorize all 26 elements, it is important to remember those which make up the majority of body mass. They are: 96% Carbon (C) Hydrogen (H) Oxygen (O) Nitrogen (N); 3.9% Calcium (Ca) Phosphorus (P) Potassium (K) Sulfur (S) Sodium (Na) Chlorine (Cl) Magnesium (Mg) Iodine (I) Iron (Fe). Carbon, hydrogen, oxygen, and nitrogen are the building blocks for all organic molecules. They make up 96% of all body mass. The nine inorganic elements account for only about 3.9% of body mass.

Thirteen **trace elements** are present only in minute concentrations, yet many of these trace elements are key components of life generating processes. The trace elements account for less than 0.1 percent of body weight. They include: Silicon (Si) Aluminum (Al) Manganese (Mn) Fluorine (F) Vanadium (V) Chromium (Cr) Copper (Cu) Boron (B) Cobalt (Co) Zinc (Zn) Selenium (Se) Molybdenum (Mo) Tin (Sn).

Quick Check Questions

1. The following is NOT a naturally occurring element in the human body.
   A. carbon
   B. plutonium
   C. sulfur
   D. iodine

2. Chemical elements present in minute concentrations are called _____ elements.

2.4.1 Atomic Structure

10 minutes

Atoms are the smallest units of matter that enter into chemical reactions. Each element is made up of the same type of atoms. For example, a bit of elemental carbon contains only carbon atoms. It is helpful to think of the composition and structure of different types of atoms (that is, the **sub-atomic structure**) when you try to understand how and why atoms tend to bond and react with one another differently.

Each individual atom is made up of a dense nucleus surrounded by electron orbitals. There are three types of **sub-atomic particles**: 1) **protons**, 2) **electrons**, and 3) **neutrons**. Protons are positively charged particles which reside in the nucleus along with uncharged (or neutral) neutrons. Negatively charged electrons (abbreviated **e-**) orbit the nucleus in electron orbitals.

Electron shells refer to the specific atomic regions (or **orbitals**) around the nucleus within which electrons spend most of their time. Two-dimensionally, electron shells are conventionally represented as circles lying at various distances from the nucleus. However, it is important to remember that atoms actually exist as spheres with concentric layers of electron shells surrounding the nuclear core.

There are four basic rules of atomic organization which provide the foundation for understanding the human body at the chemical level. Please take some time to study the following rules and the corresponding illustrations of the atomic structures of several important atoms.

Rules of Chemical Organization

Rule 1. The number of electrons in an atom always equals the number of protons. Since electrons are negative and protons are positive, each atom is "balanced," or electrically neutral.

Rule 2. Adding the masses of all protons, neutrons, and electrons in an atom gives the **atomic mass**.

Rule 3. Adding the numbers of protons and neutrons gives the **mass number**. Note: Since the mass of an electron is negligible (that is, 1/2000 of the mass of a neutron or proton), the atomic mass of an atom is nearly equal to its mass number.

Rule 4. The number of protons in an atom determines its **atomic number**. The atomic number is the number which characterizes each atom, making one different from the next.

Isotopes

Isotope is the name for atoms of an element which have the same number of protons, but a different number of neutrons. All isotopes of an element have the same chemical properties because they have the same number of electrons. (Chemical properties are the result of interactions among electrons).

Clinical Note:
Radioactive isotopes emit particles of radiation that can be monitored with radiation detectors. In a process called **medical imaging**, isotopes are introduced into the cells of certain tissues to study both structure and function of the body. (Recall that cells cannot distinguish radioactive isotopes of an element because all isotopes have identical chemical properties).

Quick Check Questions

1. Positively charged subatomic particles are:
   A. neutrons
   B. protons
   C. electrons
   D. isotopes

2. If an atom is not electrically neutral, it is called an ion. Ions vary in the number of ________ they contain.
   A. neutrons
   B. protons
   C. electrons
   D. isotopes

3. An atom which varies in its number of neutrons is called a(n):
   A. ion
   B. isotope
   C. element
   D. inert element

4. To get the mass number, you add the protons and neutrons. The atomic mass also includes the mass of the _________.

2.4.2 Chemical Reactions

5 minutes

A **chemical reaction** occurs when atoms combine with or break apart from each other. The number of electrons in an atom governs its chemical properties. Hence, electron interactions are the basis of all chemical reactions. There are as many as seven **electron shells** in an atom. Each shell can hold a certain number of electrons. The first shell (which is nearest to the nucleus) can hold a maximum of two electrons. The second shell can hold eight. The third can hold up to eighteen. The electrons in an atom arrange themselves from the first shell outwards. As each shell reaches its maximum number of electrons, it is called "filled," and leftover electrons move to the next shell.

In order to achieve stability, atoms tend to either empty their outermost shell or fill it to the maximum. Elements which already have completely filled outer shells, such as neon, are called **inert elements**. Inert elements usually do not participate in chemical reactions. Atoms with incompletely filled outer shells tend to combine with each other in chemical reactions. They may give up, accept, or share electrons, thus forming **chemical bonds**. The combining capacity (the **valence**) is the number of extra or deficient electrons in the outermost shell -- the **valence shell**. Chemical bonds are a form of potential energy: forming bonds can create energy, while breaking them may require the input of energy.

Quick Check Questions

1. Helium and neon are called inert elements because:
   A. they have equal numbers of neutrons and protons
   B. they have equal numbers of protons and electrons
   C. their valence shells are completely filled
   D. they only chemically bond with one another

2. The innermost electron shell can hold up to ___ electrons.

2.4.3 Chemical Bonds

7 minutes

Ionic bonds, **covalent bonds**, and **hydrogen bonds** are three important types of chemical bonds which join atoms into **molecules**. Molecules are formed when two or more atoms combine together in a chemical reaction. Molecules may contain atoms of the same kind or of different kinds. A **compound** is a molecule that contains atoms of two or more different elements. **Ions** form when atoms gain or lose electrons. If an atom gains an electron it acquires a negative charge and is called an **anion**. An atom which loses an electron and acquires a positive charge is called a **cation**.

Ions in solution (dissolved in water) are called **electrolytes** because of their ability to conduct an electric current. An ionic bond is formed when ions of opposite charges attract and associate with one another. Atoms in **covalent bonds**, more common in the body than ionic bonds, "share" one or more pairs of electrons. The electrons of covalently bonded atoms orbit the nuclei of both atoms, but tend to linger in the region between the two nuclei. A **single covalent bond** occurs when two atoms share one pair of electrons. A **double or triple covalent bond** occurs when two or three pairs of electrons are shared between atoms.

Quick Check Questions

1. ______ are negatively charged ions.

2. Compounds sometimes contain only atoms of the same kind. *True or False*

3. An atom which has lost an electron in order to become more stable is called a(n) ______.

4. When electron pairs are shared between atoms, the resulting bond is:
   A. ionic
   B. covalent
   C. permanent
   D. hydrogen bonded

2.4.4 Chemical Bonds (Cont.)

8 minutes

In a covalently bonded compound, one atom often attracts the shared electrons more than the others. This type of molecule is called **polar**. **Polarity** occurs because the atom that attracts the electrons carries a slight negative charge, while the other atoms carry a slight positive charge. Water is a classic polar molecule. It has a partial negative charge nearer to the oxygen and partial positive charges nearer to the hydrogens. Electric charges travel easily through water because of its polarity. In **non-polar** substances such as oils, the electrons are shared equally among the atoms. Polar liquids like water tend to dissolve other polar substances (such as sodium chloride) much more readily than non-polar substances. This is why oil will not easily dissolve in water (like dissolves like).

Water molecules are held together in droplets by **hydrogen bonds**. These bonds are formed when the partial positive charges of the hydrogen atoms are attracted to the partial negative charges of oxygen atoms in adjacent water molecules. Hydrogen bonds are only about 5 percent as strong as covalent bonds. This is not strong enough to bind atoms into molecules, but hydrogen bonds do cause attraction between molecules.

The combined force of multiple hydrogen bonds can confer considerable strength and stability to a compound, despite the relative weakness of a single bond. (The **surface tension** of a large body of water is caused by the same attractive force that holds polar water molecules together in droplets). Hydrogen bonds can also cause attraction between atoms within the same molecule. This effect helps determine the three dimensional shape of large biological molecules, and increases their structural stability.

Quick Check Questions

1. Most of the unique qualities of the compound water can be attributed to the fact that:
   A. it contains carbon atoms
   B. it forms multiple hydrogen bonds
   C. it forms ionic bonds easily
   D. it contains hydrogen and oxygen in a 3 to 1 ratio

2. Polar liquids tend to dissolve large non-polar substances readily. *True or False*

3. Water is polar because:
   A. the sharing of electrons within a molecule is equal
   B. there is no sharing of electrons within a molecule
   C. the sharing of electrons within a molecule is unequal
   D. the intramolecular bonds (the bonds within the molecule) are unstable

2.5.1 Inorganic Compounds

10 minutes

The chemicals which make up the human body exist in two principle classes of compounds: 1) **inorganic**, and 2) **organic**. Inorganic compounds lack the element carbon, while organic compounds always contain carbon and hydrogen. Small molecules including water, oxygen, carbon dioxide, mineral salts, acids, and bases comprise the important inorganic compounds in living systems. Water is the most abundant substance in your body. It accounts for most of the volume of cells and tissues, and the greatest percent of body weight. It participates in many important body functions. Water is such a unique and significant compound in living systems because:

1) It is the most versatile **solvent** and suspending medium. A solvent is a liquid or a gas in which another material (solid, liquid, or gas) called the **solute** has been dissolved: Solvent + Solute = Solution. In a **suspension**, the solute does not stay mixed, but eventually settles out.

2) It participates in important decomposition and synthesis chemical reactions.

3) It absorbs and releases heat very slowly (it has a high heat capacity), so a large amount of energy is required to change it from a liquid to a gas. Therefore, with its abundance of water, the human body is less affected by environmental temperature changes.

4) It is a major component of mucus and other lubricating fluids, needed in places where internal organs and joints slide over each other. Water is also needed for digestion. It moistens the food so that it can pass through the digestive tract smoothly.

Quick Check Questions

1. A liquid that needs to be shaken to be evenly distributed before someone drinks it is probably a __________ .

2. Water is a universal solvent because anything will dissolve in it. *True or False*

2.5.2 Acidity and Alkalinity

8 minutes

Electrolytes are molecules which **ionize** or dissociate into ions when they are dissolved in water. Ionizable molecules may be acids, bases, or salts. By definition, when **acids** dissociate they release one or more **hydrogen ions** (H+). Hydrogen ions are also called protons. When bases dissociate, they release one or more **hydroxide ions** (OH-). When a salt is dissolved in water, it releases neither H+

nor OH-, but rather, dissociates into its component cations and anions. Hydroxide ions have a strong attraction for protons, so an acid will readily react with a base in solution. The products are molecules of salt and water:

$$HCl + KOH$$
(acid) (base)

V

$$(H^+, Cl^-, K^+, OH^-)$$
(dissolved ions)

V

$$KCl + HOH$$
(salt) (water)

The reactions which occur in living systems, called **biochemical reactions**, are extremely sensitive to the concentration of protons (called acidity) and of hydroxide ions (called alkalinity). Thus, acids and bases, which are constantly formed in the body, must be maintained in their proper balance. **Buffer systems** function to prevent disruption of the acid and base concentrations.

The **pH scale** expresses a solution's acidity or alkalinity as a number. The scale runs from 0 to 14. The midpoint of the pH scale is 7. At this point, the concentrations of H+ and OH- are equal and the solution is considered **neutral**. A solution with more H+ than OH- is **acidic** and has a pH below 7. Conversely, a solution with more OH- than H+ is **alkaline** and has a pH greater than 7. The normal pH of blood and many body fluids is about 7.4.

Quick Check Questions

1. An alkaline solution has a pH:
   A. below 7
   B. above 7
   C. at 7
   D. below 2

2. Blood is:
   A. slightly acidic
   B. extremely basic
   C. slightly basic
   D. neutral

3. Digestive juice is:
   A. very acidic
   B. slightly acidic
   C. very basic
   D. exactly neutral

4. A solution is acidic if it:
   A. has more hydroxide ions than protons
   B. has more protons than hydroxide ions
   C. has an equal number of protons and hydroxide ions
   D. is unsafe to ingest

2.5.3 Organic Compounds

10 minutes

Recall that organic compounds always contain carbon and hydrogen. The four electrons in its valence shell give carbon properties which make it useful to living organisms. Carbon is able to combine with thousands of other carbon atoms to form large molecules in varying shapes. Many large carbon-containing molecules are particularly useful for building body structures because they do not easily dissolve in water. Covalent bonds hold carbon atoms together, so organic compounds are also a good source of energy. (Recall that energy is released when bonds are broken). Organic compounds commonly contain a variety of other atoms which bond to carbon. Hydrogen atoms form one covalent bond with carbon. Oxygen and sulfur each form two bonds, and nitrogen forms three bonds.

The next sections examine the four main categories of organic compounds important in living systems: 1) **carbohydrates**, 2) **lipids**, 3) **proteins**, and 4) **nucleic acids**.

Carbohydrates represent 2 to 3 percent of body weight. They include sugars, starches, **glycogen**, and **cellulose**. These compounds have several functions:

1. Providing energy (particularly in the form of glucose) to drive metabolic reactions.

2. Serving as a building block of deoxyribonucleic acid or **DNA**, the molecule that carries hereditary information (**deoxyribose** is a sugar).

3. Creating bulk. For example, cellulose (or **fiber**) is indigestible plant material which helps to move food along the digestive tract.

As a general rule, carbohydrates ("watered carbon") contain one water molecule, split into hydrogen and hydroxide units, bonded to every carbon atom.

Monosaccharides are the basic building block of carbohydrates. They contain three to seven carbon atoms, and have an atomic ratio of 1 C : 2 H : 1 O. **Disaccharides** are formed from the combination of two monosaccharides. Monosaccharides and disaccharides are known as **simple sugars**. **Polysaccharides** contain tens or hundreds of monosaccharides. The principal polysaccharide in the human body is glycogen, a molecule which stores the simple sugar glucose. Plants store sugars in the form of starch and they use cellulose to build cell walls.

Quick Check Questions

1. Glucose is a:
   A. monosaccharide
   B. disaccharide
   C. starch
   D. polysaccharide

2. Carbohydrates contain carbon, hydrogen, and ______.

3. Most of our body weight is attributable to carbohydrates. *True or False*

2.6.1 Lipids

8 minutes

Lipids, or fats, comprise 18 to 25 percent of body weight in lean adults. Since they have few polar covalent bonds, most lipids are insoluble in water, or **hydrophobic** (water fearing). Thus, lipids cannot travel freely in the watery blood and must combine with protein carriers to form **lipoproteins** which are more water soluble, or **hydrophilic** (water loving). Like carbohydrates, lipids also contain carbon, hydrogen, and oxygen atoms (although in a different ratio) and come in a variety of forms.

Triglycerides function in 1) metabolism, 2) protection, and 3) insulation. Triglycerides are the most concentrated form of energy storage in the body. All excess dietary nutrients are converted to triglycerides for storage in adipose tissue. Phospholipids (containing phosphorous) are a major component of cell membranes and are found in high concentrations in nervous tissue.

Steroids are another major class of lipids which serve a variety of important functions:

1) **Cholesterol** is a major component of cell membranes.

2) **Bile salts** emulsify fats and assist in the absorption of fat soluble vitamins.

3) **Cortisol** is a hormone that helps regulate metabolism.

4) The sex hormones such as **estrogen** and **testosterone** stimulate reproductive functions and sexual characteristics.

Vitamin D is a steroid hormone necessary for bone growth and repair. It is produced in the skin upon exposure to UV radiation from the sun, and helps in calcium absorption. Other fat-soluble vitamins require steroids for transport and absorption. Among these are the **carotenes** and **vitamin A**, essential components of visual pigments, **vitamin E** which promotes wound healing, and **vitamin K,** vital for blood clotting.

Quick Check Questions

1. Most of our body weight is attributable to:
   A. lipids
   B. carbohydrates
   C. water
   D. our brain mass

2. Since lipids generally do not dissolve well in water they are considered ____________.

3. Phospholipids and cholesterol are both key components of cell membranes. *True or False*

4. This is NOT a fat soluble vitamin:
   A. carotene
   B. thiamine
   C. E
   D. K

2.6.2 Proteins

10 minutes

Much more complex in structure than carbohydrates or lipids, **proteins** (12 to 18 percent of the body weight in a lean adult) always contain carbon, oxygen, hydrogen, nitrogen, and sometimes sulfur. Twenty **amino acids** are the building blocks of proteins. Proteins are formed from chains of amino acids. **Peptide bonds** are the covalent bonds which join each adjacent pair of amino acids in a protein chain. A **polypeptide** is a protein chain which may contain from 10 to more than 2000 amino acids. A huge variety of protein structures is possible because different proteins result from variation in the number and the sequence of the 20 amino acids.

Proteins display four levels of structural organization. The **primary structure** is simply the unique linear sequence of amino acids in a particular polypeptide strand. **Secondary structure** is the repeated twisting or folding of neighboring amino acids in a polypeptide chain. The most common forms are **alpha helices** and **beta pleated sheets. Tertiary structure** refers to the three-dimensional or "folded" shape of a protein. **Quaternary structure** refers to the arrangement of a protein which contains more than one polypeptide chain. **Hemoglobin**, the molecule that transports oxygen in the blood, is an example of a protein with quaternary structure. There are four polypeptide chains in hemoglobin.

The primary structure of a protein is maintained by covalent peptide bonds. Hydrogen bonding stabilizes the secondary structure. The tertiary and quaternary structures are held together by interactions of the side chains (or R groups) of the amino acids. These groups chemically bond by hydrogen bonds, ionic bonds, disulfide bonds (covalent bonds between two sulfurs), and other interactions.

Denaturation is the process by which a protein unravels and loses its secondary, tertiary, or quaternary structure. This can occur when a protein encounters a "hostile" environment: one which does not have a suitable temperature, pH, or electrolyte (dissolved ion) concentration. These conditions affect the stability of non-covalent chemical bonds. Once denatured, a protein is no longer functional. Proteins have both structural and functional roles in the human body. Structurally, they are cellular building materials. Functionally, a protein can be classified in one of five physiologic groups:

1) **Regulatory proteins** are hormones which regulate various physiological processes. (Note: Steroid hormones and protein hormones each affect tissues by different mechanisms).

2) **Contractile proteins** such as myosin and actin enable shortening of muscle tissue.

3) **Immunological proteins**, like antibodies and interleukins, aid processes that protect the body against foreign substances.

4) **Transport proteins** carry essential substances through the blood system.

5) **Catalytic proteins** are the enzymes which catalyze biochemical reactions in the body.

Quick Check Questions

1. All hormones are made of proteins. *True or False*

2. If a protein becomes overheated (or cooked) it may ________.

3. The three dimensional shape of a protein is described by its:
   A. primary structure
   B. secondary structure
   C. tertiary structure
   D. quaternary structure

4. Enzymes are:
   A. lipids which catalyze reactions
   B. proteins which stop reactions
   C. proteins which catalyze reactions
   D. proteins which carry vital substance in the blood

2.7.1 Nucleic Acids

7 minutes

Nucleic acids contain carbon, hydrogen, oxygen, nitrogen, and phosphorus. Their basic building blocks are called **nucleotide** units. Nucleic acids come in two forms: **DNA** or deoxyribonucleic acid, and **RNA** or ribonucleic acid. DNA forms the genetic code inside the cell's nucleus. RNA relays instructions from DNA to the cell's ribosomes for protein synthesis (discussed further in the chapters on *Cells and Tissues* and *Inheritance*).

Each nucleotide unit in a nucleic acid consists of three parts: a **pentose** (5 carbon) **sugar**, either ribose (RNA) or deoxyribose (DNA), is attached to a **nitrogenous base** and a **phosphate group**. The **double helix** structure of DNA is formed by two strands of nucleotides. Phosphate and sugar groups alternate along each strand. The bases from each nucleotide arrange opposite each other, in pairs, to form **rungs** between the strands. The two strands on the outside of the molecule then twist around each other, with base pairs on the inside. The helix is held together by hydrogen bonds which form between the pairs of bases, as well as along each strand.

DNA contains four bases: **adenosine (A)**, which always forms double hydrogen bonds with **thymine (T)**, and **cytosine (C)**, which triple hydrogen-bonds to **guanine (G)**. In RNA, the thymine is substituted by **uracil (U)**, and the structure is single as opposed to double stranded. The genetic code simply consists of the particular sequence of bases in a DNA molecule.

Quick Check Questions

1. DNA:
   A. is a single stranded
   B. contains a lot of the element potassium
   C. contains sugar ribose
   D. forms a double-helix

2. In RNA, the thymine is substituted by ______.

3. The paired bases in the double helix model are held together by:
   A. covalent bonds
   B. hydrogen bonds
   C. serous fluid
   D. ionic bonds

2.7.2 ATP

6 minutes

Adenosine triphosphate (ATP) functions in all living systems to provide energy for various cellular activities. ATP is known as the "energy currency" of living systems, because of its two high energy phosphate bonds. (These bonds are represented by ~). When a terminal phosphate group (the phosphate on the end of the compound) is hydrolyzed by the addition of water, the decomposition reaction produces a phosphate group and **adenosine diphosphate (ADP)**. But most importantly, energy is liberated from the bond-breaking! So, where does the necessary supply of ATP come from?

ATP is regenerated by **dehydration** synthesis of ADP and a phosphate group. But reformation of the high-energy bond requires the input of energy. The required energy is provided by the metabolic breakdown of glucose in a process called **cellular respiration**. Depending on the availability of oxygen during cellular respiration, either 2 or 38 molecules of ATP are produced per molecule of glucose metabolized.

The overall chemical equation for **aerobic** (in the presence of oxygen) cellular respiration is shown in the illustration to the right (in software). (This reaction proceeds by many intermediate steps). Energy can be produced from glucose in the absence of oxygen through **anaerobic** reactions. Only two ATP molecules are produced, however.

Quick Check Questions

1. ATP is important in the body because it provides:
   A. part of the genetic code
   B. energy for cellular processes
   C. a storage form for glucose

2. Regeneration of ATP by cellular respiration requires the presence of oxygen.
   True or False

Chapter 3
Cells and Tissues

3.1.1 Cells - Overview

10 minutes

The **cell** is the smallest living structure within the human body. Cells carry out all the vital life functions necessary for their own survival. **Cytology** (cyte = cell, ology = study of) refers to the study of cells. The complex physiology of the human body results from the many specialized functions performed by nearly seventy-five trillion cells.

Ranging in diameter from only 0.008 millimeters (red blood cells) to 0.3 millimeters (the female sex cell: ovum), almost all human cells are microscopic in size. The point on the end of a pencil is about five times the size of the largest ovum, just barely visible to the human eye.

Many cells are structurally specialized to carry out unique functions. For example, nerve cells which transmit impulses over long distances in the body have extended projections called **axons** and **dendrites**. Specialized structures allow each cell to make a unique contribution to tissue and organ physiology. However, most cells share certain basic components which enable them to carry out life's processes. Some of these common structures are: 1) the **plasma membrane**, 2) the **nucleus**, 3) the **cytoplasm**, and 4) the **organelles**.

Organelles

Organelles are structures in the cytoplasm which have specific cellular functions. Although different cell types may lack one or more organelle, the following are common to most cells: 1) **mitochondria**, 2) **endoplasmic reticulum** (ER), 3) **ribosomes**, 4) **Golgi apparatus**, 5) **centrosomes**, and 6) **lysosomes**.

Quick Check Questions

1. Most cells include a plasma membrane, nucleus, and cytoplasm, as well as cytoplasmic structures such as the endoplasmic reticulum, ribosomes, lysosomes, and centrosomes. These structures are generally referred to as __________.

2. The human body contains cells on the order of ________.
   A. hundreds
   B. millions
   C. billions
   D. trillions

3. No human cell is large enough to be visualized without the aid of a light microscope. *True or False*

3.2.1 Plasma Membrane: Anatomy

10 minutes

The cell membrane (or **plasma membrane**) encloses all structures within the cell, gives form to the cell, and is specialized to communicate with, and transport substances to and from, the external environment. The **phospholipid bilayer** chemical structure of the plasma membrane enables it to function as a "gate-keeper," which regulates the passage of substances into and out of the cell.

The plasma membrane is the barrier which separates the cell's **intracellular** components (structures within the cell) from the **extracellular** environment (the medium surrounding the cell). The plasma membrane consists of a phospholipid bilayer which is embedded with **proteins**, **cholesterol**, **glycoproteins** and **glycolipids** (proteins and lipids with one or more sugar groups attached). Each of these large molecules has a particular function.

Each phospholipid molecule in the bilayer is simply a lipid molecule attached to a phosphate group. Since the phosphate end (or head) of the molecule is **polar**, it is also **hydrophilic**. The lipid tail, however, is **hydrophobic**. Both the interior and the surrounding exterior environments of cells are watery (or **aqueous**).

Recall that hydrophobic molecules are repelled by water. So the hydrophobic tails of the phospholipid molecules associate together, like droplets of oil added to water. This structure leaves the hydrophilic heads facing the interior and exterior of the cell in two parallel rows.

The cell membrane is best conceptualized as a **fluid mosaic model**. The membrane is somewhat fluid, or dynamic in structure, and so allows the proteins to float freely within the bilayer of smaller lipid molecules. The membrane is considered to be mosaic because it is composed of many different types of molecules.

Quick Check Questions

1. The plasma membrane is comprised principally of membrane proteins, cholesterol, and glycoproteins in a bilayer of _____________.

2. The plasma membrane is made up of phospholipids, proteins, and nucleic acids. *True or False*

3. The plasma ________ of a cell acts as a barrier and as a "gatekeeper"of the movement of substances in and out of the cell.

3.2.2 Membrane Proteins

15 minutes

The membrane proteins, more than the membrane lipids, contribute significantly to a particular cell's function. There are two classes of membrane proteins: 1) **integral proteins**, and 2) **peripheral proteins**. Integral membrane proteins extend across the entire bilayer of the cell and protrude into the interior and out to the exterior of the cell. Peripheral membrane proteins rest more loosely among the fatty acid tails of the phospholipids. Thus, they are more easily separated from the inner and outer surfaces of the cell's membrane. The following few screens (in software) list major functions of some of the different types of membrane proteins.

1) **Channel** proteins (**pores**). These proteins form the walls of tiny holes that span the cell's membrane. Channels may be "selective," allowing only certain substances to cross, or "passive," permitting free diffusion of materials into or out of the cell.

2) **Transport** (carrier) proteins move substances across a cell's membrane. This process may be active, thus requiring cellular energy, or passive (driven by a concentration gradient).

3) **Receptor** proteins serve as recognition sites for external **ligands** such as **hormones** and **neurotransmitters**. Such ligands carry messages to the cell which trigger metabolic changes.

4) **Cytoskeletal anchors** are peripheral membrane proteins located on the interior of the plasma membrane. They form attachments between the membrane and the cytoskeleton, or support structure, of a cell.

5) **Cell identity markers**. Certain proteins on the outer surface of the plasma membrane enable cells to distinguish other cells as "self" or "non-self." These proteins are called cell identity markers.

Clinical Note:
Cell identity marker proteins are especially important when tissue type matches are required for transfusing blood or transplanting organs from one person to another.

Quick Check Questions

1. Large molecules of cholesterol in cell membranes can function as channels, transporters, and receptors, for the movement of substances into and out of cells. *True or False*

2. __________ membrane proteins are loosely attached to, and easily separated from, the inner and outer surfaces of the membrane.
   A. peripheral
   B. integral

3. This type of membrane protein enables cells to distinguish self from non-self.
   A. cell identity markers
   B. cytoskeletal anchors
   C. receptors
   D. carriers

3.3.1 Passive Transport

20 minutes

Mechanisms that move substances across the lipid bilayer enable the plasma membrane to fulfill its role as the functional gatekeeper of the cell. **Passive** and **active transport** are the two mechanisms by which substances can cross the plasma membrane. Passive processes DO NOT require the use of cellular energy, while active processes DO require the input of energy. The energy needed for passive transport across a cell membrane is provided by forces due to pressure or **concentration gradients** across the membrane. Cellular energy is provided in the form of **adenosine triphosphate** (ATP). Active transport processes make use of the energy released during the breakage of one of the high energy phosphate bonds of ATP.

Passive Transport

Passive transport processes include: 1) **diffusion**, 2) **facilitated diffusion** , 3) **osmosis**, and 4) **filtration**. These subjects are addressed in the remainder of this lesson and in the following lesson.

Diffusion

Diffusion is a process in which particles in solution move about randomly until they become evenly distributed throughout the solution. The driving force of diffusion is **kinetic energy**, the energy of motion. Although the movement of each particle is random, the overall effect is movement from areas of high concentration to areas of lower concentration. When the particles become evenly distributed in the solution (or across a cell's membrane), they have reached a state of **equilibrium**.

The movement of substances across a membrane depends upon the membrane's **permeability**. An impermeable membrane maintains the concentration of solutes on either side. A semi-permeable membrane may allow some substances to cross, but keeps others out. Cell membranes are of this variety.

When ions in a cell are present in higher concentration in one area compared to another, the difference in concentration between the two areas is called a **concentration gradient**. If there is no barrier impeding their passage, the particles will pass down the gradient from areas of higher concentration to areas of lower concentration. For example, imagine two rooms and a fragrance (perfume) sprayed in one of the rooms. If the door between the rooms is closed, then the fragrance particles will remain in one room. However, if the door is opened, the fragrance can enter the second room. The particles will move around (diffuse) until they become evenly distributed between the rooms.

The plasma membrane is like a wall around the cell, separating the interior from the extracellular environment. What substances are able to diffuse into and out of the cell depend upon the permeability of the membrane. When the membrane is permeable to a substance, it is as though the door between the two rooms is open. In cells, substances either diffuse through the phospholipid bilayer or through water-filled protein channels called **pores**.

Water and non-polar (lipid soluble) substances like oxygen, carbon dioxide, nitrogen, steroid hormones, fat-soluble vitamins (A, E, D and K), urea (a product of protein metabolism), glycerol (a sweet oily fluid), small alcohols, and ammonia are all able to diffuse by dissolving directly through the membrane. Other small substances, typically ions, can pass through the cell's pores by simple diffusion. These substances include sodium, potassium, calcium, chloride, and bicarbonate ions.

Facilitated Diffusion

Some substances are too large to pass through the pores in the cell membrane. Others are too **hydrophilic** (polar) to diffuse directly across the membrane by dissolving in the phospholipid bilayer. These substances need the assistance of **carrier proteins**, or **transporters**, which span the membrane and allow for **facilitated diffusion** of the solutes across the membrane. This mechanism is still considered passive transport because it is driven by a concentration gradient and does not require cellular energy.

Glucose (sugar) is the most important substance which enters cells by facilitated diffusion. Since glucose is chemically altered immediately upon entering the cell, its concentration is always higher on the outside of the cell. Therefore, the concentration gradient favors the transport of glucose into, not out of, cells.

Quick Check Questions

1. Cellular energy is imparted to membrane transport proteins by the splitting of molecules of:
   A. AZT
   B. cAMP
   C. ATP
   D. ATPase

2. All of the following substances can pass through the plasma membrane by way of simple diffusion, EXCEPT:
   A. oxygen
   B. small alcohols
   C. large proteins like albumin
   D. calcium ions

3. When a substance is evenly distributed on either side of a membrane, this state is called:
   A. the concentration gradient
   B. equilibrium
   C. the diffusion factor
   D. the permeability quotient

4. The most important substance which enters the body by facilitated diffusion is:
   A. carbon dioxide
   B. glucose
   C. sodium ions
   D. bicarbonate ions

3.3.2 Osmosis and Filtration

10 minutes

Osmosis is a process with the same result as diffusion (that is, a solute reaches equilibrium in solution or across the cell membrane). However, instead of the solute moving down its concentration gradient, in osmosis the solvent (water) molecules move to achieve equilibrium. In osmosis, water moves across a membrane from an area of higher water concentration to an area of lower water concentration. (Note that if a solute, such as salt, is mixed with water, the concentration of water is less than in pure water because some water molecules are displaced by salt).

Isotonic Solution

The relative concentrations of water across a cell membrane affect the shape of the cell. If the concentrations of water and solute inside the cell are the same as they are outside the cell, there is no concentration difference and the cell maintains its normal shape. In this case, the fluid in which the cell is bathed is called **isotonic** (particles are at the same concentration as in the fluid inside of the cell).

Hypotonic Solution

If a cell is placed in a **hypotonic** solution (a solution with a lower concentration of solutes and a higher concentration of water than exists within the cell), water will enter the cell by osmosis in an effort to equalize the concentration. The water entering increases the cell's volume, and the membrane stretches. This causes the cell to swell and eventually burst. Cell bursting is called **lysis**.

Hypertonic Solution

Now, if the cell is placed in a **hypertonic** solution (with a higher concentration of solutes and a lower concentration of water than inside the cell), water will exit the cell by osmosis, causing the cell to shrink and the membrane to shrivel. Cell shrinkage is called **crenation**.

Filtration

Filtration is the passive process by which substances move in and out of cells down **hydrostatic pressure gradients** (differences in water pressure), instead of down concentration gradients. The movement of water and solutes is always from an area of higher water pressure to an area of lower water pressure. The pressure gradient forces permeable substances through the cell membrane.

Quick Check Questions

1. Cell swelling or bursting is called _____.

2. If a cell is placed in a __________ solution, the net flow of water will be out of the cell.

3. Substances move into and out of cells down water pressure gradients via:
   A. diffusion
   B. osmosis
   C. facilitated diffusion
   D. filtration

3.3.3 Active Transport

15 minutes

There are also processes by which substances are actively transported across cell membranes. These processes are mediated by carrier proteins. Since particle movement is against the concentration gradient, energy is required. Such processes may be: 1) **primary active transport**, or 2) **secondary active transport**. Primary active transport is the only mechanism in which energy is derived directly from splitting a molecule of ATP. In secondary active transport, energy from ATP is still used, but indirectly: it is stored in ion gradients that are maintained across the cell membrane, and is available for later use.

The most common primary active transport pump goes by various names: 1) the **sodium pump**, 2) the **sodium/potassium pump**, or 3) the **sodium/potassium ATPase** pump. All cells have many sodium/potassium pumps (hundreds per each square micrometer of membrane). The pumps remove sodium ions from the cell and pump potassium ions in. Both of the ions (sodium and potassium) are transported against their concentration gradients, so energy is required. The pump consists of an **enzyme complex**. It derives the energy it needs from the splitting of ATP (hence the name, ATPase).

The sodium/potassium pump has binding sites for three sodium (Na+) ions, two potassium (K+) ions, and one ATP molecule. After ATP binds to the pump, a high-energy phosphate bond is cleaved (ATP becomes ADP). This releases energy which is used by the pump to change its shape, thereby creating binding sites on the cell surface for two potassium ions.

The changing shape of the pump also causes the sodium ions to be transferred from the interior to the exterior side of the cell's membrane. Two potassium ions bind to the pump's potassium (K+) binding sites, while the three sodium ions are released into the extracellular fluid. Finally, the pump returns to its original shape, with release of the two potassium ions to the cell's interior. This change back to normal does not require energy. The pump is ready to transport more sodium and potassium ions across the membrane.

Symports and Antiports

Symports and **antiports** are integral membrane proteins which function as **secondary active transport** mechanisms These mechanisms use energy which is created as a by-product of the primary active pumping system. For example, the sodium pump maintains a large concentration of sodium ions outside the cell. This concentration gradient is a form of stored energy that can be used by the cell (just as water collected behind a dam is a source of energy that can be used to generate electric power).

Secondary active transport uses this stored energy to transport a substance against its concentration gradient. Symport occurs when two substances (one of which is usually sodium) are transported in the same direction across a membrane. The symport pump binds both substances at the same time. Then, the sodium concentration gradient created by the primary pump causes both substances to be transported. When the two substances travel in opposite directions across the membrane, the process is called antiport. As an example, the cytoplasmic pH level is regulated by sodium/hydrogen antiporters, which move sodium ions into the cell and hydrogen ions out.

Quick Check Questions

1. The most common primary active transport pump moves ______ out of the cell and potassium into the cell.

2. Secondary active transport mechanisms use energy stored in the form of concentration gradients. *True or False*

3.3.4 Bulk Transport

10 minutes

Large substances move across plasma membranes by various active transport processes known as **bulk transport**. The types of bulk transport include: 1) **phagocytosis**, 2) **pinocytosis**, 3) **receptor-mediated endocytosis**, and 4) **exo-cytosis**.

Phagocytosis ("cell eating") is the process by which large solid particles are transported into the cell for digestion by enzymes. Projections of the plasma membrane called **pseudopods** extend toward, and then surround, particles targeted for phagocytosis. The plasma membrane forms a bubble, called a **phagocytic vesicle**, around the particle as it is engulfed. Cytoplasmic **lysosomes** containing enzymes (lysozymes) then join with the phagocytic vesicle and digest its contents. The entire process of phagocytosis is illustrated in the diagram on this screen.

Pinocytosis is similar to phagocytosis, except that the engulfed material is extracellular liquid (hence the nickname "cell drinking"). No pseudopods form in pinocytosis. Rather, the plasma membrane simply involutes, thus drawing the liquid inside and creating a **pinocytic vesicle**. **Receptor-mediated endocytosis** is a more selective version of pinocytosis. **Ligands** in the fluid bind to a specific receptor protein on the extracellular surface. This binding triggers the infolding and engulfing process of pinocytosis.

Clinical Note:
Receptor-mediated endocytosis is designed to import needed materials to the cell. However, a "clever" virus such as HIV (the virus that causes AIDS) can

manipulate this mechanism to its own advantage. The virus binds to **CD4**, a **glycoprotein** receptor located on the surface of certain white blood cells called **helper T cells**. The virus is then able to enter (infect) the cell. Over time, HIV may kill many helper T cells, resulting in progressive failure of the immune system which leaves the person extremely susceptible to **opportunistic infections.**

Exocytosis describes the bulk transport mechanism by which material is expelled from cells. **Secretory vesicles** are membrane-enclosed structures within the cytoplasm. They transport substances destined for secretion outside the cell. During exocytosis, secretory vesicles fuse with the plasma membrane and then open, releasing their contents into the extracellular fluid.

Quick Check Questions

1. Large solid particles are engulfed by a cell and then digested by an active process called:
   A. pinocytosis
   B. antiporting
   C. phagocytosis
   D. active diffusion

2. __________ describes the mechanism by which bulk material exits cells in secretory vesicles.

3.4.1 Cytoplasm and Nucleus

10 minutes

Gel-like in its consistency, the cytoplasm is the contents of the cell's interior, enclosed by the plasma membrane. The fluid portion of the cytoplasm, the **cytosol**, is about 75 to 90 percent water. It contains many dissolved **metabolites** (organic compounds involved in the cell's energy-producing processes) as well as molecules such as proteins, carbohydrates, and lipids.

Each cell has a complex internal network of **filamentous** proteins throughout the cytoplasm. This framework, the **cytoskeleton**, provides cellular shape and integrity, and aids in cellular movement and internal transport. **Microtubules,**

microfilaments and **intermediate filaments** are the three main types of protein filaments which comprise the cytoskeleton.

The Nucleus

The nucleus, the "mastermind" of the cell, contains the genes which dictate cellular structure and function. Most cells contain one nucleus. Exceptions include mature red blood cells which lose their nuclei in the course of **erythropoiesis** (red blood cell development), and multinucleated cells (such as skeletal muscle fibers) which contain more than one nucleus.

The **nuclear envelope** is a double membrane (composed of both inner and outer phospholipid bilayers) which contains the nucleus. The nuclear envelope contains many **nuclear pores** allowing ions, polar molecules, and large molecules (such as RNA) to pass in and out of the nucleus. Nuclear pores are much larger than the channels in the plasma membrane.

Within a cell's nucleus is at least one **nucleolus** where **ribosomes** are synthesized. The spherical bodies which form nucleoli are made of protein and **ribonucleic acid** (RNA). Nucleoli are not bound by a membrane; they dissolve and disappear prior to cell division (**mitosis**).

Quick Check Questions

1. The cytoskeleton is comprised of all of the following, EXCEPT:
   A. microtubules
   B. microfilaments
   C. mitochondria
   D. intermediate filaments

2. The nuclear envelope is a single membrane with many nuclear pores, which surrounds the nucleus of a cell. *True or False*

3. The _________, inside the nucleus of a cell, is the site of ribosomal synthesis.

3.4.2 Ribosomes

10 minutes

Ribosomes reside in the cytoplasm and consist of protein and **ribosomal RNA (rRNA)**. This rRNA is synthesized within the nucleolus of the cell, using DNA as a template. Structurally, ribosomes consist of two spherical subunits. Their function is to synthesize proteins based on information contained in the genetic code of the cell. The **free ribosomes** occur singly or in clusters sprinkled throughout the cytoplasm, where they are involved with synthesis of internal cellular proteins. Ribosomes may also be attached to the **endoplasmic reticulum** (ER), making it look "rough." Membrane-bound or secreted proteins are synthesized by those ribosomes attached to the ER.

Endoplasmic Reticulum

The endoplasmic reticulum (ER) is a system of **cisterns**, or membrane-enclosed channels, attached to the nuclear envelope. These channels function to: 1) provide a surface area for chemical reactions, and 2) transport various products from one portion of the cell to another.

Endoplasmic reticulum is referred to either as **rough ER** or **smooth ER**, depending on whether it is embedded with ribosomes. Besides protein synthesis, the rough ER may process newly formed proteins by trimming the amino acid chain or adding sugar groups to form glycoproteins. In addition, rough ER forms pockets for the storage of new proteins and vesicles for their transport. Fatty acid, phospholipid, and steroid synthesis occurs in the smooth ER. In certain cells, the smooth ER also functions in chemical detoxification and muscle contraction.

Golgi Complex

The **Golgi complex** (or **Golgi apparatus**) completes the processing, sorting, and packaging of proteins and lipids which were synthesized on the ER. Structurally, the Golgi complex consists of several cisterns piled upon one another, like a stack of pancakes with bulging ends. The expanded ends of the cisterns are pinched off, forming clusters of Golgi vesicles, which function to transport the Golgi contents. All proteins destined for secretion are packaged in Golgi vesicles. These secretory vesicles migrate to the plasma membrane, and the proteins are released from the cell by exocytosis.

The packaging of newly manufactured secretory proteins helps protect the cell of origin from the proteins' enzymatic action. Digestive proteins that will remain in the cytoplasm are packaged in Golgi vesicles which become lysosomes. Other proteins and lipids pass through the Golgi complex before being incorporated within the plasma membrane. Besides sorting and packaging of proteins based on their functions, the Golgi apparatus also performs various final modifications of its newly synthesized contents.

Quick Check Questions

1. Fatty acid and steroid synthesis occur on the:
   A. rough ER
   B. smooth ER
   C. ribosomes
   D. nucleolus

2. Proteins destined for secretion by the cell are packaged in the Golgi complex and then released from the cell in a process called __________.

3. Some glycosylation of newly synthesized proteins occurs on the:
   A. rough ER
   B. smooth ER
   C. ribosomes
   D. nucleolus

3.4.3 Lysosomes and Mitochondria

10 minutes

Lysosomes

Lysosomes are Golgi vesicles loaded with extremely potent digestive enzymes intended for use within the cell. These **hydrolytic enzymes** (enzymes which cleave large molecules by adding water) work best at an acidic pH. Since the cytoplasmic pH is neutral, active transport pumps move hydrogen ions into the vesicle's interior, and so facilitate the function of the enzymes.

Lysosomes perform three essential functions: 1) they digest foreign substances and nutrients that enter the cell via endocytosis, 2) they recycle the cell's own organelles by digestion, returning the breakdown products to the cytoplasm for reuse, and 3) they digest extracellular debris at sites of injury, thus preparing the area for wound healing.

Mitochondria

Mitochondria generate ATP, and are therefore referred to as the "powerhouses" of the cell. Very active cells, such as muscle cells, are packed with mitochondria which provide a lot of energy in the form of ATP. In times of high energy demand, mitochondria have the unique ability to self-replicate. Mitochondria are the only organelle with this capacity. This is possible because they have their own DNA called **mitochondrial DNA**.

Each mitochondrion contains two membranes, both similar in structure to the plasma membrane. The inner membrane surrounds the **matrix**, or internal compartment, of the mitochondrion. It is folded into **cristae** which serve to increase its surface area. The enzymes which catalyze the catabolism of nutrients (such as glucose) for generation of ATP are embedded within the cristae.

Quick Check Questions

1. ____________ are known as the powerhouses of the cell because of their ability to generate ATP.

2. Lysosomes are cellular organelles containing ________ which function to digest material within the cell.

3. The only DNA found in the cell is in the nucleus. *True or False*

3.5.1 Protein Synthesis

12 minutes

Of all the chemicals synthesized by cells, proteins are the most numerous and in many ways the most significant. Proteins determine the physical and chemical characteristics of cells, and therefore of organisms.

Cells are essentially "protein factories," forming proteins by stringing together long chains of amino acids. The amino acid sequence gives the protein its unique structure and function.

Transcription

A protein's amino acid sequence is determined by information in the cell's genetic code. **Transcription** is the first step in the expression of this code. In this process, a **messenger RNA molecule (mRNA)** is synthesized within the nucleus. The nucleotide sequence of one gene in a DNA molecule is copied (**transcribed**) to form an mRNA molecule. This nucleotide sequence is later **translated** into a corresponding amino acid sequence. Recall that DNA is formed from two parallel strands of phosphate and sugar molecules, with paired nucleotide bases joining the two strands like the rungs of a ladder. The bases are **guanine**, which always pairs with **cytosine**, and **adenine**, which pairs with **thymine** in DNA and **uracil** in RNA. The language of the nucleic acids is contained in particular sequences of bases called **genes**.

One of the DNA strands (called the **template strand**) is copied to form the mRNA molecule. Since bases always pair in a specific way, the nucleotide sequence of the new single-stranded RNA is **complementary** to the starting DNA sequence. The transcription process is catalyzed by an enzyme complex known as **RNA polymerase**. Almost as soon as it is formed, mRNA separates from the DNA and leaves the nucleus through the nuclear pores. It enters the cytoplasm and binds to a ribosome.

Translation

The nucleotide sequence of mRNA specifies the amino acid sequence of the protein to be synthesized. The process of **translating** the message carried by mRNA into an amino acid sequence is carried out by ribosomes in the cytoplasm. A ribosome is made up of proteins and **ribosomal RNA (rRNA)** which is copied from DNA. It contains a large and small subunit. Both free ribosomes and those attached to rough endoplasmic reticulum can synthesize proteins from an mRNA sequence.

A third type of RNA, called **transfer RNA (tRNA)**, is also formed from a DNA template. It functions to carry amino acids which are free in the cytoplasm into position on the ribosome. Each tRNA has two critical binding sites: one for a specific amino acid, and one at the other end for the corresponding binding site on mRNA. The mRNA binding sites, called **codons**, are sequences of three nucleotide bases. The binding site on each tRNA is a triplet of bases complementary to a codon, and is called the **anticodon**.

The nucleotide sequence which was copied from DNA to mRNA is divided into groups of three bases called codons. Each codon corresponds to an anticodon on a tRNA molecule, which in turn carries a specific amino acid. Thus, since a codon specifics one of the twenty amino acids where are the building blocks of proteins, we see how the base sequence of DNA specifies the amino acid sequence of all proteins.

Therefore, a ribosome binds to a portion of mRNA, and amino acids are delivered to the site in their correct sequence, by tRNAs. Consecutive pairs of amino acids are joined together by peptide bonds, forming **polypeptide chains**. (The bonds are formed by dehydration synthesis reactions catalyzed by enzymes in the large subunit.) As each amino acid is added to the polypeptide, its tRNA is released, the ribosome moves to another unit (a codon with tRNA attached) along the mRNA chain, and another tRNA binds further along. Eventually, the complete primary structure of a protein molecule is synthesized, and the protein is ready for packaging and further processing in the endoplasmic reticulum or Golgi apparatus.

Quick Check Questions

1. The sequence of bases in a DNA "template" strand is __________ to form messenger RNA.

2. Translation of messenger RNA into a sequence of amino acids occurs within the cytoplasm. *True or False*

3. A codon is made of:
   A. two amino acids linked by a peptide bond
   B. three ribonucleic acids which code for one amino acid
   C. three amino acids which code for one nucleic acid
   D. two chromosomes which make up one gene

4. ________ RNA has an anticodon which matches a codon on mRNA, and which corresponds to the specific amino acid it carries to the ribosome.

3.5.2 Mitosis

8 minutes

Cells reproduce themselves by means of **cell division**. Cell division involves two steps. During **mitosis** (nuclear division), DNA is organized and distributed into two identical nuclei. **Cytokinesis** completes the process by splitting the plasma membrane and cytoplasm. This results in two **daughter cells** that each contain identical genetic information.

Prior to cell division, the cell is in a quiescent growth phase called **interphase**. During interphase, the cell engages in growth, metabolism, and preparation for its reproductive phase. Since each daughter cell will receive a complete set of genes, the entire **genome** is copied during interphase in a process called **DNA replication**. This ensures that the cell's genetic traits are passed on to succeeding generations. In addition, the cell replicates structures such as the centrosomes and other organelles in preparation for division.

DNA replication proceeds by a mechanism similar to the **transcription** steps in **mRNA** synthesis, with the **complementary** base sequence being copied from a **template strand**. It is directed by **DNA polymerase**. The helical DNA molecule unwinds in the region of replication. Free nucleotides base-pair with one DNA strand, and then are joined together to form a new sugar-phosphate backbone. (Recall that **cytosine** always pairs with **guanine**, and **thymine** with **adenine**.)

This process proceeds along each of the original chains, until each has a new, complementary strand attached. The molecule separates into two molecules, each containing the same set of **genes** as the original. Finally, both DNA molecules coil back into the helical form.

There are four sequential phases that occur during mitosis: 1) **prophase**, 2) **metaphase**, 3) **anaphase**, and 4) **telophase**. After cell division is completed, the daughter cells enter interphase and prepare for another round of replication. The entire process is known as the **cell cycle**.

Quick Check Questions

1. The sequence of the stages of mitosis is as follows:
   A. interphase, prophase, metaphase, anaphase, telophase
   B. prophase, interphase, telophase, anaphase, metaphase
   C. interphase, metaphase, anaphase, telophase, prophase

2. ___________ is the process by which the plasma membrane and the cytoplasm are split into two parts during cell division.

3. The process of DNA __________ during interphase ensures that the daughter cells will carry the same genetic information as the original cell.

3.5.3 Mitosis (Continued)

8 minutes

During prophase, the nucleoli and the nuclear envelope break down and disappear. The replicated centrioles move to opposite sides, or poles, of the cell. **Spindle fibers**, a type of microtubule, begin to appear and orient between the opposing poles. The 46 replicated chromosomes shorten and thicken into a form which consists of two **chromatids** (condensed DNA molecules) attached by a **centromere.**

During metaphase, the chromosomes align along the equator of the cell, between the two centrosomes. Spindle fibers from both poles attach to each centromere. This is followed by anaphase, in which the spindle fibers contract, splitting the centromeres and separating the sister chromatids of each chromosome. The sister chromatids then move toward opposite poles of the dividing cell.

In telophase, the processes of prophase are reversed. Condensed chromosomes loosen, unwinding into long strands of DNA called **chromatin threads**. The nuclear envelope reappears around each new set of chromosomes, nucleoli form, and the spindle fibers disappear. Cytokinesis continues as the two sides of the plasma membrane meet and fuse. Finally, the daughter cells are complete and ready to begin another period of growth.

Meiosis is another form of cell division which only occurs when primitive sex cells divide to become mature sex cells or **gametes**. Meiosis is discussed in the chapter on the *Reproductive System*.

Quick Check Questions

1. The chromosomes align along the equatorial plane during:
   A. anaphase
   B. metaphase
   C. interphase
   D. telophase

2. The nuclear envelope breaks down during:
   A. prophase
   B. telophase
   C. metaphase
   D. anaphase

3. The structure of DNA during interphase is long strands called _________ threads.

3.6.1 Tissues - Overview

12 minutes

Tissues are groups of similar cell types which work together to carry out specific activities. For example, nervous tissue is a combination of **neurons**, which conduct impulses, and support cells (**glial cells**). Together, neurons and glial cells carry out the functions of nervous tissue: to coordinate body movements and activities.

Histology refers to the study of tissues (histos = web, ology = study of). A fluid medium, **extracellular fluid** (ECF), surrounds the cells of a body, providing a means for cell to cell communication via dissolved chemicals. ECF may be **interstitial fluid**, which fills the microscopic spaces between cells in tissues, or

plasma, which is the liquid (non-cellular) portion of the blood.

There are four principle types of body tissue, classified according to function and structure. These are: 1) **epithelial tissue**, 2) **connective tissue**, 3) **muscle tissue**, and 4) **nervous tissue**. The skin, which is shown here (in software), is an organ composed of epithelial, connective, muscle and nervous tissue. Bone is a type of connective tissue that forms the relatively lightweight framework of the body. Muscle tissue is vital for body movement and production of heat. Nervous tissue is specialized for conducting impulses throughout the body. Note: Muscle tissue and nervous tissue will be discussed in more detail in subsequent chapters.

Most cells within a tissue are anchored in place either to other cells or to a **basement membrane** of connective tissue. The points of contact between cells are called **cell junctions**. There are three distinct types of cell junctions: 1) **tight junctions** which form fluid tight seals, 2) **anchoring junctions** which hold cells together or fasten them to the extracellular material, and 3) **communicating junctions** (or **gap junctions**), which permit electrical or chemical signals to pass from cell to cell.

Quick Check Questions

1. The four principal types of body tissue are muscle, nervous, __________, and connective.

2. The following type of cell junction permits electrical or chemical signals to pass from cell to cell.
   A. communicating junctions (gap junctions)
   B. tight junctions
   C. anchoring junctions
   D. basement membranes

3. Cytology refers to the study of cells, while _________ refers to the study of tissues.

3.6.2 Epithelial Tissue

20 minutes

There are two types of epithelial tissue, which differ in both structure and function. These are: 1) **covering** and **lining epithelium**, and 2) **glandular epithelium**. Covering or lining epithelium forms the outer layer of skin and of some internal organs.

Covering Epithelium

Covering epithelium also lines the inner surfaces of blood vessels, ducts, body cavities, as well as the digestive, respiratory, urinary, and reproductive tracts. **Glandular epithelium** is the **secretory** tissue of glands such as the sweat, adrenal, thyroid, salivary, and mammary glands. The structure of covering epithelium is reflective of its function. The more wear and tear an epithelial surface receives, the more **stratified** (layered) it will be. Thus, epithelium on the palms of the hands has many more layers than that covering the internal organs.

If the primary function of epithelial tissue is absorption or filtration, then a single layer of stratified epithelium is formed. Tissue composed of a single layer of epithelium is called **simple epithelium. Pseudostratified epithelium** is also tissue with a single layer of cells. However, some of the cells do not reach the surface of the tissue, resulting in a stratified appearance. Covering epithelial tissue is classified by the shape of its cells, as well as by their layering arrangement. **Squamous** describes cells that are flattened or scale-like. **Cuboidal** cells appear square in cross-section, while **columnar** cells are tall and cylindrical. Since **transitional** cells easily change shape, they are found where there is a great degree of stretching (such as in the urinary bladder).

Ciliated epithelium is a modified form of simple and pseudostratified columnar epithelium. This tissue is capable of moving fluids and small particles of debris along its surface by the action of hair-like projections on the cells called **cilia**. For example, ciliated columnar epithelium lines the respiratory tract, where it helps particulate matter from the lungs. Similarly, ciliated simple columnar epithelium which lines the **fallopian tubes** of the female reproductive system. Movement of the cilia helps to propel **gametes** (eggs) along the passageway of the fallopian tubes.

Glandular Epithelium

Both **exocrine** (outwardly secreting) and **endocrine** (internally secreting) glands are composed of glandular epithelial tissue. Exocrine glands secrete mucus, perspiration, oil, wax, or digestive enzymes onto free tissue surfaces, either directly or through ducts. Endocrine glands secrete **hormones** (chemical messengers) directly into the extracellular fluid, where they diffuse into the **systemic circulation**.

There are three functional types of exocrine glands:

1) The cells of **holocrine glands** accumulate cellular products in their cytosol The cells then die, discharging their contents as glandular secretions.

2) **Merocrine glands**, the most common type, discharge their cells' products by exocytosis.

3) In **apocrine glands**, cells pinch off a portion of their **apical surface** filled with secretory product. (The apical surface of a cell is the side facing the **lumen**, or inner chamber, of a glandular structure).

Endocrine glands do not have ducts. Their secretory products simply diffuse into the extracellular fluid and then into the blood capillaries, where they are carried to all the cells of the body. The secretions of endocrine glands are called hormones: they are discussed in detail in the *Endocrine System* chapter.

Location of Covering Epithelial Tissue

Simple squamous epithelium is found lining the inner side of the heart and the blood vessels. Here, it is called **endothelium**. The linings of the lungs and the Bowman's capsules of the kidney are also constructed of simple squamous epithelium.

Stratified squamous epithelium is found as the outer layer of the skin and the inner lining of the nose, mouth, vagina, and anal canal. Stratified squamous epithelia may be **keratinized** or **non-keratinized**. Keratin is a protein that makes the epithelium tough, hard, and water-tight enough to withstand bacterial invasion. The skin is keratinized, but the nose, mouth, vagina, and anal canal are not. This is why some pathogens are more easily transmitted through these epithelial areas (for example, sexually transmitted diseases).

Simple cuboidal epithelium is found lining the secretory ducts of glands, in the tubules of the kidneys, and as the tissue covering the ovary. Simple columnar epithelium is found in the lining of the digestive tract. Ciliated simple or pseudostratified columnar tissue lines the internal part of the spinal column, the respiratory tract, and the uterus.

Quick Check Questions

1. Holocrine, apocrine, and _________ glands are three different types of exocrine glands.

2. ________ cells are flat epithelial cells, while columnar cells are more cylindrical in shape.

3. The type of epithelial tissue which lines the respiratory tract is called ciliated pseudo__________ columnar epithelium.

4. The outer layer of the skin (epidermis) is made of this type of epithelium.
   A. simple columnar
   B. simple squamous
   C. stratified squamous
   D. ciliated cuboidal

3.6.3 Connective Tissue

8 minutes

Connective tissue performs a variety of functions: it provides support, protection, and flexibility to a particular structure, transports and stores materials, and provides insulation. **Bone**, **cartilage**, **adipose** (fat), **blood**, and **lymph** are some of the major forms of connective tissue found in the body. These tissues are discussed in the next three sections.

Connective tissue is made up of various types of cells and fibers, and a mixture of polysaccharides and proteins called **intercellular material** or **matrix**. Intercellular matrix can exist as: 1) a fluid (the plasma in blood), 2) a semifluid (hyaluronic acid which lubricates the joints), 3) a gelatinous substance (chondroitin sulfate, which provides adhesion between bone, cartilage, and skin cells), or 4) a solid (the calcified areas of bone found between living cells). **Loose connective tissue** acts as a packing material in the body. It is composed of strong protein fibers made of **collagen** and **elastin** cells. Cells such as **fibroblasts** (which manufacture fibers), and macrophages (the scavengers of the circulatory and immune systems) are found scattered among the fibers in a semi-fluid matrix.

Collagen fibers are strong, while elastin fibers have the capacity to stretch and bend. Elastin is found within the dermis of the skin. It also surrounds and supports various organs, as well as networks of nerves and blood vessels.

Quick Check Questions

1. Cells called fibroblasts produce strong white protein fibers called ________.

2. Each of the following are major forms of connective tissue, EXCEPT:
   A. endothelium
   B. blood
   C. bone
   D. cartilage

3.6.4 Adipose, Blood, and Fibrous Tissues

8 minutes

Widely distributed around the body, fat or **adipose tissue** accounts for a large percentage of total body weight (on average 18 percent in males and 28 percent in females). Each adipose cell has a relatively large single **vacuole** (a pocket) of fat. Adipose tissue is found wherever **areolar** connective tissue is located.

Adipose tissue cells play three significant roles in the body: 1) it provides a reserve supply of energy, 2) it acts as protective padding to absorb the energy of jolting body movements, and 3) it is an insulator, preventing loss of heat. Adipose tissue can be found around the eyes, in the palms of the hands and soles of the feet, between the joints, and beneath the skin virtually all over the body.

Blood

Liquid or **circulating connective tissue**, known as **blood**, provides nutrients and oxygen to all cells and removes their waste products. Blood consists of a fluid matrix called **plasma** and three types of blood cells or **corpuscles**: 1) red corpuscles or **erythrocytes**, 2) white corpuscles or **leukocytes**, and 3) platelets or **thrombocytes**.

Fibrous Tissue

Fibrous connective tissue or **white fibrous tissue** is composed of densely packed longitudinal white collagen fibers. Since the fibers are arranged in parallel, they give longitudinal strength to the tissue. **Ligaments**, **tendons**, and **fascia** (a sheet of tissue which cover and enclose the muscles), keep muscles in place and help in their movement. These structures are composed of strong, flexible fibrous connective tissue.

Quick Check Questions

1. This type of connective tissue serves as an insulator.
   A. blood
   B. adipose
   C. white fibrous tissue
   D. ligaments

2. Blood is made of three types of cells in a fluid matrix called ______.

3. On average, men are heavier than women because they have a higher percentage body fat. *True or False*

3.6.5 Cartilage and Bone Tissue

8 minutes

Cartilage and **bone** are two types of connective tissue which form the framework of the body, the skeleton. Cartilage, commonly called "gristle," is an extremely firm, yet flexible, material which provides movement, flexibility, and support. Cartilage is composed of a fiber matrix and a scattered group of cartilage cells called **chondrocytes**. Most of the bones of the skeleton first develop in embryo as cartilage structures. During development and throughout adulthood the cartilage is transformed into bone through a process called **ossification**.

Cartilage persists in certain regions of the body, such as the tip of the nose, the external ear, and the spinal column, throughout one's lifetime. Cartilage also remains in the **costal** area, where the ribs are connected to the breastbone. The flexibility of cartilage permits the ribcage to move during breathing.

Bone tissue is composed of two general types of cells within a matrix of water, fibers, and mineral salts. **Osteoblasts** form hard bony tissue from deposition of calcium salts in the collagen fiber framework. **Osteoclasts** break bones down into their matrix components, which can be used elsewhere in the body. Therefore, growth of the skeleton is a continuous process of synthesis of new bone and reabsorption of old material.

Quick Check Question

1. By the time a person is 50 years old, all of the body's cartilage has been replaced by bone. *True or False*

2. ___________ build bone, while osteoclasts break it down.

Chapter 4
The Integumentary System

4.1.1 Integumentary System - Overview

10 minutes

The **skin** is the body's largest organ, weighing 4.5 to 5 kilograms (10 to 11 lbs) and covering an area of about 2 square meters (22 square feet) in an average sized-adult. This **integument**, or "covering," of the body is comprised of skin tissue, nerve endings, blood vessels, and the **appendages** of the skin: hair, nails, and glands. Together, these structures aid in temperature regulation, protect the body, permit sensation of the environment, excrete wastes, and manufacture vitamin D.

Functions of the Skin

Skin cells produce (or synthesize) **keratin**, a tough protein which helps keep moisture in and bacteria out. Skin cells also produce **melanin**, a pigment derived from the amino acid tyrosine. Melanin blocks the sun's ultraviolet (UV) rays from damaging the skin's underlying tissues. Sweat glands in the skin promote cooling of the body by evaporating warm water from the skin's surface. Some waste products are also excreted in the sweat.

Blood vessels in the skin dilate in hot weather, allowing more blood to flow near the surface where it can be cooled by the air. During cold weather, blood vessels in the skin constrict. When blood vessels constrict, the amount of blood flowing to the surface of the skin is decreased, and heat is preserved.

Nerve endings in skin are sensitive to pain, heat, cold, and pressure (whether hard enough to compress the tissue, or a light touch on the skin's surface). These sensory messages are necessary for responding to the environment. When exposed to the ultraviolet (UV) rays in sunlight, a compound in the skin's cells is converted to vitamin D, an essential aid in the absorption of calcium from foods.

Quick Check Questions

1. The integumentary system includes:
   A. skin, hair, nails, teeth, and eyes
   B. skin, blood vessels, and glands
   C. skin, hair, nails, glands, blood vessels, and nerve endings
   D. skin only

2. The functions of the integumentary system are: protection, sensation, excretion, vitamin D synthesis, and ___________ regulation.

3. Keratin and melanin are compounds produced by skin cells that aid in:
   A. sensation
   B. temperature regulation
   C. excretion
   D. protection

4. Blood vessels in the skin play an important role in regulation of body temperature. *True or False*

5. Sunlight is required for the synthesis of vitamin D in skin cells. *True or False*

4.2.1 Structure of the Skin

15 minutes

The skin is made up of two layers. The outer **epidermis** is a thin protective layer containing many dead cells, and the inner **dermis** is thicker, living tissue capable of supplying the skin with nutrients. A layer of dense connective tissue , known as the **subcutaneous layer**, **hypodermis**, or **superficial fascia**, lies under the dermis. The subcutaneous layer attaches the skin to underlying structures.

The Epidermis

This outer covering of the skin is thinner than a piece of paper: 0.17 millimeters (1/200 of an inch) over most areas of the body. The epidermis is thicker on the palms and soles of the feet, where friction and wear are heavy. Classified as a membranous tissue, the epidermis is composed of **stratified squamous epithelium** cells (meaning layered and plate-like, as if covered with scales). There are no blood vessels passing thorough the epidermis, so it relies on the underlying dermis for its supply of nutrients and oxygen.

Four Cell Types in the Epidermis

Keratinocytes are cells that produce keratin. They protect underlying cells from injury, water loss, and infection. Originating in the deepest part of the epidermis, keratinocytes are pushed upward toward the surface where they are sloughed off 3 to 4 weeks later. On the way up keratinocytes become smaller and more flattened. Eventually, they lose their nuclei and die. By the time they reach the surface, the keratin they have produced makes the cells hard, tough, and waterproof.

Melanocytes produce the pigment, melanin, which gives skin its color. The enzyme **tyrosinase** converts the amino acid tyrosine into melanin within the melanocytes. Melanin is then transferred to other skin cells, where it collects around the nuclei to protect the cells' genetic material, and the underlying tissue, from the sun's UV rays.

The epidermis also contains cells that perform specialized functions. **Langerhans cells** aid in fighting infection in the skin by participating in the immune response. **Merkel cells** are specialized for the sensation of touch and are found only in sensitive, hairless areas of the skin.

Five Layers of the Epidermis

The external **stratum corneum** (horny layer) contains only dead keratinocytes which are continually shed and replaced. The **stratum lucidum** (clear layer), present only on the palms and soles of the feet. It is also composed of dead keratinocytes that contain a gel-like substance, **eleiden**, which is later transformed into keratin. In the **stratum granulosum** (granular layer), keratinocytes lose their nuclei and die. At this stage, they are filled with **keratohyalin**, the initial keratin precursor.

In the **stratum spinosum** (spiny layer), the spine-like projections of the melanocytes extend among the living keratinocytes. Melanin is transferred to the keratinocytes at cellular junctions called **desmosomes**. The **stratum basale** (base layer) is a single cell layer which produce keratinocytes and melanocytes through constant cell division (**mitosis**). The term, **stratum germinativum** (growth layer) is sometimes used to describe the stratum basale and stratum spinosum together.

Quick Check Questions

1. The layer of skin located between the epidermis and the hypodermis is the _______.

2. All of the cells of the epidermis are dead. *True or False*

3. The protein which gives skin its color is called:
   A. keratin
   B. melanin
   C. eleiden
   D. keratohyalin

4. Which of the following is NOT one of the cell types in the epidermis?
   A. melanocyte
   B. keratinocyte
   C. Langerhan's cells
   D. desmosome

5. Dead or dying keratinocytes may be found in all of the epidermal cell layers, EXCEPT:
   A. stratum spinosum
   B. stratum corneum
   C. stratum lucidum
   D. stratum granulosum

6. Keratohyalin and eleiden are precursors of _______.

7. _______ cells are specialized for the sensation of touch, and are found in sensitive, hairless areas of the epidermis.

4.3.1 The Dermis

15 minutes

The **dermis** or **corium** is living tissue which lies beneath the epidermis. The dermis ranges from 0.5 to 4 millimeters in depth, much thicker than the epidermis. In general, the dermis is thicker on the dorsal side than on the ventral side of the body. It is thickest on the palms and soles of the feet, and thinnest on the eyelids, penis, and scrotum.

The dermis is composed of two layers, the papillary and the reticular regions. Both are made of strong flexible connective tissue containing **collagen, elastin fibers**, and **adipocytes** (fat cells). Rich innervation enables dermis to process sensory information. Its extensive network of blood vessels is important in regulation of body temperature and delivery of nutrients. **Hair follicles, muscle fibers, sweat glands**, and **sebaceous glands** are embedded in the dermis at various levels in.

Fibroblasts are the cells responsible for wound healing and scar formation. Fibroblasts can very quickly produce large amounts of collagen and elastin fibers for connective tissue to repair injuries. **Macrophages** (or **histiocytes**) are immune cells. In the dermis they engulf bacteria and other foreign material, protecting the skin from infection and debris. **Mast cells** are immune cells involved in allergic reactions and blood clot formation in the skin.

Two Layers of the Dermis

The outer dermis is known as the **papillary region**. This region of the skin is named for its finger-like projections, **dermal papillae**, that extend into the epidermis. Dermal papillae increase the surface area available for transferring nutrients and oxygen from dermal blood vessels to the epidermis. **Epidermal ridges** reflect the patterns of dermal papillae below. They are especially pronounced on the fingertips, palms, and soles of the feet, where they improve gripping ability (and form finger, hand and footprints).

The inner dermis, or **reticular layer** is a dense network of tough collagen and elastin fibers that give skin its strength and its ability to stretch and spring back. Nerve cells, smooth muscle fibers, and glands are interspersed within the fiber network. Muscles attached to each hair follicle (**arrector pili muscles**) cause hair to stand on end, forming "goose bumps" in cold conditions.

The Subcutaneous Layer

The subcutaneous layer, also known as the **hypodermis** or **superficial fascia**, is composed of **adipose** (fat) and **areolar** (loose connective) tissue. In this layer, collagen and elastin fibers are loosely packed and liberally interspersed with fat cells (known as **adipocytes** or **lipocytes**). Fat formed and stored in the subcutaneous layer is an important energy source and a heat insulator, and provides protection for underlying structures. Characteristic male and female body shapes result from varying patterns of subcutaneous fat storage.

Quick Check Questions

1. Another name for the corium is the ______.

2. The dermis is generally thinner than the outer epidermis. *True or False*

3. The dermis contains all but which of the following cell types?
   A. histiocytes
   B. keratinocytes
   C. mast cells
   D. fibroblasts

4. The layer of the dermis which is directly attached to the epidermis is called the _________ region.

5. Which of the following are NOT found in the dermis?
   A. arrector pili muscles
   B. sebaceous glands
   C. blood vessels
   D. melanocytes

6. The subcutaneous layer is mostly composed of areolar and ______ tissue.

4.3.2 Hair, Nails, and Sweat Glands

20 minutes

The main functions of hairs on the body (**pili**, singular = **pilus**) are protection from foreign objects entering the eyes, prevention of heat loss from the head, and sensation of touch. Sensitive touch receptors in the skin are activated by movement of the hair. The hairless areas of the body are the palms of the hands, soles of the feet, lips, nipples, penis, and labia minora.

Hair

Each hair grows from a **follicle**, a tubular structure formed by specialized epidermal cells that spread down into the dermis. Hair cells are formed at the bottom of the tube, in a section of the **stratum germinativum** called the **germinal matrix**. Each growing hair gets it's blood supply from the **papilla** (plural = **papillae**), an indentation of capillary-rich dermal tissue which extends into the base of the follicle.

The **root** of the hair is the section within the follicle, while the **shaft** projects above the epidermis. All of the cells of the hair shaft are dead. Straight hair has a round shaft, while curly hair has a flat shaft which is not as strong and breaks more easily. Each hair has three layers: 1) the inner **medulla** contains loosely packed cells, 2) the **cortex** is made of elongated cells, and 3) the **cuticle**, or outer surface has scale-like cells. Hair cells are hard, keratinized, and pigmented with melanin, which is contributed by melanocytes in the follicle. Melanocytes stop manufacturing melanin as part of the aging process, and thus hair turns grey.

Nails

Nails help protect the ends of the fingers and toes from being injured, and also aid in gripping. Nails are formed from hard, keratinized cells of the epidermis that are cemented tightly together. The **nail body** is the translucent part of the nail visible on the dorsal surface. The nail body appears pink because of capillaries carrying blood underneath it. The **free edge** of the nail body extends past the end of the finger. The **nail root** is not visible on the surface, because it is buried in a fold of skin.

The **lunula** is a half-moon shaped, whitish area where active nail growth occurs. The lunula appears white because the stratum basale in this area is thickened so underlying capillaries do not show through. The keratinized cells of the nail grow from the **nail matrix**, the epithelial tissue beneath the nail root. The **cuticle** or **eponychium** is a section of the skin's stratum corneum that adheres to the proximal end of the nail surface. Fingernails grow about 1 millimeter each week. Interestingly, the longer the digit, the faster the nail grows so the growth rate of toenails is slower.

Sebaceous Glands

Sebaceous glands are oil-producing glands in the dermis that secrete **sebum** directly into the hair follicles. Sebum is an oily substance rich in proteins, fats, and cholesterol. Sebum prevents hair from becoming too brittle, keeps the skin from becoming too dry, and discourages the growth of some bacteria and fungi. In some areas of the body (lips, eyelids, penis and labia minor), the ducts of sebaceous glands open directly onto the skin's surface. There are no sebaceous glands on the palms of the hands or soles of the feet. Sex hormones stimulate the production of sebum, so when the levels of sex hormones increase at puberty, sebaceous glands manufacture excessive amounts of sebum. The sebaceous glands enlarge, resulting in pimples, or **acne**.

Sudoriferous (Sweat) Glands

There are two types of sudoriferous (sweat-producing) glands: 1) **eccrine sweat glands**, and 2) **apocrine sweat glands**.

The Eccrine Glands

The eccrine glands are small and quite plentiful. They are most numerous on the palms and soles of the feet: one square inch of skin on the palm contains about 3000 eccrine glands. Eccrine glands occur on all body surfaces except the lips, ear canal, nail beds, and parts of the genitalia. Each eccrine gland is formed from a coiled tube that originates in the dermis and extends up into the epidermis. The tube or **excretory duct** opens to the surface in a **pore**. Sweat released from the pores is mostly water, but with some dissolved waste products such as salts and polar organic substances. Sweat functions in cooling the body. As the hot water in sweat evaporates, a great deal of heat leaves the body along with it. (Note that body odor does not come from sweat, but from bacteria on the skin that respond to the moisture.)

Apocrine Sweat Glands

Apocrine sweat glands are larger than eccrine glands and they release a more viscous secretion. Apocrine glands originate deep in the subcutaneous layer. Instead of secreting directly onto the surface through pores, apocrine glands secrete into hair follicles. Apocrine glands are concentrated around the pubic area, the nipples and the armpits. Apocrine glands only begin to function at puberty, and are stimulated by stress and sexual arousal. Besides the eccrine and apocrine glands, note that both the **mammary glands**, which produce milk, and **ceruminous glands**, which produce wax in the ear canal, are modified apocrine sweat glands.

Quick Check Questions

1. Each growing hair gets its blood supply from the:
   A. germinal matrix
   B. hair papilla
   C. lunula
   D. stratum corneum

2. The three layers of a hair are the medulla, the cortex, and the outer surface, the _______.

3. The half-moon shaped, whitish area visible on the surface where active nail growth occurs is called the:
   A. nail body
   B. free edge
   C. nail root
   D. lunula

4. The eponychium is a section of the skin's stratum corneum that adheres to the proximal end of the nail surface. It is also known as the _______.

5. Eccrine sweat glands are stimulated by sex hormones. *True or False*

6. Mammary glands and ceruminous glands are related to ________ glands.

Chapter 5
The Skeletal System

5.1.1 Skeletal System - Overview

10 minutes

How can a human being stand straight as a tree or run a 4-minute mile? Why might a 75 year old woman notice the joints of her fingers are larger and painful to move? The answers lie in the **skeletal system**: the light-weight, dynamic framework of the human body. The skeletal system contains a variety of tissues: 1) **bone**, 2) **cartilage**, 3) **tendons**, and 4) **ligaments**.

Bone

Bone functions in a number of capacities. Much like the steel framework of a building, bone provides structural "support" for the body as a whole. Bone also serves as "protection" for soft tissue structures in the body. For example, the brain is enclosed and protected by the skull, the heart is encased in the rib cage, and the vertebral column protects the soft tissue of the spinal cord. Bones are also essential for "movement."

By serving as rods to which muscles and tendons attach, bones act as "levers" to help move our limbs. In addition to their mechanical functions, bones are the center for the manufacture of blood cells. **Hemopoiesis** (or **hematopoiesis**), the formation of new **red blood cells**, **white blood cells**, and **platelets**, occurs within the inner structure of bones referred to as the **red bone marrow**. In addition, minerals such as calcium and phosphorous are stored in bone matrix. When these minerals are needed in the body, their extraction from bone is activated by **parathyroid hormone**. When calcium and phosphorous are abundant, their storage in bone is stimulated by the hormone **calcitonin**.

Quick Check Questions

1. Components of the skeletal system include all of the following tissues, EXCEPT:
   A. cartilage
   B. tendons
   C. muscles
   D. connective tissue

2. Hemopoiesis:
   A. is carried out by parathyroid hormone
   B. is the synthesis of hemoglobin
   C. occurs within the red bone marrow
   D. is the destruction of red blood cells

5.2.1 Types of Bones

7 minutes

There are several different types of bones. **Long bones** include all the bones of the extremities that serve as levers. For example, the **humerus**, **radius**, and **ulna** in the arm, the **femur**, **tibia** and **fibula** in the leg, and the **metacarpals** and **metatarsals** in the hands and feet, respectively, are all long bones. Examples of **flat bones** include the bones of the **cranium**, which encase the brain, the **scapula** in the shoulder area and the **ribs**. Short bones are small somewhat cube-shaped, with about equal length and width. Short bones in the wrist and the ankle function to transfer forces between long bones. **Sesamoid bones** are a type of small bones that are enclosed within tendons. Examples are the **patella** in the knee and the **pisiform** in the wrist. Bones with more complex shapes, such as the vertebrae of the back, are known as **irregular bones**.

Quick Check Questions

1. The scaphoid (a small bone in the wrist) would be categorized as which type of bone:
   A. flat bone
   B. sesamoid bone
   C. long bone
   D. short bone

2. The patella, which is enclosed in the patellar tendon of the knee, is a:
   A. flat bone
   B. sesamoid bone
   C. long bone

5.2.2 The Structure of the Bone

12 minutes

There are two forms of bone tissue: **compact** (dense) bone, and spongy or **cancellous** bone. Compact bone is dense and very strong. It forms a hard cylinder on the outside of long bones. Microscopically, compact bone is composed of a **matrix** of calcium phosphate crystals. These crystals form tiny cylinders called **osteons**, each of which circle a **central (Haversian) canal**, where blood and nerves travel. Spaces in the bone matrix, called **lacunae**, house the living bone cells, or **osteocytes**. Osteocytes nourish the bone matrix and regulate calcium levels in the body by releasing or sequestering calcium in the matrix of bone tissue.

The spongy or cancellous bone is light and not as strong as compact bone. The ends of the long bones are filled with spongy bone to decrease the overall weight of the skeleton. Flat bones contain a layer of cancellous bone (called **diploe**) sandwiched between two layers of compact bone. Cancellous bone consists of **trabeculae**, or **spicules** of bone, in between tiny chambers. Filling these chambers is the **red bone marrow**, where hemopoiesis occurs. Long bones contain a large **medullary cavity**. This cavity is lined by a thin membrane called the **endosteum** and contains fatty **yellow bone marrow**, which includes cells which help remodel bone and repair bone fractures. Bone is covered by a dense layer called the **periosteum**. This fibrous tissue provides a strong point of attachment for muscles, tendons, and ligaments. The periosteum also contains cells responsible for remodeling and repairing bone.

Quick Check Questions

1. The types of bone include:
   A. long, short, flat, pisiform, and regular bones
   B. long, short, flat, sesamoid, and irregular bones
   C. spongy, cancellous, and non-cancellous bones
   D. pisiform, sesamoid, triquetral bones

2. This kind of bone is covered by periosteum:
   A. long bone
   B. flat bone
   C. spongy bone
   D. A and B

3. Osteocytes:
   A. are involved in hydroxyapetite crystal formation
   B. reside within the bone marrow
   C. cause production of red blood cells
   D. reside the lacunae in compact bone

4. The endosteum does all of the following, EXCEPT:
   A. line the inside of the compact bone
   B. assist in repairing bone
   C. enclose yellow bone marrow
   D. regulate serum calcium levels

5.2.3 The Growth of Bone

8 minutes

Between the **diaphysis** (shaft) and the two **epiphyses** (ends) of a long bone is an **epiphyseal line**. Long bones develop first as cartilage, which then **calcifies** and hardens to become bone. In a growing child, bones lengthen from the **epiphyseal plate** or **growth plate**, which contains growing and calcifying cartilage at various stages. When growth ceases, the epiphyseal plate calcifies to become the epiphyseal line. Unlike long bones, flat bones are not derived from cartilage, but directly from a membrane of **undifferentiated** cells, which become **osteoblasts**, (matrix-producing cells which form bone). Spaces of membrane between the growing cranial bones are visible on a baby's head, as soft spots, or **fontanels** (to be discussed in more detail later).

Cells of Bone

Bone is a dynamic tissue, continually being broken down and rebuilt to release or store minerals. In addition to the **osteocytes**, two other types of bone cell are responsible for these processes. These are **osteoblasts** and **osteoclasts**. Osteoblasts are responsible for building the bone. They secrete organic material, which then calcifies to form the bone matrix. Osteoblast cells mature into the osteocytes, which regulate the release of calcium into the bloodstream. Osteoclasts live mainly on the surface of bones. They are **phagocytic** cells, which erode and absorb old bone tissue, so that bone is constantly being remodeled. None of the bone cell types are capable of **mitosis** (that is, the usual process of cell reproduction, nuclear division).

Quick Check Questions

1. Osteocytes are mature:
   A. osteoblasts
   B. osteoclasts
   C. osteoprogenitor cells
   D. erythroblasts

2. The bone cell type which is capable of phagocytosis is an:
   A. osteoclast
   B. osteoblast
   C. osteocyte
   D. osteophyte

5.2.4 The Skeletal System

10 minutes

The skeletal system is divided into two major components: the **axial skeleton** and the **appendicular skeleton**. The axial skeleton makes up the **axis** of the body, including the bones of the head, **vertebral column**, and rib cage. The appendicular skeleton includes bones of the shoulder and hip **girdles** and the upper and lower **appendages** (arms and legs).

More specifically, the axial skeleton includes: 1) the **cranial** and **facial** bones, 2) the three **ear ossicles**, 3) the **hyoid bone**, 4) the **vertebrae** including those of the **sacrum**, 5) the **ribs**, and 6) the **sternum**. The appendicular skeleton specifically includes: 1) the bones of the upper **pectoral girdle** (the **clavicle** and **scapula**), 2) bones of the arm and hand, or **upper extremity**, 3) the **pelvic girdle**, and 4) the bones of the leg and foot, or **lower extremity**.

The Axial Skeleton

We begin the study of the axial skeleton with the head and work down the body from top to bottom.

The Cranium

The most complex skeletal structure is the skull. The skull is a configuration of 8 cranial bones and 14 facial bones, some of which are paired on the left and right sides. The cranial bones, which encase the brain on all sides, include: 1) the **frontal** bone, 2) the paired **parietal** bones, 3) the paired **temporal** bones, 4) the **occipital** bone, 5) the **sphenoid** bone, and 6) the **ethmoid** bone. The frontal, parietal, temporal, and occipital bones are named for the parts of the brain which they protect. The facial bones include: 1) the paired **maxillae**, 2) the paired **palatine** bones, 3) the paired **lacrimal** bones, 4) the paired **nasal** bones, 5) the paired **inferior nasal conchae**, 6) the paired **zygomatic** bones, 7) the **mandible**, and 8) the **vomer**.

Quick Check Questions

1. All of the following are cranial bones, EXCEPT:
   A. parietal bones
   B. sphenoid bone
   C. maxilla
   D. temporal

2. The axial skeleton includes the cranial bone, the ________ bones, the ear ossicles, the hyoid bone, the vertebrae, the ribs, and the sternum.

3. The most complex skeletal structure is the skull. *True or False*

5.3.1 Frontal, Parietal, and Temporal Bones

12 minutes

The **frontal bone** surrounds the frontal lobe of the cerebrum, extending above, below, and to the sides of this portion of the brain. The frontal bone constitutes the forehead and the superior portions of the bony **orbits**, or eye sockets. The frontal bone also contains the **frontal sinus**, an open, mucus-filled space that forms the sound cavity that gives the voice **resonance**. The parietal bones make up the sides and roof of the cranium. The irregular temporal bones are inferior to the parietal bones, forming the lower sides of the cranium and housing the structures of the inner ear.

The temporal bones contain four distinct parts: 1) the flat **squamous portion** from which the **zygomatic process** extends, 2) the **tympanic portion** which contains the bony outer ear canal called the **external auditory meatus**, 3) the inferior **mastoid** portion with its inferior **mastoid process**, and 4) the **petrous** part of the temporal bone which houses the middle and inner ear. The petrous portion of the temporal bone is visible from the cranial cavity. At the medial border of the temporal bone, there are two important **foramina** (or holes). The **carotid canal** provides a passage for the internal carotid artery. The **internal jugular vein** and three of the **cranial nerves** travel through the **jugular foramen**.

Quick Check Questions

1. The part of the temporal bone which houses the structures of the inner ear is the _______ portion.
   A. squamous
   B. tympanic
   C. mastoid
   D. petrous

2. The part of the temporal bone which contains a bony canal called the external auditory meatus is the ______ portion.
   A. squamous
   B. tympanic
   C. mastoid
   D. petrous

3. The bone which constitutes the major part of the forehead is the _______ bone.
   A. orbital
   B. maxilla
   C. frontal
   D. sphenoid

4. The part of the temporal bone from which the zygomatic bone extends is the _______ portion.
   A. squamous
   B. tympanic
   C. mastoid
   D. sphenoid

5. The ________ bone houses the middle and inner ear.

6. The _______ bone contains the frontal sinus.

5.3.2 The Occipital Bone

10 minutes

The occipital bone forms the back of the skull and the posterior base of the skull. The occipital bone allows the attachment of the brain to the spinal cord via the **foramen magnum**, a large opening through which the spinal cord enters the skull. The **occipital condyles**, on the inferior aspect of the occipital bone, articulate with the **atlas**, which is the uppermost vertebral bone of the spinal column.

Bones of the Skull

The sphenoid bone forms the base of the skull between the anterior frontal bone, the lateral temporal bones, and the posterior occipital bone. A bony projection from the center of the sphenoid bone, called the **sella turcica** (or **dorsum sellae**), borders the **pituitary gland**. The sphenoid bone is notable because it articulates with twelve other bones. These are the frontal, occipital, vomer, and ethmoid bones, in addition to the paired parietal, temporal, zygomatic, and palatine bones.

Quick Check Questions

1. The spinal cord runs into the brain through the hole called the foramen ______.

2. The two projections which extend inferiorly at the back of the occipital bone are called the occipital ________.

3. In the center of the sphenoid, the sella turcica projects upward to the border of the _________ gland.

4. The sphenoid articulates with all of the following bones, EXCEPT:
   A. the frontal bone
   B. the mandible
   C. the ethmoid
   D. the vomer

5. The _________ bone is the most posterior bone of the skull.

5.3.3 The Sphenoid Bone

5 minutes

The sphenoid bone contains four types of foramina: 1) the **optic foramen**, through which the **ophthalmic artery** and **optic nerve** enter the orbit, 2) the **superior orbital fissure** where the nerves of eye movement and sensation run, 3) the **foramen rotundum**, a round hole traversed by the middle (maxillary) branch of the **trigeminal nerve** which supplies sensation to the face, and 4) the **foramen ovale**, through which the lower (mandibular) branch of the trigeminal nerve runs to supply sensation to the mouth, tongue, and chin.

Quick Check Questions

1. The optic nerve runs through the superior orbital fissure. *True or False*

2. The nerve supplying sensation to the face runs through the foramen rotundum. *True or False*

3. The nerve that controls eye movements runs through the foramen magnum. *True or False*

4. The nerve that supplies sensation to the tongue runs through the foramen-ovale. *True or False*

5.3.4 The Ethmoid Bone

5 minutes

The **ethmoid bone** gets its name from its sieve-like structure of bone interspersed with open spaces. The ethmoid is located between the two orbits and forms the roof, and part of the walls of, the nasal cavity. The ethmoid bone contains the **superior nasal conchae**, the **middle nasal conchae** and the **perpendicular plate**, a downward projection which forms the upper part of the nasal septum.

At its superior margin, the ethmoid bone is the upward projecting **crista galli** bordered on either side by the **cribriform plate**. The **olfactory nerves**, carrying smell sensation from the nasal cavity, pass through tiny holes in the cribriform plate to **synapse** in the olfactory bulb with other olfactory neurons.

Quick Check Questions

1. The cribriform plate, perpendicular plate, and crista galli are parts of the _______ bone.

2. The part of the ethmoid bone through which the olfactory nerves pass is the __________ plate.

3. The superior and middle nasal conchae are parts of the _______ bone.

5.4.1 Facial Bones: Bones of the Jaw

10 minutes

Unlike the cranial bones, the 14 facial bones are not in contact with the brain. Of all the bones of the head, only the **mandible** (the lower jaw) and the bones of the inner ear are movable. The two **maxilla** join to form the upper jaw. They each contain a large **maxillary sinus** (the most common site for sinus infections). The maxilla also have sockets which hold the upper teeth in place. The mandible is composed of the **body**, which forms the chin, and two **rami**, which branch upward to articulate with the rest of the skull. The **condyloid process** of the mandible is the extension that articulates with the temporal bone at the **temporomandibular joint**. The **coronoid process** is just anterior, and serves as a point of attachment for muscles of **mastication** (chewing).

The Bones of the Mouth

The paired maxilla, along with the paired **palatine bones**, form the **hard palate**, or roof of the mouth. The palatine bones form the **horizontal plate** which separates the nasal and oral cavities.

The Hyoid Bone

The **hyoid bone** is a horseshoe-shaped bone located in the neck. The hyoid bone is unique because it is not closely connected to any other bones of the skull. It functions in swallowing, to support the tongue, and to provide a site of attachment for muscles of the pharynx.

Quick Check Questions

1. The maxillary sinuses are spaces within the:
   A. maxilla
   B. mandible
   C. ethmoid

2. The part of the mandible that articulates with the temporal bone is the:
   A. condyloid process
   B. ramus
   C. coronoid process

3. The two _______ join to form the upper jaw.

5.4.2 Facial Bones: Bones of the Orbit

8 minutes

The eyes are protected by the **bony orbits**, made up of the seven bones which encircle them. The maxillae and frontal bone form the top and bottom of the orbits. On the lateral side of each orbit are the zygomatic bones. From each zygomatic bone, a process extends posteriorly, called the **temporal process**. The temporal process joins with the zygomatic process of the temporal bone to form the **zygomatic arch**, or cheekbone.

The sphenoid and ethmoid bone make up the posterior, and part of the medial aspect, of the orbit. On the medial side, there are also two small bones contributing to the orbit. These are the **nasal** bone, which forms the bridge of the nose, and the thin lacrimal bone. The **lacrimal foramen** is a small hole in the lacrimal bones through which the tear ducts pass.

The Vomer and Nasal Septum

The vomer is a flat, thin, elongated bone. The **nasal septum** is formed by the **perpendicular plate** of the ethmoid, which joins with the **vomer** to support the **septal cartilage**. Together, these structures separate the left and right nasal cavities.

Quick Check Questions

1. The nasal septum is composed of three separate structures. These are the:
   A. nasal conchae, ethmoid plate, and external nares
   B. cribriform plate, vomer, and septal cartilage
   C. perpendicular plate, vomer, and septal cartilage
   D. hard palate, crista galli, and cribriform

2. The lacrimal foramen is a small hole in the lacrimal bones through which the tear ducts pass. *True or False*

5.4.3 Cavities of the Head

5 minutes

The cranial bones protect the brain and other important structures in the head. The large **cranial cavity** protects and encloses the brain. The eyes are protected by the **orbital cavities** (or bony orbits). The delicate structures of the inner ears are housed in the **middle** and **inner ear chambers**. The **nasal cavity** and the four **paranasal sinuses** function in respiration, smell, and voice resonance. The mouth, or **oral cavity**, serves the functions of digestion, speech, smell, and taste.

Quick Check Questions

1. The cranial cavity is surrounded by the frontal bone, and superolaterally by the two ________ bones .

2. The eyes are protected by the:
   A. cranial cavity
   B. orbital cavities
   C. nasal sinus
   D. paranasal sinus

5.4.4 The Skull Sutures

8 minutes

All of the bones of the skull (except the mandible) are joined to adjacent bones by immovable joints called **sutures**. The most prominent sutures are those between the cranial bones. The **coronal suture** runs transversely between the frontal bone and the two parietal bones. The **sagittal suture** runs sagittally between the two parietal bones. At the back of the skull, the **lambdoidal suture** runs transversely between the parietal bones and the occipital bone. The **squamosal sutures** run laterally, separating the temporal bone from the parietal bone on each side.

Quick Check Questions

1. The __________ suture runs transversely between the parietal bones and the occipital bone on each side.

2. The most anterior transverse suture is the:
   A. coronal
   B. sagittal
   C. lambdoidal
   D. squamosal

3. Which suture runs longitudinally from the frontal bone to the occipital bone?
   A. coronal suture
   B. squamosal suture
   C. lambdoidal suture
   D. sagittal suture

5.4.5 The Fontanels

7 minutes

In a baby, the cranial bones have not yet become sutured together. The six **fontanels** are the areas of undifferentiated membrane where the bones do not meet. The fontanels allow the head to change shape during birth, and leave room for the rapid brain growth during infancy. The fontanels ultimately **ossify** (that is, the sutures knit together) after two years of life.

The largest of the fontanels is the **anterior fontanel**, a diamond shaped structure at the juncture of the frontal bone and the two parietal bones. The **posterior fontanel** is triangular in shape, located between the parietal bones and the occipital bone. The other four fontanels are on the sides of the skull. The left and right **anterolateral fontanels** occur at the junctions of the frontal, parietal, and temporal bones. The **posterolateral fontanels** are between the parietal, occipital, and temporal bones.

Quick Check Questions

1. The spaces where the bones of an infant's skull do not join together are called __________.

2. The largest fontanel is the:
   A. anterior
   B. posterior
   C. anterolateral
   D. posterolateral

5.5.1 The Vertebral Column

5 minutes

The **vertebral column** is a chain of bones in the back, which extend from the base of the skull to the pelvis. The vertebral column is strong but flexible. It is designed to protect the spinal cord, support the head, and provide attachment sites for the ribs and many muscles. Ligaments between each pair of **vertebrae** (singular = **vertebra**) stabilize the column. The **intervertebral discs** between the vertebrae, are fibrous cartilage pads which allow lateral movement and act as shock absorbers. The structure of the vertebral column allows for flexibility of the trunk of the body.

Quick Check Questions

1. Movement of the spinal column occurs at spaces between each vertebra, called the ____________ discs.

2. The vertebral column is stabilized and vertebrae are held in place by ________ between the vertebrae.
   A. intervertebral discs
   B. muscles
   C. ligaments
   D. both A and C
   E. both A and B

5.5.2 The Vertebrae

10 minutes

There are a total of 33 **vertebrae** in the adult vertebral column. Twenty-four of the 33 vertebrae are moveable. The vertebrae are categorized by region and structure. There are: 7 **cervical vertebrae**, 12 **thoracic vertebrae** (each of which is attached to a pair of ribs), 5 **lumbar vertebrae**, and 5 **sacral vertebrae** (which are fused together to form the **sacrum**, the back of the pelvis).

Below the sacrum is the **coccyx** (or **tailbone**), which generally contains 4 fused **coccygeal vertebrae**. The vertebrae become larger as they descend to the lumbar region, and then, in the sacrum, they begin to get smaller. This size differentiation of the vertebrae reflects the need to carry more weight in the lower back region.

Quick Check Questions

1. There are ___ vertebrae in a normal adult spinal column.

2. How many of the 33 vertebrae are movable?
   A. 33
   B. 12
   C. 23
   D. 24

3. There are ___ cervical vertebrae.

4. There are ___ thoracic vertebrae.

5. There are ___ lumbar vertebrae.

6. The vertebrae are largest in the ________ region.
   A. cervical
   B. thoracic
   C. lumbar

7. The back of the pelvis is formed by the ________.
   A. sacrum
   B. coccyx
   C. atlas

5.5.3 Function of Vertebral Column

8 minutes

The vertebral column of an adult is curved to provide support and balance. Curvatures of the spine are named according to their vertebral region. For example, the **cervical curvature** is the uppermost **flexure**, corresponding to the cervical vertebrae in the neck region. Relative to the front of the body, the cervical curvature is **convex**. In the thoracic region, or upper back, the **thoracic curvature** is **concave**. The **lumbar curvature** of the lower back is convex, and the **sacral curvature**, at the back of the pelvis, is concave.

The spinal column is capable of movements in several directions. **Extension** refers to straightening the spine or bending backward. (Ligaments between the vertebrae prevent **hyperextension** or excessive backward bending). **Flexion** is forward bending. The spine also bends to the sides, called **lateral bending**. Lastly, the spine can twist to move the shoulders or hips off the coronal plane, which is called **rotation**.

The cervical and lumbar regions are the most movable parts of the spine. Because of this, they are the most frequent sites for backaches. The thoracic vertebrae are somewhat fixed because they are held in place by the ribs, and their rotation is limited by the shape of their **vertebral processes**.

Quick Check Questions

1. A person who has **kyphosis** (or a **hunchback**) may have an excessive:
   A. cervical curvature
   B. thoracic curvature
   C. lumbar curvature
   D. sacral curvature

2. Someone who develops a **swayback** probably has an excessive:
   A. cervical curvature
   B. thoracic curvature
   C. lumbar curvature
   D. sacral curvature

3. Movements allowed by the spinal column include all of the following, EXCEPT:
   A. lateral rotation
   B. hyperextension
   C. lateral bending
   D. extension

5.6.1 The Structure of Vertebrae

22 minutes

There are similarities in basic structure of the vertebrae in the four regions of the back. Each vertebra has a solid, round **body**, which is positioned anteriorly, toward the viscera. On the dorsal side is the **vertebral arch** supported by two **pedicles**. The spinal cord passes through the space between the two pedicles called the **vertebral foramen**.

When the vertebrae are stacked on top of one another, spaces between them form the lateral **intervertebral foramina** through which the **spinal nerves** pass. From each foramen, a single **spinal nerve** extends laterally. Several processes extend from the dorsal side of each vertebra, providing sites for the attachment of ligaments and muscles and for articulation with other vertebrae.

The large, central **spinous processes** are visible on the dorsal side of the vertebral arch. The spinous processes are easily palpable. The cervical, thoracic, and lumbar regions each have differently shaped processes. Ligaments attached to the spinous processes strengthen the posterior aspect of the column.

Two **transverse processes** extend from the sides of the vertebral arch, and attach to numerous back muscles. The four **articular processes** (two superior and two inferior) terminate in surfaces called **facets**. The inferior facets of one vertebra rest on the superior facets of the vertebra below, providing increased stability and allowing some movement between the vertebrae.

Regional Characteristics of the Vertebrae

The **cervical vertebrae** have a **transverse foramen** in each transverse process through which the **vertebral arteries** pass, supplying blood to the brain. Cervical vertebrae have large vertebral foramina to accommodate the thick superior end of the spinal cord. Most cervical vertebrae have a forked spinous process. Note that these individual vertebrae are numbered in series from top to bottom, as "C1-C7."

Vertebrae C1 and C2 are the **atlas** and the **axis**. The atlas (C1) articulates with the **occipital condyles** in a way that allows nodding of the head. The atlas has no spinous process or body. The axis (C2) contains an upward projecting process called the **dens** or **odontoid process**, which fits into the vertebral foramen of the atlas. This arrangement allows lateral rotation of the head. The axis has a large, forked spinous process.

The spinous process of the seventh cervical vertebra (C7 or the **vertebra prominens**) can be felt as a bump at the base of the neck. The **thoracic vertebrae** (T1-T12) articulate with the **ribs**. The upper ten ribs and T1 through T10 have two points of attachment with each other: 1) the **facet** on the vertebral body articulates with the **head** of a rib, and 2) a facet on the transverse process of the vertebrae articulates with the **tubercle** of a rib. The lowest two ribs have a head but no tubercle, and thus articulate only on the vertebral body. The thoracic vertebrae are larger and stronger than the cervical vertebrae. Their spinous processes are narrow and are directed inferiorly.

The **lumbar vertebrae** (L1-L5) are the largest and strongest of the vertebrae. Their spinous processes are thick and blunt. The **sacrum**, made up of the fused sacral vertebrae (S1-S5), is a wedge-shaped bone forming the back of the pelvis. The sacrum provides strong support for the vertebral column and transmits the weight of the upper body to the pelvic girdle. Four pairs of foramina leave the sacrum anteriorly and posteriorly, allowing the sacral nerves to pass through.

The **median sacral crest** is formed from the spinous processes of the sacral vertebrae. The **sacral promontory**, at the anterior superior portion of S1, is an important **obstetrical** reference point for obtaining measurements of the pelvis. The base of the sacrum is joined by ligaments to the **coccyx**. The coccyx is triangular in shape, consisting of 3 to 4 fused vertebrae, and provides an anchor for some muscles of the pelvic floor.

The Rib Cage

The ribs articulate with the thoracic vertebrae and join anteriorly to meet at the **sternum**, thus forming the walls of the **thoracic cavity**. The rib cage protects the thoracic organs and assists in breathing. The sternum contains three separate fused bones: 1) the **manubrium**, 2) the **body**, and 3) the **xiphoid process**.

There are twelve **ribs**. The top seven ribs are called **true ribs** because they attach directly to the sternum, each via a separate **costal cartilage**. The bottom five ribs are called **false ribs** because their costal cartilages are either not attached to the sternum or attached indirectly. Ribs 8, 9, and 10 join the sternum indirectly via a common costal cartilage, which merges with that of the seventh rib. Ribs 11 and 12 do not join the sternum at all, and thus are called **floating ribs**.

Typical Ribs

A typical rib has a wedge-shaped **head**, a **neck** with its **tubercle** for articulation to the vertebra, and a **body** or shaft. On the inferior surface of each rib, there is a **costal groove**. In this costal groove lie the intercostal vein, artery, and nerve.

Quick Check Questions

1. All ribs are attached to two vertebrae on one end and to the sternum via a costal cartilage on the other end. *True or False*

2. The largest vertebrae are the ________ vertebrae.
   A. C1 and C2
   B. thoracic
   C. lumbar
   D. sacral

3. The vertebral foramina is larger in the _______ vertebra(e).
   A. atlas
   B. cervical
   C. lumbar
   D. sacral

4. Which has no spinous process?
   A. atlas
   B. axis
   C. a thoracic vertebra
   D. a sacral vertebra

5. The ________ vertebrae are fused in adult life.
   A. thoracic
   B. cervical
   C. lumbar
   D. sacral

5.7.1 The Appendicular Skeleton

5 minutes

The **appendicular skeleton** consists of: 1) the upper and lower **appendages** (arms and legs), and 2) the **pectoral** and **pelvic girdles** (the shoulder and hip, respectively).

The Pectoral Girdle

The pectoral girdle connects the upper extremity to the axial skeleton and provides sites of attachment for the many muscles of the arm. The pectoral girdle is comprised of two bones, the anterior **clavicle** and the posterior **scapula**.

The Clavicle

The clavicle (or collar bone) is an S-shaped bone connecting the upper limb to the trunk. It is easy to **palpate** the clavicle at the top of the chest. The medial end of the clavicle is rounded and attaches to the **sternum**, and the lateral end articulates with the **acromion process** of the scapula. The clavicle is the most frequently broken bone in the body.

Quick Check Questions

1. The clavicle articulates with the:
   A. acromion process of the scapula and the vertebral column
   B. sternum and acromion process of the scapula
   C. vertebral column and the costal cartilage
   D. sternum and the first two ribs

2. The ________ is often broken by a fall on an outstretched arm, and is the most frequently broken bone in the body.

3. The pectoral girdle is comprised of the:
   A. ilium, ischium, and pubis
   B. sacrum and os coxae
   C. clavicle and scapula
   D. scapula, clavicle, and sternum

5.7.2 The Clavicle and Scapula

8 minutes

The **scapulae** (singular = **scapula**) or shoulder blades are flat, triangular bones which lie on the sides of the upper back. The scapulae cover the lateral parts of ribs 2 through 7. The scapulae articulate with the clavicles to form the **acromio-clavicular joint**.

The scapula itself is extremely mobile. The posterior surface of the scapula contains a prominent **spine**, which becomes the **acromion process** at its superior and lateral end. Another extension of the scapula, the **coracoid process**, extends anterior and medial to the acromion process. The coracoid process is an important attachment site for muscles of the arm. Below the acromion and the coracoid process is a depression called the **glenoid cavity** which articulates with the **humerus**. This extremely flexible articulation forms the **shoulder joint**.

Quick Check Questions

1. The humerus and the glenoid cavity of the ________, form the shoulder joint.

2. Three major processes of the scapula are the spine of the scapula, the acromion process, and the ________ process.

3. Both the mandible and the scapula have a coracoid process. *True or False*

4. The scapula and the clavicle articulate at the ________clavicular joint.

5.8.1 The Upper Extremity

8 minutes

Each arm contains a total of 30 bones. The arm bones include the long bones of the arm, as well as the bones of the wrist and hand.

The Brachium

The **brachium** or upper arm contains the humerus, the largest bone of the arm. The ball like **head** of the humerus articulates with the **glenoid fossa** of the scapula. Two projections arise close to the head of the humerus: the **greater tubercle** (the most lateral point of the shoulder) and the **lesser tubercle**, anteriorly. Muscles of the arm insert on both of these tubercles. The **neck** of the humerus is divided into an **anatomical neck** and, more distally, a **surgical neck**. The surgical neck is aptly named, for it is a common site of fractures.

The distal end of the humerus widens and ends in two processes, the **trochlea** (where the ulna articulates) and the **capitulum** (where the radius articulates). On the side of these structures are two palpable knobs, the **epicondyles**, where many muscles of the forearm attach. The **medial epicondyle** which attaches to the trochlea is the more prominent. The **lateral epicondyle** attaches to the capitulum.

Quick Check Questions

1. The tubercles are proximal projections of the humerus, and the epicondyles are distal projections. *True or False*

2. Muscles of the arm insert on all of the following, EXCEPT:
   A. the greater tubercle
   B. the sacrum
   C. the lateral epicondyle
   D. the shaft of the humerus

3. The trochlea attaches to the medial epicondyle and articulates with the ____.

5.8.2 The Forearm

8 minutes

The **forearm** is the portion of the arm that lies between the distal end of the humerus and the **carpal bones** of the wrist. The forearm contains two bones, the **radius** and the **ulna**. In the anatomic position, they are parallel. When the hand is **pronated** (that is, when the hand is rotated inward from anatomical position, with the thumb pointing towards the body and the palm facing backward), the radius crosses over the ulna.

The ulna contains two processes that articulate with the humerus: 1) the **olecranon process**, and 2) the **coronoid process**. The **body** of the ulna is thicker proximally, but narrows distally. The distal end of the ulna contains the **head** and the **styloid process of the ulna**, and articulates with the **ulnar notch** of the radius.

The radius of the forearm has a proximal head, a neck, a **radial tuberosity** (the point of attachment of the biceps muscle), a **shaft**, a **styloid process**, and an **ulnar notch**. The radius of the forearm articulates with two bones of the wrist, the **scaphoid** and the **lunate**. The **styloid process of the radius** is more distal than that of the ulna. For this reason, a fall on an outstretched hand may break the distal fragment of the radius (which is called a **Colles' fracture**).

Quick Check Questions

1. The ulna projects more distally than the radius. For this reason it is fractured more often. *True or False*

2. The head of the ulna, like the heads of all bones, is on the proximal end. *True or False*

3. The distal end of the radius articulates with all of the following, EXCEPT:
   A. scaphoid
   B. the head of the ulna
   C. the styloid process of the ulna
   D. the lunate

5.8.3 The Wrist

8 minutes

In addition to the scaphoid and the lunate, the wrist contains six other **carpal bones**. The carpal bones are small short bones, arranged in two rows of four, and connected to each other by ligaments. They are found between the forearm and the **metacarpal** bones of the hand.

The carpal bones are named for their shapes (lateral to medial) the proximal row includes: 1) the **scaphoid** (boat-shaped), 2) the **lunate** (moon-shaped), 3) the **triquetrum** (triangular), and 4) the **pisiform** (pea-shaped: the pisiform is a sesamoid bone). The carpal bones in the distal row articulate with the hand. From lateral to medial, these are: 1) the **trapezium** (four-sided), 2) the **trapezoid** (also four sided), 3) the **capitate** (caput = head), and 4) the **hamate** (hook-shaped).

Quick Check Questions

1. All of the following bones of the wrist articulate with metacarpals, EXCEPT:
   A. the hamate
   B. the triquetrum
   C. the trapezium
   D. the capitate

2. The bones of the wrist are connected to each other by:
   A. ligaments
   B. articulations
   C. tendons
   D. cartilage

3. Which bone of the wrist is a sesamoid bone?
   A. scaphoid
   B. lunate
   C. hamate
   D. pisiform

5.8.4 The Carpal Tunnel

4 minutes

The walls of a conduit called the **carpal tunnel** are formed by the **flexor retinaculum**. The flexor retinaculum is comprised of a tendon on the palmar surface of the hand and the concave surface of the hamate, pisiform, scaphoid, and trapezium. Within this channel run all of the long **flexor tendons** of the digits and the median nerve, which innervates part of the hand.

Clinical Note:
Trauma to the wrist or repeated flexion may cause swelling within the carpal tunnel and result in a painful condition called **carpal tunnel syndrome**. On a separate note, the scaphoid is the most frequently fractured bone of the wrist.

Quick Check Questions

1. All of the following are true about the carpal tunnel, EXCEPT:
   A. its anterior wall is the flexor retinaculum
   B. it contains the median nerve
   C. it posterior wall is formed by four bones
   D. the flexor tendons of the digits do not pass through it

2. The walls of a conduit called the "carpal tunnel" are formed by the ______ retinaculum.

5.8.5 The Hand

6 minutes

The five **metacarpals** are miniature, long bones which make up the bones of the hand. The metacarpals articulate proximally with the bones of the wrist and distally with the **phalanges** (small bones of the fingers). The distal ends of the metacarpals are called **heads**, commonly known as the knuckles.

The **phalanges**, the bones of the fingers, are an even smaller set of long bones. The thumb has two phalanges: the **proximal phalanx** and the **distal phalanx**. In addition to having a proximal and distal phalanx, all of the other fingers also have a **middle phalanx**. The total number of phalanges in the hand is 14.

Quick Check Questions

1. The heads of the metacarpals articulate with the distal bones of the wrist. *True or False*

2. The thumb does not have a metacarpal bone. *True or False*

3. The thumb does not have a middle phalanx. *True or False*

4. How many phalanges are there in the hand?
   A. 12
   B. 14
   C. 16

5.9.1 The Pelvic Girdle and Ilium

8 minutes

The hip, the thigh, the leg, and the foot are major divisions of the lower limb. These bones are specialized for supporting the weight of the body, maintaining equilibrium, and locomotion. Since weight-bearing is a major function of these bones and joints, some mobility is sacrificed in exchange for stability.

The Pelvic Girdle

The **pelvic girdle**, or hip, consists of the left and right **os coxae** (hip bones). The os coxae are fused anteriorly at the **pubic symphysis**. Posteriorly, they are joined to the sacrum. Laterally, each hip bone contains a cup-shaped **acetabulum** which articulates with the ball-like head of the **femur**. Each os coxae is composed of three bones that fuse together during the course of development: the **ilium**, the **ischium**, and the **pubis**.

The Ilium

The ilium is the largest bone of the pelvic girdle. The ilium forms the top two thirds of the hip bone and the top two fifths of the acetabulum. The top portion is the palpable **iliac crest**. Anteriorly, the ilium ends in the **anterior superior iliac spine**, which extends inferiorly and becomes the **anterior inferior iliac spine**. Posteriorly, the iliac crest becomes the **posterior superior iliac spine**, and then the **posterior inferior iliac spine**. This spine terminates at the **greater sciatic notch**, through which the sciatic nerve passes. On the medial surface of the ilium, the ilium articulates with the sacrum at the **sacroiliac joint**.

Quick Check Questions

1. The part of the hip bone which articulates with the head of the femur (thigh bone) is called the __________.

2. Anteriorly, the ilia fuse with the sacrum at the sacroiliac joints, and posteriorly, they join at the pubic symphysis. *True or False*

3. When you rest your hands on your hip, you may feel:
   A. the anterior superior iliac spine
   B. the acetabulum
   C. the posterior superior iliac spine
   D. the iliac crest

4. The sciatic nerve passes through the greater _______ notch.

5.9.2 The Ischium and Pubis

The **ischium** forms the posterioinferior part of the os coxae and the posterior two-fifths of the acetabulum. The ischium is an L-shaped bone containing a **body** and a **ramus**. On the body, there is an **ischial spine**, separating the greater sciatic notch and the lesser sciatic notch. At the inferior part of the ischium is a U-shaped prominence called the **ischial tuberosity**. This structure supports the body in the sitting position. The top of the U is covered by the **superior ramus of the pubis**. The resulting "O" is the **obturator foramen**, where muscles insert and through which the obturator nerve passes. The two rami of the ischia join at the **inferior rami of the pubis.**

The Pubis

The **pubis** forms the anterior part of the hip bone and the anterior one-fifth of the acetabulum. The pubis contains three parts: a flattened **pubic body**, and two **pubic rami**. The body of the pubis is its anterior portion. Laterally, the body merges into the **superior ramus**. Medially, it fuses with the other hip bone at the **pubis symphysis**, a cartilage joint. A projection on the lateral aspect of the pubic body is called the **pubic tubercle**. This serves as an attachment for the **inguinal ligament**. The **inferior ramus** of the pubis runs posterioinferiorly to join the ramus of the ischium.

Quick Check Questions

1. The two pubic bones meet medially at a cartilage joint called the pubic _________.

2. All three parts of the os coxae contribute to the acetabulum. The top part comes from the _____.

3. All three parts of the os coxae contribute to the acetabulum. The posterior part comes from the _______.

4. All three parts of the os coxae contribute to the acetabulum. The anterior part comes from the _____.

5.9.3 The Pelvis

7 minutes

Together with the sacrum and coccyx, the two hip bones form a bowl called the **pelvis** (which contains the pelvic viscera). The pelvis is divided into the **pelvis major** (false pelvis) above, and a **pelvis minor** (true pelvis) below. The plane dividing the false pelvis from the true pelvis is called the **pelvic brim**.

Gender Differences in the Pelvis

The male and female pelvises have significantly different shapes. The structural differences are mainly adaptations related to pregnancy and childbirth. In the female, the angle of the **pubic arch** is greater than 90 degrees, and the iliac crest is less curved than in the male. These differences make for a female pelvis that is somewhat bowl-shaped. By contrast, the pubic arch in the male is less than 90 degrees and the iliac crest has a greater curvature. The male pelvic inlet is smaller and narrower along the medial / lateral axis, and the acetabulum is larger.

Quick Check Questions

1. The true pelvis and the false pelvis are divided by a plane called the pelvic ____.

2. The hip bones, ______, and coccyx form a bowl called the pelvis.

3. The gender differences in the pelvis are mainly an adaptation for pregnancy and __________.

4. The angle of the pubic arch of the pelvis is greater in the female. *True or False*

5.9.4 The Lower Extremity

6 minutes

Like the upper extremities, each lower extremity contains of 30 bones. There are many structural similarities between bones of the leg and arm.

The Thigh

The **femur** (thigh bone) is the longest, strongest, and heaviest bone in the human body. In an adult, the length of the thigh bone is about one-fourth the height of the body. The femur extends from the acetabulum of the hip to the **tibia** in the knee. The proximal end of the femur contains a rounded **head** which articulates with the acetabulum in a **ball-and-socket** joint. The head of the femur is connected to its **body** by the **neck**. The neck is a frequent site of hip fractures in elderly people who develop **osteoporosis**. At the base of the neck is the **intertrochanteric line** which runs between the lateral **greater trochanter** and the medial **lesser trochanter**.

Quick Check Questions

1. The ball-and-socket joint of the hip contains the ____ of the femur articulating with the acetabulum (the cup) of the hip.

2. Compared to other bones in the body, the femur is long, heavy, and ______.

3. Hip fractures, which tend to happen in elderly people, usually involve the ____ of the femur.

5.9.5 The Femur Bone

6 minutes

The body, or shaft, of the femur is smooth except for a rough posterior ridge, called the **linea aspera**. Here, a number of muscles of the thigh attach. At the distal end, the femur broadens and is divided at the **intracondylar notch** into two posteriorly directed knobs, the **medial** and **lateral condyles**. The condyles merge anteriorly, forming the **patellar surface**, on which the **patella** (a sesamoid bone) articulates. The medial and lateral condyles also articulate with the tibia. At the upper edge of each condyle is an **epicondyle**, a small bump that projects away from the intercondylar notch. The **medial** and **lateral epicondyles** are key attachment sites for the ligaments of the knee.

Quick Check Questions

1. The linea aspera is a rough line which runs along the _________ surface of the shaft of the femur.

2. The medial and lateral condyles of the femur are important attachment sites for muscles and ligaments of the pelvis. *True or False*

3. The patella is positioned anterior to the femur. *True or False*

5.9.6 The Leg

8 minutes

Anatomically, the **leg** refers to the lower appendage between the knee and ankle. Like the forearm, the leg contains two bones: 1) the medial **tibia**, and 2) the smaller, lateral **fibula**. The tibia is the second largest bone in the body. The proximal end of the tibia is large and flat, forming a **tibial plateau**. The tibia has a central **intracondylar eminence** which joins the intracondylar notch of the femur bone for added joint stability.

The **medial** and **lateral condyles of the tibia** articulate with the condyles of the femur. The lateral condyle of the tibia also articulates with the **head** of the fibula.

The **tibial tuberosity** is the insertion point of the patellar ligament. The distal end of the tibia forms a prominent medial knob, the **medial malleolus** (that is, the medial part of the ankle bone). The medial malleolus articulates with the **talus** bone of the ankle and also has a facet for articulation with the fibula. The fibula is a long thin bone. It articulates proximally with the lateral condyle of the tibia. Distally, the fibula forms the **lateral malleolus**, the lateral part of the ankle. The distal end of the fibula is sometimes fractured in a **Pott's fracture**.

Quick Check Questions

1. The fibula is connected to the tibia in ___ places.

2. Proximally, the head of the fibula articulates with:
   A. the lateral condyle of the tibia
   B. the lateral condyle of the femur
   C. the patella
   D. the medial condyle of the tibia

3. The patellar ligament inserts onto the:
   A. the lateral condyle of the femur
   B. the patella
   C. the tibial tuberosity
   D. the lateral epicondyle of the femur

5.9.7 The Ankle and Foot

7 minutes

The bones of the ankle, or **tarsus**, unlike the wrist bones, are adapted for weight bearing and locomotion. The tarsus consists of seven bones: 1) the **talus**, 2) the **calcaneus**, 3) the **cuboid**, 4) three **cuneiforms**, and 5) the **navicular**.

The talus bone articulates with the bones of the leg. The talus rests on the calcaneus and the navicular bone. The calcaneus (heel bone) is the largest, strongest bone of the foot. The navicular is anterior to the talus and connects the talus to the three cuneiform bones. The cuboid is lateral to the navicular and lateral to the three cuneiforms. The **metatarsals** are long bones, like the metacarpals in the hand. Underneath the first metatarsal are two sesamoid bones, which carry some of the weight of the body while walking. The phalanges are the bones of the toes, analogous to the phalanges of the fingers. There are two phalanges in the great toe (proximal and distal), and three in all the other toes (proximal, middle, and distal).

Quick Check Questions

1. The ______ of the ankle articulates with the bones of the leg.

2. There are ___ phalanges in the small toes.

3. Two sesamoid bones carry some of the body weight during walking. They lie under the _____ metatarsal.

5.10.1 Articulation

6 minutes

Bones may be joined together, or **articulate**, in several different ways. Points of contact between bones are called **articulations** or **joints**. The structure of a joint dictates the potential range of motion of the bones involved. Some joints, such as the hips and shoulders, enable movement in many directions. Other joints, such as the **sutures** between the bones of the skull, allow no movement at all.

Joints are categorized into three classes based upon the degree of movement they permit. The three major types of joints are: 1) **synarthroses** which permit no movement, 2) **amphiarthroses** which permit limited movement, and 3) **diarthroses**, which permit full movement.

Quick Check Questions

1. The joints of the body are also called ____________.

2. Joints are classified according to the degree of ________ they permit.

3. The three functional classes of joints are:
   A. articulations, sutures, and epiphyseal plates
   B. amphiarthroses, synarthroses, and diarthroses
   C. biarthroses, triarthroses, and diarthroses

5.10.2 Types of Joints

30 minutes

Synarthroses

Synarthroses are immobile joints. Three types of synarthrodial joints include: 1) **sutures**, 2) **gomphoses**, and 3) **synchondroses**.

Sutures join the cranial bones of the skull. For example, the coronal suture binds the frontal and parietal bones. Structurally, sutures are classified as **fibrous joints**, because the bones of the joint are bound together by fibrous connective tissue. The jagged, interlocking edges of a suture enhance its strength. Immovable joints called gomphoses hold the teeth securely in the skull. Each tooth inserts into an **alveolus**, a socket in the mandible or maxilla, and is held there by the **periodontal ligament**. Synchondroses are the temporary joints between the epiphyses (ends) and the diaphysis (shaft) of growing long bones. The bones in synchondrosis joints are held together by **hyaline cartilage**, so they fall within the structural category of **cartilaginous joint**. The hyaline cartilage ossifies to become bone during the course of bone formation. The **epiphyseal plate**, visible on an X-ray, is the site of a former synchondrotic joint.

Amphiarthroses

Amphiarthroses are joints that are partially movable, having a very limited range of motion. These joints allow the skeleton to be somewhat flexible in response to twisting, bending, and compression forces. Amphiarthroses joints include: 1) **symphyses**, and 2) **syndesmoses**. The pubis symphysis and the intervertebral discs are examples of symphyses. Symphyses joints are cartilaginous joints constructed of a thick **fibrocartilage** pad which cushions movements of the articulating bones.

Individual symphysis joints permit only limited movements. In the spinal column, however, the many adjacent intervertebral discs allow ample mobility of the spine.

Another type of amphiarthrotic joint, the syndesmoses, is a fibrous joint: ligaments and **interosseous membranes** hold the adjacent bones together. The distal ends of the ulna and the radius articulate in a syndesmotic joint. The interosseous membrane and ligament which form this joint keep the two bones from separating, yet are flexible enough to allow the radius to cross over the ulna when the hand is **pronated**.

Diarthrotic Joints

The **diarthrotic joints**, which are freely movable, include the knee, elbow, and shoulder. All of the diarthrotic joints have common structural features, which serve to decrease friction between the moving parts of the joint. They belong to the structural class of **synovial joints**.

Surfaces of the articulating bones of synovial joints are coated with **articular cartilages**, and these moving surfaces are enclosed within a fluid-filled **joint capsule**. The joint capsule is formed of fibrous tissue and lined by a **synovial membrane**, which secretes the slippery **synovial fluid**. Synovial fluid functions to lubricate the joint, to provide nutrients to the cartilage of the joint, and to help clear debris from the synovial space. Normally, there is only a minute amount of synovial fluid in a synovial joint.

There are six categories of diarthrotic joints, based on the structure and mobility allowed by the shapes of the articulating surfaces. They are: 1) **gliding joints** (also called **plane joints**), 2) **hinge joints**, 3) **pivot joints**, 4) **condyloid joints**, 5) **saddle joints**, and 6) **ball-and-socket joints**.

Plane or Gliding Joints

Plane or gliding joints exist between two flat bone surfaces and generally permit motion in only one plane. For example, plane joints exist among the bones of the wrist and between the scapula and clavicle.

Hinge Joints

Hinge joints occur between the concave surface of one bone and the convex surface of another. For example, the **trochlear notch** (or **semilunar notch**) of the ulna forms a hinge joint with the **trochlea** of the humerus. This joint permits motion in only one direction, that is, the elbow can move only in one plane. Other examples of hinge joints are the knee and the **interphalangeal joints** of the fingers.

Pivot Joints

Pivot joints permit only rotation around an axis (like a wheel rotates on an axle). A good example of a pivot joint is the articulation between the atlas and the axis which allows the head to turn from side to side (as one does when indicating the physical gesture "no"). Another example of a pivot joint is the proximal articulation of the radius and ulna. In this joint, the head of the radius turns in the radial notch of the ulna during rotation of the forearm.

Condyloid Joints

Condyloid joints (also called **ellipsoid joints**) are another type of articulation between the concave and convex surfaces of two bones. Condyloid joints allow movement along two perpendicular axes. The articulations of the metacarpal bones of the hand with the phalanges of the fingers (the **knuckles**) are examples of condyloid joints. These joints allow hinge-like movements of the fingers (as in making a fist), and sideways movement of the fingers (as in fanning the fingers). Another example of a condyloid joint is that between the radius and the carpal bones of the wrist.

Saddle Joints

Saddle joints also have a concave surface opposing a convex surface, but the two surfaces fit together like a rider in a saddle. Like condyloid joints, saddle joints permit movement in two directions, however, they allow more motion than the condyloid joints. The articulation at the base of the thumb (the first metacarpal bone with the trapezium in the wrist) is a saddle joint.

Ball-and-Socket Joints

The ball-and-socket joint allows motion in more than two planes, a greater range of motion than any other type of joint. The ball-and-socket joint consists of a cup-shaped surface which articulates with the ball-shaped head of a long bone.
The only two ball-and-socket joints in the body are the two shoulder joints and the two hip joints.

Quick Check Questions

1. Synarthroses are partially movable joints. *True or False*

2. The type of joint that occurs where the teeth articulate with the skull is called a ________.

3. The three types of synarthroses, or immovable joints, are:
   A. sutures, gomphoses, synchondroses
   B. alveoli, epiphyseal plates, and rigamortars
   C. symphyses, synchondroses, and syndesmoses
   D. sutures, lumphoses, and gomphoses

4. Amphiarthroses are joints that are:
   A. immovable
   B. partially movable
   C. freely movable

5. The symphyses and syndesmoses fall under which of the following joint classifications?
   A. synarthroses
   B. amphiarthroses
   C. diarthroses

6. The pubis symphysis and the intervertebral discs are examples of:
   A. syndesmoses
   B. symphyses

7. A type of amphiarthrotic joint, the __________, is formed of ligaments and interosseous membranes which hold adjacent bones together.

8. Which of the following structures are common to all types of diarthrotic joints?
   A. a synovial membrane
   B. synovial fluid
   C. articular cartilage
   D. all of the above

9. The six categories of diarthrotic joints include:
   A. gliding, hinge, pivot, condyloid, saddle, and ball-and-socket
   B. gliding, shearing, rotational, condyloid, saddle, and ball-and-socket
   C. hinge, pivot, cuboid, saddle, biplanar, and ball-and-socket

10. A major function of synovial fluid is to decrease ________ between the moving surfaces of the joint.

11. The following type(s) of joint permit motion in only two planes:
    A. gliding, hinge, and pivot joints
    B. condyloid and saddle joints
    C. ball-and-socket joints

12. The articulations of the metacarpal bones of the hand with the phalanges of the fingers (the knuckles) are hinge joints. *True or False*

13. The articulation at the base of the thumb (the first metacarpal bone with the trapezium in the wrist) is a ______ joint.

14. The following type(s) of joints permit motion in only one plane:
    A. gliding, hinge, and pivot joints
    B. condyloid and saddle joints
    C. ball-and-socket joints

15. The articulation of the flat surfaces of the clavicle and scapula is a _______ joint.

16. The articulations of the metacarpal bones of the hand with the phalanges of the fingers (the knuckles) are _________ joints.

17. Saddle joints have a concave surface opposing a convex surface, and like condyloid joints, they permit movement in two directions. *True or False*

18. The type of diarthrotic joint which permits the greatest range of motion is the:
    A. gliding joint
    B. ball-and-socket joint
    C. pivot joint
    D. saddle joint

5.10.3 Ligaments

8 minutes

Ligaments are strong bands of tough, dense fibrous connective tissue that attach bones to other bones. Ligaments increase the strength of joints. Indeed, much of the stability of an articulation such as the shoulder is due to the ligaments, tendons, and muscles which traverse it.

Tendons, also made of dense fibrous connective tissue, attach muscles to bones. Tendons are discussed in more detail in the *Muscular System Chapter*. Ligaments in a diarthrosis may exist as extensions of the fibrous joint capsule, or may be located entirely outside of the joint capsule. Some joints such as the amphiarthrotic joint between the radius and ulna are formed exclusively of ligament. The bones of the ankle are firmly held in place by ligaments. A **sprain** is a tearing of the ligaments that surround a joint. It is sometimes accompanied by damage to the articular cartilage and inflammation of the joint capsule.

Quick Check Questions

1. Ligaments connect:
   A. muscles to bones
   B. muscles to muscles
   C. bones to bones

2. Some joints are composed entirely of ligaments. *True or False*

3. The stability of a joint may be improved by:
   A. ligaments only
   B. ligaments and tendons
   C. ligaments, tendons, and muscles

5.10.4 Naming of Joints

8 minutes

Many of the joints in the body are named for the articulating bones with which they are associated. For example, the **temporomandibular joint** refers to the articulation of the mandible with the temporal bone.

Shoulder Joint

One possible name for the shoulder joint is the **humeroscapular joint**, since it involves the humerus and the scapula. However, note that the clavicle and several important ligaments are also integral components of the humeroscapular joint.

Elbow Joint

The elbow is formed by the articulation of the humerus with both the radius and the ulna.

Hip Joint

The hip is also known as the **coxal** joint. The coxal joint is formed by the head of the femur (the ball), and the acetabulum of the os coxae (the socket).

Knee, Leg, and Foot Joints

The **tibiofemoral joint** is another name for the knee (the articulation of the tibia and femur). The **talocrural joint** refers to the ankle, where both the tibia and fibula articulate with the **talus** in the foot.

Quick Check Questions

1. The tibiofemoral joint is another name for the:
   A. hip
   B. knee
   C. elbow
   D. ankle

2. The hip is also known as the _____ joint.

3. Another name for the shoulder is the:
   A. humeroscapular joint
   B. talocrural joint
   C. temporomandibular joint
   D. tibiofemoral joint

5.10.5 Joint Movements

20 minutes

Movements of Diarthrotic Joints

Most movements of synovial joints may be classified as **angular** and **circular**. There are four distinct movements which either increase or decrease the angle of the articulating bones in relation to each other. These four angular movements are: **flexion** and its opposite, **extension,** and **adduction** and its opposite, **abduction**.

Flexion

Flexion decreases the joint angle along a sagittal plane. For example, if the knee is flexed the foot moves up and backward, and if the hip is flexed the knee moves up and forward. Each motion decreases the angle between the bones in the joint.

Extension

Extension of the knee moves the foot down and forward again, increasing the angle between the femur and the tibia. **Hyperextension** is extension of a limb beyond the normal limits. In the ankle joint, flexion is upward movement of the foot (sometimes called **dorsiflexion**). Extension of the ankle (also called **plantar flexion**) occurs when pointing the toes.

Adduction and Abduction

Adduction is the movement of a limb or part of the body that brings it closer to the midline of the body along a frontal plane. Abduction is the lateral movement of the limbs away from the body's midline. For example, abduction of the thigh and leg, occurs when they are raised away from the sides of the body. Adduction occurs when bringing them back to the sides. The fingers are adducted or abducted in relation to the midline of the hand.

Circular Movements
Rotation and **circumduction** are the two kinds of circular movements which occur in relation to a central axis. Rotation occurs when a bone rotates around its own axis. For example rotation of the forearm causes movement of the hand from the anatomical position to one in which the palm is facing backwards . This movement of the hand itself is called **pronation**, and the reverse (turning the palms up or forward) is called **supination**.

Circumduction
Circumduction describes the movement of a limb around a central axis. The distal end of the limb moves in a circle while the fixed proximal end acts as a pivot point. Drawing circles in the air is an example of circumduction of the arm.

Multiple Movements

The coxal (or hip) joint is **triaxial**, because it permits movement on three different axes: 1) flexion and extension along the sagittal plane, 2) abduction and adduction along the coronal plane, and 3) rotation and circumduction on the axis of the femur.

Other Joint Movements

There are several specialized movements that occur at some joints. These include the opposing movements: 1) **inversion** and **eversion**, 2) **elevation** and **depression**, and 3) **protraction** and **retraction**. Inversion is movement of the foot so that the sole faces inward, while eversion causes the sole to face outward. Ankle sprains commonly occur due to excessive inversion of the foot. Elevation is the upward movement of any body part and depression is downward movement. For example, shrugging causes elevation of the shoulders, and opening the mouth causes depression of the mandible. Protraction is movement of a body part in the anterior direction, while retraction is movement in the posterior direction. For example, the mandible is protracted and retracted during the chewing of food.

Quick Check Questions

1. Flexion and extension occur on a ________ plane, while adduction and abduction occur on a coronal plane.

2. Extension of the knee is the same as:
   A. bending the knee
   B. straightening the knee
   C. moving the knee away from the midline
   D. moving the knee toward the midline

3 Flexion and adduction are:
   A. angular movements
   B. circular movements

4. Adduction is:
   A. movement of a limb closer to the midline
   B. lateral movement of the limb away from the midline
   C. a bone rotating upon its own axis

5. Abduction of the leg is the same as:
   A. bending the knee
   B. straightening the knee
   C moving the leg away from the midline
   D. moving the leg toward the midline

6. Abduction is:
   A. movement of a limb closer to the midline
   B. lateral movement of the limb away from the midline
   C. a bone rotating upon its own axis

7. Which of the following movements of the ankle is commonly associated with sprain injuries?
   A. inversion
   B. elevation
   C. depression
   D. protraction

8. The opposite of protraction is __________.

9. Abduction is the opposite of flexion. *True or False*

Chapter 6
The Muscular System

6.1.1 Muscle Histology and Physiology

15 minutes

The skeleton provides the framework for the body, but it is the muscles which allow us to move. **Muscles** have the unique capacity to generate physical movement from chemical energy. In addition to overt movement, muscles help to circulate blood and lymph, move food through the gastrointestinal tract, expel bile from the gallbladder, and contract the uterus during childbirth (to name just a few functions).

Muscles enable us to maintain body position (posture), and to retain the fluid contents of various organs. More than 600 skeletal muscles also provide an important source of body heat, which they generate during contraction. The specialized properties of muscle tissue which allow it to perform these functions include:

1) **Contractility**, the ability to contract or shorten in length. The interaction between two proteins, **actin** and **myosin**, gives muscle cells their contractility.

2) **Excitability** (or **irritability**), the ability to respond to a chemical or electrical signal. This property is unique to nerve and muscle cells.

3) **Extensibility**, the ability of a contracted muscle to stretch back to its original length when at rest. This process is passive (requires no energy): muscles are extended by the contraction of an opposing muscle.

4) **Elasticity**, the innate tension in muscles that allows them to return to their original length and shape.

These four properties give muscle tissue the ability to work in a coordinated fashion, under regulatory control of the nervous system, to perform a wide range of tasks.

Types of Muscle Tissue

There are three types of muscle tissue: 1) **skeletal muscle tissue**, 2) **cardiac muscle tissue,** and 3) **smooth muscle tissue**. These differ in the type and arrangement of their cells, as well as in their mechanisms. Muscle cells are long filaments that bundle together in a parallel arrangement, so they are called **muscle fibers**. All muscle is permanent tissue. That is, the cells developed in the fetus may continue to grow after birth, but no new cells are formed.

Skeletal muscle is responsible for movement of the skeleton and for movement of a few organs such as the eye and tongue. Since skeletal muscle is under conscious control, it is also called voluntary muscle. One exception is the diaphragm, the main muscle of respiration, which is subject to both voluntary and involuntary control. Skeletal muscle is also called **striated muscle**, because it has microscopically visible light and dark bands formed by overlapping filaments of the fibrous proteins actin and myosin. Each skeletal muscle fiber contains many nuclei. The bundles of muscle fibers are wrapped by connective tissue.

Cardiac muscle is the tissue of which the heart is made. It has an intrinsic, involuntary (though modifiable) rhythm. This property is called **autorhythmicity**. Cardiac muscle tissue is striated like skeletal muscle, but cardiac muscle fibers are branched and contain just one nucleus. The ends of different cells are connected by **gap junctions** called **intercalated discs**. These electrical synapses quickly transmit signals throughout the tissue, resulting in autorhymicity.

Smooth muscle is responsible for muscular control of the viscera, including the digestive, respiratory, urinary and reproductive organs, the blood vessels, and even the hair in the skin. (**Goose bumps** are due to **piloerection** caused by smooth muscle contraction). Smooth muscle fibers are smaller and spindle-shaped, contain a single nucleus, and communicate across gap junctions. Smooth muscle tissue is not striated. **Micturition** (urination), **peristalsis** (intestinal contraction), and **vasoconstriction** (the narrowing of blood vessels) all occur by smooth muscle contraction. Control of smooth muscle tissue is ordinarily involuntary, and smooth muscle displays autorhythmicity.

Quick Check Questions

1. Functions of the muscular system include voluntary movement, ____ generation, maintenance of posture, and retention of organ fluids.

2. Autorhythmicity is a characteristic of all types of muscle tissue. *True or False*

3. Excitability, extensibility, elasticity, and ____________ are the fundamental properties of muscle tissue.

4. In the eyelids you would expect to find ________ muscle tissue.

5. Around the bronchi in the respiratory tree you would expect to find ______ muscle tissue.

6.2.1 Organization of Skeletal Muscle

8 minutes

Skeletal muscle is organized into successive levels of bundles. Each bundle contains long, parallel fibers wrapped by connective tissue. The **epimysium** covers and protects an entire muscle. It also contains the blood vessels and motor neurons for the muscle. The muscle consists of several bundles called **fasciculi** (singular = **fasciculus**). Each fasciculus is surrounded by connective tissue called the **perimysium**.

A fasciculus is a bundle of skeletal muscle cells. Each individual muscle fiber is wrapped by a third layer of connective tissue, the **endomysium**, which also carries small blood vessels and nerves to the cells. All three connective tissue layers (epimysium, perimysium, and endomysium) are continuous with each other. They join at the end of the muscle to form attachments to tendons, bones, and adjacent muscles.

Quick Check Questions

1. Which connective tissue layer encircles an individual muscle cell?
   A. epimysium
   B. perimysium
   C. endomysium

2. A muscle fiber is bigger than a fasciculus. *True or False*

3. Capillaries that supply individual muscle cells are contained in the __________.

6.2.2 Fine Structure of Skeletal Muscle

15 minutes

We have moved through organizational levels from the muscle to the fasciculi to the muscle fibers. The cell membrane of a muscle fiber is called the **sarcolemma**, and its cytoplasm is called **sarcoplasm**. Most of the sarcoplasm is filled with hundreds of smaller fibers called **myofibrils**. Nuclei, mitochondria, and other organelles are found among the fibers. Skeletal muscle fibers are multinucleated, with the nuclei lying just beneath the sarcolemma.

Myofibrils are composed the of muscle proteins. Actin and myosin are the contractile proteins, while **troponin** and **tropomyosin** are regulatory proteins. Myofibrils have alternating **light bands** (called **I bands**) and **dark bands** (or **A bands**). In the center of the light band is a dark stripe called the **Z line**. The center of the dark band contains a lighter area called the **H zone**, with the darker **M line** running through it. The basic functional unit of muscles is the **sarcomere**, which extends from one Z line to the next Z line.

Quick Check Questions

1. The H zone is a light area which lies within the:
   A. A band
   B. I band

2. Through the center of the H zone runs a dark line called the:
   A. Z line
   B. M line

3. Skeletal muscle cells have a single central nucleus. *True or False*

4. The sarcomere extends from:
   A. A band to A band
   B. I band to I band
   C. M line to M line
   D. Z line to Z line
   E. H zone to H zone

6.2.3 Histology of Muscle Cells

10 minutes

Each myofibril is composed of many **thick filaments** and **thin filaments** that run in alternating, parallel rows. The thick filaments contain long, fibrous myosin molecules. Myosin has a straight chain tail with a large cluster (head) on one end. Two tails twist around each other, with both heads together, to make a filament. The tails of the filament point towards the dark M line in the H zone. The pair of heads is called a **cross bridge**: its binding to the thin filaments leads to contraction of the muscle. The thin filaments of the myofibril contain bean-shaped actin molecules, along with troponin and tropomyosin, arranged into chains. Each actin molecule contains a **myosin-binding site**, where the myosin heads can potentially bind. However, in a resting muscle, this site is blocked by tropomyosin.

How do the thick and thin filaments relate to the alternating dark and light bands? The I band is an area where only thin filaments lie, while the A band contains the thick filaments. The edges of each A band are regions of overlap between thick and thin filaments. The center of the band has no overlapping thin filaments, so it appears lighter in color: this is the H zone. The Z lines form where adjacent thin filaments meet.

Quick Check Questions

1. The A band contains only thick filaments. *True or* False

2. The I band contains only thin filaments. *True or False*

3. In resting muscle, the myosin-binding sites of actin molecules do NOT bind with the cross-bridges of myosin molecules because another protein, _________, is bound to the site on the ______, obstructing the interaction.
   A. tropomyosin, myosin
   B. troponin, actin
   C. elastin, myosin
   D. tropomyosin, actin

6.2.4 Physiology of Muscle Contraction

10 minutes

The muscle cell contains a maze of tubules surrounding the myofibrils. This is the **sarcoplasmic reticulum**: it corresponds to the endoplasmic reticulum of other cells. The sarcoplasmic reticulum forms expanded sacs called **terminal cisternae** that contain a high level of calcium ions. The cells also have structures called **transverse tubules** (or **T tubules**), that run perpendicular to the myofibrils. The T tubules are continuous with the sarcolemma. They open to the extracellular space through pores, and are filled with extracellular fluid. T tubules associate closely with two adjacent terminal cisternae, forming a structure called a **triad**.

Nerve cells provide the excitation impulse that causes a skeletal muscle cell to contract. A motor neuron releases a chemical messenger across its synapse with the muscle fiber. This sets up an electrical signal (a flow of ions) that passes into the pores and through the T tubules. This signal causes a release of calcium ions from the cisternae into the sarcoplasm. Finally, the increase in Ca++ concentration triggers contraction of the fiber.

Quick Check Questions

1. The __________ is a maze of tubules.
   A. sarcolemma
   B. sarcoplasmic reticulum
   C. sarcoplasm

2. The signal from a nerve cell is transmitted through the pores directly into the myofibrils. *True or False*

3. Terminal cisternae:
   A. are continuous with the T tubules
   B. contain extracellular fluid
   C. contain a high concentration of calcium ions
   D. are sacs made from the sarcolemma

6.2.5 The Sliding Filament Model

6 minutes

The accepted mechanism of skeletal muscle contraction is the **sliding filament model**. This model states that contraction is caused by the thick filaments and the thin filaments sliding past each other, with no change in the lengths of the filaments themselves. The sliding occurs when the myosin cross-bridges bind to the actin molecules, then undergo a conformational change that pulls the filaments past each other. Contraction is regulated by the calcium level, and driven by the energy of ATP hydrolysis.

The cross-bridges pull the thin filaments in closer to the centers of the thick filaments. So as the filaments slide and overlap, the I bands and the H zones become narrower and disappear. The sarcomeres shorten until they are the length of the A bands. In this way, the entire muscle fiber shortens.

Quick Check Questions

1. Muscle contraction is caused by the shortening of myosin filaments. *True or False*

2. The I bands are composed of ______. They ______ in length during contraction.
   A. actin, increase
   B. myosin, increase
   C. actin, decrease
   D. myosin, decrease

6.2.6 Biochemistry of Contraction

8 minutes

We can now examine contraction at the molecular level. The energy required for the process is provided by ATP. An ATP molecule binds to a myosin head, where it is hydrolyzed to ADP and phosphate. The phosphate bond energy is transferred to myosin, leaving the head in its "activated" position.

The myosin is ready to bind to actin. But the binding site on actin is blocked by tropomyosin, which is held in place by troponin molecules while the muscle is at rest. When a signal to contract is received from a motor neuron, we saw how calcium ions are released into the sarcoplasm. These ions bind to troponin and cause a conformational change in the troponin-tropomyosin complex. Actin's binding site is unblocked.

The myosin head now binds an actin unit. ADP is released, and the head springs back to its original position, pulling the actin filament along. This is the **power stroke** of contraction. As long as ATP is available and the Ca^{++} level remains high, these power strokes repeat and contraction is sustained.

Quick Check Questions

1. In the resting state, calcium is bound to troponin. *True or False*

2. When the T tubules receive a nerve signal, calcium is released from the terminal cisternae. *True or False*

3. Muscle contraction continues as long as there is sufficient ______ to provide energy.

4. The power stroke of the contraction comes when:
   A. ATP is hydrolyzed to ADP and phosphate
   B. tropomyosin changes its conformation
   C. the myosin head changes its conformation

6.2.7 Neurophysiology of Contraction

5 minutes

As we saw, muscle contraction is triggered when a nerve impulse is transmitted along a motor neuron to the muscle fiber. The number of muscle fibers innervated by a motor neuron is highly variable, although each muscle fiber is contacted by only one motor neuron. A **motor unit** is defined as a motor neuron and all the muscle fibers it innervates. In muscles which require fine control, such as the extraocular muscles that control eye movement, there can be as few as six muscle fibers per motor neuron. A muscle whose purpose is power rather than precise movement, such as the gastrocnemius muscle in the leg, may have as many as 2000 muscle fibers per motor neuron.

Quick Check Questions

1. A motor neuron consists of a motor unit and the associated muscle fibers.
   True or False

2. Muscles used for fine movement have _____ fibers per neuron than those used primarily for power.
   A. more
   B. fewer
   C. the same number of

6.3.1 Types of Skeletal Muscle Tissue

5 minutes

There are two types of skeletal muscle fibers: 1) dark muscle fibers, and 2) light muscle fibers. They differ in the mechanism used to regenerate their supplies of

ATP. Most muscle tissue contains both types of fiber. Dark muscle tissue has **slow twitch** fibers, also called **aerobic fibers**. Aerobic fibers have a rich blood supply, they contain many mitochondria, and their color is due to an abundance of the oxygen-carrying protein **myoglobin**. They are found in muscles which contract continuously, such as the soleus muscle in the calf, which helps maintain posture while standing. Light muscle tissue contains **fast twitch** fibers, also called **anaerobic fibers**. These fibers have few mitochondria and little myoglobin, but contain **glycogen** and **glycolytic enzymes**. Muscles with fast twitch fibers are responsible for rapid, intense contractions, such as those of the biceps brachii.

Quick Check Questions

1. Mitochondria are oxygen-carrying proteins. *True or False*

2. Muscles which must contract steadily over long periods of time, such as muscles controlling posture, have a richer blood supply than those with short, intense contractions. *True or False*

6.3.2 Organization of Cardiac Muscle

8 minutes

We return now to the other types of muscle tissue. Cardiac muscle is the muscle that makes up the ventricles and atria of the heart. The organization of cardiac muscle fibers is similar to that of skeletal muscle. The arrangement of the actin and myosin gives the fibers a striated appearance. The T tubules are larger, but work in the same way. There are several ways in which cardiac muscle differs from skeletal muscle:

1) A cardiac muscle fiber is branched, and contains a single central nucleus.

2) Cardiac muscle fibers are connected by **intercalated discs**, thickenings of the sarcolemma between cells. The discs contain **gap junctions**, through which **action potentials** (contraction signals) are transmitted. Because of gap junctions, the fibers in a given chamber of the heart contract almost simultaneously.

3) Contraction of cardiac muscle is not voluntary, nor is it controlled by input from a motor neuron. Instead, the heart has its own specialized area (the **sinoatrial** or **SA node**) which periodically sends signals to the rest of the cardiac fibers and causes them to contract. (Even without the SA node, cardiac fibers contract simultaneously because of autorhythmicity).

4) Cardiac muscle has a longer period of calcium influx, because calcium comes from the extracellular fluid as well as from the sarcoplasmic reticulum.

5) Cardiac muscle has a longer **refractory period** (obligatory period of relaxation) than skeletal muscle.

Quick Check Questions

1. All of the following are true of cardiac muscle, EXCEPT:
   A. the cardiac fiber receives all of its calcium from the extracellular space
   B. cardiac muscle fibers are striped with light and dark bands
   C. cardiac cells have a single, centrally located nucleus

2. Contraction of cardiac muscle is controlled by motor neurons from the brain.
   True or False

6.3.3 Organization of Smooth Muscle

12 minutes

The structure of smooth muscle is very different from that of skeletal muscle. Its sarcoplasm contains thick and thin filaments as well as **intermediate filaments**, and the filaments are not regularly arranged. For this reason, smooth muscle does not have a striated appearance. There are two functional types of smooth muscle: 1) **visceral single-unit smooth muscle**, and 2) **multi-unit smooth muscle**.

Visceral single-unit smooth muscle contains many gap junctions between its fibers. The fibers are arranged in sheets of muscle through which a contraction signal is rapidly transmitted. Single-unit smooth muscle is the more common type: it is found in arterioles and venules (the areas of the cardiovascular system where vasoconstriction is the most important), and in hollow viscera, such as the stomach, uterus, and bladder.

The other kind of smooth muscle, multi-unit smooth muscle, contains only a few gap junctions. Each fiber receives its own innervation from a motor neuron, so the cells do not contract in unison. Multi-unit smooth muscle is found in the muscles that constrict the pupil, as well as in the arrector pili muscles which make the hair on the skin stand up.

Mechanism of Contraction

The mechanism of smooth muscle contraction is different from that of skeletal muscle. Smooth muscle contraction does depend on the calcium ion concentration and ATP hydrolysis, but the cells have no T tubules and little sarcoplasmic reticulum. They do not contain troponin: instead they have the proteins **calmodulin** and **myosin light-chain kinase (MLCK)**. Calmodulin binds calcium, and thereby activates MLCK. MLCK catalyzes the binding of phosphate groups (from ATP) to the myosin cross-bridges, which is required prior to binding to actin.

Quick Check Questions

1. Single-unit smooth muscle has many gap ________ between the fibers.

2. Multi-unit smooth muscle tissue lacks separate innervation by motor neurons. *True or False*

3. Single-unit smooth muscle is much ____ common than multi-unit.
   A. more
   B. less

4. Smooth muscles do NOT have _______ and do NOT contain _______.
   A. sarcoplasmic reticulum, MLCK
   B. T tubules, troponin

5. MLCK catalyzes binding of phosphate to the myosin head. *True or False*

6.4.1 Anatomy of the Muscular System

25 minutes

The muscular system is made up of the **skeletal muscle organs** of the body (the skeletal muscles), which are under voluntary control. Each of these organs is composed of striated muscle tissue, a connective tissue framework, and an abundant supply of blood vessels, lymphatic vessels, and nerves. The skeletal muscles make up about 40 percent of the body weight, and are responsible for all voluntary movements essential to performance of many body functions.

Each muscle is comprised of two parts: 1) the **belly**, which is composed predominantly of muscle fibers, where the strength of contraction is generated, and 2) the **tendons**, consisting of fibrous connective tissue which attaches the muscles firmly to bones or other structures. When they contract, muscles move the bones in relation to each other. Though there are a few exceptions, most muscles are attached to two different bones of the skeleton. Thus, they usually have two tendons. The tendon that attaches to the less movable (or **proximal**) structure is called the **tendon of origin**, and the one that attaches to the more mobile (**distant**) structure is referred to as the **tendon of insertion**.

Blood Supply to Muscles

Since the muscular system is responsible for movement and generation of body heat, it is richly supplied with blood vessels. The connective tissue framework of the belly of the muscle serves to carry, support, and protect these vessels. Arteries and veins enter the muscle together along the connective tissue **trabeculae,** and then break up to form a fine network of capillaries in the endomysium surrounding individual muscle fibers. These vessels constrict and dilate, regulating the blood supply to muscles. Muscular activity helps to pump blood from these vessels towards the heart, thereby increasing the blood flow to the heart and speeding the flow of the entire circulation.

Nerve Supply to Muscles

Nerves travel along the **intermuscular septa** and usually enter muscles with the blood vessels. Then they branch through the connective tissue framework and eventually reach the individual muscle fibers. The **sensory nerve fibers** (or **afferent** nerve fibers) come from groups of specialized muscle fibers, and carry impulses to the **central nervous system** (CNS). They are stimulated by muscular contraction and stretching, and are responsible for providing data regarding the status of the muscles' activity.

The **motor nerve fibers** are **efferent** fibers, and are of two types: 1) **alpha motor neurons**, which end in **motor end-plates** or **myoneural junctions** on regular muscle fibers, and 2) **gamma motor neurons**, which end in the motor end-plates on the smaller muscle fibers of **muscle spindles**. Motor neurons send signals from the nervous system to the muscles.

Muscle Types

Muscles may be grouped according to the role they play in different actions of the body. If a muscle contracts to produce a desired movement, it is called a **prime mover** or **agonist** for that movement. If a muscle serves to counteract or slow the action of a prime mover, it is referred to as an **antagonist**. If a muscle steadies a movement, or eliminates an undesired movement of a joint, it is said to be a **synergist**. Muscles which maintain the position of other body parts but do not actually take part in the action are called **fixators**.

Structure of Skeletal Muscles

We saw that skeletal muscle fibers are arranged within the muscle in bundles called **fasciculi**. The muscle fibers are parallel to each other within a bundle, but the arrangement of fasciculi with respect to the tendons may vary. The muscles may be divided into groups on this basis.

Muscle Groups

ARRANGEMENT: Parallel
DESCRIPTION: Fasciculi run parallel to longitudinal axis of muscle and terminate in flat tendons at either end.
EXAMPLE: Stylohyoid.

ARRANGEMENT: Fusiform
DESCRIPTION: Fasciculi arranged as above, but muscle tapers towards tendons, so diameter at the ends is less than at the belly.
EXAMPLE: Digastric.

ARRANGEMENT: Pennate
DESCRIPTION: Fasciculi short as compared to muscle length, and tendon extends nearly the entire length of the muscle.
EXAMPLE: The three categories of pennate musclesare described below.

ARRANGEMENT: Unipennate
DESCRIPTION: Fasciculi arranged on one side of the tendon.
EXAMPLE: Extensor digitorum longus.

ARRANGEMENT: Bipennate
DESCRIPTION: Fasciculi arranged on both sides of a centrally positioned tendon.
EXAMPLE: Rectus femoris.

ARRANGEMENT: Multipennate
DESCRIPTION: Fasciculi attached obliquely from many directions to several tendons.
EXAMPLE: Deltoid.

ARRANGEMENT: Circular
DESCRIPTION: Fasciculi arranged in a circular pattern to enclose an orifice.
EXAMPLE: Orbicularis oris.

ARRANGEMENT: Convergent
DESCRIPTION: A tendon is shared by more than one muscle.
EXAMPLE: Rectus femoris, vastus medialis, vastus lateralis, and vastus intermedius all attach to the patellar tendon.

Quick Check Questions

1. Muscle organs are composed of the _____ and the tendons.

2. The tendon attached proximally is referred to as the tendon of origin, and the tendon attached distally is referred to as the tendon of _________.

3. Constriction and ________ of blood vessels regulates the blood supply to the muscle.

4. The afferent nerve fibers from muscles are also called _______ neurons, and the efferent fibers are also called motor neurons.

5. Efferent motor neurons which end on regular muscle fibers are referred to as type _____, and those that end on smaller fibers are referred to as type gamma.

6. Muscles which maintain the position of body parts while not actually taking part in a given movement are referred to as ________.

7. In a pennate arrangement, the fasciculi are short in comparison to the length of the tendons. *True or False*

6.4.2 Classification of Muscles

20 minutes

Orientation

The orientation of muscle fibers is described in relation to the midline.

Description:	*Example*:
Parallel (rectus)	Rectus
Perpendicular (transverse)	Transversus
Diagonal (oblique)	External oblique

Location

Location of a muscle is described in relation to the structure near where the muscle is found.

Examples: Frontal bone (frontalis); in front of the tibia (tibialis anterior).

Size

Size of a muscle is described in relative terms.

Examples: Largest = Maximus (Gluteus maximus); Smallest = Minimus (Gluteus minimus); Longest = Longus (Adductor longus); Shortest = Brevis (Peroneus brevis).

Number of Origins

Examples: Two = Biceps (Biceps brachii); Three = Triceps (Triceps brachii); Four = Quadriceps (Quadratus femoris).

Shape

The shape of a muscle refers to its overall shape.

Examples: Triangular = Deltoid (Deltoid); Saw-toothed = Serratus (Serratus anterior).

Origin and Insertion

The origin and insertion of a muscle refer to the sites where its tendons attach.

Action:	*(Example)*:
Flexor	(F. carpi radialis)
Extensor	(E. carpi ulnaris)
Abductor	(A. pollicis brevis)
Adductor	(A. longus)
Levator	(L. scapulae)
Depressor	(D. labii inferioris)
Supinator	(Supinator)
Pronator	(P. teres)
Sphincter	(External anal)
Tensor	(T. fascia lata)
Rotator	(Obturator externus)

Classification of Muscles

Muscles of the axial skeleton include:
Muscles of the head and neck. Muscles of the vertebral column. Muscles of the thorax. Muscles of the abdomen. Muscles of the pelvic floor.

Muscles of the upper extremity include:
Muscles that act on the pectoral girdle. Muscles that act on the arm. Muscles that act on the forearm. Muscles that move the wrist, hand, and fingers. Muscles of the hand.

Muscles of the lower extremity include:
Muscles that move the thigh. Muscles that move the leg. Muscles that move the ankle, foot, and toes. Muscles of the foot.

Axial Skeleton: Muscles that move the head

Sternocleidomastoid: There are two of these muscles, one on either side of the neck. When one contracts alone, the face rotates to the opposite side; when the two contract together, they bend the head forward on the vertebral column.
Semispinalis capitis: Contraction of one muscle alone rotates the face to the same side; contraction of both together extends the head.
Splenius capitis: Contraction of one alone laterally flexes the head and rotates it to the same side; acting together, both muscles extend the head.
Longissimus capitis: These muscles extend the head and rotate the face towards the same side as the contracting muscle.

Axial Skeleton: Muscles of facial expression

Frontalis: Draws scalp forward, raises eyebrows and wrinkles skin of forehead horizontally.
Occipitalis: Draws scalp backward.
Orbicularis oris: Closes lips, compresses lips against teeth, protrudes lips and shapes lips during speech.
Zygomaticus: Draws angle of mouth upward and outward, as in smiling, laughing.
Levator labii superioris: elevates upper lip.
Depressor labii inferioris: depresses lower lip.

Buccinator: major cheek muscle - compresses cheeks and causes them to cave in.
Mentalis: elevates and protrudes lower lip.
Platysma: draws outer part of lower lip downward and backward; depresses mandible.
Risorius: draws angle of mouth laterally.
Orbicularis oculi: closes eye.
Corrugator supercilii: draws eyebrow downward.
Levator palpebrae superioris: elevates upper eyelid.

Axial Skeleton: Muscles that move the lower jaw

Masseter: elevates and protracts mandible, and assists in side to side movement.
Temporalis: elevates and retracts mandible, and assists in side to side movement.
Medial pterygoid: elevates and protracts mandible, and moves it from side to side.
Lateral pterygoid: opens mouth, protracts mandible and moves it from side to side.

Axial Skeleton: Muscles that move the eyeball

Superior rectus: rolls eyeball upward.
Inferior rectus: rolls eyeball downward.
Lateral rectus: rolls eyeball laterally.
Medial rectus: rolls eyeball medially.
Superior oblique: rotates eyeball and directs cornea downward and laterally.
Inferior oblique: rotates eyeball and directs cornea upward and laterally.

Quick Check Questions

1. When the sternocleidomastoid of one side contracts alone, the face moves to the same side. *True or False*

2. The frontalis muscle raises the eyebrows and wrinkles the skin of the forehead horizontally. *True or False*

3. The zygomaticus draws the angle of the mouth upwards and outwards. *True or False*

4. The orbicularis oculi opens the eye. *True or False*

5. The masseter and medial pterygoid elevate and protract the mandible and assist in side to side movement. *True or False*

6. The inferior rectus rolls the eyeball downwards. *True or False*

7. The inferior oblique rolls the eyeball downwards. *True or False*

6.4.3 Classification of Muscles (Cont.)

10 minutes

Axial Skeleton: Muscles of the Vertebral Column

Splenius: Together, they extend the head and neck, and acting singly, each laterally flexes and rotates head to the same side.

Erector spinae: This is the largest muscular mass of the back and consists of three groupings: 1) **Iliocostalis**: Extends cervical and lumbar region and maintains erect position of spine, 2) **Longissimus**: Extends cervical and thoracic region of vertebral column; extends head and rotates it to opposite side, and 3) **Spinalis**: Extends vertebral column.

Transversospinalis: extends vertebral column and rotates it to the opposite side.
Segmental: extends and laterally flexes vertebral column.
Scalene: flexes and rotates neck, and assists in inspiration.

Axial Skeleton: Muscles of the Thorax

Diaphragm: forms floor of thoracic cavity; pulls central tendon downwards during inspiration, thereby increasing vertical length of thorax.

External intercostals: elevate ribs during inspiration, increasing both anteroposterior and lateral dimensions of the thorax.

Internal intercostals: Draw adjacent ribs together during expiration, thereby decreasing both anteroposterior and lateral dimensions of thorax.

Axial Skeleton: Muscles of the Abdomen

Rectus abdominis: compresses abdomen and flexes vertebral column.
External obliques: contraction of both together causes compression of the abdomen; when they contract alone, they cause bending and lateral rotation of the vertebral column.
Internal obliques: contraction of both together causes compression of the abdomen; when they contract alone, they cause bending and lateral rotation of the vertebral column.
Transversus abdominis: compresses abdomen.
Quadratus lumborum: during expiration, pulls downward on the twelfth rib, and during inspiration, prevents its elevation. Contraction of one side bends the vertebral column laterally.

Axial Skeleton: Muscles of the Pelvic Floor

1) **Levator ani**: Supports and slightly raises the pelvic floor; resists increased intraabdominal pressure, draws the anus towards the pubis, and constricts it.

2) **Coccygeus**: Aids the levator ani; pulls coccyx forward following defecation or parturition.

Quick Check Questions

1. The largest muscular mass of the back is formed by the _______ spinae.

2. The erector spinae consists of three muscle groups: the spinalis, the longissimus, and the ____________.

3. The _________ forms the floor of the thoracic cavity.

4. When the rectus abdominis contracts, it compresses the abdomen and ______ the vertebral column.

5. The quadratus lumborum acts on the _______ rib.

6. The levator ani and the __________ support the pelvic floor.

6.5.1 Muscles - Upper Extremity

6 minutes

Muscles that act on the pectoral girdle anteriorly include:

Subclavius: depresses clavicle.
Pectoralis: depresses and moves scapula anteriorly; when scapula is fixed, elevates ribs 3 - 5 during inspiration.
Serratus: rotates scapula upwards and anterior laterally; when scapula is fixed, elevates the ribs.

Muscles that act on the pectoral girdle posteriorly include:

Trapezius: elevates clavicle, depresses head; adducts, elevates, rotates, and depresses scapula.
Levator scapulae: elevates scapula and rotates it downward.
Rhomboideus (major): adducts scapula and major rotates it downward.
Rhomboideus (minor): adduction and downward minor rotation of scapula.

Muscles that act on the arm include:

Axial:
Pectoralis: flexion, adduction, and medial major rotation.
Latissimus dorsi: extension, abduction, and medial rotation.

Scapular:
Deltoid: abduction, flexion, and extension; medial and lateral rotation.
Subscapularis: medial rotation.
Supraspinatus: assists deltoid in abduction.
Infraspinatus: adduction and lateral rotation.
Teres major: extension; assists in adduction and medial rotation.
Teres minor: lateral rotation, adduction and extension.
Coracobrachialis: flexion and adduction.

Quick Check Questions

1. The levator scapulae causes depression of the scapula. *True or False*

2. The infraspinatus causes abduction and medial rotation of the arm. *True or False*

6.5.2 Muscles - Upper Extremity (Cont.)

15 minutes

Muscles that act on the forearm include:

Flexors:
Biceps brachii: flexion and supination.
Brachialis: flexion.
Brachioradialis: flexion; semi-supination and semi-pronation.

Extensors:
Triceps brachii: extension of arm and forearm.
Anconeus: extension of the forearm.

Pronators:
Pronator teres: pronation and flexion.
Pronator quadratus: pronation.

Supinators:
Supinator: supination.

Muscles that move the wrist, hand, and fingers include:

Flexors:
Superficial:
F. carpi radialis: flexion and abduction.
Palmaris longus: flexion.

F. digitorum superficialis: flexes middle phalanges.
F. carpi ulnaris: flexion and adduction.

Deep:
F. digitorum profundus: flexes distal phalanges.
F. pollicis longus: flexes thumb.

Extensors:
Superficial:
E. carpi radialis longus: extension and abduction of wrist.
E. carpi radialis brevis: extension and abduction of wrist.
E. digitorum: extension of phalanges.
E. digiti minimi: extension of little finger.
E. carpi ulnaris: extension and adduction of wrist.

Deep:
Abductor pollicis: extension of thumb, abduction of wrist.
E. pollicis brevis: extension of thumb, abduction of wrist.
E. pollicis longus: extension of thumb, abduction of wrist.
E. indicis: extension of index finger.

Muscles of the hand include:

Thenar:
Abductor pollicis brevis: abduction of thumb.
Opponens pollicis: opposition of thumb, little finger.
Flexor pollicis brevis: flexion and adduction of thumb.
Adductor pollicis: adduction of thumb.

Hypothenar:
Palmaris brevis: draws skin to middle of palm.
Abductor digiti minimi: abduction of little finger.
Flexor digiti minimi: flexion of little finger.
Opponens digiti minimi: draws little finger to meet thumb.

Intermediate (Midpalmar):
Lumbricals: extension of interphalangeal (IP) joints, flexion of metacarpophalangeal (MP) joints.
Dorsal interossei: abduction from middle finger, extension of IP and flexion of

MP joints.
Palmar interossei: adduction to middle finger, extension of IP and flexion of MP joints.

Quick Check Questions

1. The biceps brachii, the supinator, and the ________________ muscles contribute to supination of the arm.

2. Pronation of the arm is caused by the contraction of the brachioradialis, the pronator teres, and the pronator _________ muscles.

3. The thumb is flexed by the flexor pollicis ______.

4. Flexion and adduction of the thumb is caused by the flexor pollicis ______.

5. The opponens digiti ______ muscle draws the little finger to meet the thumb.

6. The interossei cause _________ at the IP joints and flexion at the MP joints.

6.5.3 Muscles - Lower Extremity

10 minutes

Muscles that move the thigh include:

Psoas major: flexion and lateral rotation of thigh, flexion of vertebral column.
Iliacus: flexion and lateral rotation of thigh, flexion of vertebral column.
Gluteus maximus: extension, lateral rotation.
Gluteus medius: abduction, medial rotation.
Gluteus minimus: abduction, medial rotation.
Tensor fascia lata: flexion and abduction.
Piriformis: abduction and lateral rotation.
Obturator internus: abduction and lateral rotation.
Obturator externus: lateral rotation.
Quadratus femoris: lateral rotation and adduction.
Adductor longus: adduction, flexion, medial rotation.
Adductor brevis: adduction, flexion, medial rotation.

Adductor magnus: adduction, flexion, medial rotation, extension.
Pectineus: flexion and adduction.

Muscles that move the leg include:

Adductor compartment (Note: All adduct the thigh and flex the leg):
Adductor magnus.
Adductor longus.
Adductor brevis.
Pectineus.
Gracilis.

Extensor compartment:
Quadriceps femoris: extension of leg.
Rectus femoris: flexion of thigh, extension of leg.
Vastus lateralis: extension of leg.
Vastus medialis: extension of leg.
Vastus intermedius: extension of leg.
Sartorius: flexion of leg, flexion and lateral rotation of thigh.

Flexor compartment (Note: All flex leg and extend thigh):
Hamstrings: **Biceps femoris, Semitendinosus, Semimembranosus.**

Quick Check Questions

1. Contraction of the gluteus maximus causes extension and lateral rotation of the _____.

2. The tensor fascia lata causes flexion and _________ of the thigh.

3. The obturator externus causes _______ rotation of the thigh.

4. The vasti together cause _________ of the leg.

5. The __________ consist of the biceps femoris, semitendinosus and semi-membranosus muscles.

6.5.4 Muscles - Lower Extremity (Cont.)

12 minutes

Muscles that move the ankle, foot and toes include:

Anterior compartment:
Tibialis anterior: dorsiflexion and inversion of foot.
Extensor hallucis longus: dorsiflexion and inversion of foot, extension of great toe.
Extensor digitorum longus: dorsiflexion and eversion of foot, extension of toes.
Peroneus tertius: dorsiflexion and eversion of foot.
Peroneus longus: plantar flexion and eversion of foot.
Peroneus brevis: plantar flexion and eversion of foot.

Posterior compartment:
Superficial:
Gastrocnemius: plantar flexion of foot, flexion of leg.
Soleus: plantar flexion of foot.
Plantaris: plantar flexion of foot.

Deep:
Popliteus: flexion and medial rotation of leg.
Flexor hallucis longus: plantar flexion and inversion of foot, flexion of great toe.
Flexor digitorum longus: plantar flexion and inversion of foot, flexion of toes.
Tibialis posterior: plantar flexion and inversion of foot.

Intrinsic muscles of the foot include:

Dorsal:
Extensor digitorum brevis: extension, toes 1 - 4.

Plantar:
First layer:
Abductor hallucis: abduction of great toe, flexion of metatarsophalangeal joint.
Flexor digitorum brevis: flexion of toes 2 - 5.
Abductor digiti minimi: abduction and flexion of small toe.

Second layer:
Quadratus plantae: flexion of toes 2 - 5.
Lumbricals: extension of interphalangeal, flexion of MT joints and toes 2 - 5.

Third layer:
Flexor hallucis brevis: flexion of great toe.
Adductor hallucis: adduction and flexion of great toe.
Flexor digiti minimi brevis: flexion of small toe.

Fourth layer:
Dorsal interossei: abduction of toes, flexion of proximal phalanges.
Plantar interossei: adduction of toes 3 - 5, flexion of proximal phalanges.

Quick Check Questions

1. The tibialis anterior and extensor hallucis longus cause dorsiflexion and inversion of the foot. *True or False*

2. The peronei cause plantar flexion and eversion of the foot. *True or False*

3. The quadratus plantae and lumbricals form the first plantar layer of intrinsic muscles of the foot. *True or False*

4. Both the plantar and dorsal interossei cause flexion of the proximal phalanges of the toes. *True or False*

Chapter 7
The Nervous System Organization

7.1.1 Nervous System - Overview

15 minutes

The nervous system is a vast network of connected cells which comprise: 1) the **brain** (our most complex and least well understood organ), 2) the **spinal cord**, and 3) the **peripheral nerves**. The nervous system can "sense changes," both in the body and in the outside environment. The nervous system also integrates information and controls body movement and internal body functions. In order to sustain life, the nervous system must maintain a state of **homeostasis** (that is, balance or equilibrium) in response to changes of the outside world.

Anatomical Divisions of the Nervous System

The nervous system is divided anatomically between: 1) the **central nervous system** (CNS), which includes the brain and spinal cord, and 2) the **peripheral nervous system** (PNS). The PNS includes the **cranial nerves**, that are connected to the brain and the **spinal nerves**, joined to the spinal cord. Many peripheral nerves carry "two-way" information: both into and outwards from the CNS. Incoming information from various sensory receptors is carried by the **sensory** (or **afferent**) nerves. Outgoing impulses to muscles and glands are carried by **motor** (or **efferent**) nerves.

Functional Divisions of the Nervous System

The nervous system may also be divided according to function. The **somatic nervous system** and the **autonomic nervous system** are two functional classifications of the nervous system. The somatic nervous system is involved in **conscious** perception of the environment and **voluntary** movement of the body. The autonomic nervous system senses the body's internal environment and controls **involuntary** functions such as heart rate, gastrointestinal contractions, and glandular secretions.

Divisions of the Autonomic Nervous System

The efferent (motor) portion of the autonomic nervous system is further divided into the **sympathetic** and **parasympathetic** systems. Many internal organs receive input from both of these systems. In general, the effects of sympathetic and parasympathetic activity are opposite. The sympathetic division increases the body's available energy, and is active when a person is under stress. It is thus named the **fight or flight** system. The parasympathetic division, however, increases the storage of energy and controls normal resting activities such as the digestion of food. It is sometimes called the **rest and repair** system.

Quick Check Questions

1. Which of the following is a functional division of the nervous system?
   A. the central nervous system
   B. the peripheral nervous system
   C. the somatic nervous system
   D. the cranial nerves

2. Three major functions of the nervous system are sensation, integration, and _______ of body functions.

3. The cranial and spinal nerves make up the anatomical division called the __________ nervous system.

4. Sensory or ________ nerves conduct information into the CNS from various sensory receptors.

5. The _______ nervous system is important for conscious perception and voluntary movement.

6. The division of the efferent autonomic nervous system that can increase the energy storage processes involved in "rest and repair" is the ____________ nervous system.

7.2.1 Cells of the Nervous System

15 minutes

The nervous system is comprised of two major types of cells: 1) **neurons** and 2) **neuroglia**. Neurons are very specialized cells which have the ability to conduct electrical impulses. Neuroglia, or **glial cells**, function in the protection, and support of the impulse-conducting neurons. Glial cells are smaller and much more numerous than neurons. Glial cells are able to multiply and regenerate, while most neurons are incapable of **mitosis** (cell division). There are six types of neuroglia: four exist in the central nervous system (CNS), and two are part of the peripheral nervous system (PNS).

Four Types of CNS Neuroglia

Astrocytes are glial cells in the CNS that help repair damaged nerve tissue and may contribute to the formation of a barrier between neurons and blood vessels. The barrier is called the **blood-brain barrier**. The blood brain barrier allows only certain substances to pass from the blood into the **interstitial fluid** of the CNS. One type of neuroglia found in the brain is **microglia**, which is a **phagocytic** glial cells. Microglia destroy microbes and consume the debris of dead brain cells.

Ependymal cells line the fluid-filled cavities of the brain (the ventricles), and the fluid-filled **central canal** of the spinal cord. Many ependymal cells are equipped with beating, hair-like **cilia** which help to keep fluid moving through these spaces. **Oligodendrocytes** are glial cells which wind around neurons, forming a wrapping which increases the speed of nerve impulse conduction. This wrapping is called a **myelin sheath**. Each oligodendrocyte has many extensions which form myelin sheaths around different neurons.

Two Types of PNS Neuroglia

The glial cells in the PNS are **neurolemmocytes** (or **Schwann cells**), and **satellite cells**. Much like oligodendrocytes, neurolemmocytes wrap around neurons to form myelin sheaths in the PNS. As many as 500 adjacent neurolemmocytes may form a myelin sheath around the long process of a single PNS neuron. Satellite cells are found in **nerve ganglia** (aggregations of nerve cell bodies), where they support neurons.

Myelination

Oligodendrocytes and neurolemmocytes produce a lipoprotein called **myelin**. These cells wrap themselves around and around the process of a neuron to form many myelin layers. The outermost layer of the myelin sheath, called the **neurilemma**, contains the nuclei of the glial cells.

Myelinated neurons are able to conduct impulses much faster than those that are **unmyelinated**. Each glial cell covers a 1 millimeter length of the neuron. Small gaps of neural membrane are left uncovered between glial cells. These gaps are known as **neurofibril nodes** or **nodes of Ranvier**. Since myelin is white in color, the portions of the brain containing many myelinated nerve fibers are reffered to as **white matter**. Unmyelinated portions are called **gray matter**.

Quick Check Questions

1. The two major types of cells in the nervous system are neurons and __________.

2. Neuroglial cells are capable of multiplying and dividing. *True or False*

3. Which of the following line the fluid-filled cavities of the brain?
   A. astrocytes
   B. microglia
   C. ependymal cells
   D. oligodendrocytes

4. Which of the following contribute the **blood-brain barrier**?
   A. astrocytes
   B. microglia
   C. ependymal cells
   D. oligodendrocytes

5. In myelinated neurons, the small gaps of neural membrane left uncovered between glial cells are called ___________ nodes, or nodes of Ranvier.

7.3.1 Neurons

12 minutes

Neurons are the cells that conduct electrical nerve impulses. Neurons may relay information over distances as short as 1 millimeter, or as long as 1 meter or more. For example, a single neuron carries sensory information from the toes to the base of the brain. The neural impulses can travel at speeds anywhere from 0.5 to 130 meters per second (1 to 290 miles per hour). The **contact point** between neurons, or between a neuron and a muscle or gland, is called a **synapse**. When a motor neuron synapses with a muscle fiber, the union is called a **neuromuscular junction**. When a motor neuron synapses with a gland, the union is called a **neuroglandular junction**.

Parts of a Neuron

The major parts of a neuron are the **cell body**, **dendrites**, and **axon**. The cell body contains the nucleus, cytoplasm, and organelles (such as mitochondria), characteristic of most body cells. In addition neurons also have specialized organelles called the **chromatophilic substance**, or **Nissl bodies**, formed of rough endoplasmic reticulum and ribosomes. Nissl bodies manufacture proteins called **neurifibrils** and **microtubules**, tiny fibers and tubes involved in transporting substances within the neuron.

Dendrites

Dendrites and axons are processes extending from a nerve cell body, which aid in receiving and conducting impulses. Neurons may have many dendrites, which form tapering branches extending from the cell body. Dendrites are usually not myelinated, although, they may be covered with tiny projections called

dendritic spines, which increase their surface area for contacting other neurons. Impulses are conducted along the dendrites toward the cell body.

Axons

An **axon** is a long, thin, cylindrical process that conducts impulses away from the nerve cell body. Axons are often myelinated. An axon joins the cell body within a cone-shaped structure called the **axon hillock**. Branches called **axon collaterals** may emanate at right angles along the length of an axon branches into many **axon terminals**.

Neurons with branched axons can transmit impulses to many cells at once. At the end of each axon terminal is an enlarged area called the **synaptic end bulb** (also called the **synaptic knob** or **synaptic button**). Each synaptic knob contains many enclosed sacs (vesicles), for the storage of **neurotransmitter** molecules. Neurotransmitters are a chemicals that enable information transmission between neurons.

Quick Check Questions

1. The contact point between two neurons is called the:
   A. synapse
   B. neuromuscular junction
   C. neuroglandular junction
   D. association fiber

2. Which of the following is not found in the cytoplasm of a neuron?
   A. mitochondria
   B. Nissl bodies
   C. neurifibrils
   D. myelin

3. Neurons differ from glial cells in their ability to conduct ________.

4. Three major parts of a neuron are the cell body, axon, and _________.

5. Dendrites are more likely to be myelinated than are axons. *True or False*

6. Which of the following is a storage site for neurotransmitters?
   A. synaptic end-bulb
   B. axon hillock
   C. dendritic spines
   D. axon collaterals

7.3.2 Terminology

10 minutes

A **nerve fiber** refers to any process of a nerve cell, whether an axon or dendrite. A **nerve** is a bundle of axons with connective tissue wrapping them together. **Ganglia** are clusters of nerve cell bodies in the PNS. **Tracts** are bundles of nerve fibers without connective tissue wrapping in the CNS.

Classification of Neurons

Neurons may be classified according to their structure. **Multipolar neurons**, most common in the brain and spinal cord, have many dendrites and one axon. **Bipolar neurons**, which are found in the retina of the eye, the inner ear (for balance), and the olfactory area (for smell), have one dendrite and one axon. **Unipolar** (or **pseudounipolar**) **neurons** start out in embryo as bipolar, but their processes become fused during the course of development, leaving only one process extending from the cell body. Unipolar neurons are always sensory neurons.

Neurons may also be classified functionally: 1) **Afferent** (or **sensory**) neurons transmit information from sensory receptors to the CNS. 2) **Efferent** (or **motor**) neuron carry impulses to the muscles and glands. 3) **Association** neurons (or **interneurons**) convey signals from afferent neurons to efferent neurons. About 90% of the neurons in the body are association neurons. Many of these are located in the brain.

Quick Check Questions

1. Which of the following is the name for a bundle of nerve fibers in the CNS?
   A. nerve fiber
   B. nerve
   C. ganglion
   D. nerve tract

2. Clusters of nerve cell bodies in the PNS are called _______.

3. The structural classification of neurons with only one dendrite and one axon is called _______.

4. Ninety percent of neurons in the body are:
   A. multipolar
   B. interneurons
   C. bipolar
   D. afferent

7.4.1 Neurophysiology

15 minutes

Neurons are specialized for conducting impulses. Two properties which are unique to neurons are: 1) **irritability**, which refers to their ability to respond to a stimulus, and 2) **conductivity**, or their ability to transmit an impulse.

Irritability of Neurons

Even when no impulses are being conducted, a neuron's membrane is **polarized**. Polarization means that there is an excess of (negative) charge on the inner face relative to the outer face of the membrane. This polarization is due to the unequal distribution of ions such as Na+ (sodium ions) and K+ (potassium ions) across the membrane. Polarization creates a small build-up of negative charges on the inside of the cell's membrane. Thus, there are differences in the concentration of charged ions on either side of the membrane, and the membrane is said to be polarized.

Since opposite charges attract each other, the separation of positive and negative charges across the membrane sets up a situation of potential energy, called a **potential**. This **membrane potential** is an electrical charge on the membrane which exists when no nerve impulses are being conducted, thus it is called the **resting membrane potential**. The resting membrane potential can be measured in millivolts.

Several factors help to maintain the resting membrane potential: one is the relative "concentration of Na+ and K+ ions" in the fluid just inside and outside the cell, just described. Another factor that helps maintain the resting membrane potential is the membrane's **selective permeability**. In its resting state, the membrane has **ion channels** which allow K+ and Na+ to pass through it. There is a far greater number of open K+ channels than Na+ channels. Therefore, the membrane is much more permeable to K+ than it is to N+. Lastly, the membrane is equipped with protein molecules which actively pump Na+ ions out of the cell into the **extracellular fluid** and K+ ions into the cell. These **Na+ / K+ active transport pumps** help maintain the resting membrane potential.

Conductivity of Neurons

A neuron's conductivity depends on its ability to propagate an impulse along the length of its fibers. A nerve impulse is actually a brief disruption of the resting membrane potential. During the conduction of an impulse, the **permeability** of the membrane to Na+ ions changes transiently, yet dramatically, and Na+ ions rush into the cell. K+ ions then rush out of the cell. Thus, the exchange of Na+ and K+ ions across the membrane, which occurs progressively along a nerve fiber, constitutes a nerve impulse. A nerve impulse, which is **propagated** along the complete length of a neuron, is called an **action potential**.

Quick Check Questions

1. Irritability refers to a neuron's ability to respond to a stimulus, and ____________ refers to its ability to transmit an impulse.

2. The resting membrane potential of a neuron is characterized by:
   A. more sodium ions (Na+) outside the cell than inside
   B. more potassium ions (K+) inside the cell than outside
   C. a small build-up of negative charges on the inside the cell
   D. all of the above

3. The resting membrane potential is an electrical charge on the neuronal membrane which exists when no nerve impulses are being conducted. *True or False*

4. Which of the following is NOT a factor which helps maintain the resting membrane potential?
   A. There is more Na+ outside and more K+ inside the membrane
   B. The membrane is more permeable to Na+ than to K+
   C. Na+ ions are actively pumped out of the cell
   D. Some K+ ions are actively pumped into the cell

5. When an action potential is initiated, the permeability of the membrane to sodium ions:
   A. increases
   B. decreases
   C. does not change
   D. none of the above

6. An impulse is propagated along the length of a nerve fiber via the exchange of Na+ and K+ ions across the membrane. *True or False*

7. A nerve impulse which is propagated along the complete length of a neuron is called a(n) ______ potential.

7.4.2 How Neurons Respond to Stimuli

15 minutes

Three types of stimuli have the capacity to produce action potentials, these are: 1) electrical voltage, 2) chemicals, and 3) mechanical pressure.

When a stimulus is applied to a neuron, some Na+ ion channels open, allowing Na+ ions to enter the cell. This produces a localized change in the polarization of the membrane, or in other words, a **depolarization**. In neurons, if the magnitude of the local depolarization exceeds a limit called the **threshold potential**, then many Na+ channels will open, and an action potential is initiated. An action potential is not generated in neurons with no axons. Neural cells without axons contain few or no Na+ channels and instead generate a **graded potential** through non-Na+ channels.

There are some important differences between action potentials and graded potentials. First, action potentials are **propagated** along the complete length of the neuron, whereas graded potentials are not. Second, for a particular neuron, every action potential has the same **amplitude**. That is, the magnitude of voltage change is the same every time the neuron fires, because action potentials are "all or none." However, graded potentials may be above or below threshold level; they do not involve the whole neuron and, they have varied amplitudes.

The passage of an action potential is a rapid, progressive wave of depolarization of the membrane. Almost immediately after the action potential passes, there is a **repolarization** of the membrane which restores the resting concentrations of Na+ and K+ ions so that the neuron is ready to transmit another impulse. During the brief period when the neuron is undergoing repolarization, another impulse cannot be conducted, and the neuron is said to be **refractory**. Neurons exhibit a short refractory period after an action potential, but no refractory period after a graded potential.

Saltatory Conduction

When a nerve impulse is transmitted along a myelinated axon, the myelin casing around the axon acts much like the insulation on a telephone wire, allowing the current to flow farther down the axon without leaking out. Specifically, complete depolarization of the neuronal membrane occurs only at each exposed **neurilemmal node**. Where neurolemmocytes cover the axon, the impulse flows quickly over the myelin sheath as the ionic current travels through the surrounding extracellular fluid. Thus, the impulse appears to jump from node to node. This fast type of impulse conduction is characteristic of myelinated fibers, and is called **saltatory** (or jumping) **conduction**.

Quick Check Questions

1. Which of the following is NOT a distinguishing characteristic of action potentials as compared to graded potentials?
   A. The presence of a refractory period
   B. Amplitude is "all or none"
   C. The neural membrane is depolarized
   D. The potential is propagated the length of the neuron

2. During a neuron's refractory period, it is more sensitive to stimuli than at other times. *True or False*

3. Neurons are sensitive to all of the following types of stimuli, EXCEPT:
   A. heat
   B. chemicals
   C. mechanical pressure
   D. light

4. If the local depolarization of a neural membrane has a magnitude sufficient to produce an action potential, it is called a(n) _________ potential.

5. Graded potentials are "all or none" depolarizations of the neural membrane. *True or False*

6. The fast type of impulse transmission characteristic of myelinated fibers is called _________ conduction.

7.4.3 Transmission Across the Synapse

15 minutes

Impulses are passed from one neuron to another across a **synapse**. The neuron sending the impulse is the **presynaptic neuron**, and the one receiving the impulse is the **postsynaptic neuron**. Most synapses are **axodendritic**, meaning that the axon of the presynaptic neuron synapses on a dendrite of the postsynaptic cell. Synapses, however, can also be **axosomatic**, occurring from an axon to the cell body of another neuron or, more rarely, **axoaxonic**, where one axon synapses upon another axon. Synapses are designed to convey impulses by either **chemical or electrical transmission**.

Electrical Synapses

In the heart muscle and in the smooth muscle of the viscera, neurons deliver coordinated impulses via electrical synapses. In an electrical synapse, the impulse is transferred from one cell to another through **gap junctions**. Gap junctions are tiny channels through which the ionic current of an action potential may flow between the cells. Transmission of impulses is faster through electrical synapses than through chemical synapses.

Chemical Synapses

The three functioning parts of a chemical synapse are: 1) the **synaptic knob**, 2) the **synaptic cleft**, and 3) the plasma membrane of the postsynaptic neuron, or the **postsynaptic membrane**. The synaptic cleft is a space between the presynaptic and postsynaptic membranes which is only about one-millionth of an inch wide.

An action potential cannot jump the synaptic cleft. However, when an action potential reaches the synaptic knob, the voltage change triggers **calcium (Ca^{++}) channels** to open. Ca^{++} ions rush into the synaptic knob, stimulating **microtubules** to draw **synaptic vesicles** toward the membrane of the synaptic knob. The vesicles then fuse with the membrane, depositing their neurotransmitter molecules into the synaptic cleft.

When neurotransmitters cross the synaptic cleft, they act on the postsynaptic membrane to either stimulate or inhibit the postsynaptic neuron. Neurotransmitter molecules must be removed from the synaptic cleft so that their effects on the postsynaptic cell are not sustained. Transmitter molecules may simply **diffuse** out of the synaptic cleft, they may be degraded by **enzymes**, or the presynaptic neuron may draw them back into the synaptic knob for reuse, (called **reuptake** of the neurotransmitter).

Different neurons release different neurotransmitters. These chemicals may stimulate or inhibit the postsynaptic cell. **Excitatory neurotransmitters** cause Na^+ and K^+ ion channels to open in the postsynaptic membrane, provoking an **excitatory postsynaptic potential** (EPSP), or a local depolarization of the membrane. Inhibitory neurotransmitters cause the opening of ion channels which actually increase the polarization of the resting membrane. For example, the opening of **chloride (Cl-) ion channels** allows more negatively charged ions into the cell. As the inside of the neuron becomes more negatively charged, a **local hyperpolarization**, or **inhibitory postsynaptic potential** (IPSP) occurs.

Quick Check Questions

1. A neuron which receives an impulse across a synapse from another neuron is called the ____________ neuron.

2. A synapse from an axon onto the cell body of another neuron is called:
   A. axoaxonic
   B. axodendritic
   C. axosomatic
   D. a gap junction

3. In electrical synapses, impulses are transferred from one cell to another through gap _________.

4. Neurotransmitter molecules which are left in the synaptic cleft after an impulse has been transmitted:
   A. are allowed to diffuse away
   B. are degraded
   C. are taken up by the presynaptic cell
   D. all of the above

5. When ion channels open which allow the inside of the cell to become more negatively charged, this is called:
   A. an EPSP
   B. hyperpolarization
   C. depolarization
   D. an excitatory potential

6. An action potential is most likely to be initiated by:
   A. an EPSP
   B. an IPSP
   C. inhibitory neurotransmitters
   D. Cl- ions entering the cell

7.4.4 Summation

8 minutes

Thousands of synaptic knobs from many different neurons may synapse with a single postsynaptic cell. Although the EPSP of one neuron is not enough to initiate an action potential in the postsynaptic neuron, the effects of many different excitatory synapses firing at once may produce enough depolarization to initiate an action potential. This phenomenon is called **spatial summation** of impulses. Alternatively, if several synapses fire in rapid secession, their effects may add up in a brief period of time to initiate an action potential. This is called **temporal summation**. Spatial and temporal summation of impulses (EPSP's and IPSP's) coming from the dendrites and cell body will occur at the axon hillock of the neuron.

Neurotransmitters

There are more than 30 known neurotransmitter compounds, and possibly many more. Some are excitatory while others are inhibitory. Some neurotransmitters act directly to open or close ion channels, and others initiate changes in the postsynaptic cell via a **second messenger** mechanism. Second messengers are intracellular molecules which cause ion channels to open or close by a series of chemical steps. The four major chemical classes of neurotransmitters are: 1) **acetylcholine**, 2) **amines**, 3) **amino acids**, and 4) **neuropeptides**.

Quick Check Questions

1. When the effects of many different excitatory synapses firing at once produce an action potential, this phenomenon is called _______ summation.

2. When several synapses fire in rapid secession, and their effects add up to initiate an action potential, this phenomenon is called ________ summation.

3. Which of the following types of molecules are NOT released from the synaptic vesicles of presynaptic neurons?
   A. amines
   B. amino acids
   C. neuropeptides
   D. second messengers

Chapter 8
The Central Nervous System

8.1.1 Central Nervous System - Overview

25 minutes

The **central nervous system** (CNS) and the **peripheral nervous system** (PNS) are the two major anatomical divisions of the nervous system. The CNS consists of the brain and spinal cord. In addition to integrating all sensory input and motor output, the CNS is the seat of memory, emotion, and intellect. The PNS includes the cranial and spinal nerves and their branches. The PNS carries sensory and motor impulses to and from receptors, muscles, and glands of the head, neck, and viscera (internal organs). This chapter addresses the CNS. The anatomy and physiology of the PNS are addressed in the following chapter.

Functional Divisions of the CNS

Functions of the central nervous system correspond to its three structural levels: 1) the **spinal cord**, 2) the **lower brain**, and 3) the **higher brain**. The functions of the spinal cord are relatively simple compared to the increasingly complex functions of the lower brain and the higher brain.

Development of the CNS

During the fourth and fifth weeks of pregnancy, the brain and spinal cord begin to form the **neural tube**, a hollow segmented tube. These segments eventually differentiate into the component parts of the spinal cord, the lower brain, and the higher brain. Structures at the anterior end of the neural tube tend to have more complex functions after development.

The Neural Tube

The most posterior segment of the neural tube becomes the spinal cord and the **brain stem**. The middle and part of the anterior segments of the brain stem eventually form the structures of the lower brain: 1) the **medulla**, 2) the **cerebellum**, 3) the **pons**, 4) the **midbrain**, 5) the **hypothalamus**, and 6) the **thalamus**. The most anterior segment of the neural tube differentiates into the **cerebrum**, or higher brain.

The Spinal Cord

The spinal cord transports information to and from the brain. The spinal cord also contains nerve circuits which permit reflexes to direct basic functions like walking, upright posture, and gastrointestinal contractions.

The Lower Brain

The lower brain performs **subconscious** functions which regulate activities of the viscera. For example, regulation of blood pressure, body temperature, hunger and thirst, sleep/wakefulness cycles, and respiration are under lower brain control. In addition, the lower brain is active during **emotional** responses. The lower brain includes the three structures commonly referred to as the **brain stem**. They are: 1) the **medulla**, 2) the **pons**, and 3) the **cerebellum**. In addition to the brain stem, other structures involved in lower brain functions include: 1) the **midbrain**, 2) the **hypothalamus**, 3) the **thalamus**, 4) the **basal ganglia**, and 5) the **limbic system**.

The Higher Brain

The higher brain consists of the cerebrum. The **cerebrum** is partially separated into left and right **cerebral hemispheres** by a deep sagittal groove called the **longitudinal fissure**. The cerebrum governs the function of the lower brain and spinal cord. For instance, when the display of a certain emotion is appropriate, the cerebrum "turns on" the lower brain response for that emotion. The cerebrum controls all voluntary movement, stores memory, and is the seat of intelligence.

Quick Check Questions

1. Which of the following integrates all sensory input and motor output and is the seat of memory and intellect?
   A. the PNS
   B. the thalamus
   C. the limbic system
   D. the cerebrum

2. The central nervous system (CNS) includes the brain and ______ cord.

3. Central nervous system activities may be categorized into what three levels of function?
   A. lower brain, midbrain, and higher brain
   B. spinal cord, lower brain, and higher brain
   C. prosencephalon, mesencephalon, and rhombencephalon
   D. peripheral nerves, middle nerves, and central nerves

4. During the fourth and fifth weeks of pregnancy, the brain and spinal cord begin to form in the shape of a segmented, hollow tube called the ______ tube.

5. More complex neural structures develop from what end of the neural tube?
   A. anterior
   B. posterior
   C. left
   D. right

6. What division of the CNS do the medulla, cerebellum, pons, midbrain, hypothalamus, and thalamus form?
   A. higher brain
   B. lower brain
   C. spinal cord
   D. neural tube

7. The most posterior segment of the neural tube will become the spinal cord and the _________.

8. Which of the following structures contains nerve reflex circuits which permit involuntary control of walking, upright posture, and gastrointestinal contractions?
   A. higher brain
   B. limbic system
   C. spinal cord
   D. neural tube

9. What part of the brain controls all voluntary movement, stores memory, and is the seat of intelligence?
   A. cerebrum
   B. cerebellum
   C. medulla oblongata
   D. lower brain

10. Which of the following is responsible for the involuntary control of blood pressure, body temperature, hunger and thirst, sleep / wakefulness cycles, and respiration?
    A. higher brain
    B. lower brain
    C. spinal cord
    D. neural tube

11. The medulla, pons, and _________ are collectively referred to as the brainstem.

12. The longitudinal fissure separates the cerebrum into the right and left cerebral _____spheres.

8.2.1 Protective Coverings of the Brain

12 minutes

With the cranial bones covering the brain and each vertebrae circling the spinal cord, the entire CNS is protected by a casing of bone. Under the bone are three membranes of connective tissue, called the **meninges**, which enclose the brain and the spinal cord in fluid, protecting them from impact.

The liquid in which the brain and spinal cord are bathed is called **cerebrospinal fluid** (CSF). Cerebrospinal fluid buoys the brain so that its delicate nerve tissue is not crushed by its own weight. Cerebrospinal fluid also provides a nutritive function, and along with the blood, it monitors changes in **carbon dioxide** levels and **pH** balance throughout the body.

The Dura Mater

The most external of the three meninges is named for its toughness, the **dura mater**, a membrane composed of dense fibrous connective tissue. The small space between vertebral and cranial bones and the dura mater is called the **epidural space**. The dura mater extends down into the longitudinal fissure as well as the two other large fissures in the brain's surface.

The Subdural Space

There is a **subdural space** between the dura mater and a second membrane. This second membrane is named for its resemblance to spider webs, the **arachnoid membrane**. It is delicate, with net-like filaments which extend inward into the **subarachnoid space**, which is filled with cerebrospinal fluid.

The Pia Mater

The third, innermost membrane is named for its softness, the **pia mater**. Pia mater is composed of loose fibrous connective tissue which serves to anchor blood vessels to the brain's surface. This thin membrane extends into the grooves (or **sulci**) and fissures on the surface of the brain.

Quick Check Questions

1. The three connective tissue membranes which enclose the brain and the spinal cord are called the ________.

2. The function of the meninges is to:
   A. protect the CNS
   B. enclose the CNS
   C. allow the CNS to be bathed in fluid
   D. all of the above

3. The liquid in which the brain and spinal cord are bathed is called _____________ fluid.

4. Which of the following brain structures is filled with cerebrospinal fluid?
   A. pia mater
   B. dura mater
   C. epidural space
   D. subarachnoid space

5. Named for its toughness, which of the following is the outermost of the three meninges of the brain?
   A. pia mater
   B. arachnoid mater
   C. dura mater
   D. subarachnoid space

6. Which of the following is between the vertebrae and the dura mater?
   A. pia mater
   B. arachnoid mater
   C. epidural space
   D. subarachnoid space

7. Which of the following membranes lies directly on the external surface of the brain and supports the blood vessels anchored there?
   A. pia mater
   B. arachnoid mater
   C. dura mater
   D. subarachnoid space

8. Which of the following structures of the brain is comprised partly of web-like filaments bathed in cerebrospinal fluid?
   A. pia mater
   B. arachnoid mater
   C. dura mater
   D. epidural space

8.2.2 The Blood-Brain Barrier

20 minutes

The delicate brain tissue must be protected from many substances circulating in the blood. Cerebrospinal fluid and brain tissue fluid are kept separate by the **blood-brain barrier**. This barrier is formed by tight junctions between the endothelial cells lining blood vessels. Contributing to the selectivity of the blood-brain barrier are **astrocytes**. The astrocyte extensions covering the brain capillaries may influence the selection of which substances can enter from the blood into the tissue fluid of the brain. Generally, they allow small molecules like water, oxygen, and glucose in, but keep large molecules and solid particles out. Many drugs, including most antibiotics, are unable to cross the blood-brain barrier.

The Cerebrum

The cerebrum is the largest, most highly developed part of the brain. Each of the two cerebral hemispheres has an outer layer of **gray matter**, called the **cerebral cortex**, composed mostly of nerve cell bodies. Within an underlying layer of **white matter**, composed mostly of **myelinated** nerve cell **axons**, lie the nuclei (or nerve cell bodies) of gray matter, the **basal ganglia**.

Gyri, Sulci, and Fissures

The cerebral cortex has many grooves and bumpy **convolutions**. Since the cerebral cortex grows so big, the gray matter relative to the underlying white matter and brain stem needs increased cortical surface area. The elevated ridges of the convolutions are called **gyri** (singular = gyrus), and the grooves are called **sulci** (singular = sulcus).

Fissures

In addition to the small gyri and sulci, the brain has several large **fissures**, or deep grooves, which separate the cerebrum into **lobes**. One of these grooves is the transverse fissure, which separates the cerebrum and the cerebellum. Another large groove is the **longitudinal fissure**, which separates the left and right cerebral hemispheres. The two hemispheres of the brain are connected at the bottom of the longitudinal fissure by the **corpus callosum**. The corpus callosum is a wide band of nerve tracts running between cells in opposite hemispheres. These nerve tracts facilitate communication between the two hemispheres.

There are four ventricles, fluid-filled cavities, within the brain. Each hemisphere of the brain contains a large **lateral ventricle**. The two other ventricles are the **third and fourth ventricles**. The third ventricle is located between the lower portions of the lateral ventricles. The fourth ventricle is located beneath the third ventricle (connected by the **cerebral aqueduct**) and at the top of the **central canal**, where the cerebellum is attached to the brain stem.

The two lateral ventricles are located on either side of this sagittal section. However, the interventricular foramen, where the lateral ventricles drain into the third ventricle, is visible. Cerebrospinal fluid from the third ventricle drains through the cerebral aqueduct into the fourth ventricle. From there it circulates down the central canal of the spinal cord and into the subarachnoid space surrounding the spinal cord and brain. The ciliated ependymal cells which line the ventricles help to circulate the cerebrospinal fluid.

Cerebrospinal Fluid

The majority of cerebrospinal fluid (CSF) is produced within the **choroid plexus** of the ventricles. CSF is a clear, colorless liquid that resembles blood plasma and the interstitial fluid of cells. Structures inside the cranium, such as the brain, and the vertebral canal (the spinal cord), float in the CSF.

Clinical Note:
A diagnostic procedure called a **lumbar puncture** is performed for the detection of certain nervous system disorders by removing (with a needle) cerebrospinal fluid from the **subarachnoid space** adjacent to the third and fourth lumbar vertebrae.

Quick Check Questions

1. Which types of cells make up the blood-brain barrier?
   A. microglia
   B. astrocytes
   C. ependymal
   D. Schwann

2. The outer layer of the cerebrum which is made up of gray matter is called the ________ cortex.

3. White matter of the brain is comprised mainly of:
   A. basal ganglia
   B. choroid plexus
   C. degenerated gray matter
   D. myelinated nerve cell axons

4. The elevated ridges in the surface of the brain are called gyri, while the small grooves are called _____.

5. The small band of nerve tracts that runs between the two hemispheres of the brain is the corpus ________.

6. Cerebrospinal fluid in the brain is produced mainly in the:
   A. vertebrae
   B. synapses
   C. blood-brain barrier
   D. choroid plexus

7. What separates the cerebrum of the brain into lobes?
   A. ventricles
   B. fissures
   C. gray matter
   D. corpus callosum

8. The lateral ventricle is located in which hemisphere of the brain?
   A. right
   B. left
   C. both left and right hemispheres
   D. lateral hemisphere

8.2.3 Blood Supply to the Brain

12 minutes

The brain receives about 20 percent of the body's entire blood supply. Carbon dioxide in the blood assures an adequate blood supply to the central nervous system because it is an efficient vasodilator. The brain receives its blood supply from the heart through the **internal carotid arteries** and the **vertebral arteries.**

The carotid arteries supply the largest portion of blood to the brain. The carotid arteries enter the brain at the base of the skull and branch off into the **anterior and middle cerebral arteries**. The vertebral arteries are a continuation of the **subclavian arteries**. The vertebral arteries enter the brain at a large opening in the **cranium** called the **foramen magnum**, and join at the pons to form the **basilar artery**.

The **circle of Willis** is formed by the anterior and posterior communicating arteries, cerebral arteries, and the internal carotid arteries. The circle of Willis can compensate for a reduction of blood flow from any of the other major arteries. The spinal cord receives its blood supply from branches, or spinal arteries off the vertebral arteries, and from the **aorta**. The cerebral blood drainage occurs in the dural sinuses between the dural layers and eventually into the internal jugular veins. Blood drains into **venous sinuses**, located between the dura and the **periosteum** of the vertebrae in the spinal cord.

Quick Check Questions

1. The brain receives most of its blood supply from the internal _______ arteries.

2. The _________ arteries enter the cranium through the foramen magnum.

3. The structure which has the ability to compensate for arterial blood flow loss from another major source is called **circle of** _______.

4. The basilar artery is the union of the:
   A. internal carotid arteries
   B. anterior and posterior communicating arteries
   C. vertebral arteries

5. The spinal cord receives its blood supply mainly through the __________ arteries and the aorta.

6. Blood drains from the cerebrum through dural sinuses and into the _______ veins.

7. In the spinal cord, blood drains through venous sinuses which are located between the dura and __________ of the vertebrae.

8.3.1 The Brain Stem

18 minutes

The brain stem is comprised of the following four structures: 1) the **medulla oblongata**, 2) the **pons**, 3) the **reticular formation**, and 4) the **midbrain.**

The Medulla Oblongata

The medulla oblongata is a continuation of the spinal cord which forms the lowest part of the brain stem. Two large bulges on the anterior side of the medulla, called **pyramids**, carry the largest **motor tracts** on the outside of the cerebrum to the spinal cord. To the right and left sides of the pyramids is an oval projection called the **olive**. Nuclei in the olive connect to the cerebellum by paired bundles of fibers (tracts), called the **inferior cerebellar peduncles.**

The dorsal (or posterior) side of the medulla contains two areas of nuclei, the **nucleus gracilis** and the **nucleus cuneatus**. Sensory nerve fibers pass through these cell bodies and convey information to the thalamus. The pons is the bulging, round structure located directly above the medulla and in front of the cerebellum. Like the medulla, the pons consists of white fiber tracts and nuclei associated with specific cranial nerves. The **pneumotaxic** and **apneustic** areas of the pons help control respiration. Fiber tracts in the pons include the **middle cerebellar peduncles**, transverse fibers connecting both sides of the cerebellum.

Reticular Formation

Throughout the brain stem are small areas of gray matter within the white matter fibers. This region is called the reticular formation, and contains a structure called the **reticular activating system** (RAS), which is responsible for maintaining consciousness and sleep arousal. The RAS is made up of gray matter within white matter fibers.

The Midbrain

The midbrain lies above the pons and below the cerebrum. The midbrain contains the **cerebral peduncles**, tracts which convey impulses from the midbrain to the cerebrum. The two superior and two inferior **colliculi** form the **corpora quadregemina**, located in the posterior portion of the midbrain and above the cerebellum. Visual centers are located in the superior colliculi and auditory centers are associated with the inferior colliculi.

Next to the cerebral peduncles is the **substantia nigra**, named for its darkly pigmented nuclei. This area also contains the **red nucleus**, a structure named for its rich supply of blood. These two clusters of neurons (the substantia nigra and the red nucleus) are involved in muscular control.

Quick Check Questions

1. The medulla is an extension of the spinal cord. *True or False*

2. The reticular activating system is made up of white matter within gray matter fibers. *True or False*

3. Large projections on the front of the medulla are called ________.

4. The midbrain contains all of these structures, EXCEPT:
   A. the cerebral peduncles
   B. the olive
   C. the red nucleus
   D. the superior colliculi

5. This structure is involved in respiratory control.
   A. reticular formation
   B. substantia nigra
   C. pons
   D. medulla oblongata

6. The superior and inferior colliculi form the _______ quadregemina.

8.3.2 The Diencephalon

18 minutes

The diencephalon is made up primarily of the thalamus and the hypothalamus. The thalamus is an oval structure located above the midbrain. The thalamus serves as the major relay center (for sensory impulses projecting to the cerebral cortex) as well as between the basal ganglia and the cerebellum. Most of the thalamus is composed of gray matter masses which form nuclei. These nuclei form the lateral walls of the third ventricle.

The paired masses of the thalamus are joined together by the **intermediate mass,** a strip of gray matter that traverses the third ventricle. The **interior medullary lamina**, a white matter portion of the thalamus, divides the gray matter masses into **medial and lateral geniculate nuclei**. The medial and lateral **geniculate nuclei** are involved in relaying hearing and vision sensory impulses. **Ventral posterior and anterior nuclei** of the thalamus relay taste, somatic sensations, and motor actions to the cortex.

The hypothalamus forms the bottom, and a portion of the lateral walls, of the third ventricle. The nuclei of the hypothalamus contain **neurosecretions** which control different functions of the human body. The hypothalamus is one of the main regulators of **homeostasis** (equilibrium). One region of the hypothalamus contains the **mamillary bodies**, two small rounded structures that relay information involved in the sense of smell. The tuberal region of the hypothalamus contains the **infundibulum**. The infundibulum is an elongated structure which connects the hypothalamus to the **pituitary gland**.

The main functions of the hypothalamus are:

1) It regulates the activities of the autonomic nervous system. By controlling the secretions of certain glands and the contraction of muscles, the hypothalamus affects heart rate, the movement of food through the intestinal tract, and urine formation by the kidney.

2) It is associated with emotions such as rage and anger, and pain and pleasure.

3) It regulates internal body temperature.

4) As the **hunger center**, it is responsible for sensations such as hunger and satiation.

5) It produces sensations of thirst when it receives signals of an increase in osmotic pressure of the extracellular fluid.

6) It helps to maintain the body's sleep-wake cycle.

7) It is involved in sexual responses such as arousal and orgasm.

Quick Check Questions

1. The ____________ is one of the most important regulators of homeostasis.

2. The ________ makes up four-fifths of the diencephalon.

3. The infundibulum connects the thalamus to the hypothalamus.
   True or False

4. The mamillary bodies of the brain are:
   A. paired gray matter structures in the thalamus
   B. connected to the hypothalamus by the infundibulum
   C. part of the tuberal region of the hypothalamus
   D. involved in the sense of smell

5. The lateral and medial geniculate nuclei are located in the ________.

6. Hunger and thirst are regulated through the:
   A. pituitary gland
   B. hypothalamus
   C. lateral geniculate nuclei
   D. mamillary bodies

8.3.3 The Cerebral Lobes

15 minutes

The cerebral lobes are named after the bones of the skull which cover them. The central sulcus separates the frontal and parietal lobes. The **prefrontal area** of the frontal lobe is credited with the responsibility for goal-oriented behavior and thought processing. It also inhibits the response of the limbic system.

Also located in the frontal lobe is the **premotor area**, which contains cells that are part of the **extrapyramidal system**, which controls fine motor movements. These pathways, which meet at the pyramids of the medulla, connect the cortex and the spinal nerve tracts. A primary area of motor function is located in the precentral gyrus, which lies directly in front of the central sulcus. **Broca's speech area**, which is responsible for the motor aspects of speech, is located here on the left hemisphere. Damage to this area can result in an inability to form words.

The **parietal lobe** lies between the borders of the central sulcus, the occipital lobe, and the lateral (sylvian) fissure. The major area for somatosensory input is located along the **postcentral gyrus**. The **primary gustatory area** receives input related to taste. The **temporal lobe**, the auditory association area, lies just below the lateral fissure and is a major area for memory, balance, and smell. The **primary olfactory area** is also located here. **Wernicke's area** lies partially in the posterior portion of the temporal lobe of the left hemisphere. This area is responsible for the recognition and interpretation of speech, music, and noise.

The **occipital lobe** lies above the cerebellum and behind the parietooccipital fissure. The areas responsible for visual association and visual reception (primary visual cortex) are located here. For example, axons from the optic nerve terminate in the lateral geniculate nuclei of the thalamus, which relays all visual sensory impulses to the visual area of the cerebral cortex.

Quick Check Questions

1. The premotor area contains neurons which are part of the extra_________ system.

2. The central sulcus separates the temporal lobe from the parietal lobe.
   True or False

3. The temporal lobe is responsible for the motor functions of speech.
   True or False

4. The occipital lobe contains:
   A. the primary visual cortex
   B. Wernicke's area
   C. Broca's area
   D. the auditory association area

5. The temporal lobe contains all of these, EXCEPT:
   A. the auditory association area
   B. Wernicke's area
   C. the somatosensory area
   D. the major areas for memory, balance, and smell

6. The somatosensory area is located along the ____________ gyrus.

8.4.1 The Limbic System

15 minutes

The **limbic system** is a collection of brain nuclei connected by fiber tracts, surrounding the brain stem. These brain centers are activated during basic emotional responses such as fear and anger. Limbic connections to the viscera (through the autonomic nervous system) are responsible for the common manifestations of emotion (such as, increased heart rate, or "butterflies in the stomach").

The regions of gray matter which comprise the limbic system include:

1) The **limbic lobe**, which is made up of the **parahippocampal gyrus** and **cingulate gyri** of the cerebral hemispheres, and the **hippocampus**.

2) The **dentate gyrus**, located between the hippocampus and the parahippocampal gyrus.

3) The amygdala or **amygdaloid body**, a group of neurons above the parahippocampal gyrus and at the end of the **caudate nucleus.**

4) The **mamillary bodies**, part of the **mamillothalamic tract** of the hippocampus.

5) The **olfactory bulbs**, part of the olfactory tracts that rest on the cribriform plate.

6) The **fornix**, which connects other groups with myelinated axons.

As the primary emotional center of the brain, the limbic system is active in both the overt expression of emotions, as well as our subjective experience of them. Sex drive, hunger, pleasure, anxiety or fear, sorrow, and anger are emotional responses that are propagated by activity of neurons in the limbic system. It is likely that cortical areas of the frontal lobe modulate limbic activity. Thus, the higher brain determines the appropriateness of an emotional response, and may regulate the timing and intensity of emotional expression by the limbic system.

External stimulation of one area of the limbic system (with an electrode) can result in a pleasurable sensation, while stimulation of another area can result in pain or rage. Involuntary or autonomic emotional responses, such as blushing, involve the tracts of the limbic system. The hippocampus extends into the lower part of the lateral ventricle. Along with certain parts of the cerebrum, it aids memory of events which are emotionally linked. Thus, damage to this area of the limbic system can result in memory loss.

Quick Check Questions

1. The limbic system encircles the:
   A. brain stem
   B. fornix
   C. corpus callosum
   D. cerebrum

2. The cingulate gyrus is located in the:
   A. hypothalamus
   B. lateral ventricle
   C. limbic node

3. The corpus callosum is part of the limbic system. *True or False*

4. The ___________ and parts of the cerebrum are involved in memory functions.

5. The limbic system would most likely be involved in all of the following functions, EXCEPT:
   A. blushing
   B. emotional memories
   C. digesting food
   D. "butterflies in the stomach"

6. The ________ is located at the end of the caudate nucleus.

8.4.2 Lateralization

7 minutes

Although the brain may appear to be identical on both sides, there are anatomical and functional differences between the two hemispheres. In left-handed individuals, the parietal and occipital lobes of the left hemisphere are usually wider than in the right hemisphere. Conversely, the right-hemisphere frontal lobe is usually wider than that of the left hemisphere, in these individuals.

The right side of the brain has been shown to control the left side of the body. The left side of the brain has been shown to control the right side of the body. For most people, the left side of the brain is important for language, math, scientific skills, and reasoning. The right side of the brain is involved in musical and artistic awareness and ability, spatial and pattern recognition, insight, creativity, and images of sight, sound, and smell that are compared with spatial relationships.

Quick Check Questions

1. In left-handed individuals, the right-hemisphere frontal lobe is wider than its equivalent lobe in the left-hemisphere. *True or False*

2. The right side typically controls the ____ side of the body.

3. In most people, the left side of the brain is important for all of these, EXCEPT:
   A. language
   B. mathematics
   C. spoken language
   D. musical ability

8.4.3 Cerebellum

12 minutes

The cerebellum is the second largest portion of the brain. The cerebellum is located posterior to the medulla and pons and inferior to the occipital lobe. The **transverse fissure** and a continuation of the cranial dura matter called the **tentorium cerebelli** separate the cerebellum from the cerebrum. The cerebellum has the appearance of a butterfly and is divided into two lobes or cerebellar hemispheres, which are connected by a structure called the **vermis.**

The gray matter of the **cerebellar cortex** or surface is made up of parallel ridges called **folia.** The white matter is called **arbor vitae**, as it resembles branches of a tree. The **cerebellar nuclei** are gray matter masses which are deep within the arbor vitae.

The cerebellum is responsible for fine-tuning of motor control, and receives extensive sensory input from the brain to maintain coordination, posture, and balance. Fine-tuning of motor control is accomplished by the cerebellum through bundles of fiber tracts called the **cerebellar peduncles.** The cerebellum is connected to the medulla by the **inferior cerebellar peduncle**, and to the midbrain by the **superior cerebellar peduncle.** The pons connects with the two hemispheres by the middle cerebellar peduncle.

Quick Check Questions

1. The two lobes of the cerebellum are connected by the tentorium cerebelli. *True or False*

2. The ridges of gray matter on the surface of the cerebellum are called _____.

3. The ________ connects the cerebellum to the medulla.
   A. superior cerebellar peduncle
   B. inferior cerebellar peduncle
   C. pons
   D. vermis

4. _____ vitae is white matter within the cerebellum.

5. The __________ nuclei are located deep within the white matter of the cerebellum.

8.5.1 Neurotransmitters

10 minutes

Neurotransmitters are chemicals released from the **axon terminals** of conducting neurons. There are several chemicals that function as neurotransmitters in the CNS. Among them are: **acetylcholine**, the **amines** (**norepinephrine**, **epinephrine**, **dopamine** and **serotonin**), **amino acids** (**GABA**, **glycine**, and **glutamate**), and **polypeptides** (**substance P**, **somatostatin**, and the **endorphins**). Some **hormones**, such as **glucagon** and **vasopressin** found in the brain, may also function as neurotransmitters.

Neurotransmitters have excitatory or inhibitory effects on **postsynaptic cells**. When a neurotransmitter is released at the synaptic site, the **postsynaptic response** will either be an increase of activity (excitation) or a decrease in activity (inhibition) of the postsynaptic cell. The type of postsynaptic response elicited depends upon how the **receptor** affects a cell's membrane.

For example, of the two receptors which bind acetylcholine (ACH), one may cause a slight **depolarization** of the membrane (excitation), while the other may produce **hyperpolarization** (inhibition). Such changes in the **membrane potential** are localized at the site of the receptor. Thus, for an **action potential** to be initiated in the postsynaptic cell, **summation (temporal summation** and **spatial summation**) of impulses must occur. It is through neurotransmitters that nerve cells communicate with each other, and exert effects upon other tissues such as muscle or visceral organs.

The effects of various neurotransmitters are diverse. For example, serotonin, a neurotransmitter which is concentrated in neurons in the **raphe nucleus** of the brain stem, is thought to help induce sleep, aid in sensory perception, and control moods. The largest family of neurotransmitters is the **neuropeptides**. These are short chains of amino acids which typically serve to regulate digestive functioning. In addition, they may act as pain killers by attaching to opiate receptors, as well as enhance the actions of other hormones.

Quick Check Questions

1. Some chemicals which are traditionally known as "hormones" may also function as neurotransmitters. *True or False*

2. Norepinephrine and epinephrine, both of which are classified as ________, double as hormones and as CNS neurotransmitters.

3. Acetylcholine, norepinephrine, glutamate, and dopamine are examples of __________________.

4. The ____________ is a neurotransmitter constructed from a short chain of amino acids.

8.5.2 The Spinal Cord

10 minutes

The spinal cord is located within the **vertebral column**, the **spinal cavity**. Along with the spinal cord, it contains **meninges**, **cerebrospinal fluid**, and **adipose tissue**, which acts as a cushion for spinal tracts, and blood vessels. The **anterior median fissure** and the **posterior median sulcus** nearly divide the spinal cord into symmetrical halves. The anterior fissure is the deeper of the two, and is an important anatomical marker, in that it enables one to distinguish at a glance which is the anterior and which is the posterior part of the spinal cord.

Each side of the spinal cord carries fibers called **nerve roots**. The **dorsal nerve root** channels sensory information to the spinal cord through regions of unipolar, gray matter cells called dorsal root ganglia. By contrast, the **ventral nerve root** carries motor information out of the spinal cord through multipolar motor neurons which form the spinal cord's inner core of gray matter.

The spinal cord's gray matter extends the length of the cord. It has three dimensions. They are: 1) the **anterior horns**, 2) the **posterior horns**, and 3) the **lateral horns**. These horns are made up mostly of interneurons and motor neurons. White matter, which is composed of axons, surrounds the horns of gray matter. Bundles of white matter axons compose both the ascending and descending tracts of the spinal cord. Each tract serves a specific function.

The **spinothalamic tracts** are ascending tracts which transmit sensations such as pain, touch, and pressure. Descending tracts of the spinal cord are motor tracts, some of which are as follows: 1) **corticospinal tracts**, which allow voluntary movement or contraction of small or individual muscle groups, 2) **reticulospinal tracts** transmit impulses through anterior horn motor neurons to skeletal muscles, and 3) **rubrospinal tracts**, which allow coordination of posture and movement.

Quick Check Questions

1. The dorsal nerve root contains multipolar gray matter neurons.
   True or False

2. The ____thalamic tracts transmit impulses of pain and pressure.

3. The reticulo______ tracts transmit impulses to the skeletal muscles.

4. Spinothalamic tracts are composed of gray matter nuclei, while corticospinal tracts are white matter axons. *True or False*

Chapter 9
The Peripheral Nervous System

9.1.1 PNS - Overview

12 minutes

The **peripheral nervous system** (PNS), a structural division of the entire nervous system, consists of the **cranial** and **spinal** nerves, and the several smaller branches which arise from and feed into these nerves. Emerging from the inferior surface of the brain, the 12 paired cranial nerves carry sensory and motor impulses to and from receptors, muscles and glands of the head, the neck, and viscera (body organs). The 31 paired spinal nerves emerge from the spinal cord, carrying information to and from the rest of the body, which include parts of the neck and the viscera. The **sensory receptors** may also be considered part of the peripheral nervous system, but will be discussed in the *Integumentary System* chapter.

The Cranial Nerves

Although each of the 12 paired cranial nerves has a name, they are also numbered with roman numerals I through XII. This numbering system is based on where each pair of nerves exits the brain, from anterior to posterior. Some cranial nerves contain only **afferent** fibers and are thus called **sensory nerves**. Most contain both afferent and **efferent** fibers and are called **mixed nerves**. Some of these mixed nerves are chiefly motor in function, and contain only a few **proprioceptive** sensory fibers, which indicate the position of muscles.

Of the 12 paired cranial nerves, two emerge from the brain, and ten, from the brain stem. All the cranial nerves exit the cranial cavity through small **foramina** (holes) in the skull. Each nerve, with its name, number, sensory / motor classification, **distribution** (the area it innervates), and function, will be described next.

Olfactory Nerve (I) (sensory)

The olfactory nerves carry the sensation of smell to the brain. Axons of these sensory neurons in the **nasal mucosa** enter the cranial cavity through the **cribriform plate**. They synapse with other neurons over the cribriform plate, which collectively form the pair of, or left and right, **olfactory bulbs**. The axons of this second set of neurons make up the **olfactory tracts**, which transmit sensations of smell to the brain.

Optic Nerve (II) (sensory)

The optic nerves carry visual information from sensory neurons of the retina to the **visual cortex** of the brain. After entering the cranial cavity, the two optic nerves merge at the **optic chiasm**, where some fibers cross to opposite sides. Posterior to the optic chiasm, the **optic tracts** carry visual information to the **thalamus**. Once the visual information reaches the thalamus, the thalamus associates, synthesizes, and then relays the information to the visual cortex of the **occipital lobe**. The optic nerve traverses the cranium via the optic foramen.

Quick Check Questions

1. The peripheral nervous system consists of 12 pairs of cranial nerves, 31 pairs of ______ nerves, and all of their branches.

2. Nerves which contain both motor and sensory fibers are called _____ nerves.

3. The cranial nerve which passes through the cribriform plate, and carries the sensation of smell is called the:
   A. optic nerve
   B. optic tract
   C. olfactory nerve
   D. olfactory tract

4. Some afferent fibers which carry visual impulses cross over from left to right and vice versa at the:
   A. optic nerve
   B. optic chiasm
   C. optic tract
   D. cribriform plate

9.1.2 The Cranial Nerves

Oculomotor Nerve (III) (mixed, mostly motor)

25 minutes

The **oculomotor nerve** carries motor impulses to the muscles which move the eye. The oculomotor nerve controls movement of the eyeball, focusing, and regulation of the amount of light entering through the iris. The oculomotor nerve traverses the skull through the **superior orbital fissure**.

Trochlear Nerve (IV) (mixed, mostly motor)

The **trochlear nerve** innervates muscles which also direct movement of the eyeball. The trochlear nerve passes through the superior orbital fissure.

Trigeminal Nerve (V) (mixed)

The **trigeminal nerve** has three major branches which carry sensory and motor information to the face and jaw. The three branches of the trigeminal nerve are the: 1) **ophthalmic nerve**, 2) **maxillary nerve**, and 3) **mandibular nerve**.

Sensations of the head and face, and the motor functions of chewing are carried by the trigeminal nerve. The ophthalmic nerve carries sensation from the **cornea** of the eye, and the skin of the nose, scalp, and forehead. The maxillary branch carries sensation from the nasal and oval cavities, the upper lip, and skin of the cheeks. The mandibular nerve transmits sensory information from the tongue, the lower teeth and lip, and the skin of the jaw. The ophthalmic nerve traverses the superior orbital fissure. The mandibular nerve crosses the skull via the **foramen rotundum**, and the maxillary branch exits through the **foramen ovale**.

Abducens Nerve (VI) (mixed, mainly motor)

The **abducens nerve** carries impulses to muscles which move the eyeball laterally.

Facial Nerve (VII) (mixed)

The **facial nerve** innervates superficial muscles of the head. It also carries the sensation of taste and is responsible for stimulating the secretion of saliva and for producing tears. The facial nerve traverses the **stylomastoid foramen**.

Vestibulocochlear Nerve (VIII) (sensory)

The **vestibulocochlear nerve** carries the sensations of hearing from the **cochlea** and of balance, or **equilibrium**, from the **vestibule** of the inner ear. The vestibule is a sensory organ which detects our physical orientation in space (that is, what is up and what is down). It is important in the control of posture and **righting responses**. The cochlea is the organ of hearing. The vestibulocochlear nerve enters the cranium via the **internal auditory meatus**.

Glossopharyngeal Nerve (IX) (mixed)

The **glossopharyngeal nerve** extends to the tongue and **pharynx** (throat). The glossopharyngeal nerve carries the sensation of taste, and stimulates motor functions in swallowing and secretion of saliva. In addition, the glossopharyngeal nerve has a role in controlling blood pressure via receptors in the **carotid sinus**. The glossopharyngeal nerve traverses the **jugular foramen**.

Vagus Nerve (X) (mixed)

The **vagus nerve** has many branches, which carry sensations from respiratory structures, the heart and blood vessels, and parts of the digestive tract. Based on sensations from receptors in these areas, the motor component of the vagus nerve helps to control respiration, heart rate, and gastrointestinal activity. The vagus nerve traverses the jugular foramen.

Accessory (or Spinal Accessory) Nerve (XI) (mixed, mainly motor)

The **accessory nerve** innervates muscles which move the shoulders and head. The accessory nerve traverses the jugular foramen.

Hypoglossal Nerve (XII) (mixed, mainly motor)

The **hypoglossal nerve** controls movement of the tongue. The hypoglossal nerve exits the cranium through the **hypoglossal canal**.

Quick Check Questions

1. Which of the following cranial nerves does NOT carry impulses to the muscles which move the eyeball?
   A. oculomotor
   B. trochlear
   C. abducens
   D. vagus

2. The facial nerve innervates superficial muscles of the head and carries the sensation of taste. *True or False*

3. The spinal accessory nerve allows movement of the tongue. *True or False*

4. The ________________ nerve carries the sensations of hearing from the cochlea and of equilibrium from the vestibule.

5. Which of the following cranial nerves helps control respiration, heart rate, and gastrointestinal activity?
   A. vagus
   B. glossopharyngeal
   C. trigeminal
   D. abducens

6. Which of the following cranial nerves does NOT carry impulses to or from the mouth?
   A. glossopharyngeal
   B. optic
   C. hypoglossal
   D. trigeminal

7. The three branches of the trigeminal nerve are the ________, ________, and ________ nerves:
   A. ophthalmic, maxillary, and mandibular
   B. optic, olfactory, and oculomotor
   C. optic, olfactory, and maxillary
   D. optic, olfactory, and mandibular

9.2.1 The Spinal Nerves

15 minutes

Spinal nerves allow communication between the central nervous system (CNS) and receptors, glands, and muscles of the body. All spinal nerves are mixed nerves which carry both sensory and motor information. Spinal nerves are named for the region of the spinal cord from which they emerge.

The spinal nerves are also numbered by group. There are: eight **cervical spinal nerves** (labeled C1-C8), twelve **thoracic spinal nerves** (T1-T12), five **lumbar spinal nerves** (L1-L5), five **sacral spinal nerves** (S1-S5), and one pair of **coccygeal spinal nerves**. Except for spinal nerve C1, which emerges from the spinal cord between the **atlas** (first vertebra) and the **occipital bone**, all spinal nerves exit through the **intervertebral foramina** between adjacent vertebrae.

Each spinal nerve has two **roots**, which attach to the spinal cord. The **dorsal root** (on the dorsal side of the body) is made up of sensory (afferent) fibers, while the **ventral root** is made up of motor (efferent) fibers. The dorsal and ventral roots join to exit the spinal column as one spinal nerve. After they exit the vertebral column, however, all of the spinal nerves split into branches.

Spinal Efferent Nerve Plexuses

The ventral roots of all spinal nerves, except the thoracic nerves T2-T12, join and split to form four nerve networks or **plexuses** -- the **cervical**, **brachial**, **lumbar**, and **sacral** plexuses. Nerves which arise from these plexuses contain fibers which originate from different spinal nerves. After emerging from a plexus, the peripheral nerves are named for the structures which they innervate.

The **cervical plexus** carries sensory information from parts of the head, neck, shoulders, and chest. The cervical plexus also sends motor impulses to muscles in these areas. The **brachial plexus** carries sensory from and motor innervation to the shoulder, arm, and hand. The **lumbar plexus** carries sensory and motor impulses for the abdominal and pelvic regions, and parts of the thigh. The **sacral plexus** carries impulses to and from parts of the thigh, leg, and foot.

Dermatomes

The dorsal root of each spinal nerve receives sensory information from a different area of the body. Each section of skin surface supplied by a different spinal nerve is called a **dermatome**.

Clinical Note:
The dermatome pattern is important for diagnosing spinal nerve problems. It helps physicians know which spinal nerves to anesthetize in order to numb a particular section of the body.

Quick Check Questions

1. There are ___ pairs of spinal nerves.
   A. 12
   B. 24
   C. 31
   D. 36

2. All spinal nerves contain both afferent and efferent fibers. *True or False*

3. The dorsal root of a spinal nerve is made up of ________ fibers, and the ventral root is made up of ________ fibers.
   A. sensory or afferent, motor or efferent
   B. motor or efferent, sensory or afferent
   C. both sensory and motor, motor
   D. sensory, both sensory and motor

4. A network of nerves is called a ______.

Chapter 10
The Somatic and Autonomic Nervous System

10.1.1 SNS and ANS - Overview

25 minutes

We have already examined two anatomical divisions of the nervous system: 1) the central nervous system (CNS), and 2) the peripheral nervous system (PNS). The entire nervous system may be studied, alternatively, according to its functional divisions. Two functional divisions of the nervous system are the somatic nervous system (SNS) and the autonomic nervous system (ANS). Structures of the somatic and autonomic systems exist in both of the anatomical divisions: that is, tracts in the CNS and nerves in the PNS carry both somatic and autonomic information.

A Comparison of Somatic and Autonomic Functions

In general, the somatic nervous system functions in conscious perception and voluntary control of the body (that is, movement of the limbs), while the autonomic nervous system functions in **involuntary** control (such as, digestion and heart rate). These somatic and autonomic functions rely upon **efferent** as well as **afferent** neurons. The efferent portion of the autonomic nervous system is divided into the **sympathetic** and **parasympathetic** divisions.

Somatic Sensory Neurons

The **special senses** -- hearing, equilibrium (balance), gustation (taste), olfaction (smell), and vision -- as well as proprioception (sense of body position), and general sensation (pain, touch, temperature) are all carried by somatic afferent nerves.

Somatic Motor Neurons

Voluntary control of skeletal muscles occurs via somatic efferents.

Autonomic Sensory Neurons

The autonomic nervous system senses internal bodily conditions (such as oxygen and carbon dioxide levels in the blood, or presence of food in the digestive tract) via afferent neurons.

Autonomic Motor Neurons

Autonomic efferents control the action of cardiac muscle, smooth muscle, and glands. Generally, autonomic functions are not under direct, conscious control. However, a limited degree of voluntary control over autonomic functions can be achieved. For example, a person connected to a machine that produces an audible beep as their heart contracts may be able to consciously slow down or speed up their heart rate. This is an example of **biofeedback**.

Autonomic Control Mechanisms

Efferent neurons of the autonomic nervous system may be either excitatory or inhibitory. The sympathetic and parasympathetic divisions generally have opposite effects upon the smooth muscle, cardiac muscle, and glands which they innervate. Many organs receive both sympathetic and parasympathetic input.

Somatic Control Mechanisms

In contrast to the efferent neurons of the autonomic system, somatic efferents are always excitatory. Thus, when a somatic motor neuron fires, muscle fibers contract: when the somatic motor neuron ceases its activity, the muscle relaxes.

Somatic vs. Autonomic Systems: Structure of Efferent Pathways

The efferent pathways of the autonomic nervous system consists of at least two neurons, while those of the somatic nervous system generally consist of a single neuron. A single motor neuron will traverse the entire distance to the muscle it innervates, synapsing on the muscle at a **motor end plate**. In the autonomic nervous system, the first neuron (called the **preganglionic neuron**) exits the spinal cord and travels to an **autonomic ganglion**, where it synapses on the cell body of the second (**postganglionic**) neuron.

The postganglionic neuron then extends directly to an **end organ** (the target of a neural pathway, such as a muscle or a gland). Autonomic ganglia are located either adjacent to the spinal cord (in the sympathetic division) or embedded within the end organ (in the parasympathetic division).

Somatic vs. Autonomic Neurotransmitters

Where they synapse on an end organ, somatic motor neurons always release the neurotransmitter **acetylcholine** (Ach). Ach causes skeletal muscle fibers to contract. Autonomic neurons, however, release either norepinephrine (in the sympathetic division) or Ach (in the parasympathetic division) at the end organ.

Somatic vs. Autonomic Pathways

Afferent and efferent neurons of the somatic and the autonomic nervous system follow discrete pathways: 1) peripheral pathways consist of nerves and ganglia, and 2) central pathways consist of **tracts** and **nuclei** in the brain and spinal cord. Some of these pathways are visible in transverse sections of the spinal cord, or in sections of the brain stem, where they show up as characteristic patterns of **gray matter** and **white matter**. In the following discussion, various somatic and autonomic pathways will be presented along with their functions.

Quick Check Questions

1. There are two centers for somatic control. One is the sensory pathway, the other is the _____ pathway.

2. In general, movement and control of involuntary muscles is a function of the _________ nervous system.

3. Efferent neurons of both nervous systems have excitatory effects. Autonomic efferents may also be __________.

4. Neurons in the autonomic efferent pathway synapse each other at the:
   A. motor end plate
   B. autonomic ganglion

10.2.1 The Somatic Nervous System

15 minutes

The sensory cortex (the **postcentral gyrus**) and motor cortex (the **precentral gyrus**) are important areas for the processing of sensory information. The **thalamus** contains two major somatic nervous system centers through which information is relayed to and from the cortex. These are the **somatosensory center** and the **motor center**. Most sensory input **decussates** (crosses from one side of the body to the other) in the spinal cord or brain stem, before it reaches the thalamus. Most motor signals also decussate.

Sensory Pathways of the Somatic Nervous System

Two afferent pathways carry information to the sensory cortex: one is the **medial lemniscal pathway**, and the other is called the **spinothalamic pathway**. The medial lemniscal pathway carries the sensations of touch and **proprioception** (muscle and joint position). The spinothalamic pathway carries pain, temperature, itch, tickle, and pressure. Both of these somatosensory pathways are comprised of three sets of neurons: first-order, second-order, and third-order neurons.

First-order and second-order neurons synapse in the **nucleus cuneatus** and the **nucleus gracilis**, which comprise the **posterior column** of the spinal cord. The nucleus cuneatus receives sensory information from the neck, arms, and upper chest via axons in the **fasciculus cuneatus**. The nucleus gracilis receives information from the trunk and legs via the **fasciculus gracilis**. The medial lemniscal system is made up of fasciculus cuneatus and fasciculus gracilis which are posterior white columns (axons) of the spinal cord, and the medial lemniscus, which is a flattened band of white fibers which runs through the medulla, pons, and midbrain.

Second order cell bodies of the medial lemniscus originate in the medulla, cross and travel upward to the thalamus. Once there, they synapse with third order neurons, whose axons connect with gray matter of the cerebral cortex, more specifically from the thalamus to the postcentral gyrus of the parietal lobe. The functions of the medial lemniscal system include the following: 1) the conduction of impulses which produce discriminating, or fine touch and pressure sensations such as **stereognosis** (awareness of an object's size, shape, texture), precise localization, and two-point discrimination, 2) the ability to detect vibration, 3) proprioception, and 4) **kinesthesia**, which is the sense of movement and body position.

The spinothalamic (or anterolateral) pathways also contain first, second, and third order neurons. The lateral spinothalamic fibers carry input for sensory impulses of pain and temperature, and the anterior spinothalamic tracts carry impulses for tickle, itch, and the less sensitive sensations of touch and pressure. Most sensory pathways from second order to third order neurons decussate (they cross from left to right and vice versa). That is, sensations originating on the right side of the body are experienced by the left somatic sensory area, etc. The posterior spinocerebellar tract is an exception. This uncrossed pathway allows the cerebellum to provide input necessary for adjusting balance, posture and muscle coordination. From the medulla, spinocerebellar fibers enter the inferior cerebellar peduncles and terminate at the cerebellar cortex.

Quick Check Questions

1. The first order neurons in the somatosensory pathways extend up through:
   A. white matter in the cerebral cortex
   B. the final common path
   C. the post central gyrus of the parietal lobe
   D. the dorsal gray columns

2. All of the following are functions of the medial lemniscus, EXCEPT:
   A. conduct impulses to the parietal lobe
   B. kinesthesia
   C. two-point discrimination
   D. all of the above

3. One function of the spinothalamic tract is kinesthesia. *True or False*

4. The fasciculi cuneatus and fasciculi gracilis are mostly gray matter dorsal columns of the spinal cord. *True or False*

10.2.2 Somatic Motor Pathways

20 minutes

The motor cortex, or precentral gyrus, is the major region of control for all voluntary motor pathways. Pathways originating in the motor cortex conduct impulses to the skeletal muscles via tracts in the spinal cord. Impulses from cortical motor neurons are transmitted through synapses in the **anterior gray horn** of the spinal cord. Motor tracts emerge from the **ventral root** of the spinal cord. The ventral root contains motor neurons with long axons which often extend all the way to the skeletal muscle.

Skeletal muscles are stimulated by the **direct** or **pyramidal** pathways, the simplest of which consist of just an upper and a lower motor neuron. The axon bundles of the upper motor neurons form the pyramids, and cross to the opposite side of the medulla. They terminate either in the anterior gray horn of the spinal cord or in the nuclei of the cranial nerves. Lower motor neurons leave the cranial nerves or the anterior horn and synapse with the motor end plates on skeletal muscles. The motor neurons release acetylcholine at their axon terminals, which has an excitatory action upon the motor end plates.

Upper motor neurons may synapse either with an association neuron or with a lower motor neuron. These neurons channel impulses into three distinct tracts: 1) lateral corticospinal tracts, 2) anterior corticospinal tracts, and 3) corticobulbar tracts. Lower motor neurons are activated either by direct or indirect pathways, they are sometimes referred to as the **final common pathway**.

Lateral Corticospinal Tracts

These pathways begin in the motor cortex and descend through the internal capsule of the cerebrum, the cerebral peduncle, and the pons before decussating. Most of the upper motor neurons cross at the medulla, at which point they form tracts, visible as lateral white columns in the spinal cord. The lateral corticospinal pathway controls precise motor contractions in the extremities.

Anterior Corticospinal Tracts

The anterior corticospinal tracts, formed by a group of about fifteen percent (15%) of all upper motor neurons do not decussate in the brain stem. Rather they extend through the medulla on the same side and form the anterior white columns of the spinal cord. At various levels of the spinal cord, these neurons eventually decussate and synapse with association or lower motor neurons in the anterior gray. The lower motor neurons extend their axons from the cervical and upper thoracic segments of the spinal cord into the skeletal muscles of the upper body and neck.

Corticobulbar Tracts

These tracts run along the path of the corticospinal tracts, from the motor cortex, through the internal capsule to the brain stem. The corticobulbar tracts decussate and terminate within the nuclei of the cranial nerves. These tracts carry impulses for voluntary head and neck movement. The indirect (extrapyramidal) pathways also carry motor output from the brain, but they are multi-synaptic and more complex than the direct pathways. Indirect pathways have upper neurons which always begin in one of the nuclei of the brain stem. The lower neurons of the indirect pathways are the same as those used by the direct pathways, which is why they are called the **final common pathway**. The five indirect pathways are as follows:

Rubrospinal Tract

The rubrospinal tract originates in the red nucleus of the midbrain, which in turn receives impulses from the cerebellum and cortex. Like the lateral corticospinal tract, it projects nerve impulses to the opposite side of the body and controls fine motor movements of the distal extremities.

Tectospinal Tract

The tectospinal tract starts in the superior colliculi. This tract transmits impulses to the opposite side of the body and controls reflex responses of the head and eyes to visual stimulation.

Vestibulospinal Tract

The vestibulospinal tract begins in the vestibular nucleus of the medulla, which receives input from the balance receptors in the ear. This pathway plays a role in regulating muscle tone and maintaining balance in response to head movement. Unlike most nerve pathways, this tract controls muscles on the same side of the body.

Lateral Reticulospinal Tract

The lateral reticulospinal tract starts in the reticular formation of the medulla. This tract facilitates flexor reflexes, inhibits extensor reflexes, and decreases muscle tone in the axial skeleton and **proximal limb**.

Anterior and Medial Reticulospinal Tract

The anterior (ventral) and medial reticulospinal tract originates in the pons and facilitates extensor reflexes, inhibits flexor reflexes, and increases muscle tone in muscles of the axial skeleton and the proximal limb. The cerebellum plays a key role in somatic motor control. The cerebellum is active in learning and performing coordinated, quick, skilled movements such as running or speaking. It also helps maintain posture and balance. The cerebellum receives input about motor functions from the higher brain and the peripheral nervous system. If there is a discrepancy, signals are sent out from the thalamus to the cerebrum, which initiates processes to decrease the discrepancy and smooth motion.

Quick Check Questions

1. Most of the tracts of the somatic motor system are crossed. *True or False*

2. This tract regulates reflex responses of the head and neck to visual stimulation:
   A. rubrospinal tract
   B. vestibulospinal tract
   C. tectospinal tract
   D. corticobulbar tracts

3. The anterior or medial reticulospinal tract of the brain begins in the:
   A. cerebellum
   B. axial skeleton
   C. reticular formation
   D. pons

4. The lateral reticulospinal tract of the brain originates in the:
   A. cerebellum
   B. pons
   C. reticular formation
   D. red nucleus

5. These neurons are also called the final common pathway:
   A. lower motor neurons
   B. upper motor neurons
   C. association neurons
   D. corticobulbar tracts

6. Anterior or medial reticulospinal tracts facilitate ________ reflexes.

7. _____________ tracts accompany the corticospinal tracts from the motor cortex, through the internal capsule, and on to the brain stem.

8. The __________ receives input from the higher brain and the peripheral nervous system to facilitate motor control.

10.2.3 The Reflex Arc

10 minutes

A fast, predictable, automatic response to a stimulus is called a **reflex**. A reflex consists of a nerve impulse passing over a **reflex arc**. Normally this refers only to involuntary responses -- those which involve no cerebral cortex activity. A **cranial reflex** refers to responses in which the center of the reflex arc is located in the brain.

Spinal reflexes refer to responses from reflex arcs which are centered in the spinal cord. Autonomic (or visceral) reflexes are initiated by contractions of smooth or cardiac muscle, or by glandular secretion. These reflex arcs involve components of the autonomic nervous system. Somatic reflexes are initiated by sensory stimulation or muscular contraction, and these reflex arcs pass through the spinal cord or the brain stem. A somatic reflex can serve as a valuable diagnostic tool.

A somatic reflex provides a visible, standard physiological response, and deviations from this standard can be indicative of particular diseases.

The following are some commonly tested reflexes:

1) Knee jerk or **patellar** reflex. A rapid extension outward of the lower leg in response to tapping the patellar tendon.

2) Ankle jerk or Achilles reflex. An extension of the foot as a result of a tap to the **Achilles tendon.**

3) The **Babinski reflex**. This reflex results from stimulation of the outer sole of the foot, which causes extension of the big toe. This reflex is considered abnormal after 1 1/2 years of age, and a positive test indicates degradation of the corticospinal fibers (the pyramidal tract).

4) **Corneal** reflex. Blinking in response to touching the cornea.

5) **Abdominal** reflex. A drawing in of the abdominal area, brought on by stimulating the side of the abdomen.

Quick Check Questions

1. The Babinski reflex is normal until about 8 years of age. *True or False*

2. A positive Babinski test is characteristic of damage to spinocerebellar tracts. *True or False*

3. Somatic reflexes are produced by reflex arcs involving the spinal cord or __________ neurons.

4. Autonomic or visceral reflexes are produced by contractions of cardiac or ______ muscle.

5. A reflex may be conscious, although the term usually refers to involuntary movements. *True or False*

10.3.1 The Autonomic Nervous System

10 minutes

The **autonomic nervous system** (ANS) regulates heartbeat, smooth muscle contraction, and glandular secretion, helping to maintain homeostasis. Like somatic motor regulation, autonomic regulation depends on sensory feedback. The visceral organs and blood vessels are well innervated with sensory neurons which relay information to the autonomic nervous system. The efferent autonomic pathways, the sympathetic and parasympathetic divisions of the autonomic nervous system, will be discussed in detail.

The **sympathetic** and the **parasympathetic** divisions of the autonomic nervous system consist of distinct pathways. Commonly, one division has an inhibitory action on muscles or glands (the **end organs**) while the other stimulates them. This allows for efficient, sensitive control of responses: for example, in the sexual response cycle, organs are rapidly stimulated and then inhibited from arousal through orgasm.

Unlike the somatic motor system, which requires only one efferent neuron to conduct impulses from the CNS, recall that at least two autonomic neurons make up the pathway to conduct impulses from the CNS to autonomic effectors. Autonomic preganglionic neurons are most often myelinated, while post ganglionic neurons are often unmyelinated. Preganglionic neurons, conduct impulses from the brain or spinal cord to synapse with a postganglionic neuron in an autonomic ganglion. The preganglionic neuron then synapses with a second efferent neuron which carries the impulse away from the ganglion. This postganglionic neuron, which is unmyelinated, carries the impulse from the ganglion to the effector.

Quick Check Questions

1. The autonomic nervous system is a subdivision of the __________ nervous system.

2. The sympathetic and para___________ divisions make up the autonomic nervous system.

3. The autonomic nervous system requires two neurons to conduct impulses from the CNS to the autonomic effectors. *True or False*

4. ______________ neurons conduct impulses from the spinal cord to an autonomic ganglion.

5. _______________ neurons carry impulses from the ganglion to an effector.

6. The autonomic nervous system contains efferent and afferent neurons. *True or False*

10.3.2 Sympathetic and Parasympathetic

15 minutes

Sympathetic preganglionic neurons have cell bodies and dendrites which are located in the lateral gray horns of the spinal cord. Axons from these neurons exit the spinal cord through the ventral roots of the first four lumbar and the thoracic vertebrae. From the ventral roots, preganglionic nerve fibers branch by way of the white ramus, named for its large number of myelinated axons. After passing through the **gray and white rami** nerve fibers enter one of a series of ganglia located adjacent to the spinal cord, the **sympathetic chain ganglia.**

Inside the sympathetic chain ganglia, preganglionic neurons follow one of three paths: 1) they may synapse with a postganglionic neuron, or 2) they may ascend or descend within the sympathetic chain (or **sympathetic trunk)** and then synapse with postganglionic neurons higher or lower in the chain, or 3) they may pass through ganglia without synapsing, continuing on as **splanchnic nerves** which terminate in other sympathetic ganglia called **collateral** (or **prevertebral**) ganglia. Collateral ganglia are named after the blood vessels they are near. Below the diaphragm, the **celiac ganglion** (or solar plexus) lies next to the celiac artery. Other examples of collateral ganglia are the superior and inferior mesenteric ganglia.

The **adrenal medulla** of the kidney releases **epinephrine** and norepinephrine when the sympathetic nervous system is activated. Much like a sympathetic ganglion, the adrenal medulla receives preganglionic fibers from the thoracic level of the spinal cord. Instead of snyapsing with a postganglionic neuron, these fibers release their products directly into the bloodstream. Epinephrine may act synergistically on sympathetic end organs, increasing the effects of norepinephrine released by sympathetic postganglionic cells.

Structure of the Parasympathetic System

Parasympathetic preganglionic neurons have cell bodies in the nuclei in the brain stem or in the lateral gray columns of the sacral portion of the spinal cord. The axons of these nerves are found in cranial nerves III, VII, IX, X, and XI, and in a few pelvic nerves. In comparison to the sympathetic system, parasympathetic preganglionic neurons are long and postganglionic neurons are short. About three-fourths of all parasympathetic preganglionic fibers travel through the vagus nerve for at least 12 inches before they synapse with postganglionic neurons in the terminal ganglia of the chest or abdominal areas.

Postganglionic neurons of the parasympathetic system do not lie near the spinal cord, but are located in or near autonomic effectors. One example is the submandibular ganglion, located in the lower jaw. This ganglion serves parasympathetic fibers which innervate the salivary glands. Parasympathetic postganglionic neurons typically synapse with a single effector. This means that responses from parasympathetic stimulation usually involves only one organ, as opposed to sympathetic stimulation, which can affect a number of organs.

Quick Check Questions

1. The **sympathetic chain ganglia** are made up of:
   A. gray myelinated rami
   B. white myelinated rami
   C. both gray and white myelinated rami
   D. corticobulbar fibers

2. The submandibular ganglion is one example of a __________ ganglia.

3. ___________ system stimulation usually affects more than one organ.

4. Axons of preganglionic neurons in the parasympathetic division are located in the cranial nerves and the ______ nerves.

5. Sympathetic postganglionic neurons have which of the following characteristics?
   A. Some of their axons return to spinal nerve fibers.
   B. Their cell bodies are located in the collateral ganglia.
   C. Some of their axons stimulate other sympathetic ganglia.
   D. All are characteristics of sympathetic postganglionic neurons.

6. The ciliary ganglion is located in the _____.

10.3.3 ANS Innervation

10 minutes

All sympathetic and parasympathetic preganglionic neurons are **cholinergic**, that is, they release acetylcholine as a neurotransmitter. Postganglionic neurons release either acetylcholine or norepinephrine. The autonomic nervous system response to neurotransmitters is excitatory or inhibitory, depending on the type of receptor on the postsynaptic cell.

Stimulation of **alpha-adrenergic** receptors by neurotransmitters causes contraction of smooth muscle (an excitatory effect). **Beta-adrenergic** receptors inhibit the contraction of smooth muscles, causing them to relax. However, beta-adrenergic receptors also stimulate the contraction of cardiac muscle and increase the heart rate. These effects can be observed together in the **fight or flight** response. The **beta** effect is noted by an increased cardiac output, while the **alpha** effect is seen in the reduction of blood flow to the **visceral** organs.

The sympathetic division is most commonly known for its role in the fight or flight response. When the body is in homeostasis, the sympathetic system overrides the parasympathetic division just enough to carry out normal physical processes requiring energy. However, during increased physical or emotional stress the sympathetic response dominates, initiating a characteristic set of physiological changes.

Characteristic signs of sympathetic stimulation during the fight or flight response include:

1) Dilation of the pupils.
2) Increased heart rate and blood pressure.
3) Constriction of blood vessels of the skin and less essential organs.
4) Dilation of blood vessels of organs involved in rigorous physical activity such as skeletal muscles, cardiac muscle, liver and adipose tissue.
5) Breathing becomes more rapid and deep as the bronchioles dilate.
6) Liver glycogen converts to glucose and blood sugar level rises.
7) These sympathetic effects are increased and prolonged as the adrenal gland is stimulated to release epinephrine and norepinephrine.
8) Processes which are inessential for meeting the demands of the stress situation are decreased. For instance, digestion slows down or stops completely.

The parasympathetic system is responsible for maintaining normal body functions and for restoring and conserving the body's energy during recovery periods. Normally, the parasympathetic system dominates over the sympathetic reactions, particularly in smooth muscle or digestive functioning. It is mainly involved with the digestion and absorption of food, and the elimination of wastes. It is also involved in emotional reactions, such as lacrimation (tear production). Intense fear can increase the activity of this system so much that one loses control over bodily functions.

Quick Check Questions

1. The autonomic nervous system responds to neurotransmitters by ________ action.

   A. excitatory
   B. both excitatory and inhibitory depending on the synaptic receptor
   C. inhibitory
   D. "fight or flight"

2. The ______________ system is involved in tear production.

3. The sympathetic system is responsible for all of these, EXCEPT:
   A. digestion and absorption of food
   B. "fight or flight" response
   C. dilation of blood vessels
   D. beta-adrenergic effects

4. Normally, the ______________ system dominates in autonomic functioning
   A. sympathetic
   B. parasympathetic

10.3.4 Control of Autonomic Activation

10 minutes

Despite its name, the autonomic nervous system (ANS) does not function on its own. The central nervous system (CNS) plays a large role in controlling the ANS, and many CNS axons connect to both the sympathetic and parasympathetic divisions. The hypothalamus controls and integrates the ANS through fibers in the medulla and spinal cord.

Somatic or visceral sensory neurons provide input to these centers, and the ANS adjusts activity accordingly, usually without conscious awareness. The posterior and lateral portions of the hypothalamus control responses from the sympathetic division. Messages from the cortex related to emotional stress stimulate the limbic system, which activates cardiac and vasomotor centers of the medulla. Cortical stimulation caused by hearing very bad news or witnessing a severely disturbing sight may cause constriction of blood vessels, which in turn can cause fainting.

The anterior and medial portions of the hypothalamus control the parasympathetic division. Under normal, less stressful conditions, more impulses are carried by way of acetylcholine, the neurotransmitter of the parasympathetic system, rather than by adrenergic fibers of the sympathetic system. Just as the sympathetic system is responsible for fight or flight, it can be said that the parasympathetic system is responsible for **recoup and repair**. Parasympathetic activity tends to slow the heartbeat, but enhances smooth muscle contractions for activities such as glandular secretion and digestion.

Quick Check Questions

1. The autonomic nervous system usually operates without conscious awareness. *True or False*

2. The ____________ controls the ANS through fibers in the medulla and the spinal cord.

3. Which portions of the hypothalamus control the parasympathetic division?
   A. posterior and lateral
   B. anterior and medial
   C. anterior and lateral
   D. posterior and anterior

4. Messages from the ______ related to emotional arousal stimulate the limbic-system.

5. Which system is responsible for increasing the secretion of epinephrine and norepinephrine from the adrenal medulla?
   A. limbic system
   B. sympathetic system
   C. parasympathetic system

6. _____________ is the neurotransmitter of the postganglionic neurons in the parasympathetic system.

Chapter 11
Sensory Organs

11.1.1 Sensory Organs - Overview

7 minutes

The **sensory organs** represent evolutionary adaptations which have been essential to the survival of the human species. Sensory organs provide the awareness of our internal and external environments needed for successfully responding to environmental and physiological challenges. In particular, sensory organs allow us to recognize life-threatening circumstances, whether from external predators or internal problems so that we may flee from a bear or feed an empty stomach.

Sensory Receptors

The body's sense organs, also called **sensory receptors**, can be classified into two main categories: 1) the general or **somatic senses**, and 2) the **special senses**.

The Somatic Sense Organs

The somatic sense organs comprise millions of receptors which produce sensations of touch, temperature, pain, and pressure. These general senses are associated with fairly simple receptors, including free nerve endings.

The Special Sense Organs

The special sense organs, which perceive vision, hearing, equilibrium, taste and smell, are composed of structurally complex, localized receptors (such as the eyes, ears, and tongue).

Quick Check Questions

1. _______ receptors perceive touch, temperature, vision, pressure and equilibrium.

2. Which of the following is NOT considered a special sense organ?
   A. ear
   B. skin
   C. eye
   D. nose

11.2.1 Sensory Receptors

8 minutes

In most cases, sensory receptors are specialized to respond selectively to particular types of stimuli. Sensory receptors can be categorized by their location, or by the type of stimuli that activate them.

Categorization of Sensory Receptors by Location

Exteroceptors are located on the body surface. **Proprioceptors** are located within muscles and joints. **Visceroceptors** are found in visceral organs.

Categorization of Sensory Receptors by Type of Stimuli

Mechanoreceptors are activated by mechanical stimuli which change the position or shape of the receptor, such as pressure to the skin or stretching of a muscle. **Chemoreceptors**, such as those involved in taste or smell, are activated by the amount or concentration of certain chemicals. **Thermoreceptors** are activated by heat or cold. **Nociceptors** are activated by stimuli accompanying tissue damage, producing a sensation of pain). **Photoreceptors**, found in the eye, respond to light stimuli. When a stimulus reaches a receptor, the response is converted into nerve impulses which are conducted into the central nervous system. Once the nerve impulses reach the CNS, they are interpreted as a sensation, which may trigger a reflex response.

Adaptation refers to a change in the intensity of a sensation from a prolonged or continuous stimulus. For example, one is able to become less distracted by the noise of an air conditioner, reducing it to **background noise**, after it has been on for a while. Similarly, one will become less aware of the scent of a cologne after wearing it all day.

Quick Check Questions

1. A sensory receptor which facilitates the sense of smell is most likely a:
   A. mechanoreceptor
   B. chemoreceptor
   C. proprioceptor

2. Receptors can be categorized by their location and the amount of stimuli they receive. *True or False*

11.2.2 Somatic Sense Receptors

10 minutes

Many somatic sense receptors, respond to external stimuli, so they are classified as **exteroceptors**. Since somatic exteroceptors are located in the skin, they are called **cutaneous receptors**. They may have structures such as bulbs, or spindle-like **corpuscles**. Stimuli such as touch, pressure, or vibration move or alter the shape of the corpuscles, thus triggering a nervous impulse.

Types of Somatic Sense Receptors

Meissner's corpuscles are found in the dermis of the skin, particularly in the fingertips and lips. They sense fine touch and low frequency vibration. **Krause's end bulbs** are found in the dermis and subcutaneous tissue, particularly the lips, eyelids, and external genitalia. They sense touch and low-frequency vibration. **Free nerve endings** are the most superficial touch receptors in the skin. They do not form distinctive structures or perform specialized functions but are generic receptors for sensations such as pain, tickle, temperature, and itch.

Touch and Pressure Receptors

Ruffini's corpuscles are found in the dermis and subcutaneous tissues of the fingers. These receptors are involved in the sensations of touch, deep pressure, and stretch. The ability to grasp an object for an extended period of time, while remaiing sensitive to its presence is aided by these receptors. **Pacinian corpuscles** are found in the skin, and external genitalia, as well as in the digestive tract, muscle tendons, and mammary glands (visceroceptors). These receptors sense pressure, high frequency vibration, and stretch.

Although touch and pressure receptors are involved in the sensation of stretch, muscle length and the strength of muscle contractions are sensed by proprioceptors there are two specialized stretch receptors or **proprioceptors**. These proprioceptors are called the **muscle spindles** and **Golgi tendon receptors**.

Muscle spindles located within skeletal muscle sense muscle length. Muscle spindles function as the afferent component of the **stretch reflex**, a nerve pathway which unconsciously aids in maintaining body posture and position in opposition to gravity. Stimulated by muscle tension, Golgi tendon receptors oppose muscle spindles by causing muscles to relax. Golgi tendon receptors are located near the junction of tendons and muscles. Golgi tendon receptors serve a protective function by preventing muscles from being torn from their bony attachments as a result of contraction.

Quick Check Questions

1. Two types of proprioceptors are:
   A. photoreceptors and mechanoreceptors
   B. Golgi tendon receptors and nociceptors
   C. muscle spindles and Golgi tendon receptors

2. Muscle spindles are a part of a stretch reflex which is:
   A. conscious
   B. unconscious
   C. semiconscious

3. Which type of pressure receptor allows us to grasp a steering wheel for a long period of time and still remain sensitive to its presence?
   A. Pacinian corpuscle
   B. Free nerve ending
   C. Ruffini's corpuscle

11.3.1 Special Senses

10 minutes

The special senses are classified as: 1) smell or **olfaction**, 2) taste or **gustation**, 3) **hearing**, 4) balance or **equilibrium**, and 5) **vision**.

Olfaction and Gustation

The olfactory receptors are chemoreceptors embedded within the olfactory epithelium in the superior part of the nasal cavity. These specialized sensory neurons have extremely sensitive **olfactory hairs or cilia** protruding into the nasal cavity that convert stimuli into nerve signals. The cilia are stimulated by chemicals that dissolve in the mucus which covers the nasal cavity. Unlike most neurons in the adult nervous system, olfactory receptors only live for about a month before being replaced by new receptors. New receptor cells are continually produced by basal cells, also called **stem cells**, through **mitosis** and **differentiation**.

As with the other special senses, olfaction has a low stimulation threshold. Olfactory receptors can be stimulated by even a few molecules of some chemicals. Sensory **adaptation** also occurs quickly, with about a 50 percent decrease in intensity within the first second of stimulation. The brain is able to distinguish between thousands of different odors. Most smells can be considered as complex mixtures of primary or pure scents. The primary scents include camphoraceous, ethereal, floral, peppermint, pungent, putrid, and musky.

The olfactory nerve fibers pass through the **foramina** in the cribriform plate of the ethmoid bone. Olfactory nerves synapse as paired **rostral** enlargements, called **olfactory bulbs**. From here the **olfactory tract** extends back into the thalamic and olfactory centers of the brain, where interpretation, integration, and short and long-term memory storage of the signals occur. Olfactory input can contribute to autonomic responses such as salivation or nausea.

Clinical Note:
Sufficient impact, such as falling and hitting one's head on concrete, can cause anteroposterior movement of the brain which shears the olfactory fibers traversing the cribriform plate. A fracture of this sort would not only cause olfactory loss, but could create a passageway through which air and infectious agents could enter the cranial cavity and cerebrospinal fluid could leave it.

Quick Check Questions

1. Chemicals in the nasal cavity are detected by olfactory hairs called _____.

2. The following cranial nerve is known as the olfactory nerve.
   A. I
   B. II
   C. X

3. Floral, peppermint, and musky are examples of:
   A. pretty scents
   B. perfume scents
   C. primary scents

11.3.2 Taste

8 minutes

Taste buds (organs comprised of **taste cells** are chemoreceptors stimulated by chemicals dissolved in the saliva. Taste cells are mostly located on **papillae** (elevated projections) of the tongue, but can also be found in the lining of the mouth and the throat.

While most taste cells respond to all taste stimuli, each cell responds most efficiently to just one of the primary taste stimuli: **bitter**, **salty**, **sour**, **sweet** (and possibly **metallic**). Humans are most sensitive to bitter tastes this may be an evolutionary adaptation to protect us from swallowing bitter-tasting poisonous compounds. Specific areas of the tongue are associated with receptors for the primary taste sensations.

As is the case with olfaction, our ability to distinguish flavors is due to a complex blending of the primary sensations. There is a strong interaction between gustation and olfaction. Gustatory information travels to the **gustatory area** of the parietal **cortex** where it is integrated and processed. This sensory information is carried by cranial nerves via the medulla and the thalamus. Three nerves are involved for different areas of the tongue: cranial nerve VII (the **facial nerve**), cranial nerve IX (the **glossopharyngeal nerve**), and cranial nerve X (the **vagus nerve**). A lesion to any one of these cranial nerves, particularly to the facial nerve, can result in loss of the taste sensation.

Quick Check Questions

1. There is a strong interaction between:
   A. hearing and gustation
   B. olfaction and equilibrium
   C. olfaction and gustation

2. The gustatory area of the cortex is located within the ________ lobe of the brain.

3. Which of the following terms is NOT a primary taste stimuli?
   A. sweet
   B. musky
   C. sour
   D. bitter

11.3.3 Hearing and Equilibrium

10 minutes

The ear is conventionally divided into three anatomical parts: 1) the **external ear**, 2) the **middle ear**, and 3) the **inner ear**. The ear functions in both hearing and equilibrium.

Hearing

The external ear is comprised of the **auricle** or **pinna**, and the **external auditory meatus** or ear canal. The ear canal terminates at the **tympanic membrane** (the ear drum), which separates it from the middle ear. The pinna facilitates the funneling of **sound waves** (vibrations that occur within air, fluid, or solid material) through the ear canal. Sound waves strike the tympanic membrane, causing the ear drum to vibrate. The middle ear contains three small bones called **auditory ossicles**: 1) the **malleus** (hammer), 2) the **incus** (anvil), and 3) the **stapes** (stirrup). Vibrations of the tympanic membrane are transmitted to the inner ear by triggering vibration of the malleus, then the incus, then the stapes which moves against the **oval window**. This causes motion of inner ear fluid, which stimulates the hearing receptors.

Besides the tympanic membrane, from the outer ear, openings to the middle ear include: 1) the **oval window** (into which the stapes fits), and 2) the **round window**, both of which open to the inner ear, 3) the **Eustachian tube** (or auditory tube) to the throat, and 4) the **tympanic antrum** a posterior chamber that communicates with air spaces in the temporal bone. The latter openings can provide routes for spreading infection to and from the middle ear. Infection of the middle ear is referred to as **otitis media**.

Composed of bony, **cartilaginous** and fibrous tissue, the Eustachian tubes connect the middle ear to the throat, or **nasopharynx**. The tubes function to equalize pressure against the inner and outer parts of the tympanic membrane, preventing discomfort and potential rupture. Swallowing or yawning causes the Eustachian tubes to open allowing the middle ear to equilibrate to atmospheric pressure. Infection can travel from the throat to the middle ear through the Eustachian tubes.

Quick Check Questions

1. The outer ear is also known as the _______.

2. The tympanic membrane is more commonly known as the ear ____.

3. The following are the bones of the middle ear:
   A. malleus, incus, and orbit
   B. malleus, stapes, and incus
   C. malleus, humerus, stapes.

11.4.1 The Inner Ear

10 minutes

The inner ear, also called the **labyrinth**, consists of a bony canal with a membranous tube in it. The **cochlea, semicircular canals**, and **vestibule** comprise the **bony** or **osseous labyrinth**. The **membranous labyrinth** includes the **cochlear duct** (within the cochlea), the membranous semicircular canals (within the osseous semicircular canals), and the **utricle** and **saccule** (within the vestibule). **Endolymph** is the potassium-rich fluid which fills the membranous labyrinth. **Perilymph**, similar in composition to **cerebrospinal fluid**, fills the spaces between the membranous and bony labyrinth.

The cochlea is involved with hearing, while the vestibule and the semicircular canals are participate in balance. Sound waves enter the external auditory meatus and cause the tympanic membrane to vibrate. The vibrations are transmitted through the ossicles, to the oval window, causing waves of pressure to form in the perilymph. These waves pass to the endolymph within the **scala vestibuli**, and eventually they the **basilar membrane** of the **organ of Corti**, which is the actual hearing sense organ.

The cochlea is essentially a spiral tube wound around a cone-shaped bone, the **modiolus**. The **modiolus** contains the **spiral ganglion**, the cell bodies of the sensory neurons of the **vestibulocochlear** or **auditory nerve (Cranial Nerve VIII)**.

Quick Check Questions

1. The inner ear is comprised of the:
   A. malleus, incus, and stapes
   B. auricles and the ear drum
   C. ear drum only
   D. cochlea, vestibule, and semicircular canals

2. The actual hearing sense organ is the:
   A. pinna
   B. organ of Corti
   C. ear drum

3. The vestibulocochlear nerve is Cranial Nerve number ___.

11.4.2 The Cochlear Duct

15 minutes

The Cochlea

The **cochlea** is a bony coiled tube which looks like a snail's shell. The cochlea transforms mechanical sound waves to nerve impulses. Three separate fluid-filled chambers run through the length of the cochlear tube.

The Cochlear Duct

The **cochlear duct** is roofed by the **vestibular membrane**, which separates it from the **scala vestibuli**. The cochlear duct is floored by the **basilar membrane**, which separates it from the **scala tympani**. The cochlear duct is filled with endolymph. The organ of Corti rests on the basilar membrane and has specialized sensory **hair cells** which project upward into the endolymph.

The scala vestibuli, which begins at the **oval window**, is filled with perilymph. The scala vestibuli is continuous with the **vestibule**. The scala tympani, also filled with perilymph, is connected to the scala vestibuli at the narrow, distal end of the cochlea. Thus, perilymph in the two chambers is continuous. The balloons on this illustration (which show an uncoiled cochlea in the software) point to the major cochlear structures. The **tectorial membrane** is a gelatinous membrane which lies gently on top of the hair cells.

Sound waves in the air cause movement of the tympanic membrane. Mechanical vibrations then occur in the incus, malleus, stapes and oval window, causing pressure waves in the perilymph of the scala vestibuli and the scala tympani. As the basilar membrane flexes in response to fluid pressure, pressure waves occur in the endolymph and the hair cells move against the tectorial membrane. It is the movement which initiates impulses in the cochlear nerve. The sensation of hearing results from stimulation of the auditory area in the cerebral cortex by sound impulses transmitted through the cochlear nerve.

Clinical Note:
Skull fractures or infections may damage the auditory apparatus or the vestibulocochlear nerve. Tumors within the internal auditory meatus, called **acoustic neuromas**, can also damage the nerve. Either of these conditions may result in loss or decrease of hearing ability in the affected ear.

Conduction impairment refers to the blockage of sound waves before they reach the receptors of the inner ear. This condition can be caused by a buildup of **cerumen** (or wax) which blocks the external auditory meatus, or by middle ear infections that produce swelling and pus thus blocking the middle ear. Inherited or acquired **nerve impairment** will cause insensitivity to sound due to nerve damage. Both normal aging and chronic exposure to loud noises can cause nerve damage.

Quick Check Questions

1. The following structure is filled with endolymph.
   A. scala vestibuli
   B. cochlear duct
   C. scala tympani

2. Chronic exposure to loud noises can cause:
   A. nerve impairment
   B. conduction impairment

11.4.3 Balance

8 minutes

The three semicircular canals lie within the temporal bone at approximately right angles to one another. Each canal contains the fluid endolymph, and joins the vestibular utricle at an enlargement called an **ampulla**. The sensing of **static equilibrium** or balance, a function of the utricle and the saccule chambers of membranous labyrinth found within the vestibule. Static equilibrium senses the position of the head in space and helps maintain posture while motionless. In addition, it is involved in **righting reflexes** which restore the body and its parts to their normal positions after displacement.

In each ear, there are two **maculae** (specialized patches of epithelium), located almost at right angles to one another. One is found in the utricle and the other in the saccule. Each macula contains hair cells covered with a gelatinous matrix that is embedded with tiny calcium carbonate crystals called **otoliths** (ear stones). As the position of the head changes, the otoliths move, and the amount of pressure they exert on the matrix varies. This pressure stimulates the vestibulocochlear nerve to conduct impulses to the **central nervous system** (CNS). The impulses convey positional information, which is then used to maintain balance and equilibrium.

Quick Check Questions

1. The calcium carbonate crystals within the macula are called ________.

2. Restoring the body to its normal position after displacement is referred to as a:
   A. lefting reflex
   B. reorientation adjustment
   C. righting reflex

11.4.4 Semicircular Canals

5 minutes

The semicircular canals maintain balance when the head or the body is subjected to sudden movement. This accounts for both the direction and rate at which motion occurs. This is called **dynamic equilibrium**. The **crista ampullaris,** found within the ampulla, is a sensory organ similar to a macula (of each semicircular canal). These cone-shaped structures are composed of many hair cells in contact with a gelatinous covering called the **cupula**.

Detection of movement in all directions is possible because the three semicircular canals are oriented at nearly right angles to each other. The cupula floats within and moves with the flow of endolymph that fills the canals. When the cupula moves, it distorts the shape of the underlying hair cells, and a nerve impulse is sent to the vestibulocochlear nerve.

Quick Check Questions

1. The following structures are components of the semicircular canals.
   A. otoliths and cupula
   B. crista ampullaris and cupula
   C. crista ampullaris and otoliths

2. Semicircular canals are involved with _______ equilibrium.

11.5.1 Sight

10 minutes

The body's only sense organ for vision, the eye, converts light energy into electrical nerve impulses which are interpreted by the brain as sight. The eyeball is made up of several **circumferential** coats or layers. Each eyeball, measuring about one inch in diameter, lies protected in the bony socket of the skull called the orbit.

Layers of the Eye

The three major layers of the eyeball include: 1) the outer **sclera**, 2) the middle **choroid**, and 3) the inner **retina**. The sclera, is a tough, white, opaque fibrous tissue called the **white of the eye**. The anterior portion of the eyeball consists of the transparent **cornea**, which lies in front of the **iris**, the colored portion of the eye.

The Choroid Layer

The middle choroid layer of the eye contains many blood vessels, and has a modified anterior portion called the **ciliary body**. This muscular thickening of the choroid, anchors the **suspensory ligaments** and the iris.

Suspensory Ligaments

The **suspensory ligaments** attach to the lens and suspend it in place. The ciliary body controls the focal length of the lens by contracting and relaxing. When the ciliary body relaxes, it pulls on the suspensory ligaments. These pull the lens, which then becomes flatter, and the eye focuses upon more distant objects. The iris has both circular and radial **smooth muscle fibers**, which vary the circumference of the hole in the middle (called the **pupil**).

Accessory Structures

The following **accessory structures** of the eye function in its protection. The eyebrows and eyelashes prevent foreign objects from entering the eye. The eyelids (or **palpebrae)** moisturize the eye. They contain inner, mucous membranes, or **conjunctivae**, which are continuous with the surface of the eyeball. The conjunctivae also protect the eye against the entry of foreign objects. The **lacrimal apparatus** secretes tears for lubrication, which drain into the **nasal cavity** via the lacrimal duct.

Quick Check Questions

1. The three layers of the eyeball are the sclera, the _______, and the retina.

2. The transparent anterior portion of the sclera is the:
   A. lens
   B. pupil
   C. cornea

3. The iris surrounds the opening of the eyeball called the _____.

11.5.2 The Retina

8 minutes

The **retina** coats the inner surface of the back of the eyeball and is divided into sensory and pigmented portions. The **pigmented retina** lies next to the choroid. The **sensory retina** is made up of three layers of sensory neurons which translate light impulses into electrical impulses. These impulses are conducted to the brain for processing and integration. The three cell types of the sensory retina are: 1) **photoreceptor cells**, 2) **bipolar cells**, and 3) **ganglion cells**.

Visual impulses, coded from light that enters the iris, are conducted through the following structures in the following order: Photoreceptor cells, Bipolar cells, Ganglion cells, Optic nerve, and Brain. The photoreceptor neurons, called **rods** and **cones**, are visual receptors highly specialized for stimulation by light. Rods and cones contain **photopigments**, pigmented compounds which undergo structural changes in response to light resulting in the generation of nerve impulses. These nerve impulses travel through the optic nerves to the brain.

Rhodopsin is the pigment in rods, which is important for vision of shades of gray, but not colors. There are three cone photopigments, one for each of the primary colors (red, green, and blue). These pigments are less sensitive to light and dark, but they produce sharper color images in bright light. Combined neural inputs from the different cone types makes our perception of a range of colors possible.

Clinical Note:
Color blindness is caused by missing or deficient photopigments: affected individuals see colors, but are unable to distinguish them correctly.

Quick Check Questions

1. The following cells are NOT components of the sensory retina:
   A. photoreceptor cells
   B. hair cells
   C. bipolar cells

2. Rhodopsin is a photopigment found in:
   A. rods
   B. cones
   C. the pigmented retina

3. The retina covers only the ___________ portion of the inner eye.

11.5.3 Cones

5 minutes

Less numerous than rods, **cones** are concentrated in the **fovea centralis** within the **macula lutea**, a yellowish area found near the center of the retina. Rods, absent from this region, increase in density toward the periphery of the retina. To see an object clearly in the daytime, we look at it directly, focusing the image on the

fovea. But to see in dim light or darkness, we need to look slightly to the side, focusing near the periphery of the retina.

The bipolar neurons connect the photoreceptor neurons to the ganglion neurons. The bipolar neurons extend back to the **optic disc**, the region on the posterior part of the eyeball, where the fibers emerge as the **optic nerve** (Cranial Nerve II). This region is also called the **blind spot** because photoreceptor neurons are absent here: there are only nerve fibers in this area.

Quick Check Questions

1. The blind spot of the eye refers to the:
   A. macula lutea
   B. optic disc
   C. fovea centralis

2. The _____ are responsible for color vision.

11.5.4 Cavities of the Eye

7 minutes

In addition to the three layers of the eye, there are two cavities, separated by the lens and its apparatus: the **anterior cavity**, and the **posterior cavity**. The anterior cavity consists of both an **anterior chamber** (anterior to the iris) and a **posterior chamber** (posterior to the iris). Both chambers in the anterior cavity are filled with a clear watery substance called **aqueous humor**. The posterior chamber is filled with a soft gelatinous material called **vitreous humor**. Both aqueous and vitreous humor help the eye maintain **intra-ocular pressure** and shape, and prevent it from collapsing on itself.

The aqueous humor is continuous with the circulatory system of the body. Passive filtration from capillary blood contributes to its formation at the ciliary body. Normally, it drains into the **canal of Schlemm** (a ring shaped venous sinus located below the junction between the sclera and the cornea) at a rate equal to its formation.

Clinical Note:
Glaucoma is an eye disease that occurs when formation and drainage of aqueous humor are unmatched, resulting in a increase of intraocular pressure above the normal level (about 20 to 25 mmHg of pressure).

Quick Check Questions

1. Vitreous humor of the eye fills the:
   A. lateral cavity
   B. anterior cavity
   C. posterior cavity

2. The canal of Schlemm of the eye drains the:
   A. aqueous humor
   B. vitreous humor
   C. good humor

3. The eye disease which results from high intraocular pressure is:
   A. color blindness
   B. double vision
   C. glaucoma

11.5.5 Four Components of Vision

8 minutes

There are four components in the process of vision which work together for sight to occur: 1) **refraction** of light rays, 2) **accommodation** of the lens, 3) **constriction** of the pupil, and 4) **convergence** of the eyes. The goal of vision is to focus the light rays from an image on the retina, such that nerve impulses are transmitted to the visual cortex in the **occipital lobe** of the brain for processing.

The deflection or bending of light rays entering the eye, known as **refraction**, occurs through the cornea, aqueous humor, lens, and vitreous humor. Light rays 20 feet or more away are parallel by the time they reach the eye. A relaxed normal, **emmetropic**, eye will refract parallel rays such that they are brought to focus on the retina. When there is not enough refracting power to bring an object into focus, farsightedness or **hypermetropia** results.

Accommodation of the lens must occur for objects closer than 20 feet to be brought into focus on the retina. Light rays closer than 20 feet are divergent, rather than parallel, requiring more refracting power. Accommodation is accomplished by increasing the curvature of the lens, by contraction of the ciliary muscle and relaxation of the suspensory ligaments. The opposite accommodation occurs for far vision: relaxation of the muscle and tension on the ligaments. Eyes with too much refracting power bring images into focus anterior to the retina. This condition is known as nearsightedness or **myopia**.

The smooth muscles of the iris function to constrict the pupil in bright light. This is known as the **pupillary reflex**. The pupillary reflex also prevents divergent rays from entering the eye through the periphery of the cornea and the lens. These pupillary reflex actions create a sharper image.

Convergence is the mechanism by which the two eyeballs move in unison for light rays to strike corresponding points on the two retinas. The nearer the object, the greater the degree of convergence (eyes angled inward towards the nose) necessary for single vision to be maintained. **Diplopia** refers to double-vision, which can result when the extrinsic muscles of the eyes are unable to coordinate their movement in relation to one another.

Quick Check Questions

1. The following process refers to the bending of light rays:
   A. diplopia
   B. convergence
   C. refraction

2. The pupillary reflex is made possible by:
   A. pupillary constriction
   B. lens convergence
   C. myopia

3. Myopia is more commonly known as farsightedness. *True or False*

Chapter 12
The Endocrine System

12.1.1 Endocrine System - Overview

10 minutes

The **endocrine system** is a collection of glands that secrete substances called **hormones**. Hormones are biologically active chemicals that are released into the blood. Although all cells of the body are exposed to many hormones, only those cells having specific hormone **receptors** are affected by them. Such **target cells** are found at various locations in the body.

Unlike the nervous system, which sends messages along nerves, endocrine signals are sent through the blood. Indeed, an **endocrine gland** is defined as one that secretes its product directly into the bloodstream, as opposed to an **exocrine gland** which secretes its product through a duct.

The endocrine glands include the: 1) **hypothalamus**, 2) **pituitary gland**, 3) **thyroid glands**, 4) the paired **adrenal glands**, 5) the **pancreas**, and 6) the paired **gonads** (that is, the **ovaries** or **testes**). Several other organs, such as the heart, intestines, and during pregnancy, the placenta, also have some endocrine functions.

The functions of the endocrine system are: 1) to regulate the growth and development of the human body, 2) to maintain appropriate amounts of **metabolites** (nutrients) and **electrolytes** (such as **glucose** and **sodium**), and 3) to regulate physical responses to **stress**.

General Classes of Hormones

Hormones fall into three general classes based upon their chemical structure. These are:

1) **Amino acid derivatives** (hormones which are produced by chemical changes made to amino acids). The hormone **epinephrine** (also known as **adrenaline**) is an amino acid derivative.

2) **Steroids** (these hormones are derived from **cholesterol**). An example is **cortisol**, which has strong anti-inflammatory properties. Synthetic forms of cortisol are useful for treating inflammation.

3) **Peptides** (hormones consisting of short chains of amino acids). **Insulin**, a hormone which helps regulate blood sugar levels, is an example of a peptide hormone.

Quick Check Questions

1. Both nervous tissues and endocrine tissues send messages to distant parts of the body. *True or False*

2. The endocrine system is a collection of glands that secrete substances called ________ directly into the bloodstream.

3. All of the following are types of hormones, EXCEPT:
   A. catecholamines
   B. fatty acids
   C. cholesterol derivatives
   D. short chains of amino acids

12.1.2 The Function of Hormones

10 minutes

Hormones effect changes in their **target cells** by binding to specific **receptors** on those cells. Receptors may be located on the cell's plasma membrane, or within its **cytoplasm** (epinephrine receptors are located on the cell surface, while cortisol receptors are in the cytoplasm). In either case, a cellular **switch** is turned on when a hormone binds to its receptor. This switch causes the chemical events that amplify the **message** so that a larger effect is generated from the binding of a single hormone molecule.

One way amplification is accomplished is through a **cascade mechanism**. For example, when thyroid hormone levels are low, a message is sent to the hypothalamus gland in the brain causing it to secrete a small amount of **thyroid releasing hormone** (TRH). The TRH travels through the blood to the anterior pituitary where it binds to target cell receptors. Each interaction between TRH and a pituitary receptor causes the pituitary gland to release many **thyroid stimulating hormone** (TSH) molecules. TSH binds to receptors in the thyroid gland. Each molecule of TSH stimulates the release of many molecules of the thyroid hormones, **thyroxine** and **triiodothyronine**. Thus, the message originating from the hypothalamus, carried by TRH, is amplified many times during the cascade of events that lead to the release of thyroid hormones.

The glands of the endocrine system are scattered throughout the body. The hypothalamus is often called the **master gland**, because it receives many cellular signals and responds by secreting a variety of hormones which regulate hormone release from various other glands. These **releasing hormones** and **inhibitory hormones** control hormone release from the anterior pituitary gland.

The two lobes that comprise the pituitary gland (anterior and posterior) are located just inferior to the hypothalamus. The pituitary gland is connected to the hypothalamus by a stalk called the **infundibulum**. The anterior pituitary gland secretes several stimulating hormones directed to other glands. The posterior pituitary gland stores and releases hormones produced by the hypothalamus.

The thyroid gland is located in the neck, attached to the trachea. The thyroid gland secretes thyroid hormones, which regulate the **basal metabolic rate** (the rate of energy use in the body) as well as growth and development. The **parathyroid glands** are four small glands located on the posterior surface of the thyroid. The parathyroids are involved in monitoring and maintaining calcium levels in the blood.

The paired adrenal glands are located in the abdominal cavity, resting on top of (superior to) each kidney. The adrenal glands are divided into two functionally different parts: 1) the **adrenal cortex**, and 2) the **adrenal medulla**.

The outer layer of the adrenal gland is called the adrenal cortex. The adrenal cortex secretes **glucocorticoids** (including cortisol). In general, these hormones control energy processes such as glucose utilization. The adrenal cortex also secretes hormones involved in sodium retention and water balance. The most potent of these hormones is **aldosterone**, which acts on the kidney. In addition, the adrenal cortex releases small amounts of **sex steroids**, which supplement those released by the gonads.

The adrenal medulla is the inner part of the adrenal gland. It receives innervation from the sympathetic division of the autonomic nervous system (ANS). The sympathetic division stimulates the adrenal medulla to produce the **catecholamine** hormones, specifically, **epinephrine** (adrenaline) and **norepinephrine** (nor-adrenaline). These hormones play an important role in the body's response to stress.

The pancreas has both endocrine and exocrine functions. The pancreas secretes **insulin** and **glucagon** directly into the bloodstream (an endocrine function). These hormones regulate blood glucose levels. In addition, the pancreas secretes enzymes for the digestion of food through the **pancreatic duct** into the small intestine (an exocrine function).

The **gonads (testes** in the male and **ovaries** in the female), secrete the sex hormones. Some of these are **testosterone**, **estrogen** and **progesterone**, which control sexual development and normal sexual functions.

Quick Check Questions

1. Which endocrine gland produces hormones important in regulating sexual function?
   A. adrenal cortex
   B. pancreas
   C. posterior pituitary
   D. ovary

2. The adrenal medulla helps to regulate which of the following?
   A. stress responses
   B. basal metabolic rate
   C. calcium level
   D. blood glucose level

12.2.1 The Hypothalamus

10 minutes

The **hypothalamus** is called the master gland because it is involved in the regulation of many other endocrine glands. Its roles will be discussed as part of the sections on each of the glands it regulates.

The Pituitary

The **pituitary gland**, a dual-lobed organ about the size of a large pea, is located on the inferior aspect of the brain. The pituitary gland rests in the bony socket formed by the sella torsica of the sphenoid bone. Above the pituitary is the infundibulum, a stalk containing a network of capillaries through which the hypothalamus sends its endocrine messages to the anterior pituitary. These capillaries comprise the **hypophyseal portal system.**

The pituitary gland contains two functional divisions: 1) the anterior pituitary and 2) the posterior pituitary. The anterior pituitary (or as the **adenohypophysis**) is the larger lobe, containing about 75 percent of the mass of the pituitary. Cells of the anterior pituitary synthesize regulatory hormones, the targets of which are other endocrine glands.

Cells Types of Anterior Pituitary

All of the hormones produced in the anterior pituitary are peptides. Five types of anterior pituitary cells secrete a total of seven major hormones. They are:

1) **Somatotrophs**, the most numerous cell type, secrete **growth hormone.**

2) **Mammotrophs** secrete **prolactin**. These cells increase in number during pregnancy and lactation.

3) **Corticotrophs** release **adrenoncorticotrophic hormone** (ACTH) and **melanocyte-stimulating hormone** (MSH), which respectively stimulate the adrenal cortex to secrete glucocorticoids and increase skin pigmentation.

4) **Thyrotrophs** secrete **thyroid-stimulating hormone** (TSH).

6) **Gonadotrophs**, secrete **follicle-stimulating hormone** (FSH) and **luteinizing hormone** (LH), both of which regulate activities of the pituitary glands.

The anatomy and function of the posterior pituitary are covered in the next lesson.

Quick Check Questions

1. All of the following glands are affected by major hormones from the anterior pituitary, EXCEPT:
   A. thyroid
   B. pancreas
   C. gonads
   D. mammary glands

2. Often called the master gland, the ____________ is involved in the regulation of other endocrine glands.

3. Which of the following is the most numerous cell type in the anterior pituitary gland?
   A. mammotroph
   B. corticotroph
   C. somatotroph

12.2.2 The Posterior Pituitary

7 minutes

Unlike the anterior pituitary, the **posterior pituitary** is not a functionally separate gland. Rather, the posterior pituitary contains the axon terminals of neurons called **neurosecretory cells** which originate in the hypothalamus. The neurosecretory cell bodies are locked in regions of the hypothalamus called the **supraoptic** and **paraventricular** nuclei. The axons of these neurons, which run through the infundibulum, comprise the **supra-optico-hypophyseal tract**.

The hormones released into circulation from the posterior pituitary are manufactured in the hypothalamus and delivered to the pituitary along the axons of the neurosecretory cells. The posterior pituitary hormones are **oxytocin**, active in the mother during and after birth, and **antidiuretic hormone** (ADH, also known as **vasopressin**), which regulates the body's water level.

Quick Check Questions

1. Messages from the hypothalamus reach the posterior pituitary via a system of hypophyseal portal veins. *True or False*

2. Vasopressin is made in the:
   A. hypothalamus
   B. anterior pituitary
   C. posterior pituitary
   D. heart muscle

3. Vasopressin is released from the:
   A. hypothalamus
   B. anterior pituitary
   C. posterior pituitary
   D. heart muscle

12.2.3 Hormones - Anterior Pituitary

10 minutes

The regulating effects of the anterior pituitary hormones merit a more detailed examination. Each of the seven hormones is discussed in terms of: 1) What it does (the effects of the hormone upon target cells), 2) How it works (the hormone's mechanism of action), 3) What turns it on (the factors which stimulate release of the hormones from the anterior pituitary), and 4) What turns it off (the circumstances which inhibit release of the hormone from the anterior pituitary).

Growth Hormone (GH): What Does it Do?

The actions of GH are threefold: 1) GH promotes the build-up of lean body mass (muscle and bone), as well as organ growth, 2) GH stimulates the use of fatty acids instead of proteins to generate energy, and 3) GH causes an increase in blood glucose, and thus an increase in available energy.

Growth Hormone: How Does it Work?

GH promotes movement of amino acids into the cells, thus increasing protein synthesis. GH also restarts protein breakdown. In this way, cellular reproduction and the growth rate of muscles, bones, and other tissues is increased. GH carries out some functions in conjunction with other hormones such as the **somatomedins**, insulin-like factors synthesized in the liver.

Growth Hormone: What Turns it On?

Factors which stimulate GH secretion include: 1) decreased fatty acid levels in the blood, 2) increased amino acid levels in the blood, 3) **hypoglycemia** (low blood sugar levels), 4) increased activity of the sympathetic division of ANS, 5) **deep sleep** (as indicated by **delta brain wave** activity), and 6) hormones, including glucagon, estrogen, cortisol, and insulin.

Growth Hormone: What Turns it Off?

Factors which inhibit GH secretion are: 1) increased blood levels of fatty acids, 2) decreased levels of amino acids in the blood, 3) **hyperglycemia** (high blood sugar levels), 4) **rapid eye movement** (REM) sleep, the dream stage, 5) obesity, 6) **hypothyroidism** (low levels of thyroid hormone), and 8) emotional deprivation causing decreased SNS activity. Another factor that suppresses GH release is high blood levels of GH itself. This demonstrates a common mechanism in hormonal regulation, the **negative feedback mechanism**. Many hormones self-regulate in this way: when blood levels of a hormone are high, release of the hormone is turned off.

The negative feedback loop of GH occurs in the hypothalamus (where GH suppresses the production of **gonadotropic releasing hormone** (GnRH)), and in the anterior pituitary (where GH suppresses its own production and release).

Quick Check Questions

1. Growth Hormone (GH) causes a rise in blood glucose. *True or False*

2. A person who is deprived of REM sleep will probably have a low level of GH in their blood. *True or False*

3. All of the following inhibit growth hormone (GH) secretion, EXCEPT:
   A. obesity
   B. estrogen
   C. REM sleep
   D. growth hormone (GH)

4. All of the following promote growth hormone (GH) secretion, EXCEPT:
   A. insulin
   B. hypoglycemia
   C. deep sleep
   D. thyroid hormone

12.2.4 Effects of Growth Hormone

15 minutes

An excess of GH during childhood leads to gigantism, a condition of extreme height caused by abnormal growth of the large bones. Affected persons frequently develop problems such as diabetes mellitus (uncontrollably high serum glucose) and heart failure. An excess of GH during adulthood leads to **acromegaly**. The stature of a person with acromegaly does not increase because the skeletal growth plates (**epiphyseal plates**) have already fused. However, certain bones in the hands and feet and face grow wider and thicker. If GH secretion is inadequate during childhood, the result is **pituitary dwarfism** characterized by limited growth of the bones and other organs.

Clinical Note:
An interesting potential clinical applications of growth hormone has been proposed by some researchers. It is known that age causes, the percentage of fat in the body to increase, while muscles become smaller. The same effect occurs in from diseases such as **cancer** and **AIDS**. The mechanisms of these processes are not well understood, and neither is the function of growth hormone in the adult. But it is thought that the two things are connected, and that GH may be the key to maintaining youthful and healthy levels of growth metabolism.

Adrenocorticotrophic Hormone (ACTH): What Does it Do?

ACTH is released from the pituitary, stimulating target cells in the adrenal cortex to secrete glucocorticoid hormones. ACTH is modified a short peptide segment which is cut out of a long peptide called **proopiomelanocortin** (POMC).

Four different peptide segments from POMC form molecules with completely separate functions. These are: 1) the pituitary hormones, ACTH, and 2) MSH, **melanocyte stimulating hormone**, 3) **b-endorphins** (opioid neurotransmitters which are endogenous pain killers), and 4) **b-lipotropin** (a substance that stimulates fat breakdown).

ACTH: How Does it Work?

ACTH stimulates cells of the adrenal cortex via a **second messenger** mechanism. In general, a second messenger is a molecule within the target cell that is activated when the hormone (the first messenger, in this case ACTH) binds to its receptor. Second messengers often work by cascade mechanisms. When a molecule of ACTH binds to its receptor on the outer surface of an adrenal cells plasma membrane, **adenylate cyclase** on the inner surface are activated. Activated adenylate cyclase converts ATP in the cytoplasm into **cyclic AMP** (cAMP). Next, cAMP the second messenger goes on to alter specific cell functions. In ACTH target cells, the result is manufacture and release of glucocorticoid hormones.

ACTH: What Turns it On?

Factors which promote ACTH secretion are: 1) **corticotropin-releasing hormone** (CRH) produced by the hypothalamus, 2) emotional stress, 3) physical trauma, 4) low blood glucose, and 5) **interleukin-1** a molecule secreted by macrophages that causes fevers (a sign of bodily stress).

ACTH: What Turns it Off?

The glucocorticoid hormones exert a potent self-regulatory effect upon the pituitary, by inhibiting ACTH release. Glucocorticoids also inhibit CRH release from the hypothalamus reducing ACTH productions. Together, these negative feedback loops regulate glucocorticoid levels.

Quick Check Questions

1. A person who produces too much ACTH (from a tumor, for example) might be expected to also have:
   A. very long bones and large joints
   B. a dark tan
   C. very short stature
   D. abnormalities or carbohydrate and protein metabolism

2. All of the following promote ACTH secretion, EXCEPT:
   A. low serum cortisol
   B. interleukin-1
   C. preparation for final exams
   D. hyperglycemia (high blood sugar levels)

3. Glucocorticoids exert a potent negative feedback upon the pituitary, inhibiting ____ release.

12.2.5 Prolactin

7 minutes

Prolactin: What Does it Do?

Prolactin is responsible for **lactation** (milk production and secretion) in the **mammary glands** (breast tissue). In males, the function of prolactin is unknown.

Prolactin: How Does it Work?

Prolactin works in conjunction with a team of hormones that prepare the mammary glands for milk secretion: progesterone, estrogen, cortisol, growth hormone, thyroxine, and insulin. If a woman's nutritional needs are not met so that she does not have appropriate levels of glucose, amino acids, and fatty acids in her blood, lactation is more difficult.

Prolactin: What Turns it On?

Prolactin secretion is stimulated by an unidentified hormone, referred to as **prolactin-releasing factor**. Prolactin levels are increased during pregnancy and during nursing or breast stimulation. In addition, prolactin release is stimulated by stress, and during sleep.

Prolactin: What Turns it Off?

Lactation is inhibited by **prolactin-inhibiting hormone**, another name for the neurotransmitter dopamine. Dopamine has many functions, only one of which is inhibition of prolactin.

Quick Check Questions

1. All of the following hormones are important in milk production and lactation, EXCEPT:
   A. growth hormone
   B. progesterone
   C. oxytocin
   D. cortisol

2. Prolactin levels are _________ during pregnancy.
   A. decreased
   B. increased

12.2.6 Thyroid-Stimulating Hormone

20 minutes

Thyroid-Stimulating Hormone (TSH): What Does it Do?

Thyroid-stimulating hormone (TSH), generated in the anterior pituitary, stimulates the synthesis of the thyroid hormones **triiodothyronine** (T3) and **thyroxine** (T4). In turn, these hormones help regulate energy use in the body by increasing the basal metabolic rate.

TSH: How Does it Work?

TSH from the anterior pituitary stimulates a series of reactions that result in the synthesis of thyroid hormones T3 and T4 inside the **thyroid follicle**.

TSH: What Turns it On?

Secretion of TSH from the anterior pituitary is stimulated by **thyroid-releasing hormone** (TRH) from the hypothalamus. Levels of TSH increase with low T3, low TSH, and hypoglycemia, according to a negative feedback mechanism.

TSH: What Turns it Off?

TSH release from the anterior pituitary is inhibited by high TSH levels, low TRH from the hypothalamus, high T3, and hyperglycemia.

Follicle-Stimulating Hormone (FSH): What Does it Do?

Follicle-stimulating hormone or FSH is one of two hormones produced by the gonadotrophs cells of the anterior pituitary. FSH stimulates the **follicular cells** of the ovaries and their secretion of estrogen. In males, FSH stimulates sperm production by the **seminiferous tubules** of the testes.

FSH: How Does it Work?

FSH works together with luteinizing hormone (LH) the hormone produced by **gonadotropin**. FSH and LH are known as gonadotropins because they influence gonadal functions. The actions of FSH are carried out via an intracellular second messenger system.

FSH: What Turns it On?

FSH production is stimulated by **gonadotropin-releasing hormone** (GnRH) from the hypothalamus.

FSH: What Turns it Off?

Inhibition of FSH is triggered by estrogen levels in females and testosterone in males. FSH is controlled by negative feedback inhibition.

Luteinizing Hormone (LH): What Does it Do?

Luteinizing hormone (LH) is the second hormone produced by the gonadotrophs. LH works together with FSH, to stimulate estrogen secretion and **ovulation**, release of a secondary oocyte from the ovary. LH also controls development production and maintenance of the **corpus luteum** after ovulation, and its secretion of **progesterone** another female sex hormone. In the male, LH stimulates production of the sex hormone **testosterone** by the **interstitial cells** of the testes.

LH: How Does it Work?

As noted, LH and FSH work together to maintain sexual functions via second messenger mechanism.

LH: What Turns it On?

LH, like FSH, is stimulated by GnRH from the hypothalamus.

LH: What Turns it Off?

LH secretion is decreased when GnRH levels become lower.

Melanocyte - Stimulating Hormone (MSH)

Not a lot is known about the function of MSH in humans. When present in abnormally high levels it stimulates the production of melanin by melanocytes, but its effects at normal levels are unknown. In reptiles and amphibians MSH acts on a particular (non-human) cell type to darken the skin when needed for camouflage. MSH is regulated by hypothalamic hormones **MSH releasing hormones** (MRH) and **MSH inhibiting hormone** (MIH).

Quick Check Questions

1. Luteinizing hormone (LH) can cause all of the following, EXCEPT:
   A. stimulation of progesterone secretion
   B. stimulation of testosterone secretion
   C. release of sperm for ejaculation
   D. ovulation (release of an egg from the ovary)

2. In the male, luteinizing hormone (LH) stimulates ____________ production by interstitial cells of the testes.

3. Secretion of thyroid-stimulating hormone (TSH) is stimulated by thyroid-releasing hormone (TRH) from the hypothalamus.

4. Follicle-stimulating hormone (FSH) is one of ____ hormones produced by the gonadotroph cells of the anterior pituitary.
   A. two
   B. three
   C. four

12.2.7 Hormones - Posterior Pituitary

8 minutes

Oxytocin and antidiuretic hormone (ADH, or vasopressin) are hormones that are synthesized in the hypothalamus, and released from the posterior pituitary. After oxytocin and ADH are manufactured in the supraoptic and paraventricular nuclei, they travel down the axons to terminals in the posterior pituitary. From the posterior pituitary, they diffuse into the bloodstream.

Oxytocin: What Does it Do?

Oxytocin functions in the process of birth and lactation. During delivery, oxytocin stimulates the smooth muscle of the uterus, increasing its contractions. After the birth of a child, oxytocin causes contraction of the smooth muscle cells around the milk ducts in the breasts, pushing the milk into larger ducts which empty at the nipple. (This process is called milk **ejection** or **let down**).

Oxytocin: How Does it Work?

Oxytocin uses an intracellular second messenger to carry out its effects.

Oxytocin: What Turns it On?

Secretion of oxytocin is controlled by a **neuroendocrine reflexes** in which nerve signals trigger hormonal release. During childbirth, stretch receptors in the **cervix** (the mouth of the uterus) are stimulated and send messages to the hypothalamus for oxytocin production. During breast feeding, stimulation of touch receptors in the nipple causes oxytocin release.

Clinical Note:
An analog of oxytocin called **pitocin** is often given to induce labor when a pregnant woman is past her due date.

Oxytocin: What Turns it Off?

Oxytocin is released in response to specific nerve stimuli (cervical stretching and suckling). It is controlled through positive feedback: oxytocin release increases uterine contractions, which causes further stretching of the cervix, so that more hormone is released. Therefore, oxytocin release stops when the stimulus from the sensory receptors ends.

Quick Check Questions

1. ADH and oxytocin are manufactured in axon terminals of the posterior pituitary, where they are released on demand. *True or False*

2. When the cervix is stretched as a woman enters the last stage of labor, levels of oxytocin are already at their maximum, and thus remain unchanged. *True or False*

3. Secretion of oxytocin is controlled through a neuro__________ reflex.

12.2.8 Antidiuretic Hormone (ADH)

10 minutes

ADH: What Does it Do?

Antidiuretic hormone is the hormone responsible for conserving water in the body.

ADH: How Does it Work?

ADH decreases the volume of urine output by promoting water reabsorption in the kidneys. ADH is so effective in concentrating the urine that a normal person may produce 1 to 2 liters of urine per day, while a person without antidiuretic hormone can produce twenty liters! Once it is released from the posterior pituitary, ADH acts upon the **distal tubule** of kidney **nephrons**. Cells in this area are impermeable to water without ADH.

Some **diuretics** (drugs which increase urine volume) work by blocking ADH from binding to its receptors on kidney cells. In addition to its effects on water balance, ADH also functions to increase blood pressure by constricting blood vessels (hence its other name, vasopressin), and to decrease perspiration (another way to conserve water).

ADH: What Turns it On?

The production of ADH is controlled by **osmoreceptors** in the hypothalamus. These cells sense high **osmolarity** (ionic concentration, osmotic pressure). That is, when the concentration of solutes in the blood (such as sodium, chloride, and bicarbonate) is high, and water concentration is low, ADH secretion is stimulated. ADH secretion is also increased by stress, pain, anxiety, the neurotransmitter acetylcholine, and drugs including nicotine, morphine and tranquilizers.

ADH: What Turns it Off?

When the volume of water in the blood is high, and osmolarity is low, ADH secretion is inhibited. The kidneys increase their urine output, returning the osmotic pressure to normal. ADH production is also inhibited by alcohol consumption.

Quick Check Questions

1. Antidiuretic hormone (ADH) exerts its water-retaining effect by inhibiting bladder contraction. *True or False*

2. Release of the hormone ADH, from the posterior pituitary, causes all of the following, EXCEPT:
   A. more concentrated urine
   B. decreased perspiration
   C. increased osmolarity of the blood
   D. decreased osmolarity of the blood

3. The hormone, vasopressin, is made and stored in axon terminals in the posterior pituitary. *True or False*

4. People tend to urinate more after drinking large quantities of beer because alcohol inhibits the production of:
   A. thyroxine
   B. oxytocin
   C. parathyroid hormone
   D. vasopressin

12.3.1 The Thyroid Gland

7 minutes

The thyroid is a gland which wraps around the **trachea** just below the **larynx**: it typically weighs 15 to 20 grams. The thyroid consist of two **lateral lobes** connected by a narrow band called the **isthmus**, which crosses the anterior surface of the trachea.

The thyroid gland has a rich blood supply, which facilitates quick movement of thyroid hormones into the bloodstream. The thyroid gland contains two cell types and two classes of hormones:

1) The iodine containing hormones **triiodothyronine** (also called **T3** because it contains three iodine molecules) and **thyroxine** (known as **T4** because it carries four iodines). These hormones are made by **follicular cells** of the thyroid.

2) **Calcitonin** (or **thyrocalcitonin**) is made by the **parafollicular cells** of the thyroid. It functions to lower the levels of calcium and phosphorous in the blood.

The follicular cells of the thyroid gland are cuboidal epithelial cells. They are arranged in a single layer around the fluid-filled **follicles**, spherical sacs that comprise the gland. Small numbers of parafollicular cells are scattered in the spaces between adjacent follicles. The thyroid follicles are enclosed by connective tissue, and the thyroid gland itself is enveloped in a capsule of connective tissue.

Quick Check Questions

1. All of the following are true about the thyroid gland, EXCEPT:
   A. it produces and secretes both thyroid hormones (T3 and T4)
   B. it contains squamous follicular cells
   C. it has an isthmus
   D. it is a collection of fluid filled sacs, called follicles

2. The thyroid is a 15 to 20 gram gland which is wrapped around the _______, just below the larynx.

3. The iodine containing hormones triiodothyronine (T3) and thyroxine (T4) are made by the parafollicular cells of the thyroid. *True or False*

12.3.2 Thyroid Gland Hormones

15 minutes

The thyroid gland is unique among the endocrine glands in that it stores large amounts of its hormones (triiodothyronine and thyroxine) in an inactive form. The inactive precursors of T3 and T4 are stored within the **lumens** (internal space) of the follicles in the thick fluid called **thyroid colloid**. Thyroid-stimulating hormone (TSH) from the anterior pituitary causes conversion of these precursors to their active forms and subsequent release of active T3 and T4.

The Synthesis of T3 and T4

Iodine, an essential constituent of thyroid hormones, is collected and stored in the thyroid gland. Iodine is trapped in the thyroid follicular cells by the active transport of iodide ions from the blood. As a result of this active transport of iodide ions from the bloodstream, the thyroid gland contains the majority of the body's iodine supply.

The precursor of the thyroid hormones is a large glycoprotein called **thyroglobulin** (TGB). Thyroglobulin is steadily synthesized by the follicular cells and released into the follicle's lumen, forming the thyroid colloid. Each molecule of thyroglobulin contains many copies or the amino acid **tyrosine**, which combine with iodine to form T3 and T4. In order to form T3 and T4 from thyroglobulin, iodine enters the colloid and combines with tyrosine. Before they can diffuse into the colloid, iodide ions must first be **oxidized** to form an iodine molecule (I2). Iodine is oxidized by the enzyme **peroxidase**. Within the lumen of the follicle, the iodine binds to one of the tyrosine residues of thyroglobulin, forming either **monoiodotyrosine** (T1, with one iodine bound), or **diiodotyrosine** (T2, with two iodines). Still within the colloid, the T1 and T2 residues combine forming T4 and T3.

After formation of T3 and T4, each thyroglobulin molecule contains one to five T4 (thyroxine) molecules, and one, or no, T3's (triiodothyronine). The follicular cells reabsorb the modified thyroglobulin by pinocytosis, engulfing some colloid into a vesicle. The vesicle is transported within the cell and joins with a lysosome containing digestive enzymes, where T3 and T4 molecules are cleaved from thyroglobulin. The thyroid hormones are released into the blood, where they bind to **thyroid-binding globulin** (TBG) for transport. Although more T4 is synthesized, T3 is the more active of the two hormones. Most of the T3 that is active in the body is not actually synthesized in the thyroid gland, but is produced in the peripheral tissues by the **deiodination** (removal of an iodine) of T4.

Quick Check Questions

1. All of the following are steps in the synthesis of thyroid hormone, EXCEPT:
   A. synthesis of thyroglobulin (TBG) in the thyroid follicles
   B. oxidation of iodine by peroxidase
   C. coupling of T1 and T2 to form T3 and T4
   D. all are true steps

2. The thyroid gland is unique among the endocrine glands in that it stores large amounts of thyroid hormones in an inactive form within the lumen of the follicles, which are filled with a fluid called _______.

12.3.3 Function of Thyroid Hormone Levels

5 minutes

There are two major functions of thyroid hormones. The first is regulation of the basal metabolic rate by stimulating ATP production. When ATP is produced the body has more available energy. Heat is generated as a by-product of ATP production. Thus, the thyroid hormones have a heat-producing **(calorigenic)** effect which acts to raise body temperature.

The second major function of thyroid hormones is regulation of normal growth and development, together with such hormones as GH and insulin. Thyroid hormones are especially important in the growth of nervous tissues. Thyroid hormones carry out their functions by influencing cellular metabolism. In general, they increase **lipolysis** (breakdown of fats) and **glycolysis** (breakdown of carbohydrates), while stimulating the synthesis of proteins.

Quick Check Questions

1. Thyroid hormones have all of the following effects, EXCEPT:
   A. increasing the basal metabolic rate
   B. increasing synthesis of ATP
   C. promoting normal growth
   D. promoting formation of adipose tissue

2. There are two major functions of thyroid hormones. The first is regulating the basal _________ rate. The second major function is regulation of normal growth and development.

12.3.4 Thyroid Hormone Regulation

5 minutes

Thyroid hormone release is regulated by negative feedback. A low blood level of T3 leads to release of thyroid-releasing hormone (TRH) from the hypothalamus. This causes release of thyroid-stimulating hormone (TSH) from the anterior pituitary, which stimulates production and release of T3 and T4. Other factors that stimulate TRH release include cold temperature, hypoglycemia, and pregnancy. TRH is inhibited by high levels of T3. TSH increases thyroid hormone levels by stimulating thyroid activity, including: 1) an increase in iodide trapping, 2) an increase in thyroid hormone secretion, and 3) growth and activation of follicular cells. (Follicular cells are flat squamous cells while at rest, but thicken to cuboidal cells when activated).

Quick Check Questions

1. Which of the following inhibits the release of thyroid hormones?
   A. pregnancy
   B. elevated T3
   C. hypoglycemia
   D. cold

2. Thyroid hormone production is regulated by negative feedback. *True or False*

12.3.5 Abnormal Thyroid Hormone Levels

10 minutes

One way to remember the numerous effects of thyroid hormones is to consider what happens when a person has abnormal thyroid hormone levels. **Hypothyroidism** (diminished production of thyroid hormones) in a fetus or young child causes **cretinism**. Entirely preventable, cretinism is characterized by dwarfism and severe mental retardation.

Measuring and supplementing **neonatal** thyroxine and TSH levels is now required in many areas. Hypothyroidism in the adult does not alter growth because brain and bone development is finished. However, adult hypothyroidism is characterized by **lethargy**, weight gain with **facial edema** (or swelling), and a lowered basal metabolic rate with increased sensitivity to cold.

On the other hand, **hyperthyroidism** (an abnormally high level of thyroid hormones), causes an increase in the basal metabolic rate accompanied by elevated body temperature, increased sweating, and intractable weight loss. It also causes protuberant eyes, called **exopthalmos**, and a fine **tremor** or shaking of the body. Hyperthyroidism is often identified by a goiter (an enlarged thyroid gland).

Calcitonin, is the other hormone produced by the thyroid gland. It is synthesized in the parafollicular cells. Calcitonin lowers serum calcium levels by inhibiting bone **osteoclasts** (which cause bone breakdown and reabsorption) and stimulating **osteoblasts** (cells which cause bone growth). Although its actions are well understood, the importance of calcitonin is not. Individuals who produce no calcitonin (for instance, after thyroid removal) have no bone or serum calcium level problems. The effects of calcitonin are opposite to those of parathyroid hormone, discussed in the next tutorial.

Quick Check Questions

1. Hyperthyroidism is the major cause of severe mental retardation in adults. *True or False*

2. Elevated body temperature may be a sign of hyperthyroidism. *True or False*

3. A ______ is an enlarged thyroid gland, which may be a sign of hyperthyroidism.

12.3.6 The Parathyroid Glands

10 minutes

The **parathyroid glands** are four pea-sized balls of tissue found on the posterior aspect of the thyroid gland. There are two parathyroid glands on each side, one superior and one inferior. They have one known function, the production of **parathyroid hormone** (PTH). It is the **chief cells** of the parathyroid glands that manufacture parathyroid hormone.

Parathyroid Hormone (PTH)

Parathyroid hormone (PTH) is the main regulator of calcium homeostasis. PTH increases serum calcium by acting upon three areas: 1) the bones, 2) the kidneys, and 3) the gastrointestinal tract. In the bones, PTH stimulates bone reabsorption (or breakdown) by increasing the number and activity of osteoclasts. Since bone is composed of calcium phosphate crystals, this results in increased serum calcium and increased serum phosphate levels.

In the kidneys, PTH has three effects: 1) PTH causes a decrease in calcium and magnesium excretion (that is, less calcium is excreted in the urine and more stays in the blood). 2) PTH promotes an increase in phosphate excretion. Since phosphate is released from the bones along with calcium, increased excretion allows serum phosphate levels to remain normal. 3) PTH promotes activation of vitamin D. The absorption of calcium from food depends on active vitamin D. Vitamin D activation occurs in the kidney. In the intestines, parathyroid hormone causes a direct increase in calcium absorption.

Regulation of parathyroid hormone depends solely on the serum calcium level, which is sensed in the parathyroids. When calcium is high, PTH levels decrease. Conversely, when calcium is low, PTH levels increase.

Quick Check Questions

1. A person who does not produce calcitonin might be expected to have _________ levels of calcium in her blood. But, surprisingly, the levels are usually normal.

2. High serum calcium causes an increase in levels of parathyroid hormone. *True or False*

12.4.1 The Adrenal Gland

7 minutes

The two adrenal glands are located superior to the kidneys (ad = near, renal = kidney). As with the pituitary, the adrenal glands have two distinct structural and functional regions. Each highly vascularized gland contains an adrenal cortex (outer layer) and an adrenal medulla (inside). The adrenal cortex produces steroid hormones, all of which are derived from the cholesterol molecule. Unlike peptide hormones, steroids diffuse through the plasma membrane of their target cells, and bind to receptors in the cytoplasm. Steroids are carried to the nucleus, where they exert their actions directly on the target cell's DNA causing a hormone-specific RNA synthesis.

The adrenal cortex is absolutely vital for life. Without the steroid hormones it produces, a person would die within a week. The **mineralocorticoids** and **glucocorticoids**, play key roles in fluid and electrolyte balance and in metabolism, respectively. Regulation of the glucocorticoid hormones is by ACTH from the pituitary.

The Adrenal Medulla

The adrenal medulla (the inner part of the adrenal gland) is derived from the same embryonic tissue as are the cells of the sympathetic division of the ANS, to which it is closely related. The adrenal medulla produces the catecholamines: epinephrine and norepinephrine. These hormones effect many areas of the body. They also act as important **neurotransmitters**. Their levels are regulated by impulses from the sympathetic division of the ANS.

Quick Check Questions

1. Hormones of both the adrenal medulla and the adrenal cortex are steroids which act on the DNA of the cell. *True or False*

2. All of the following statements are true, EXCEPT:
   A. the adrenal cortex releases mineralocorticoids
   B. the adrenal cortex releases catecholamines
   C. the adrenal medulla is closely related to the CNS
   D. all hormones produced by the adrenal cortex are steroids

12.4.2 The Adrenal Cortex

10 minutes

The adrenal cortex is divided histologically and functionally into three layers. The outermost layer, underneath the fibrous connective tissue capsule, is the **zona glomerulosa**. This is where glucocorticoids are produced. Underneath this, is the middle layer called the **zona fasciculata**, where mineralocorticoids are made. The **zona reticularis** is the innermost layer, which produces only minute quantities of sex steroids.

Glucocorticoids

Three major glucocorticoids are **cortisol**, **cortisone**, and **corticosterone**. Cortisol is the most important in humans. The metabolic effects of the glucocorticoids provide for adaptation of the body to a stressful situation.

Glucocorticoids cause the body to reduce its protein supplies, growth, and inflammatory and immune system responses. Inhibiting functions, which use a lot of energy ensures the availability of energy reserves needed for the body to react to stressors. In the presence of cortisol, proteins are broken down into their component amino acids. In the liver, the amino acids are used to synthesize other proteins, or are further broken down to produce glucose via **gluconeogenesis**. Cortisol also causes fats to undergo **lipolysis** (breakdown), with the energy used to manufacture extra ATP.

Cortisol secretion results in an increase in serum glucose levels allowing more ATP to be synthesized. The production of glucose is increased by liver gluconeogenesis, as is the storage of glucose in the liver in the form of **glycogen.** Cortisol also causes a moderate decrease in glucose use by cells all over the body.

Since both cortisol and growth hormone have significant effects on metabolism, a comparison of the two is appropriate. GH promotes protein synthesis, while cortisol promotes protein breakdown. However, both hormones promote fat breakdown and increased serum glucose levels.

It is interesting to note that the serum levels of cortisol fluctuate during the course of the day. It is at its highest levels early in the morning, and its lowest levels in the evening. In other words, cortisol, like several other hormones, has a **circadian rhythm**. Cortisol levels also increase with physical, emotional, or mental stress. Due to its structural similarity to the mineralocorticoids, cortisol can also cause blood pressure to increase.

Clinical Note:
The immune and anti-inflammatory effects of cortisol are clinically very important. Cortisol can decrease the activity of **lymphocytes,** making a person more susceptible to infections. **Exogenous** cortisol, or drugs similar to cortisol help to protect a person against potentially harmful effects of their own immune system such as **autoimmune diseases** or the chemical rejection of transplanted organs. Glucocorticoids prevent inflammation by inhibiting the synthesis of the chemical **prostaglandin alpha 2**, which is crucial for recruiting white blood cells to an area of tissue injury.

Quick Check Questions

1. All of the following are effects of cortisol, EXCEPT:
   A. breakdown of proteins
   B. suppression of inflammation
   C. increased blood glucose levels
   D. lowering of blood pressure

2. Levels of cortisol are lowest in the morning. *True or False*

12.4.3 Regulation of Hormones

6 minutes

The **hypothalamus-pituitary adrenal-axis** refers to the interaction of these three glands in the production of glucocorticoids. In response to low cortisol levels, stress, or injury, the hypothalamus secretes **corticotropin-releasing hormone** (CRH). When it reaches the anterior pituitary (after travelling through the **hypophyseal portal system**), CRH causes release of ACTH. In turn, ACTH stimulates cortisol production in the adrenal cortex.

The mineralocorticoids are produced in the middle layer of the adrenal cortex, the zona fasciculata. The most important of these is **aldosterone**. The job of aldosterone is to help retain sodium. Sodium is the most abundant electrolyte in the body. If its blood and tissue levels become too low (**hyponatremia**), seizures, coma, and death may result. Aldosterone works on the proximal tubules of the kidney nephrons, causing an increase in sodium, chloride, and bicarbonate ion reabsorption. Aldosterone also causes increased excretion of potassium and hydrogen ions.

Several interacting mechanisms control the release of aldosterone. The first is the **renin-angiotensin system**. A fall in blood pressure causes the kidney to produce the enzyme **renin**. Renin helps catalyze the conversion of the protein **angiotensin** into its active hormone form, **angiotensin II**. Angiotensin II then stimulates production and release of aldosterone from the adrenal cortex. Another mechanism for the control of aldosterone involves potassium. Potassium excretion is increased by aldosterone so blood potassium is high when aldosterone levels are low. Hence, a high potassium level is a direct signal to the adrenal gland to increase aldosterone production.

Quick Check Questions

1. Addison's disease is a condition in which there is a deficiency of all the hormones produced in the adrenal cortex. Which of the following symptoms, would NOT be associated with Addison's disease?
   A. hypertension (high blood pressure)
   B. increased inflammatory response
   C. hypoglycemia (low blood pressure)
   D. hyperkalemia (excessive amounts of potassium in the blood)

2. All of the following are true, EXCEPT:
   A. aldosterone and ADH both affect sodium and water balance
   B. aldosterone causes only calcium retention
   C. aldosterone is produced in the zona fasciculatis of the adrenal cortex
   D. aldosterone secretion is stimulated by the release of renin from the kidney

12.4.4 The Adrenal Medulla

5 minutes

The **chromaffin cells** of the adrenal medulla produce and secrete epinephrine and norepinephrine. The release of these hormones is directly stimulated by the preganglionic neurons of the sympathetic division of the ANS. Thus, the chromaffin cells themselves are functionally equivalent to postganglionic neurons.

The release of epinephrine and norepinephrine is an integral component of the body's **fight or flight** response. This response readies a person to deal with a stressful or physically taxing environmental situation. It causes an increased heart rate, stronger heart contractions, increased blood pressure, dilation of blood vessels to the skeletal muscles and lungs, and constriction of blood vessels feeding the skin and viscera.

Epinephrine and norepinephrine trigger the breakdown of carbohydrates and fats for energy. They cause the release of glucagon, and a decrease in insulin levels. All of this leads to increased serum glucose levels. Since epinephrine secretion is stimulated by nervous rather than endocrine mechanisms, it is released very quickly in response to a demanding stimulus. (Endocrine signals work more slowly because of the time required for hormones to travel through the circulatory system). Exogenous epinephrine is used as a quick antidote in some medical emergencies.

Quick Check Questions

1. All of the following are physiological effects of epinephrine, EXCEPT:
   A. increased heart rate
   B. increased blood pressure
   C. increased serum glucose levels
   D. increased insulin levels

2. The **chromaffin cells** of the adrenal medulla produce and secrete epinephrine and norepinephrine. *True or False*

12.5.1 The Pancreas

7 minutes

The **pancreas** has both exocrine and endocrine functions. Its exocrine functions are discussed in the Digestive System chapter. Here, we examine the pancreas as an endocrine organ. The pancreas produces two hormones involved in blood glucose regulation: insulin and glucagon. It also produces a hormone called **somatostatin,** which inhibits GH secretion. Within the glandular exocrine tissue of the pancreas are scattered groups of endocrine cells. These clumps, called **islets of Langerhans,** aggregate around the capillaries. The islets contain three cell types: 1) **alpha-cells** which secrete glucagon, 2) **beta-cells** which secrete insulin, and 3) **delta-cells** which secrete somatostatin.

Glucagon

Glucagon increases the blood glucose level by increasing production of glucose in the liver (via gluconeogenesis, or **glycogenolysis**). Glucagon also causes the release of glucose from the liver into the blood. The pancreas is stimulated to release glucagon by low blood glucose, high serum amino acids, and increased SNS activity. Glucagon release is inhibited by somatostatin.

Quick Check Questions

1. The following are true, EXCEPT:
   A. alpha cells of the pancreas produce glucagon
   B. beta cells of the pancreas secrete insulin
   C. delta cells of the pancreas secrete somatostatin
   D. the pancreas is solely an endocrine gland

2. Glucagon stimulates production of glucose in the brain. *True or False*

3. Levels of glucagon decrease in the presence of somatostatin. *True or False*

12.5.2 Insulin

5 minutes

In contrast to glucagon, insulin decreases elevated blood glucose levels, for example, after a high carbohydrate meal. Insulin also acts to increase the synthesis of fats, proteins, and glycogen in the liver and muscle tissue. Since it promotes synthetic reactions, insulin is an **anabolic** hormone.

In the liver, insulin causes increased levels of glycogen through glucose conversion. It stops the production of glucose from amino acids and carbohydrates. Further, it increases **triglyceride** formation. In skeletal muscle, insulin increases protein synthesis, increases glucose transport into cells, and increases glycogen synthesis. In adipose tissue, insulin increases the storage of fatty acids and triglycerides as fats.

Insulin release depends primarily upon levels of blood glucose. High blood glucose levels stimulate the pancreas to produce insulin, while a low level (hypoglycemia) stimulates glucagon release. Another influence on insulin production is a high level of some amino acids, which signals that protein building blocks are available for use by the cells. In addition, GH, thyroxine, and cortisol all promote insulin secretion indirectly because they increase glucose levels. Stimulation of the parasympathetic division of the ANS also promotes insulin secretion.

Quick Check Questions

1. One way insulin lowers serum glucose is by increasing glucose transport into the liver and brain. *True or False*

2. Insulin secretion from the pancreas is stimulated by all of the following, EXCEPT:
   A. high blood glucose levels
   B. high thyroid hormone levels
   C. high blood cortisol levels
   D. high blood epinephrine levels

12.5.3 The Ovaries and Testes

5 minutes

Many body tissues, in addition to the endocrine glands mentioned in this chapter, are capable of producing hormones which affect other tissues. The effects and regulation of the steroid hormones produced by the ovaries and testes is covered in the *Reproductive System* chapter.

Other Endocrine Organs: The Kidney

Another important hormone is erythropoietin, a peptide produced in the kidney. Erythropoietin's function is to stimulate the production of red blood cells in the bone marrow. When the amount of oxygen reaching the kidneys is decreased signalling a need for more erythrocytes to carry oxygen in the blood, the secretion of erythropoietin is stimulated.

Other Endocrine Organs: The Heart

In response to stretching of the atrial walls of the heart due to high blood pressure or volume, cells in the atria release **atrial naturitic peptice** (ANP). This substance acts upon the kidneys to decrease sodium retention, and thus, to decrease blood volume.

Quick Check Questions

1. Anemia might be caused by a lack of erythropoietin from the _______.
   A. adrenal cortex
   B. parathyroid glands
   C. testes
   D. kidney

2. Erythropoietin's function is to stimulate the production of white blood cells in the bone marrow. *True or False*

Chapter 13
Cardiovascular System: The Blood

13.1.1 The Blood - Overview

7 minutes

The **cardiovascular system** and **lymphatic system** form the two subsystems of the **circulatory system**. The cardiovascular system (the heart, arteries, and veins) pumps blood throughout the body, while the lymphatic system controls fluid balance and provides immunity against diseases (see chapter on *Lymphatic & Immune Systems*). This chapter addresses the blood and its circulation through the body.

Body Fluids

Interstitial fluid or **tissue fluid**, **blood plasma** and **lymph fluid** are the main **extracellular fluids** (ECF) of the body. The body maintains this fluid in physiological balance, a condition known as **homeostasis** (Greek, homeo = similar, stasis = standing still). The branch of science concerned with the study of the blood is called **hematology** (Greek, hema = blood, ology = study of). Tissue fluid is derived from plasma that passes out of **capillary** walls. Some of this fluid returns directly to the capillaries, while the rest is picked up by lymphatic vessels. While in the tissue, this fluid is called interstitial fluid or **intercellular fluid**.

Quick Check Questions

1. Interstitial fluid is kept in physiological balance through a condition known as homeo______.

2. The branch of science concerned with the study of the blood is called __________.

3. Blood plasma and lymph fluid are called interstitial fluids. *True or False*

4. The cardiovascular system and lymphatic system comprise the two sub-systems of the:
   A. systemic circulation
   B. circulatory system
   C. pulmonary circulation

13.2.1 The Function of the Blood

8 minutes

Blood performs three main functions in the body: 1) transportation of oxygen, carbon dioxide, nutrients, waste products, heat, and hormones, 2) regulation of pH level, body temperature, and water content of cells, and 3) protection in the form of clotting mechanisms and immune system components such as **antibodies**, **interferon**, and **complement**.

The blood transports: 1) nutrients from the gastrointestinal tract to all areas of the body, 2) oxygen from the lungs to all cells of the body, 3) carbon dioxide from cell tissues to the lungs, 4) waste products from cell tissues to the excretory organs, and 5) hormones from the **endocrine glands** to the body tissues.

The blood helps maintain body temperature and interstitial fluid balance. The blood also regulates **pH**, a measure of the acidity of the blood (a value of about 7.4 is normal) and **osmotic pressure** (the pressure created by the solute concentration of fluids, which regulates the flow of water across membranes). The blood's **clotting system** protects the body against blood loss, and special white blood cells and plasma proteins protect the body from foreign pathogens.

Characteristics of the Blood

The temperature of blood is 38 degrees Celsius (or 100.4 degrees Fahrenheit), which is higher than normal body temperature, of 37 C (98.6 F). Blood has a slightly alkaline **pH** of about 7.4 and accounts for about 8% of total body weight. **Blood volume** in adult males is about 5 to 6 liters and about 4 to 5 liters in adult females.

Quick Check Questions

1. Blood performs three main functions in the body:
   A. transportation, regulation, and circulation
   B. transportation, protection, and detection
   C. transportation, regulation, and protection

2. The blood carries carbon dioxide from cell tissues to:
   A. the gastrointestinal system
   B. the lungs
   C. lymph vessels

3. The blood's clotting system protects the body against blood ____ after injury.

4. The temperature of the blood is:
   A. 36 degrees Celsius
   B. 37 degrees Celsius
   C. 38 degrees Celsius
   D. 39 degrees Celsius

13.2.2 The Composition of Blood

8 minutes

The blood consists of three formed elements which are all suspended in a yellowish fluid called plasma. They are: 1) **erythrocytes** or red blood cells (RBCs), 2) **leukocytes** or white blood cells (WBCs), and 3) specialized cell fragments called **thrombocytes** or **platelets**.

Packed cell volume (PCV) or **hematocrit** describes the percent of RBCs in whole blood. In a normal sample of whole blood, plasma accounts for 55 percent of the volume, consisting of about 90 percent water and 10 percent protein and other solutes. PCV accounts for about 45 percent of the volume of whole blood in adult males and (42 percent in adult females). A reduced PCV is called **anemia**, and elevated PCV is called **polycythemia.** Leukocytes and platelets make up less than 1 percent of whole blood volume.

Quick Check Questions

1. The blood consists of three components which are all suspended in a yellowish fluid called plasma. They are:
   A. erythrocytes, leukocytes, and neutrophils
   B. erythrocytes, leukocytes, and thrombocytes
   C. erythrocytes, leukocytes, and dandrocytes

2. Packed cell volume (PCV) or __________ describes the percent of RBCs in whole blood.

3. In a sample of normal whole blood, plasma accounts for ___ of the volume.
   A. 45%
   B. 55%
   C. 65%
   D. 90%

4. Reduced PCV is called anemia and elevated PCV is called polycythemia.
   True or False

13.2.3 The Function of Blood Plasma

7 minutes

Blood plasma consists of about 90 percent water, 7 percent protein, and 3 percent dissolved salts, oxygen, gases, glucose, nutrients, metabolic wastes, and hormones. There are three main types of plasma proteins: 1) **albumin**, 2) **globulin**, and 3) **fibrinogen**. The proteins perform homeostatic functions to maintain normal blood volume, **viscosity**, and osmotic pressure. Some of the plasma proteins, **gamma globulins**, serve as antibodies that provide immunity against diseases.

Fibrinogens and an albumin named **prothrombin** assist in the blood clotting process. Gamma globulins are produced by lymph tissue, and the other plasma proteins are produced by the liver. As blood moves through the body's capillaries, some plasma proteins pass through the capillary walls into tissues. Other, larger protein molecules remain in the capillaries and exert an osmotic force that draws tissue fluid back into the blood stream. Hence, plasma proteins play an important role in controlling normal blood circulation and interstitial fluid balance.

Quick Check Questions

1. There are three groups of plasma proteins: albumins, globulins, and ____________.

2. Gamma globulins serve as antibodies that provide immunity against diseases. *True or False*

3. Plasma proteins play an important role in controlling:
   A. normal blood circulation
   B. blood clotting
   C. body temperature

13.3.1 The Formation of Blood Cells

10 minutes

All blood cells are formed by a process called **hemopoiesis**, also called **hematopoiesis**. **Stem cells** or **pluripotent hematopoietic cells**, also named **hemocytoblasts**, reside in the **red bone marrow** of selected bones. Stem cells are produced from **mesenchyme**, an embryonic connective tissue from which all connective tissues arise. Stem cells develop into five different cell types, each of which gives rise to different mature blood cells.

The illustration (in software) to the right shows the various transformations of the hemocytoblast into red blood cells, white blood cells and platelets. Explore the balloons on the illustration, which name each of the blood cell types as they develop through the transformations.

Quick Check Questions

1. All blood cells are formed by a process called:
   A. homeostasis
   B. hemostasis
   C. hemopoiesis

2. _____ cells or hemocytoblasts are produced from mesenchyme.

13.3.2 The Function of Erythrocytes

10 minutes

An adult body contains about 30 trillion red blood cells (RBCs). Females have slightly fewer RBCs than males. Each RBC is 7 to 8 micrometers in diameter (1500 RBCs side by side would only extend less than one-half inch). Unlike typical body cells, RBCs have no nucleus and contain no ribosomes, mitochondria, or other organelles. Mature RBCs are tiny, flexible, **biconcave** (thinner in the center than around the edge) discs.

Each RBC cell contains about 250 **hemoglobin** molecules. A hemoglobin molecule includes four protein chains or **globin**, two called alpha and two called beta. Each globin chain is bound to a non-protein pigment molecule called **heme** or **heme groups**. The heme groups contain one atom of iron that can bind to an oxygen molecule to form **oxyhemoglobin**. This is a reversible reaction. Oxyhemoglobin is transported through the blood and interstitial fluid where oxygen is ultimately released into body tissue cells.

Hemoglobin picks up about 23 percent of the body's waste carbon dioxide created by metabolic processes. CO2 from the tissues enters the blood capillaries and is transported by the RBCs to the lungs, where it is released from the cells and exhaled. In the respiratory system, carbon dioxide combines reversibly with globin chains, rather than heme groups, to form **carbaminohemoglobin.**

Oxygenated hemoglobin, which gives RBCs their red color, accounts for about 1/3 of the cell's volume. The biconcave shape of an RBC gives it a large surface compared to its volume. The sides of erythrocytes can move in and out permitting the cell to change shape so that it can move through narrow capillary vessels.

RBCs transport both oxygen and carbon dioxide in the blood stream. When blood passes through the lungs, oxygen diffuses into the RBCs and combines (reversibly) with hemoglobin to form oxyhemoglobin. As the blood passes through other body tissues that are low in oxygen, oxygen diffuses from the RBCs into the tissue cells. Oxyhemoglobin gives RBCs their red pigment. Hemoglobin without oxygen is bluish in color, hence, the color of veins and venules.

Quick Check Questions

1. Erythrocytes (RBCs) have no _______ and contain no ribosomes, mitochondria, or other organelles.

2. The formation of oxyhemoglobin is a reversible reaction. *True or False*

3. Each hemoglobin molecule includes ____ protein chains.
   A. two
   B. three
   C. four
   D. five

4. The _________ shape of RBCs gives it a large surface compared to its volume.

5. Oxyhemoglobin gives erythrocytes (RBCs) their red pigment. *True or False*

13.3.3 The Formation of Erythrocytes

15 minutes

The process of RBC formation is called **erythropoiesis**. In adults, erythrocytes mature in red bone marrow from stem cells called hemocytoblasts. The red marrow is only found in certain bones (namely, the vertebrae, sternum, skull, and ribs). In children, red bone marrow, and RBC production exists in most of the bones.

New erythrocytes are manufactured at a rate of about 2.5 million cells per second. In the process of erythropoiesis, the liver and spleen continuously recycle erythrocytes. The iron molecules in the RBCs are salvaged and returned to the red bone marrow where they are used again to make new erythrocytes. Since RBCs have no nucleus or organelles, they cannot manufacture protein, so when their proteins break down, the cells degenerate and are recycled. Others rupture as they squeeze through small capillary vessels.

Quick Check Questions

1. The process of erythrocyte formation is called _______poiesis.

2. Erythrocytes mature in _______ marrow from stem cells called hemocytoblasts.
   A. brain
   B. red bone
   C. vertebrae

13.4.1 The Function of Leukocytes

8 minutes

There are two categories of leukocytes: 1) **granulocytes**, and 2) **agranulocytes**. Both of these leukocytes have a nucleus, and they contain no hemoglobin.

Granulocytes

All granulocytes have multilobed nuclei, so they are referred to as **polymorphonuclear**. Granulocytes also have granules containing enzymes in their cytoplasm. There are three types of granulocytes: 1) neutrophils, 2) eosinophils, and 3) basophils.

Agranulocytes

Agranulocytes have a large spherical, single-lobed nuclei (referred to as **mononuclear**) surrounded by a small amount of cytoplasm. There are two types of agranulocytes: 1) lymphocytes, and 2) monocytes. Leukocytes are found primarily in blood vessels, but they also have the ability to squeeze through the capillary walls and pass into connective and epithelial tissues. The movement of leukocytes through the capillary wall is referred to as **diapedesis** or **emigration**. The proper balance of leukocytes in the blood is critical to the body's homeostasis. An increase in leukocytes in the total blood volume is called **leukocytosis** and a decrease is called **leukopenia**.

Quick Check Questions

1. There are two categories of erythrocytes: granulocytes and agranulocytes. *True or False*

2. All granulocytes have _____lobed nuclei.

3. There are three types of granulocytes: neutrophils, eosinophils, and __________.
   A. basophils
   B. monophils
   C. lymphophils

4. Agranulocytes have a large spherical, single-lobed nuclei. They are ____nuclear.

5. There are two types of agranulocytes:
   A. monocytes and thrombocytes
   B. lymphocytes and thrombocytes
   C. lymphocytes and monocytes

6. The movement of leukocytes through the capillary wall is called ___pedesis or emigration.

13.4.2 Granulocytes

8 minutes

Neutrophils

In a normal blood sample, neutrophils (about 10 to 12 micrometers in diameter) account for 65 percent of the WBC count. The smallish granules in neutrophils, which are lysosomes containing powerful enzymes, serve to digest or **phagocytize** bacteria and other damaged cells. Neutrophils are attracted to problem cells by a process called **chemotaxis**, triggered by the release of chemicals from the damaged or inflamed cells. Of all leukocytes, neutrophils respond most quickly to troubled areas.

Eosinophils

Eosinophils account for about 2 to 5 percent of WBCs. Eosinophils (which are 10 to 12 micrometers in diameter) are numerous in the digestive and respiratory tracts. The primary function of eosinophils involves protection against parasitic worms and allergic reactions. A high eosinophil count usually means the body is undergoing an allergic or parasitic infection.

Basophils

Basophils (which are about 10 to 12 um in diameter) are the least numerous leukocytes, comprising only about 1 percent of the total leukocyte count. The granules of basophil cytoplasm can release **heparin**, **histamine**, and **serotonin** (inflammatory and anticoagulant chemicals). Basophils also serve to ameliorate allergic reactions and inflammations, and are also capable of diapedesis. Once they diapedize, they are called **mast cells.**

Quick Check Questions

1. In a normal blood sample neutrophils account for ___ of the WBC count.
   A. 45%
   B. 55%
   C. 65%
   D. 75%

2. Neutrophils are attracted to problem cells by a process called chemo_____.

3. Eosinophils are numerous in the digestive and ________ tracts where their primary functions involve protection against parasitic worms and allergic reactions.
   A. endocrine
   B. respiratory
   C. circulatory

4. Basophilic granules of basophil cytoplasm can release heparin, histamine, and serotonin, which are inflammatory and anticoagulant chemicals.
   True or False

13.4.3 Agranulocytes

6 minutes

Lymphocytes

Lymphocytes are the smallest of WBCs (6 to 8 um in diameter). They have a large spherical nucleus and a little cytoplasm. After neutrophils, lymphocytes are the most numerous leukocytes, accounting for about 25 percent of all WBCs. There are two types of lymphocytes which function as combatants in immune responses: 1) **T cells** which attack infected or cancerous cells and 2) **B cells,** which produce antibodies against specific **antigens.**

Monocytes

Monocytes are the largest of leukocytes (14 to 19 um in diameter) and have a kidney bean-shaped nucleus surrounded by a large amount of cytoplasm. Monocytes are large scavenger cells that migrate into body tissues where they enlarge and develop into fixed or wandering **macrophages**. (Fixed macrophages remain in one specific tissue such as spleen or liver, whereas wandering macrophages roam the tissues and collect at areas of infection or inflammation.)

Quick Check Questions

1. There are two types of lymphocytes which function as combatants in immune responses:
   A. T cells and C cells
   B. B cells and C cells
   C. T cells and B cells

2. Lymphocytes are the largest of WBCs. *True or False*

3. Monocytes are large scavenger cells that migrate into body tissues and enlarge into _____ or wandering macrophages.

13.4.4 The Formation of Leukocytes

6 minutes

The **hemocytoblast** or stem cell is the precursor of leukocytes, including the: 1) neutrophils, 2) eosinophils, 3) basophils, and 4) some lymphocytes and monocytes. Most neutrophils, eosinophils, and basophils originate in the red bone marrow's **myeloid tissue**, which is located in the spongy (cancellous) bone.

Most lymphocytes and monocytes originate from hemocytoblasts in the **lymphoid tissue** of the lymph nodes, spleen, and liver. Once generated, lymphocytes are then carried by the bloodstream to the myeloid tissue. Myeloid and lymphatic tissue are the two **hematopoietic** (blood cell generating) tissues of the body.

Quick Check Questions

1. All leukocytes originate in red bone marrow called _______ tissue.

2. Myeloid and lymphatic tissue are the two hemopoietic (blood cell generating) tissues of the body. *True or False*

13.5.1 Thrombocytes (Platelets)

6 minutes

Thrombocytes are irregular disc-shaped cells about 2 to 4 um in diameter. Hemocytoblast stem cells differentiate into **megakaryoblasts** which transform into **metamegakaryocytes**, large cells that shed fragments of cytoplasm. Each cytoplasmic fragment forms a thrombocyte that is enclosed by a piece of cell membrane. Thrombocytes contain no nuclei, but have several granules.

Platelets break off of the metamegakaryocytes and enter the blood stream where they help repair damaged blood vessels. Their granules contain chemicals that promote **blood clotting**, or **coagulation**, when released. Platelets live only for a few days. Dead platelets are consumed in the liver and spleen by fixed macrophages.

Quick Check Questions

1. Hemocytoblasts differentiate into megakaryoblasts which then transform into _____________ .
   A. metamegakaryocytes
   B. metathrombocytes
   C. metamegakaryoblasts

2. Thrombocytes break off from metamegakaryocytes and enter the blood stream. Their granules have chemicals that promote blood ________ .

13.5.2 The Function of Thrombocytes

10 minutes

Thrombocytes are an important element in the process of **hemostasis** (stoppage of bleeding). Three actions of the body prevent blood loss: 1) **vascular spasm**, 2) **platelet plug formation**, and 3) blood clotting.

Vascular spasm occurs immediately when arteries or arterioles are damaged, causing the smooth muscle of their walls to contract. Vascular spasm results from reflexes stimulated by pain receptors. Seconds after a blood vessel is injured, platelets band together in the process of **platelet adhesion** forming a hemostatic platelet plug over the damaged area to stop blood flow.

Clotting or coagulation refers to blood outside the body that thickens and forms a gel. The gel is called a **clot** or **thrombus** and consists of platelets, other blood cells and strands of protein fibers called **fibrin**. There are two basic stages of clotting. In the first, **prothrombin** (a plasma protein) is converted into the plasma enzyme **thrombin**. Next, **fibrinogen** (a soluble plasma protein) is converted into threads of insoluble protein that combines with thrombin to form fibrin.

A blood clot dissolves by a process called **fibrinolysis**, in which the body or tissues activate a substance called **plasminogen**. Plasminogen produces an enzyme called **plasmin**, also called **fibrinolysin**. Plasmin dissolves the clot by digesting fibrin threads and also serves to inactivate the production of fibrinogen and prothrombin.

Quick Check Questions

1. Thrombocytes are an important element in the process of ________ (stoppage of bleeding).
   A. hemostasis
   B. homeostasis
   C. hemopoiesis

2. ________ spasm occurs immediately when arteries or arterioles are damaged, causing the smooth muscle of their walls to contract.

3. Seconds after a vessel is injured, platelets band together and form an hemostatic ________ plug over the damaged area to stop blood flow.

4. A blood clot (or thrombus) consists of protein fibers called fibrin. *True or False*

5. _______ dissolves a blood clot by digesting fibrin threads, and by inactivating the production of fibrinogen and prothrombin.
   A. Thrombus
   B. Plasma
   C. Plasmin

13.6.1 Blood Types and Groups

17 minutes

The term **blood type** refers to the antigens or **agglutinogens** that are found on the surface of an individual's erythrocytes. Blood types must be matched for compatibility for procedures such as blood transfusions. The most important types of antigens are A, B, and D (or Rh). The two major blood **group classifications** are **ABO** and **Rh**.

ABO Blood Grouping

All blood falls into one of four **ABO** blood types. Each blood type is named according to the antigens produced by the individual. The four ABO blood types are: **Type A** -- antigen A is found on the erythrocyte surfaces, **Type B** -- antigen B on the erythrocyte, **Type AB** -- both antigen A and B are produced, and **Type O** -- neither antigen A or B is present.

The blood plasma also contains antibodies called **agglutinins** that will react with the A and B antigens if they are mixed together. An agglutinin will only react with a specific agglutinogen. An individual's plasma does not contain antibodies against its own antigens. However, the plasma does contain antibodies against the antigens (A or B), that are not normally present. Type A blood contains anti-B antibodies in its plasma. Type B blood contains anti-A antibodies in its plasma. Type AB blood has neither anti-A or anti-B antibodies in its plasma. Type O blood contains both anti-A and anti-B antibodies in its plasma.

In the ABO system, an individual with type O blood (containing no antigens) is a universal donor, and Type AB blood is the **universal recipients**. Blood plasma can also contain agglutinins other than anti-A and anti-B antibodies. All blood that is to be transfused from a donor to a recipient is **cross-matched** prior to the transfusion. More specifically, the two bloods are mixed and observed for antigen-antibody reactions such as **agglutination** (clumping) or **hemolysis** (bursting of RBCs).

Rh Blood Grouping

The Rh blood classification system is also based on the presence of specific antigens on the surface RBCs. Blood containing antigen D is called **Rh positive**, and without antigen D is called **Rh negative**. Unlike the case for anti-A and anti-B antibodies, Rh negative blood will not develop anti-Rh antibodies unless it is exposed to Rh positive blood. However, once Rh negative blood is exposed to antigen D from Rh positive blood, Rh negative blood plasma will always contain anti-Rh antibodies. So an Rh negative individual will not react to Rh positive blood the first time it is exposed, but any subsequent exposure will cause reaction.

Quick Check Questions

1. The two major blood group classifications are ___ and Rh.

2. The four ABO blood types are:
   A. A, B, O, Rh
   B. A, B, AB, O
   C. A, B, AO, BO

3. Type O has neither antigen A or B on its erythrocytes and is referred to as the universal _____.

4. Plasma does not contain antibodies against its own antigens, but does contain antibodies against antigen A or B if they are not present on its ___________.

5. Type A blood will contain ________ antibodies in its plasma.
   A. anti-B
   B. anti-A
   C. Both anti-A and anti-B

6. In theory, Type O blood is the universal donor and Type AB blood is the universal _________.
7. Blood plasma can contain agglutinins other than anti-A and anti-B antibodies. *True or False*

8. The Rh blood classification system is also based on the presence of ________ on the surface of erythrocytes.

9. Rh negative blood will not develop anti-Rh antibodies to D antigen unless it is _______ to Rh positive blood.

13.7.1 Major Circulatory Routes

8 minutes

There are two main circulatory routes of the blood: the **systemic circulation** and the **pulmonary circulation**. The systemic circulation moves blood through blood vessels from the heart's left **ventricle** to all parts of the body (except the lungs) and returns the blood back to the heart's right **atrium**. The blood travels from the left ventricle through the **ascending aorta** into **arteries** and then into **arterioles** which feed **capillaries**.

The **capillary bed** is the site in the tissues and organs where the two-way exchange of fresh materials and waste materials takes place. (Arteries and arterioles appear as red vessels indicating oxygenated blood, while the blue vessels and venules indicate deoxygenated blood). After the exchange of substances, the blood flows out of each tissue into small **venules** then into larger **veins**, and then into the **inferior** or **superior vena cava** (the two great veins of the body). Finally, the vena cava returns venous blood to the right atrium of the heart.

In the pulmonary circulation, venous blood from the vena cava flows into the right atrium, and then into the right ventricle and through the left and right **pulmonary arteries**. The pulmonary arteries flow into arterioles which feed the capillaries of the lung. In the lung capillaries, there is an exchange of gases: deoxygenated blood is oxygenated and carbon dioxide is released for expiration. The oxygenated blood moves through lung venules into four pulmonary arteries which return the blood to the heart's left atrium. The oxygenated blood then flows into the left ventricle ready to be pumped back through the aorta to the systemic circulation.

Quick Check Questions

1. There are two main circulatory routes of the blood: systemic circulation and the __________ circulation.

2. Systemic circulation moves blood from the heart's ________ through blood vessels to all parts of the body.
   A. left ventricle
   B. right ventricle
   C. left atrium
   D. right atrium

3. Blood flows out of each body tissue from ________, into veins, and then into the inferior or superior vena cava.

13.8.1 Types of Blood Vessels

5 minutes

There are three types of blood vessels: 1) **arteries**, 2) **veins**, and 3) **capillaries**. The vessels that pass blood from the heart to the body's tissues are called arteries. The vessels that pass blood from the tissues back to the heart are called veins. Small arteries are called arterioles and small veins are called venules. The smallest vessels that carry blood through a tissue are the capillaries, which are fed from the arterioles and feed back to the venules. The network of blood capillaries in the tissues is called the capillary bed.

Quick Check Questions

1. There are three types of blood vessels: arteries, veins, and ___________.

2. The vessels that pass blood from the tissues back to the heart are called ________.

   A. arteries
   B. veins
   C. capillaries

3. The blood capillary tissue network is called the blood capillary ___.

13.8.2 The Structure of Blood Vessels

8 minutes

The walls of arteries and veins consist of three layers. The outside layer is called the **tunica adventitia**, or **tunica externa**. It is composed of a strong, fibrous, elastic connective tissue. The tunica adventitia holds blood vessels open and protects them against tearing when the body moves. Tunica adventitia is thicker in the walls of the veins than in the arteries. The **tunica media** is the middle layer of the vessel walls, consisting of smooth muscle tissue and elastic fibers. Contraction of the smooth muscle layer, which is innervated by the autonomic nervous system, changes the blood vessel diameter. The smooth muscle of the tunica media is supplied with blood by capillaries called **vasa vasorum**.

The inner most layer of blood vessel walls is called the **tunica intima** or tunica interna. The tunica intima is made of **endothelium** (simple squamous epithelial tissue of the circulatory system) which is continuous with the endothelium that forms the inner wall of the heart. The tunica intima has a smooth surface in arteries, but in the veins it forms one-way **semilunar valves** that prevent backflow of the blood. This layer is thinner in veins than in arteries.

Capillaries only contain a single thin wall made of endothelium tissue. The endothelium permits the exchange of nutrients, gases, and wastes between the blood plasma and the interstitial fluid of the tissues. These materials are only exchanged through the walls of capillaries. The internal space of blood vessels is called the **lumen**. The lumen of veins has a larger diameter than in arteries. Although capillaries are very small, they have a large lumen in relation to their wall thickness.

Quick Check Questions

1. The outside layer of a blood vessel, called the tunica adventitia, is made of strong _______ connective tissue.

2. The tunica adventitia is thicker in the arteries than in the veins. *True or False*

3. The endothelium in arteries is a smooth surface, whereas in veins it forms the ____lunar valves.

4. Capillaries only contain one thin wall (the ________) which permits the exchange between the blood plasma and the interstitial fluid.
   A. tuncia media
   B. endothelium
   C. myocardium

13.8.3 The Function of Blood Vessels

7 minutes

The capillaries, although the smallest of vessels, are functionally the most important since they transport essential materials to and from the tissue cells. The process of blood flow through the capillary bed is called **microcirculation**. The arterioles play an important role in regulating the blood flow. They are able to constrict and dilate due to the smooth muscle of the tunica media. **Precapillary sphincters**, muscle fibers near the origin of capillaries, control blood flow into the capillaries, and therefore into the tissues. The main function of arteries is the distribution of blood from the heart to the arterioles.

Veins return oxygen-poor blood to the heart from the capillaries. Veins also collect and store blood, acting as reservoirs which pool blood in the chambers formed between the semilunar valves. The heart is responsible for moving (pumping) the blood through this system of arteries, arterioles, capillaries, venules, and veins. The function of the entire circulatory system revolves around providing just the right amount of blood to meet the changing needs of each cell. In this way, the cells are kept supplied with oxygen and nutrients, and their waste materials are removed.

Quick Check Questions

1. The arterioles have an important function to constrict and ______ at pre-capillary sphincters.

2. Veins return oxyhemoglobin blood to the heart from the capillaries. *True or False*

3. The process of blood flow through the capillary bed is called micro___________.

13.9.1 Systemic Arteries of the Body

30 minutes

Systemic arteries are the major vessels that distribute oxygenated blood from the heart to the body's organs. By contrast, pulmonary circulation sends venous (deoxygenated) blood through the lungs before returning it to systemic circulation via the left atrium of the heart. The main arteries arising from the aorta and its branches are listed and illustrated on the following screens (in software).

ARTERY - **Ascending aorta** > SUPPLIES - The heart muscle, via the left and right coronary arteries

ARTERY - **Arch of aorta**, brachiocephalic trunk, right common carotid, and right subclavian branches > SUPPLIES - Upper body

ARTERY - **Common carotid**, left and right, external and internal branches > SUPPLIES - Head and neck

ARTERY - **External carotid**, left and right, occipital and facial branches > SUPPLIES - Throat, parts of the face

ARTERY - **Internal carotid**, left and right > SUPPLIES - Brain, eyes, parts of the face

ARTERY - **Occipital** > SUPPLIES - Posterior aspect of the head

ARTERY - **Facial** > SUPPLIES - Anterior aspect of the head

ARTERY - **Subclavian**, left and right, vertebral and axillary branches > SUPPLIES - Upper extremity, cervical vertebrae

ARTERY - **Axillary**, left and right > SUPPLIES - Shoulder area

ARTERY - **Brachial**, left and right, divides into radial and ulnar branches distally > SUPPLIES - Upper arm

ARTERY - **Radial**, left and right > SUPPLIES - Medial aspect of forearm

ARTERY - **Ulnar**, left and right > SUPPLIES - Lateral aspect of forearm

ARTERY - **Palmar arch**, left and right, superficial and deep branches > SUPPLIES - Palmar area of hand

ARTERY - **Digitalis**, left and right > SUPPLIES - Digits of hand

ARTERY - **Thoracic aorta**, visceral branches and parietal branches > SUPPLIES - Visceral branches: pericardium, bronchi, esophagus; Parietal branches: chest muscles, breasts, diaphragm

ARTERY - **Pulmonary**, left and right > SUPPLIES - Lungs (carries venous blood)

ARTERY - **Abdominal aorta**, celiac, renal, mesenteric branches > SUPPLIES - Abdominal viscera, back, spinal cord, and meninges, divides into left and right iliac branches

ARTERY - **Celiac**, hepatic, splenic, and gastric branches > SUPPLIES - Liver, spleen, and stomach

ARTERY - **Splenic** > SUPPLIES - Spleen

ARTERY - **Superior mesenteric** > SUPPLIES - Small intestine

ARTERY - **Inferior mesenteric** > SUPPLIES - Large intestine

ARTERY - **Renal**, right and left > SUPPLIES - Kidneys

ARTERY - **Common iliac**, right and left, external and internal (hypogastric) branches > SUPPLIES - Internal: pelvic wall and viscera; External: legs via femoral arteries

ARTERY - **Femoral**, left and right, becomes popliteal artery distally > SUPPLIES - Upper leg, genitals, abdominal wall

ARTERY - **Popliteal**, branches into anterior and posterior tibial, peroneal > SUPPLIES - Knee, lower leg

ARTERY - **Anterior tibial**, left and right > SUPPLIES - Anterior portion of lower leg, toes (via arcuate)

ARTERY - **Posterior tibial**, left and right, medial and lateral plantar branches > SUPPLIES - Posterior portion of lower leg, heel, becomes dorsalis pedis distally

ARTERY - **Peroneal**, left and right > SUPPLIES - Medial aspect of lower leg, calcaneal area

ARTERY - **Dorsalis pedis**, left and right > SUPPLIES - Toes, dorsal aspect of foot

Quick Check Questions

1. Systemic arteries distribute deoxygenated blood from the heart to the body's organs. *True or False*

2. The arch of aorta supplies blood to the:
   A. lower body
   B. upper body
   C. both A and B

3. The left and right brachial arteries supply blood to the:
   A. lower arm
   B. upper arm
   C. lower leg
   D. upper leg

4. The facial artery supplies blood to the:
   A. superior aspect of the head
   B. anterior aspect of the head
   C. both A and B
   D. neither A or B

5. The thoracic aorta supplies blood to the:
   A. visceral branches
   B. parietal branches
   C. both A and B
   D. neither A or B

6. The celiac artery supplies blood to the liver, spleen, and stomach. *True or False*

7. The superior mesenteric artery supplies blood to the:
   A. spleen
   B. large intestine
   C. small intestine
   D. liver
   E. all of the above

8. The popliteal artery supplies blood to the:
   A. thigh and lower leg
   B. knee and lower leg
   C. only to the lower leg

9. The left and right anterior tibial arteries supply blood to the lower forearm. *True or False*

13.10.1 Systemic Veins of the Body

30 minutes

The body's venous system returns deoxygenated blood from the various tissues and organs to the heart. Like the arteries, the venous system is also divided into systemic and pulmonary branches. The main veins arising from the vena cava and its branches are listed and illustrated in the following screens (in software).

VEIN - **Coronary sinus**, Anterior and posterior coronary branches > DRAINS - The heart muscle

VEIN - **Superior vena cava** > DRAINS - Upper body via the brachiocephalics

VEIN - **Jugular**, left and right, external and internal branches > DRAINS - Head (via the cerebral sinuses) and neck

VEIN - **External jugular**, left and right > DRAINS - Superficial facial tissues, scalp

VEIN - **Sagittal sinus**, superior and inferior > DRAINS - Cranial cavity

VEIN - **Transverse** (lateral) sinus > DRAINS - Occipital area

VEIN - **Straight sinus** > DRAINS - Central portion of brain

VEIN - **Anterior facial** > DRAINS - Face, frontal aspect of head

VEIN - **Brachiocephalic**, left and right > DRAINS - Head, arms, upper thorax via subclavian and jugular

VEIN - **Subclavian**, left and right > DRAINS - Upper extremities via the brachial, axillary, and basilic

VEIN - **Axillary**, left and right > DRAINS - Upper arm, axilla via the brachial and basilic

VEIN - **Cephalic**, left and right > DRAINS - Lateral aspect of upper extremity

VEIN - **Basilic**, left and right > DRAINS - Palmar arches of the hand via the radial and ulnar veins.

VEIN - **Basilic and median cubital** (basilic), left and right > DRAINS - Upper arm, lower arm, hand

VEIN - **Accessory cephalic**, right and left > DRAINS - Forearm

VEIN - **Right medial antebrachial** > DRAINS - Forearm, wrist

VEIN - **Right cephalic** > DRAINS - Wrist, hand

VEIN - **Right palmar arch** > DRAINS - Hand, fingers

VEIN - **Volar digital**, left and right > DRAINS - Digits of hand

VEIN - **Pulmonary**, left and right > DRAINS - Lungs

VEIN - **Inferior vena cava** > DRAINS - Abdomen and lower extremities via iliacs

VEIN - **Hepatic** > DRAINS - Liver via hepatic portal circulation

VEIN - **Hepatic portal** > DRAINS - Digestive organs

VEIN - **Superior mesenteric** > DRAINS - Small intestine

VEIN - **Inferior mesenteric** > DRAINS - Large intestines

VEIN - **Common iliac**, left and right, external and internal branches > DRAINS - Pelvis and lower extremities via femorals

VEIN - **External iliac**, left and right > DRAINS - Pelvis, buttocks, medial aspect of thigh

VEIN - **Internal (hypogastric) iliac**, left and right > DRAINS - Legs via femorals

VEIN - **Femoral**, left and right > DRAINS - Legs via popliteal and saphenous

VEIN - **Great saphenous**, right and left > DRAINS - Medial aspect of lower extremity

VEIN - **Popliteal**, left and right > DRAINS - Knee, lower leg via peroneal

VEIN - **Posterior tibial**, left and right > DRAINS - Foot via plantar arch

VEIN - **Anterior tibial**, left and right > DRAINS - Foot via dorsalis pedis

VEIN - **Dorsal venous arch**, left and right > DRAINS - Foot

Quick Check Questions

1. The body's venous system returns oxygenated blood from tissues and organs to the heart. *True or False*

2. The coronary sinus drains the:
   A. head muscles
   B. thoracic muscles
   C. heart muscles

3. The sagittal sinuses (superior and inferior) drain the:
   A. spinal cavity
   B. cranial cavity
   C. thoracic cavity

4. The left and right subclavian veins drain the:
   A. upper extremities
   B. lower extremities
   C. both A and B
   D. neither A or B

5. The right medial antebrachial vein drains the:
   A. upper arm and forearm
   B. forearm and hand
   C. forearm and wrist
   D. none of the above

6. The left and right pulmonary veins drain the:
   A. heart
   B. lungs
   C. brain
   D. all of the above

7. The hepatic vein drains the liver via hepatic portal circulation. *True or False*

8. The inferior mesenteric vein drains the small intestine. *True or False*

9. The left and right anterior tibial veins drain the foot via the dorsal venus arch. *True or False*

Chapter 14
The Cardiovascular System: The Heart

14.1.1 The Heart - Overview

10 minutes

The cardiovascular system circulates blood to every part of the body. Together with the lymphatic system, it comprises the circulatory system. The cardiovascular system consists of the heart (the pumping device) and the closed **vessel** system of arteries, veins, and capillaries. Blood carries oxygen from the lungs and nutrients from the digestive system to nourish the cells of the body. Blood also carries metabolic waste products away from the cells.

The term **cardiovascular** is taken from the prefix **cardio** (from the Greek term **kardia**, meaning heart) and the word **vascular** (relating to vessels). The vessels that pass blood from the heart to the body's tissues are called arteries. Vessels which return blood from the tissues to the heart are called veins. Smaller arteries are called arterioles and smaller veins are called venules. Even smaller vessels that carry blood through a tissue are called capillaries. Blood flows from the arterioles through the capillaries and back to the venules. The capillary-tissue network is called the blood capillary bed.

Quick Check Questions

1. Cardio is derived from the Greek term **kardia** which means _____.

2. Vessels that pass blood from the heart to the body's tissues are called arteries. Vessels that pass blood from the tissues back to the heart are called _____.

3. Arterioles are very small veins. *True or False*

4. The network of capillary tissue is called the:
   A. artery network
   B. blood capillary bed
   C. vein capillary bed

5. The cardiovascular system is one part of the __________ system.

14.2.1 Heart Location, Size, and Shape

5 minutes

The heart is located in the chest or thoracic cavity. Its size and shape are similar to a closed fist, weighing about 310 grams (0.7 lbs) in adult males and 225 grams (0.5 lbs) in adult females. The superior aspect of the heart (which is called the **base**, due to its comparative width) lies just below the second rib.

The bottom (or **apex**) of the heart lies on the diaphragm, pointing to the left. The posterior or back side of the heart rests against the fourth through eighth thoracic vertebrae. The anterior or front side of the heart rests against the sternum. Hence, the heart is located in the **mediastinum**, the middle region of the thoracic cavity between the two lungs.

Quick Check Questions

1. The heart is located in the _____stinum or middle region of the thoracic cavity.

2. The top of the heart (or base of the heart) is located just below the:
   A. second rib
   B. third rib
   C. fourth rib

14.2.2 Four Chambers of the Heart

10 minutes

Though the heart is a single organ, it functions as two pumps, one on the left side and one on the right. Each side has two chambers, an **atrium** (or receiving chamber) which is smaller and a **ventricle** (or dispensing chamber) which is larger. The upper atrium has thin walls, and the lower ventricle has thick, muscular walls. The walls of the left ventricle are twice as thick as the right side. These differences reflect the differences in work (pumping) required of the chambers. The chambers on the left side are called the **left atrium** and **left ventricle**, and the chambers on the right side are called the **right atrium** and **right ventricle**.

The left and right ventricles of the heart are separated by a wall called the **interventricular septum**. The left and right atria are divided by the **interatrial septum**. The double pumps of the heart are divided by the septa. The right atrium receives oxygen-depleted blood from the veins of the systemic circulation, and the right ventricle pumps that blood to the pulmonary circulation. There, in the lungs , carbon dioxide ($CO2$) is released and oxygen ($O2$) is picked up by the hemoglobin in the blood. The blood returns to the left atrium of the heart through the pulmonary veins and the left ventricle pumps the oxygen-enriched blood into the aorta, from which it branches into arteries of the systemic circulation.

Electrical impulses stimulate the heart's cardiac muscle and synchronize the **atrioventricular** pumping motions of each side. The atrial walls contract first, filling the ventricles with blood, then the ventricles contract, pumping blood into the pulmonary and systemic arteries. (The electrical components of cardiac function will be covered in more detail in Section Four).

Quick Check Questions

1. Each side of the heart has two chambers, the atrium and the _________.

2. Blood returns to the left atrium of the heart from pulmonary arteries. *True or False*

3. The two sides of the heart are separated by an interventricular wall called the ______.

4. Oxygen-rich blood is pumped through the arteries for systemic circulation. *True or False*

14.3.1 The Pericardial Sac and Heart Wall

12 minutes

The heart is enclosed in a loose-fitting sac called the **parietal pericardium**, or **pericardial sac**. The outside layer of the pericardium consists of a tough, white, fibrous sac called the **fibrous pericardium**. The inner layer of the pericardium, a smooth, moist membrane called **serous pericardium**, lines the fibrous pericardium. A similar, **visceral** layer of serous pericardium covers the **myocardium** (heart wall).

Pericardial Space

In between the parietal and visceral layers of the serous pericardium lies the **pericardial space**. The pericardial space allows the heart to move with less friction by bathing it in a lubricating fluid (**pericardial fluid**) which is secreted by the serous pericardium.

Three Layers of the Heart Wall

There are three primary layers of the heart wall: 1) the **epicardium** (the outer layer also called the visceral layer or serous pericardium), 2) the **myocardium** (the middle layer, the heart muscle), and 3) the **endocardium** (the inner lining).

The Epicardium

The outer layer, the epicardium, is a serous membrane similar to the inner side of the pericardial sac. This layer is also known as the **visceral pericardium**. The epicardium also includes the arteries and veins attached to the outer surface of the heart.

The Myocardium

The middle layer of the heart, the myocardium, consists of thick, contractile, cardiac muscle cells. The cardiac muscle cells are branched. Neighboring cells fuse together forming **intercalated discs**, through which electrical signals are transmitted. Collectively the structure of cardiac tissue is called a **syncytium** (or joined cells). The syncytium forms a continuous cover of muscle that encircles the heart can compresses the heart cavities with great force, pumping blood through the circulatory system.

Cardiac Muscle

The cardiac muscle is a special type of striated, involuntary muscle which is only found in the heart. Cardiac muscle cells contract rhythmically and continuously in a coordinated fashion, **autorhythmically** or through self-rhythm. This rhythmic action creates a pumping motion that provides a constant flow of blood through the body.

The Endocardium

The endocardium, consisting of **endothelial tissue**, lines the inside of the **myocardial wall. Endothelium** describes the simple squamous epithelium that lines the heart wall. This tissue is continuous with the endothelium that forms the inner surface of blood vessels. The endocardium forms the valves of the heart, the tendons which hold them in place, and a network of small muscle of the ventricle myocardium called **trabeculae carneae**. The Swiss cheese-like muscle projections allow more efficient pumping of blood from the ventricles.

Quick Check Questions

1. There are three main layers of the heart wall: the epicardium, myocardium, and ___________.

2. The pericardial sac consists of a fibrous pericardium and a ______ pericardium.

3. The thickest layer of the heart wall is the __________.

4. Cardiac muscle cells are also called:
   A. endothelial cells
   B. striated involuntary cells
   C. fibrous white cells

5. The branching cells of the myocardium, form a syncytium, meaning ______ **cells.**

14.3.2 Heart Valves

10 minutes

The heart valves can be viewed as mechanical devices that restrict blood flow to one direction. There are four primary valves that regulate proper functioning of the heart. Two **atrioventricular (AV) valves** regulate the passageways between the atria and the ventricles (or the **atrioventricular orifices**).

The AV valves are also called the **cuspid valves** because they consist of flaps or **cusps** of fibrous endocardium. The AV valve on the right side of the heart has three cusps, so it is called the **tricuspid valve**. The AV valve on the left side of the heart has only two cusps and is called the **bicuspid valve** (or more commonly the **mitral valve**). The other two heart valves are called the **semilunar (SL) valves**. They are located on the right and left ventricles, and they each have these flaps of endocardial tissue. The SL valve on the left ventricle prevents the backflow of blood from the **aorta**. The SL valve on the right ventricle controls passage of blood to the pulmonary artery.

Each of the AV valves of the heart consists of four kinds of tissue : 1) an **anulus** (ring) of fibrous connective tissue forms the rim of the valve, 2) cusps or leaflets of endothelial tissue are fixed to the anulus and covers the orifice, 3) thin tendon-like cords (**chordae tendinae**) connect to the free edges of the cusps, and 4) **papillary muscles** anchored to the ventricle walls connect to the chordae tendinae and function in valve opening and closing.

Quick Check Questions

1. The two AV valves regulate the passageways between the atria and the __________.

2. The two valves on the right and left ventricles are called:
   A. cuspid valves
   B. mitral valves
   C. semilunar valves

3. Papillary muscles that connect to the _______ tendinae are anchored to the ventricle walls.

4. An anulus (ring) of fibrous connective tissue forms a rim around the heart. *True or False*

14.3.3 Coronary Arteries

8 minutes

The heart is constantly recycling the body's blood supply, but it also needs a supply of blood for its own tissue. Two **coronary arteries** (meaning crown-like) and their arterioles supply blood to the heart: they branch off from the aorta as it leaves the left ventricle. Blood from the heart walls drains into **coronary veins** (called **venae cordis minimae**), that merge into one large vein called the **coronary sinus**, which empties directly into the right atrium.

The muscles of the ventricles receive oxygen and nutrients via blood from the right and left coronary arteries, whereas the atria receive blood from small branches of arterioles. The ventricles need more blood because the ventricular muscles do 3 to 4 times as much work as the atria, so their thicker myocardial walls, require more oxygen and nutrients to sustain their efforts. The left ventricle, the largest and strongest heart chamber, pumps blood to the entire body and thus receives a larger blood supply than the other chambers.

Quick Check Questions

1. Blood drains from the heart walls through coronary _____ (or venae cordis minimae).

2. Two coronary arteries and their branches supply blood to the heart from the aorta. *True or False*

3. The muscles of the atria receive their blood supply from just a small branch of the ________ arteries.

4. Blood is pumped through systemic circulation by the ________, which is the strongest heart chamber.
   A. right ventricle
   B. left ventricle
   C. right atrium
   D. left atrium

14.4.1 Conduction System of the Heart

10 minutes

The heart's "conduction system" consists of special cardiac muscle cells that generate and conduct electrical impulses throughout the **myocardium**. Each atrium and ventricle pair work together as a single pump, and each **atrioventricular** pump acts synchronously. The entire cycle of events involved in a single heart beat is called the **cardiac cycle.**

We refer to the heart's ability to initiate and coordinate its own complex series of contractions as **autorhythmicity**. Of all the muscle tissues, only the specialized cells of the heart's conduction system possesses this quality. The conduction system includes three major structures: the **sinoatrial node (SA)**, the **atrioventricular node (AV)**, and **Purkinje fibers.**

The SA node is a small mass of muscle cells in the posterior wall of the right atrium. The SA node is known as the **pacemaker** because it is the autorhythmic center that triggers each heartbeat, without any stimulation by nerve impulses from the brain. Even if the heart is removed from the body, the SA node will continue to initiate regular heartbeats! Fibers that extend from the SA node into the atrial muscle propagate the electrical impulse, inducing **depolarization** (conduction of the **action potential**) in the arterial walls. On the electrocardiogram (EKG or ECG), the depolarization creates the **P-wave.**

Fibers in one part of the atrial muscle carry the impulse to the AV node located in the septum between the atria. At the AV node, transmission of the impulse is delayed (just long enough for the atria to complete their contractions before the ventricles are stimulated to contract). As the impulse from the AV node is transmitted to both ventricles, it travels quickly through fibers called **atrioventricular bundle** (or **bundle of His**). The bundle of His divides into left and right branches and into the smaller Purkinje fibers (conduction myofibril), which conduct the impulse throughout the ventricular muscle. Thus stimulated the ventricles contract almost simultaneously.

The electrical impulses which accompany the depolarization of the ventricles is recorded on the EKG as the "QRS complex" (the letters mark sequential peaks on the EKG). The **T-wave** marks **repolarization** (return to resting membrane potential) of the ventricular muscle, and the beginning of the heart's next relaxation phase.

Quick Check Questions

1. The conduction system includes _____ nodes which generate or transmit impulses.
   A. two
   B. three
   C. four
   D. five

2. The SA node is known as the pacemaker because it possesses intrinsic rhythm. *True or False*

3. Fibers from the SA node extend into the muscle cells of the atria. When the electrical impulse spreads, it creates an atrial ___________.

4. Once the impulse passes into the ventricles, it travels quickly through a mass of fibers called atrioventricular bundle (or bundle of ___).

14.4.2 Cardiac Cycle

8 minutes

The **cardiac cycle** is the sequence of events associated with one full heartbeat. It involves the conduction system events, muscular contractions, and the flow of blood through the heart. The cardiac cycle consists of three phases: a relaxation period, **ventricular filling**, and **ventricular contraction** (or **systole**). One heartbeat takes about 0.8 seconds to complete (this corresponds to a heart rate of about 72 beats per minute). In the first phase (relaxation, or **diastole**), the ventricular muscles relax and the chambers expand, so that the pressure within them drops.

All the heart valves are closed, sealing off the ventricles and preventing blood flow from the atria or backflow from the aorta and pulmonary arteries. The ventricles continue to expand until the pressure within them drops below that of the atria. At that point, the **atrioventricular (AV) valves** open and blood flows into the ventricles. This is the second phase of the cardiac cycle, ventricular filling. During this phase, the SA node fires, triggering atrial contraction which forces the last of the blood into the ventricles.

The third phase of the cardiac cycle is ventricular contraction, or systole. The cardiac impulse passes into the ventricular muscle, initiating contraction. The blood is forced against the AV valves, causing them to close. When pressure in the ventricles rises above that of the pulmonary arteries and the aorta, the **semilunar (SL) valves** open and blood flows out to the lungs and the rest of the body. Finally, the ventricles start to relax, the SL valves close to prevent back flow, and a new cardiac cycle is ready to begin.

When you listen to the heart through a **stethoscope**, you hear a **lub-dup sound**, caused by the closing of the heart valves. The lub (a long, low-pitched sound) signals ventricular systole. It is the sound of the AV valves closing when the ventricles start to contract. The dup (a quick, snapping sound) is from ventricular diastole (relaxation), caused by the closing of the SL valves. The heart sound has important clinical significance since any irregularity might indicate a problem with the AV or SL valves.

Clinical Note:
A heart **murmur** is one abnormal sound often caused by improper valve closings (**valvular insufficiency**) or **stenosis** (restriction or narrowing) of heart valves.

Quick Check Questions

1. One complete heartbeat is called a cardiac _____.

2. The phases of a cardiac cycle are relaxation, ventricular ______, and ventricular contraction.

3. The "dup" sound of the heart is a long low-pitched sound. *True or False*

4. There are two phases for each cardiac cycle: a contraction phase, which is called systole, and a relaxation phase, which is called ________.

5. The dup (a quick snapping sound) of the heart is the ventricular relaxation, caused when the________ valves close.
   A. atrioventricular
   B. semilunar

14.4.3 Nervous System Regulation

8 minutes

Although the heart is autorhythmic, the nervous system can speed or slow the heartbeat. The heart is regulated by the autonomic nervous system's (ANS) sympathetic and parasympathetic divisions. Sympathetic fibers extend from the spinal cord to the heart via the middle, superior, and inferior "cardiac nerves," while parasympathetic fibers extend from the brain via branches of the **vagus nerve**. Together these fibers form the **cardiac plexuses** located close to the arch of the aorta.

From the cardiac plexuses, nerve fibers follow the right and left coronary arteries into the heart. Most of these nerve fibers end in the SA node, but some terminate in the AV node and in the atrial myocardium. Sympathetic heart nerves are also referred to as cardiac **accelerator nerves** because they speed the heart rate and increase its force of contraction. The parasympathetic **vagus fibers** are called cardiac **inhibitory** or cardiac **depressor** nerves, because they slow the heart rate.

The **endocrine system** can also affect the heart during stress. **Epinephrine** and **norepinephrine** from the **adrenal medulla** speed the heartbeat. Elevated body temperature, from exercise or fever, also increases heart rate. Heart rate decreases as body temperature drops. A fast heart rate (over 100 beats per minute) is called **tachycardia**, and slow heart rate (less than 60 beats per minute) is called **bradycardia**.

Quick Check Questions

1. The heart is regulated by the two divisions of the autonomic nervous system: the sympathetic and the ____sympathetic.

2. Parasympathetic fibers are found in the branches of the _____ nerve.

3. Cardiac plexuses are located close to the arch of the aorta. *True or False*

4. Sympathetic heart nerves are also referred to as accelerator nerves, and the parasympathetic vagus fibers are called:
   A. autonomic nerves
   B. inhibitory nerves
   C. coronary nerves

5. A fast heart rate is called tachycardia and slow heart rate is called _____cardia.

Chapter 15
The Lymphatic and Immune Systems

15.1.1 Lymphatic and Immune Systems - Overview

15 minutes

Most people agree that their body is their most valuable possession. Like any other prized possession, it must be protected from damage. Infection from outside organisms can compromise the health of the body. Hence, in order to survive, the body must protect itself from the effects of external **pathogens** (such as **bacteria**, **viruses** and parasites) and internal disease (such as **cancer**).

Immunity (or **resistance**) refers to the body's ability to defend itself against damage by foreign substances or microbes. The body uses several methods to resist pathogens and diseases. For the purposes of this course, the body's defenses are described in three parts: 1) the **lymphatic system**, 2) **non-specific immunity**, and 3) **specific immunity**.

Lymphatic System - Components and Functions

The two main functions of the lymphatic system are: 1) **body fluid** balance, and 2) specific immunity. In a system much like the blood circulatory system, the **lymphatic vessels** drain excess **interstitial fluid** from the tissues, acting as the body's sewage system. The lymphatic vessels also dispose of the waste products from the body's immune responses.

Once excess interstitial fluid enters the lymphatic vessels from a tissue, it becomes the composite fluid known as **lymph**. Lymph travels through an intricate network of tributaries, performing several tasks. Besides draining excess fluid, lymph transports dietary fats, fat soluble vitamins, **macrophages** (scavenger cells), and **lymphocytes** (white blood cells). As lymph fluid passes through the **lymph nodes**, it encounters concentrations of cells called lymphocytes and macrophages. Lymphocytes and macrophages are involved in powerful immune responses that prevent foreign substances from harming the body.

Lymphatic tissue is also referred to as **reticular tissue** because it is composed of a specialized network of connective tissue and lymphocytes. Lymph tissue exists in two forms: 1) **diffuse** and 2) **non-diffuse**. Diffuse lymphatic tissue is scattered in small amounts throughout the body, particularly in the mucous membranes of the respiratory, gastrointestinal, urinary, and reproductive tracts. Non-diffuse lymphatic tissue is **encapsulated** in **lymphatic nodules** such as the **tonsils** and the lymph nodes. Tonsils and lymph nodes are the main waste stations through which lymph percolates. These structures assist in the overall immune response and help protect the body from invasion.

After passing through the lymph nodes or tonsils, lymph continues to flow, eventually emptying into the **venous circulation**. Once lymph fluid mixes with the blood, additional lymphocytes and macrophages help to clean the fluid and remaining wastes are eliminated by the kidneys. The precursor cells of macrophages are **monocytes**. Both lymphocytes and monocytes are agranulocytes that arise in the bone marrow. One type of lymphocyte, the **B-cells**, develop fully before release from the bone tissue. **T-cells**, however, travel to the **thymus gland** to mature. Monocytes migrate to sites of inflammation in the body developing into mature macrophages when and where they are needed.

Quick Check Questions

1. The immune system provides the body's defense against disease-causing substances. *True or False*

2. Vessels and structures of the ________ system play an integral role in the immune system.
   A. endocrine
   B. reproductive
   C. lymphatic
   D. nervous

3. All of the following tissues have an important role in the lymphatic system, EXCEPT:
   A. lymph fluid
   B. bone marrow
   C. lymphatic tissue
   D. cardiac muscle

4. The main functions of the lymphatic system are to drain interstitial fluid, transport fats, and help carry out immune responses. *True or False*

5. A monocyte is:
   A. a single eyeglass
   B. a macrophage precursor
   C. a red blood cell
   D. a lymphocyte precursor

6. Tonsils and lymph nodes are examples of non-_______, or encapsulated lymphatic tissue.

15.2.1 Lymphatic Circulation

15 minutes

Lymphatic circulation entails the one-way flow of excess **interstitial fluid** from the body tissues back to the circulating blood. Lymph fluid flows through the **lymphatic vessels**, and eventually reaches the heart via the **subclavian veins.** As blood flows though the capillaries, a great deal of its fluid and dissolved components filters into the intercellular space of the tissues. Although much of this fluid returns to the capillary blood, some excess is always left in the **interstitium**.

The spaces between cells of the capillary walls are too small for most blood cells to pass through. The rate of flow of fluid from the blood is dependent on the permeability of the capillaries. Capillary permeability is based on **hydrostatic** and **osmotic** pressures in the capillaries and interstitium.

Approximately three liters of excess interstitial fluid accumulates each day. If this fluid is not drained by the lymphatic system, tissue swelling, or **edema,** results. The lymphatic capillaries, which drain the excess fluid from the tissues , are similar to blood capillaries, with three exceptions: 1) lymph capillaries have thinner walls, 2) lymph capillary walls only permit fluid to flow inwards, not back out, and 3) the fluid in lymph capillaries flows through nodes or filtering stations at various intervals. When fluid and osmotic pressure in the interstitium (Pi) is greater than pressure in the lymphatic capillaries (Pc), the endothelial cells of the capillaries separate, allowing inward flow of interstitial fluid.

When interstitial pressure is much higher than capillary pressure (when tissue is swollen or **edematous**) endothelial separation is enhanced by the movement of filaments anchored to cells of the capillary walls. These filaments help to separate the cells of capillary walls. These filaments help to separate the cells of capillary walls, increasing the drainage of fluid from interstitial tissue into the lymph capillaries.

Under opposite conditions, when Pc (lymph capillary pressure) is greater than Pi (interstitial pressure), the endothelial cells adhere to each other, preventing backward flow of lymph fluid into the tissues. From the lymphatic capillaries, lymph flows into the lymphatic vessels which, like veins, contain valves to prevent backward flow. In the skin, these vessels follow vein routes in the subcutaneous tissue, whereas in the viscera (body organs) they follow arteries and form plexuses. The lymphatic vessels carry lymph through nodes, where it is cleansed and filtered. The vessels later empty into **lymphatic trunks**. Lymphatic trunks converge and empty into the two large **lymphatic ducts**.

The **right lymphatic duct** drains lymph from the right side of the head, neck, thorax (including lung and heart), liver and upper extremity. Lymph from the remainder of the body (all parts except the upper right quadrant) drains through the **thoracic duct**. This large vessel begins as an enlarged area called the **cisterna chyli**. The duct is about 5 centimeters in diameter and 40 to 45 centimeters in length (compare to the right lymphatic duct, only about 1.25 cm long).

Specifically, the thoracic duct drains the left side of the head, neck, thorax (including lung, heart, anterior abdominal wall, and anterior diaphragm). The thoracic duct also drains the left upper extremity, and the entire lower body below the **diaphragm**. From the right lymphatic duct and the thoracic duct, lymph enters the bloodstream via the venous circulation, draining into the subclavian veins where they join the jugular veins. The movement of lymph through these various vessels is promoted by skeletal muscle contraction, as well as changes in thoracic pressure that occur during respiration.

Quick Check Questions

1. From the blood capillaries, plasma flows from the blood into the:
   A. interstitium
   B. circulatory system
   C. lymph nodes

2. Excess ____________ fluid is drained by lymphatic capillaries.

3. Lymph travels in lymphatic vessels which follow the routes of _____ in the subcutaneous tissue and arteries in the viscera.

4. Lymph from lymph vessels drains into larger lymphatic ______ and lymphatic ducts before emptying back into the venous circulation.

5. Lymphatic trunks converge into the right lymphatic duct and the ________ duct.

6. Lymph fluid empties into the venous system at the __________ veins.

7. The cisterna chyli marks the beginning of the thoracic duct. *True or False*

8. Inhalation promotes flow of lymph from the abdomen into the thorax. *True or False*

15.2.2 The Immune System

10 minutes

The **immune system** is the body's built-in defense system against pathogens (disease-causing organisms) and toxins. The magnitude of the immune system response depends on the body's resistance or susceptibility to the invading (or **infecting**) substance. Previous exposure to foreign substances and good overall health increase an individual's resistance to disease.

Immunological Memory

An individual may become ill due to invasion by the a particular virus. However, some time later, the person may encounter the same virus again, yet not become ill. The body recalls its previous experience with the **pathogen**, and thus mobilizes its immune responses more quickly. The infection is terminated before symptoms from the virus develop.

This capacity to recall previous exposure to a pathogen is called **immunological memory**. In some cases, the immune response to a pathogen may be **hyperacute** (abnormally sensitive). This is the basis for **hypersensitivity** or **allergic** reactions. On the other hand, if an individual has poor nutrition, is under stress, or is already dealing with another invasion, the immune response to a new pathogen may be less effective, or may not be mounted at all.

A person who is **immunocompromised** has problems mobilizing effective immune responses to pathogens. For some reason, the person lacks the biological resources to replenish and reinforce his or her arsenal of immune defenses. Such is the case for people with **acquired immune deficiency syndrome (AIDS)**, because this disease attacks the immune system.

Active Versus Passive Immunity

When a pathogen is detected, the body may generate (or mount) an **active immunity** response, in which cells replicate and produce antibodies directly in response to the invader. This type of response can prevent the person from getting the disease upon a subsequent encounter with the pathogen.

Passive immunity refers to the resistance that is conferred when a person is given antibodies that were produced **exogenously**. For example, **immunoglobulin** injections are given to protect persons who travel to areas at high risk from certain diseases. Passive immunity is also passes from a mother to fetus (antibodies from the blood can cross the placenta), or to infant child (from antibodies present in the breast milk).

Quick Check Questions

1. Pathogens are:
   A. disease causing organisms
   B. white blood cells
   C. platelets
   D. antibiotics

2. __________ is the ability of the body to protect itself against an invading pathogen.

3. A person's health has no relation to the strength of their immune responses. *True or False*

4. Immunological memory describes the body's ability to remember a previous exposure to a pathogen, and to respond strongly to a subsequent exposure. *True or False*

5. In hypersensitivity reactions, the immune response mounted exhibits less severe symptoms than normal. *True or False*

15.3.1 The Arsenal of the Immune System

12 minutes

The arsenal of the **immune system** includes the components (or weapons) used to resist invasion by substances which threaten the normal functioning of the body. These weapons are chemical substances and the cells which manufacture and release them, along with cells which kill **pathogens** directly. The immune system employs several strategies. Together, the interrelated mechanisms form a comprehensive means of defense for the body. For clarity, we divide immune mechanisms into two categories: 1) **non-specific resistance**, and 2) **specific resistance**.

Non-Specific Resistance

As its name implies, non-specific resistance is a general response to foreign substances, rather than a reaction to a particular type of pathogen. The weapons used in non-specific resistance include the skin, mucous membranes, **antimicrobial** chemicals, natural killer cells, phagocytic cells, and inflammatory and fever responses. Although not specific to a single pathogen, these defense mechanisms are complex. They protect the body and reduce its susceptibility to infection and disease.

The Skin

As the largest organ of the body, the skin covers and protects a large, vulnerable surface area. Offering both mechanical and chemical protection, the skin is the first line of defense against invading organisms. A physical barrier between the outside world and the inner body, the epidermis is formed of **keratinized** epithelial cells. Unhealthy, damaged, or wounded skin offers less protection (as would a weather-beaten overcoat in winter).

Pathogens, which are always present on the outside of the skin, can enter the body through a break in the skin's mechanical defense. For example, **staphylococcus epidermis**, a particularly persistent species, exists among the hair follicles. By shedding dead cells and rinsing the skin's surface with sweat (which contains anti-bacterial enzymes), the body is able to keep microbe levels manageably low.

To further reinforce the mechanical barrier of the skin, the **sebaceous glands** produce **sebum**, which acts as a chemical weapon. Sebum is an oily, acidic substance which is released into the hair follicles of the skin. Both sebum and sweat hinder pathogens from penetrating the skin, and may actually destroy the invading organisms.

Quick Check Questions

1. Non-specific immune responses are aimed directly at a particular invading organism. *True or False*

2. The skin and mucous membranes offer only chemical protection against invading organisms. *True or False*

3. The physical barrier provided by the skin is constructed mainly of keratinized __________ cells.

4. Burned skin offers the same protective barrier to pathogens as healthy skin. *True or False*

5. Staphylococcus ________ is a pathogen commonly found around the hair follicles in skin.

6. All of the following assist in the protective functions of skin, EXCEPT:
   A. sweat
   B. sebum
   C. shedding of dead cells
   D. saliva

15.3.2 Mucous Membranes

8 minutes

Like the skin, the **mucous membranes** provide both mechanical and chemical protection. Mucous membranes are constructed of an epithelial layer with a basement membrane of connective tissue. These membranes line the cavities of the body which are open to the outside from gastrointestinal, respiratory, urinary, and reproductive systems. More easily penetrated than the skin, the mucous membranes benefit from the added chemical protection provided by mucus that is secreted by **goblet cells**. Mucus, a viscous, sticky substance, traps organisms and acts as a physical barrier to invasion.

By continually producing mucus, the mucous membranes keep from drying out and keep their protective barrier from breaking down. Mucus traps foreign material with the assistance of hair or **cilia**. Once a substance is caught in mucus, the beating cilia sweep the particles toward the body's external openings. Saliva, tears, gastric fluid, and vaginal secretions also contain chemical defenders effective against pathogens. **Antimicrobial** substances and acidic (low pH) conditions in these bodily fluids inhibit microbial life. In addition, the normal flow of these fluids carries pathogens away from vulnerable areas of the body.

Quick Check Questions

1. Mucous membranes line all of the following, EXCEPT:
   A. gastrointestinal tract
   B. respiratory tract
   C. skin surface
   D. urinary tract

2. _____ helps prevent drying of the mucous membranes.

3. Cilia and mucus work in conjunction to trap and expel pathogens. *True or False*

15.3.3 Antimicrobial Substances

7 minutes

Chemicals called **antimicrobial** substances provide the second line of defense after skin and mucous membranes. Antimicrobial chemicals inhibit **microbial growth**. These substances include proteins classed as: 1) **transferrin**, 2) **interferons**, and 3) **complement**. Transferrin is an iron-binding protein in the blood. Less iron is available to **pathogens** for growth and survival if it is tied up with transferrin. However, the body still has access to transferrin-bound iron.

Viruses

Viruses are the most common cause of human disease. For example, most people get a case of the common cold at least once a year. Viruses are very small infectious agents that assume control of the **replication** machinery of host cells. A virus can not reproduce by itself, but only by causing its host to make copies of itself.

Interferons

Interferons are a class of hormone-like proteins that are mainly produced by cells infected with viruses. Once a cell is infected, it secrets interferons into the surrounding area. The interferons act upon other cells which are not yet infected by the virus. Interferon triggers these uninfected cells to synthesize and release **antiviral** proteins. Thus, the uninfected cells are protected.

Extremely important for defense against viruses, interferons are also produced by lymphocytes, macrophages, and fibroblasts. Interferon (INF) exists in two types, each of which has a specialized function in the immune system. Type I INF (which consists of alpha and beta interferon) suppresses the growth of tumor cells. Type II INF (also called gamma - INF) promotes **phagocytosis** and **natural killer cell** functions.

Quick Check Questions

1. Antimicrobial substances are part of the first line of defense to prevent pathogens from invading the body. *True or False*

2. Which of the following is NOT an antimicrobial substance?
   A. transferrin
   B. hair
   C. interferon
   D. complement

15.4.1 The Complement System

10 minutes

The **complement system** is a group of proteins which are carried in the plasma and other body fluids. When an immune response is mounted, it triggers a cascade or reactions by which these inactive enzymes become activated one after another. Once activated, the complement proteins organize themselves to help resist the invading "microbe." The initial event of complement activation can be triggered either by specific or by **non-specific immune** reactions. The cascade begins with activation of a protein called **C3**. This complement protein may be activated via the **classical** or **alternate pathway**. The complement proteins are named by the numbers, **C1** through **C9** as well as "Factor B," "Factor Ba," and **properdin**.

The **classical pathway**, in which C3 is activated by formation of an **antibody-antigen complex**, occurs in response to a **specific immunity** mechanism. In the alternate pathway, C3 is activated directly by **polysaccharides** on the pathogen surface, triggering a non-specific immune response. Regardless of how C3 is activated, it triggers a sequence of activation of other proteins. Several of the activated proteins join together into structures that form holes in the invading cell's membrane. Formation of this **membrane attack complex** (**MAC**) leads to complement-induced **cytolysis** of the microbe.

The hollow centers of the MACs puncture the plasma membrane, forming holes. Extracellular fluid leaks into the cell through these channels. Soon, the inflow of water increases the pressure inside the cell so much that it bursts! Note that fluid leaks into rather than out of the punctured cell due to **osmotic pressure**: the cytoplasm inside a cell has a much higher concentration of solutes than the surrounding fluid.

"Immunoglobulin G (IgG)" is one of the major **antibodies** in the immune system, making up 75 percent of of all the body's circulating antibodies. When an antibody binds to an **antigen** on the cell's surface, it changes shape just enough to expose previously hidden binding sites for complement proteins. This is how the antibody serves as a catalyst to start the complement reaction.

Activation of the complement causes all of the following immune responses: 1) **inflammation** (to be discussed later in this chapter), 2) **cytolysis** (through formation of the MACs), and 3) **opsonization** (covering of the foreign cell's surface, also called **immune adherence**. Opsonization is interesting because it makes the pathogen more attractive for consumption by **phagocytosis**. Activated C3 (C3b) binds to the surface of invading cells, and, like sugar coating, makes the microorganism more appealing to the white blood cells. **Phagocytic** cells have binding sites for C3b, so the presence of C3b on a foreign cell's surface makes it easier for the **phagocyte** to attach itself.

Natural Killer Cells

Natural killer (**NK**) cells are a type of lymphocyte found in the blood, bone marrow, spleen, and lymph nodes. NKs rupture or **lyse** pathogens and tumor cells. They also secrete **gamma INF** (gamma interferon). NKs are able to recognize and kill invaders without the aid of other immune mechanisms. However, their method of action is not completely understood. In some cancer and AIDS patients, NKs are either fewer in number or defective.

Quick Check Questions

1. Activation of the ___ complement protein triggers the activation of the entire system.

2. Antibody-antigen complexes are essential for C3 activation via the classical pathway. *True or False*

3. Opsonization is a way that pathogens are prepared for phagocytosis by white blood cells. *True or False*

4. Activated complement proteins form membrane attack complexes (MAC) which rupture or ____ foreign cells.

5. Natural killer cells are a special type of __________.

15.4.2 Phagocytosis

7 minutes

Phagocytosis occurs when a defending cell engulfs and consumes a foreign substance or microorganism. The immune system uses phagocytosis to defend the body from **pathogens** and to cleanse it of cellular debris. Phagocytosis is initiated when a foreign invasion is detected. The two main types of **phagocytes** are: 1) **granulocytes** (neutrophils and eosinophils), and 2) **macrophages** formed from agranular monocytes.

Chemical attractants, such as complement proteins or pathogen by-products, attract phagocytic cells to a site of pathogen invasion. This process of attraction is called **chemotaxis**. In response to chemotaxis, neutrophils and monocytes travel to the site of invasion. Neutrophils respond first, followed by the monocytes, which then develop into macrophages.

Phagocytes kill an invading organism by attaching to its surface, ultimately engulfing it within a **phagosome** (phagocytic vesicle). Within the phagocyte, the phagosome fuses with vesicles called **lysosomes**. Lysozymes are powerful enzymes contained in the phagocyte's lysosomes. They digest the pathogen (or a damaged native cell) down to basic components (lipids, nucleic acids, amino acids, etc.). Any remaining structure is expelled from the phagocyte as a **residual body**.

Quick Check Questions

1. Neutrophils, macrophages, and erythrocytes are all phagocytes. *True or False*

2. __________ is the mechanism by which phagocytes are drawn to the site of an infection (where chemical by-products are released).

3. A _________ is a phagocytic vesicle that fuses with a lysosome.

15.4.3 Inflammation

15 minutes

Inflammation is the body's response to tissue damage or injury. General characteristics of inflammation include: 1) redness, 2) heat, 3) swelling, 4) pain, and occasionally, 5) loss of function. Inflammation incorporates a number of cellular reactions: its main phases are: 1) increased **vasodilation** (widening of blood vessels resulting in increased blood flow) and vascular permeability, 2) phagocytic migration, and 3) tissue repair.

Several physiologically active substances (**histamine**, the **kinins**, the **prostaglandins**, the **leukotrienes**, and complement) all interact to increase vasodilation, vessel permeability, chemotaxis, migration of phagocytes, and phagocytosis. As vasodilation allows more blood to flow to the site of invasion and damage, increased vascular permeability (separation of the endothelial cells) allows the phagocytes to leave the blood vessels and migrate through the interstitial fluid. The phagocytic neutrophils attach to the inner surface of the vascular endothelium (called **margination**) so they can pass into the area of infection. Then they squeeze through the capillary walls in the process called **diapedesis** or **emigration**.

Neutrophils are attracted to the site of injury by **chemotaxis**. When neutrophils encounter pathogens and tissue debris, they assume their phagocytic role. Macrophages, which develop from monocytes a couple of hours after the initial attack by the neutrophils, continue the phagocytosis. After a few days of battle against infection, cellular and tissue debris collect as fluid called **pus**. Pus usually is usually degraded or expelled from the site of invasion through the skin, allowing tissue regeneration to begin.

Fever

Fever is defined as an oral temperature rises above the normal average of 98.6 degrees Fahrenheit (or 37 degrees Celsius). Fever actually facilitates tissue repair and interferon function by raising the metabolic rate of the damaged area. In addition, higher temperatures inhibit the growth of pathogens. Body temperature is controlled by the **temperature set point** in the hypothalamus in the brain. Fever-causing substances called **pyrogens** can cause the set point to be elevated. Macrophages secrete **interleukin-1 (IL-1)**, a pyrogen which signals the hypothalamus to raise the set point. In addition, many by-products of infection are examples of **pyrogens**, including protein breakdown products and the toxins which are secreted by **bacteria**.

Fever is often accompanied by shivering, nausea, headache, diarrhea, and constipation. Fever may result from any infectious illness caused by viruses or bacteria. When temperature rises above 105 degrees F (40.5 degrees C), delirium, convulsions, and permanent tissue damage may result. An **intermittent** fever rises and falls periodically, often reaching its peak at night, and returning to normal during the day. A **remittent** fever also fluctuates, but normal temperature does not return at any time until it runs its course.

Quick Check Questions

1. Neutrophils and eosinophils are the precursors of macrophages. *True or False*

2. The following are steps in the mechanism of phagocytosis, EXCEPT:
   A. chemotaxis
   B. vasoconstriction
   C. margination
   D. migration

3. Loss of function always accompanies inflammation. *True or False*

4. Redness, pain, heat, and ________ are characteristics of an inflammatory response.

5. All of the following EXCEPT _________ facilitate vasodilation in inflammation.
   A. histamine
   B. kinins
   C. immunoglobulins
   D. leukotrienes

6. Margination and emigration are steps in a phagocyte's migration to the site of an infection or injury. *True or False*

7. ___ is composed of dead cells remaining after phagocytosis and other by-products of infection.

8. Fever inhibits the effects of interferons. *True of False*

15.4.4 Specific Resistance

12 minutes

Unlike **non-specific immunity, specific resistance** is a defense mechanism which is triggered by a particular invading agent. Specific immune responses may be mounted against: 1) bacteria, 2) viruses, 3) toxins, or 4) foreign tissue. Specific immune responses exhibit substances as either **self** or **non-self**. A substance that triggers a specific immune response is called an **antigen**. Once the body has encountered a particular antigen, it is cataloged in the immune system's **memory** by the creation of chemicals called **antibodies**. The body's recollection of a previous encounter with a foreign substance is triggered when the antigen reacts with its corresponding antibody. The immune system response is more vigorous after the initial exposure.

Antigens

An antigen is any substance which, when introduced into the body, is recognized as foreign or non-self. Antigens are "macromolecules" that may enter the body as a membrane component of a foreign cell, or may themselves be recognized by the immune system. Chemically, antigens can be nucleic acids, lipids, polysaccharides, but most often, they are proteins. The essential characteristics of antigens are: 1) **immunogenicity** (the ability to provoke an immune response) and 2) **reactivity** (the ability to specifically react with an particular immunological agent). **Complete antigens** (or **immunogens**) possess both of these characteristics, but other antigens exhibit only one.

An antigen which is only capable of reactivity is called a **partial antigen** or a **hapten**. A hapten that combines with some other molecule to gain immunogenicity, can become a full-fledged immunogen. The part of the antigen that is recognized by the immune system is the **antigenic determinant** or **epitope**. The epitope is recognized by **antigen receptors** which are located in the plasma membrane lymphocytes.

The genetic makeup of any individual allows many different antigenic receptors to exist on each lymphocyte. The lymphocyte's potential to recognize many different antigens is multiplied by its capacity for genetic reorganization. When this occurs, the composition of its membrane proteins become even more diverse. Lymphocytes are able to reorganize their genes for antigen receptor proteins in two ways: 1) **genetic recombination**, and 2) **somatic mutations**.

Genetic recombination results from the shuffling of many gene segments to create each complete gene, which increases the diversity of the receptor proteins that result. This occurs during maturation of the lymphocytes. Somatic mutations occur in particular gene segments of B-lymphocytes after they have been mobilized. These mutations create further diversity in the antigens that a lymphocyte can recognize.

Quick Check Questions

1. Specific resistance is a type of immunity. *True or False*

2. A distinguishing feature of specific immune resistance is the ability to distinguish "self" tissue from "__________" tissue.

3. A complete antigen possesses both immunogenicity and memory. *True or False*

4. _______ are partial antigens, which only posses the "reactivity" component of immunogenicity.

5. ________ and ________ allow for diversity in antigen receptors on a single lymphocyte.
   A. genetic recombination, somatic mutation
   B. reactivity, specificity
   C. opsonization, immunogenicity
   D. cell division, somatic recombination

15.5.1 Lymphocytes

10 minutes

Every **lymphocyte** is equipped to recognize the **antigens** present on the body's own cells so that it can identify the cell as **self**. All body cells (except **erythrocytes**) carry surface glycoproteins, called **human leukocyte associated** (HLA) or **major histocompatibility complex** (MHC) antigens, that are unique for each individual. MHC proteins reside on cell surfaces. They associate with breakdown products from antigenic proteins, which allows immune system cells to recognize them.

MHC Antigens

There are two classes of MHC proteins. Class I MHC antigens are membrane proteins found on every cell but red blood cells. Class II MHC antigens are present only on **antigen-presenting cells** (APCs), thymus cells, and activated T lymphocytes. The main function of MHC antigens on cells is to help T lymphocytes (or **T cells**) to recognize foreign substances. B lymphocytes (or **B cells**) can recognize non-MHC antigens, that is, antigens circulating in body fluid.

The body cells constantly recycle their proteins by breakdown and resynthesis. Peptide fragments from this process form complexes with MHC proteins, producing additional antigens on their plasma membranes. A self protein associated with MHC is ignored by the immune system. However, a foreign protein-MHC complex is recognized as foreign and targeted for elimination.

Viruses

Viruses are very small, foreign particles composed of a core of genetic material (**DNA** or **RNA**) surrounded by a protein coat. Viruses are cellular parasites that are only able to replicate within living cells, which they then destroy. Viruses act by taking over the reproductive machinery of the cell, inserting their own nucleic acids, and causing the cell to produce many copies of the virus.

Viruses cause many diseases, from the common cold to **acquired immune deficiency syndrome (AIDS)**. Viruses are of interest in relation to the MHC system because they cause the infected cell to produce many foreign proteins. These **endogenous** proteins (produced inside the cell) are presented with Class I MHC proteins on the cell's surface as foreign antigens. Thus, virus-infected cells are killed as foreign cells would be.

Exogenous antigens which are produced by invading cells, are presented to T cells after being processed by antigen-presenting cells (APCs). APCs are macrophages, B cells, or dendritic cells of the nervous system that ingest exogenous antigens and complex their peptide fragments with Class II MCHs. These MHC-peptide groups allow T cells to recognize and mount a response against the foreign cells. Antigens remaining in circulation are often recognized by B cells, which help to eliminate them by creating specific antibodies against them.

Quick Check Questions

1. All of the following EXCEPT ______ are antigen presenting cells.
   A. erythrocytes
   B. macrophages
   C. B cells
   D. dendritic cells

2. Erythrocytes have MHC Class I antigens incorporated in their plasma membranes. *True or False*

3. Viruses take over the synthetic machinery of infected cells. *True or False*

15.5.2 Lymphocytes (Cont.)

20 minutes

Lymphocytes are white blood cells which act as agents or defenders in **specific immune** responses. The two major types of lymphocytes are: 1) **T cells** and 2) **B cells**. Lymphocytes originate from stem cells also called **hemocytoblasts**. Hemocytoblasts reside in the **red bone marrow** and in the fetal liver. Immature T cells migrate to the thymus, where they mature, and become specialized by developing specific surface proteins. These include antigen receptors, as well as special proteins called D4 and CD8. Mature T cells reside in an inactive form within the various lymphatic tissues throughout the body.

Immature B cells remain in the bone marrow. Once matured, they reside in lymphatic tissue (such as the lymph nodes, spleen, tonsils, etc.) until they are needed. In response to signals indicating a foreign presence in the body, B cells transform into **plasma cells** which are discharged into systemic circulation, targeted for the site of tissue invasion. T cells respond directly to invasion in the process called **cell mediated immunity**. B cells respond indirectly through **antibody-mediated** or **humoral immunity**. In addition T and B cells often interact in complementary ways in both types of immune response.

Cell-Mediated Immunity

Cell-mediated immunity is the specific immune mechanism carried out by T cells. Activate T cells differentiate into helper, killer or cytotoxic, suppressor, and "memory T cells." The trademark of T cells is their capacity to attack other cells. T cells are attracted to cells presenting self-MHCs complexed with non-self peptides, whether they are antigen-presenting cells (APCs) carrying exogenous antigens, cancer cells, or cells presenting endogenous antigens produced by intracellular pathogens such as viruses, fungi, and parasites.

Cell-mediated immunity can be divided into three stages. First, a receptor on the T cell's surface recognizes and binds a particular MHC-antigen combination on another cell. Second, the T cell is stimulated by one of the **cytokines**, protein hormones secreted by monocytes, macrophages and activated T helper cells, as a signal of foreign cell invasion.

The major lymphokines involved in this **co-stimulation** of T cells are **interleukin-1 (IL-1)** and **interleukin-2 (IL-2)**. Co-stimulation helps to regulate T cell function, assuring that T cells are activated only as needed. **Anergy** (lacking energy) describes the inactive state of a T cell that has recognized an antigen without co-stimulation. Once T cells are activated by antigen recognition and co-stimulation, stage three of cell mediated immunity begins. T cells prepare to attack the antigen through proliferation and **differentiation**. The few T cells that first recognized the offending antigen are propagated into a colony of thousands of cells activated against the invading substance.

These differentiated T cells carry out various roles in the attack process. The main players are: 1) **helper T cells**, and 2) **killer cells (or cytotoxic T cells)**. Maximum cell-mediated immune response requires activation of both helper T cells and killer T cells. Helper T cells are distinguished by carrying the surface protein CD4 (T helper cells are also called T4 cells for this reason). Helper T cells recognize foreign antigens that are presented by MHC-II proteins; that is, they recognize APCs. After helper T cells are costimulated by interleukin-1, they secrete interleukin-2. Then IL-2 costimulates the proliferation of killer T cells. In this way, helper cells assist in cell-mediated immunity. Helper T helper cells are also known to secrete the cytokines **interleukin-4** a B cell co-stimulator and a **transforming growth factor-beta (TGF-B)** an inhibitor of immune responses.

Killer T cells (cytotoxic T cells) are identified by the surface protein named CD8 (hence their nickname, **T8 cells**). Killer T cells recognize endogenous antigens associated with MHC-I proteins, such as those found on the surfaces of infected, transplanted, or cancerous cells. When activated, a killer T cell adheres to the antigen-MHC complex in preparation for destroying the invading cell.

Once bound to the **target cell**, the killer T cell strikes its first blow by secreting **perforin**, a cytokine which perforates the cell membrane. The holes created in the target cell allow fluid to leak in, which causes **lysis** or bursting of the cell. After the release of perforin, the killer T cell strikes another blow by releasing other cytokines. **Lymphotoxin** is discharged into target cells, which it kills by activating enzymes which destroy their DNA. In addition to these cytotoxic secretions, killer T cells release **gamma interferon**, which attracts neutrophils and macrophages to the site and activates phagocytosis.

Quick Check Questions

1. Cytokines (lymphokines and monokines) include all of the following, EXCEPT:
   A. lymphotoxin
   B. interleukin-1
   C. interleukin-2
   D. prostaglandin

2. Cell-mediated immunity involves the following T cells, EXCEPT:
   A. helper
   B. killer
   C. memory
   D. lipton

3. Killer T cells are identified by the surface protein CD4. *True or False*

4. Helper T cells are also referred to as T4 cells. *True or False*

5. The following statements are true, EXCEPT:
   A. Helper T cells produce interleukin-2
   B. T cell activation may begin without co-stimulation
   C. Helper T cells recognize foreign antigens associated with MHC II proteins
   D. Killer T cells recognize foreign antigens associated with MHC I proteins

6. Interleukin-1 is produced by monocytes and macrophages to co-stimulate B and T cells. *True or False*

15.6.1 Humoral Immunity

20 minutes

Humoral or **antibody-mediated immunity** involves the activation of **B cells** and the regulation of their antibody production. Like **T cells**, B cells reside throughout the body, circulating in various lymphatic tissues. (The term **humor** refers to the fluid components of the body.) When a B cell encounters an **antigen** which matches one of its cell-surface receptors, the receptor binds to the antigen. B cells can bind and be stimulated by either free antigens or **major histocompatibility (MHC)** bound antigens on **antigen-presenting cells (APCs)**. By incorporating the antigen into its cellular machinery, the B cell transforms into an APC using Class II MHC proteins to present the antigen to other cells. The B cell presents its antigen to **helper T cells**, which secrete **interleukin-2** and other **cytokines** that then co-stimulate B cells.

After the B cell is costimulated, it divides and proliferates into many **plasma cells** (the antibody-producing form of B cells). Plasma cells circulate through the lymph, traveling to the site of invasion. Upon arrival, plasma cells continue to multiply and, importantly, to produce thousands of antigen specific antibodies. The antibodies manufactured by B cells fit together with specific antigens like a lock and key, forming a complex which is easily recognized by phagocytic cells. The antigen-antibody complex also functions to stimulate the **complement system**, speeding the digestion of the foreign substances by neutrophils and macrophages.

It is noteworthy that not all of the activated B cells are transformed to plasma cells. A certain number of B cells remain in the lymphatic tissue as memory cells, providing a record of the antigen that was encountered. **Memory B cells** remain in a semi-alert state, from which they can quickly react when next encountering the same antigen. Stimulation of B cells to become antibody-producing cells thus occurs much faster and more efficiently in subsequent encounters with the same invaders.

Antibodies

Antibodies, also called **immunoglobulins**, are glycoproteins (that is, proteins with carbohydrate attachments). Identical in specificity to the antigen receptors on B cells, each antibody matches a specific antigen. Each B cells has surface receptors specific to only one antigen, and produces antibodies against the same substance. Antibodies are proteins constructed from polypeptide chains. Each antibody contains four chains: two identical **heavy chains** and two **identical light** chains. Each polypeptide chain contains a **variable region** and a **constant region**. The variable regions at the ends of the chains define the **antigen binding site** that is specific for each antibody. The constant regions of the chains fall into five basic types and they define which of five antibody types the molecule belongs to.

An antibody is typically in a Y or T shape. The heavy chains compose the trunk, whereas the light chains form the arms. Although strategically stabilized by **disulfide bonds**, the antibody chains also display a significant amount of flexibility. This flexibility facilitates a good **lock and key** fit of the antibody to the antigen.

Classes of Antibodies

Although each is specific to a particular antigen, antibodies are grouped according to certain defining characteristics. There are five classes of antibodies. They are: 1) IgG (abbreviation for immunoglobulin G), 2) IgM (immunoglobulin M), 3) IgA (immunoglobulin A), 4) IgE (immunoglobulin E), and 5) IgD (immunoglobulin D). IgG accounts for approximately 75 percent of the antibodies found in the blood, lymph, and intestines. IgG's function is to defend against bacteria and viruses. IgG is most noted for providing protection in newborns. (It is transferred from the mother across the **placenta**.)

IgM, which forms a pentameric (5-unit) structure, is the initial antibody produced by circulating plasma cells in the blood and lymph. IgM may also be found on the surface of B cells, serving as an antigen receptor. One example of the IgM class is the blood group antibodies A and B which recognize A and B antigens on red blood cells. IgA offers much of the local protection in mucous membranes. Existing either as one or two unit structures, IgA is found in saliva, tears, gastrointestinal fluids, mucus, milk, blood, and lymph. IgE and IgD are the least abundant antibodies. Found on mast cells and basophils (white blood cells), IgE is essential in allergic reactions. IgD acts as an antigen receptor on B cells, and is also involved in B cell activation.

Quick Check Questions

1. ______ immunity refers to immunity conferred by antibodies and B cells in circulating body fluids such as blood and lymph.

2. All of the following are true, EXCEPT:
   A. antibodies contain three heavy chains and one light chain
   B. each antibody has a constant and variable region
   C. there is one antibody produced per antigen receptor
   D. plasma cells produce antibodies

3. There are both circulating B cells and "memory" B cells which reside in tissues. *True or False*

4. The ______ cell is a mature B cell which produces antibodies.

5. An antigen-antibody complex can stimulate T cell activation. *True or False*

6. All of the following are classes of antibodies, EXCEPT:
   A. IgA
   B. IgM
   C. IgE
   D. IgB

7. The most abundant antibody is IgE. *True or False*

8. ___ is responsible for conferring immunity in newborns.

15.6.2 Aberrant Immune Responses

7 minutes

Clinically, a number of immune disorders are recognized. The **acquired immune deficiency syndrome** (**AIDS**) is one of these disorders. Infection by the **human immunodeficiency virus** (**HIV-1**) causes the destruction of T4 cells. Thus, the numbers of functioning helper T cells is periodically measured in HIV positive or AIDS patients.

There are different opportunistic infections which tend to occur when helper T cell levels are within certain ranges. Thus, these infections can serve as **prognostic indicators** of the progress of HIV disease. Also prevalent are **autoimmune disorders**. Autoimmune disorders occur when the immune system recognizes **self** antigens as being **non-self** tissue and attacks body tissues at particular sites.

Clinical Note:
Examples of autoimmune include: 1) **rheumatoid arthritis** (an inflammatory disease of the joints), 2) **systemic lupus erythematous** (an inflammatory disease of connective tissue), 3) **multiple sclerosis** (an immune system attack on the myelin sheaths of neurons), and 4) **diabetes mellitus** (autoimmune disease attacking insulin-producing cells of the pancreas).

Quick Check Questions

1. All of the following are examples of an aberrant immune response, EXCEPT:
   A. tissue transplant rejection
   B. rheumatoid arthritis
   C. opportunistic infections in AIDS patients
   D. systemic lupus erythematous

Chapter 16
The Respiratory System

16.1.1 Respiratory System - Overview

20 minutes

You have probably heard that we need to breathe **oxygen** in order to live. How does oxygen get from the air to all the cells of your body that need it? The **respiratory system**, together with the **cardiovascular system**, extract oxygen from the air and transport it to the body's tissues. At the same time, these systems move **carbon dioxide (CO2)**, a cellular waste, to the lungs where it is excreted into the air.

The process of **respiration** can be divided into three separate functions. The first function of respiration, **ventilation**, is the movement of air from outside the body into the lungs. A second function of respiration is **gas exchange**. Gas exchange is the process by which oxygen (O2) enters the blood from air in the lungs and carbon dioxide (CO2) is released from the blood into the air. The third function of respiration is **tissue respiration**. Tissue respiration occurs when the tissues themselves absorb and utilize oxygen from the blood.

The Respiratory Tree

The **respiratory tree** is a system of air passages. The respiratory tree begins with the nose and branches into successively smaller airways, terminating in the tiny **alveoli** of the lungs. The upper **conducting airways** of the respiratory tree include: the **nose**, the **pharynx**, the **larynx**, and the **trachea**. The lower conducting airways of the respiratory tree include: the **bronchi**, the **bronchioles**, the **terminal bronchioles**, the **respiratory bronchioles**, and the **alveolar ducts**.

Divisions of the Respiratory System

The respiratory system has two divisions, which are based upon the functions of ventilation and gas exchange. They are: 1) the **conducting division** and 2) the **respiratory division**. The conducting division includes the anatomical structures necessary for ventilation (that is, for the movement of air into the lungs). The respiratory division of the respiratory system includes those structures involved in gas exchange. Gas exchange involves the movement of oxygen into the blood and the movement of carbon dioxide out of the blood.

The Conducting Division

The conducting division of the respiratory system includes the major airways: the nose, pharynx, larynx, trachea, bronchi, bronchioles, and the terminal bronchioles. None of these structures are involved in gas exchange. Because gas exchange cannot occur here, the conducting division is called the **anatomic dead space** and is normally about 150 milliliters.

The Respiratory Division

The remainder of the respiratory tree (the alveoli), is involved in gas exchange, and thus falls under the respiratory division. The volume of air in the respiratory division is much greater than the conducting division, often 5 liters or more. Thus, the **total lung volume** in an average size adult is about 5 to 6 liters.

Quick Check Questions

1. One of the functions of the respiratory system is:
   A. supplying oxygen to muscles
   B. olfaction
   C. swallowing
   D. absorbing carbon dioxide in the lungs

2. The process of respiration can be divided into three separate functions. They are:
   A. ventilation, movement of air, and inspiration
   B. gas exchange, photosynthesis, and tissue respiration
   C. absorption of carbon dioxide, release of oxygen, and ventilation
   D. ventilation, gas exchange, and tissue respiration

3. __________ is the movement of air from outside the body into the lungs.

4. The process by which tissues absorb and utilize oxygen is called tissue __________.

5. The two functional divisions of the respiratory system are the __________ division and the respiratory division.

6. The volume in the conducting division, called anatomic dead space is about 500 milliliters. *True or False*

7. Which of the following is NOT a component of the conducting division of the respiratory system?
   A. terminal bronchioles
   B. alveolar ducts
   C. nose
   D. trachea

8. Which of the following is NOT a component of the respiratory division of the respiratory system?
   A. alveoli
   B. trachea
   C. alveolar ducts
   D. terminal bronchioles

16.2.1 The Nasal Cavity

15 minutes

Air enters the **nasal cavity** through the nostrils or **external nares**. The nasal cavity is a large space with three functions: 1) it warms, humidifies, and cleans incoming air, 2) it facilitates the sensation of smell, and 3) it enhances voice phonetics by acting as a resonating chamber.

The **mucous membranes** or **mucosa** of the respiratory tract begin in the nasal cavity. This moist, sticky, ciliated lining helps clean and moisten the air. Receptors for smell are located in the superior part of the nasal cavity. The nasal cavity has three inward-projecting bones called the **nasal conchae**, which are covered with **ciliated** mucosa. Cilia all over the respiratory tract function to move foreign particles toward the external nares or nostrils.

The Paranasal Sinuses

Sound resonance is aided by open spaces in the facial bones surrounding the nasal cavity, called **paranasal sinuses**. There are four major sinuses: 1) the **frontal sinus**, 2) the **sphenoid sinus**, 3) the **ethmoid sinuses**, and 4) one other sinus (shown on the next screen in software), the **maxillary sinus**.

The laterally located maxillary sinus is the largest of the nasal sinuses. The smaller sphenoid sinus and the ethmoid sinuses are located superior and lateral to the nasal cavity. The frontal sinus is visible in a sagittal section of the frontal bone.

Air Passage Through the Nasal Cavity

Air enters the nostrils and nasal cavity, then exits into the nasopharynx through a posterior opening called the **choana**.

Quick Check Questions

1. The nasal cavity and paranasal sinuses are responsible for all of the following, EXCEPT:
   A. filtering air
   B. warming air
   C. draining ear infections
   D. resonance of the voice

2. The choana is between the nasal cavity and the nasopharynx. *True or False*

3. The four paranasal sinuses are the frontal, sphenoid, ethmoid, and __________ sinuses.

4. Which of the following is NOT one of the four paranasal sinuses?
   A. frontal
   B. occipital
   C. sphenoid
   D. maxillary

5. The nasal conchae are:
   A. sinuses
   B. nerves
   C. smell receptors
   D. bones

6. In the nasal cavity, air becomes cleaner, warmer, and dryer. *True or False*

7. Another name for the nostrils is the external _____.

16.2.2 The Pharynx

15 minutes

After leaving the nasal cavity, air passes into the **pharynx**. The pharynx is subdivided into three parts: 1) the **nasopharynx**, 2) the **oropharynx**, and 3) the **laryngopharynx**.

The Nasopharynx

The nasopharynx is directly above the **soft palate** and it functions purely as an air passageway. The nasopharynx contains the **uvula**, the pink piece of tissue that hangs behind the tongue. The uvula prevents food from entering the nasal cavity during swallowing. This occurs when muscles of the pharynx press the uvula against the soft palate posteriorly, sealing the nasal cavity.

The nasopharynx also contains the **pharyngeal tonsils** or **adenoids**, which are masses of lymph tissue. The **auditory (or Eustachian) tubes** from the middle ear also open into the nasopharynx.

The Oropharynx

The oropharynx is located directly posterior to the oral cavity. The oropharynx contains the base of the tongue with the **lingual tonsils** attached. The **palatine tonsils** are located laterally, on the sides of the oropharynx. The palatine tonsils can be seen on either side of a wide-open mouth.

Clinical Note:
If infected, the palatine tonsils may become enlarged, interfering with breathing. The palatine tonsils are sometimes removed if they become a source of chronic bacterial infections. This operation is called a **tonsillectomy**.

The Laryngopharynx

The laryngopharynx is the most inferior part of the pharynx, located posterior to the larynx or voice box.

Quick Check Questions

1. The auditory (or Eustachian) tubes extend from the middle ear to the:
   A. nasal cavity
   B. nasopharynx
   C. oropharynx
   D. paranasal sinuses

2. Which of the following is a function of the uvula?
   A. prevents air from entering the esophagus during swallowing
   B. connects the nasal cavity to the nasopharynx
   C. prevents nasal secretions from entering the lower respiratory tract
   D. prevents material from entering the nasal cavity from the oral cavity

3. The _____ prevents food from entering the nasal cavity during swallowing.

4. The part of the pharynx directly above the soft palate is called the ____pharynx.

5. The pink piece of tissue that you can see hanging behind your tongue, which prevents food from entering the nasal cavity during swallowing, is called the _____.

6. A doctor who asks a child to open his mouth and say "ahhh" may see the uvula hanging down, as well as the lateral walls of the oropharynx with the two ________ tonsils.

7. The laryngopharynx lies above the oropharynx. *True or False*

16.2.3 The Larynx

20 minutes

The Larynx

The **larynx**, also called the voice box, is the entrance to the upper respiratory system. The larynx functions to produce sounds and to prevent food from entering the respiratory tract. The larynx is constructed mainly of cartilage and muscles. Part of the larynx, the **thyroid cartilage**, is apparent on the front of the neck as the *Adam's apple*. The larynx is protected anteriorly by the hard structure of the thyroid cartilage. Below the thyroid cartilage lies the **cricoid cartilage**: above it are the **thyrohyoid membrane** and the **hyoid bone**.

Vocal Cords

The **vocal cords** are two bands of connective tissue attached to the thyroid cartilage anteriorly and the paired **arytenoid cartilages** posteriorly. Sound is produced when muscles pull the vocal cords taut and air is passed through the **glottis**, the open space between the cords. This action causes the vocal cords to vibrate.

Several laryngeal muscles can move the arytenoid cartilages, changing the length, tension, and position of the vocal cords. When air passes through the glottis, different vibrations result depending on the position of the cords. Thus, vocal sounds of differing pitch are produced.

Swallowing

The larynx moves upward during swallowing, causing the **epiglottis** (a lid-like, cartilaginous structure) to be pushed over the top of the larynx where it covers the glottis. The upward movement of the larynx during swallowing helps to prevent the passage of food or liquid into the respiratory tract.

The Trachea

The **trachea** is a tube formed by 16 to 20 C-shaped rings of cartilage, which provide a flexible airway that is kept permanently open. The trachea is positioned anterior to the esophagus. Next to the esophagus is the open end of the C-shaped rings, which are covered by smooth muscle and a fibrous connective tissue membrane. The soft membrane at the back of the trachea allows the esophagus to expand for a **bolus** (chunks of food), unobstructed by the trachea. The trachea is about 12 centimeters (4.5 inches) long. The trachea extends from the larynx to the division of the **primary bronchi** which is the main branch off the trachea.

Quick Check Questions

1. The functions of the larynx are to produce vocal sounds and to prevent ____ from entering the respiratory tract.

2. The larynx is constructed mainly of _________ and muscles.

3. The Adam's apple is formed by the laryngeal prominence of the _______ cartilage.

4. During swallowing, the glottis is pushed over the top of the larynx, preventing food from entering the respiratory tract. *True or False*

5. The function of the epiglottis during swallowing is to:
   A. allow the esophagus to expand with a bolus of food
   B. prevent food from entering the esophagus
   C. prevent food from entering the larynx
   D. prevent food from entering the nasal cavity

6. The _______ extends from the larynx to the division of the primary bronchi.

7. The trachea is about 24 centimeters (9 inches) long. *True or False*

16.3.1 The Bronchial Tree: Conducting Division

18 minutes

The **bronchial tree** is named for its branched structure. The conducting airways of the bronchial tree grow progressively narrower as they branch. At about the level of the **manubrium** of the **sternum**, the **trachea** divides into the right and left **primary bronchi**. At the division of the bronchi is the **carnia**, a triangular piece of reinforcing cartilage.

The right primary bronchus enters the lung at a more vertical angle than does the left primary bronchus, allowing for space taken by the heart on the left side. The primary bronchi are similar to the trachea in that they also contain cartilage rings, and they are lined with a mucous membrane. The right primary bronchus divides into three **secondary bronchi** which feed the three lobes of the right lung. On the left side, however, the primary bronchus divides into only two secondary bronchi, which feed the two lobes of the left lung.

The secondary bronchi on both sides further divide into **tertiary bronchi**, also known as **segmental bronchi**. Compared to the larynx and trachea, the smaller bronchi and other air passages closer to the lungs have less cartilage. The hard structure of cartilage is necessary to keep the larger airways open.

The Bronchioles

The tertiary bronchi branch into smaller **bronchioles**, which contain little or no cartilage. The bronchioles have a thick smooth muscle layer which can contract or relax to dilate or constrict the airways. Of all the conducting airways, the bronchioles have the greatest capacity to regulate air flow. The highest degree of resistance to air flow occurs when the bronchioles are constricted. In this way, the bronchioles are analogous to the **arterioles** in the circulatory system. The bronchioles branch into narrower **terminal bronchioles**. Terminal bronchioles are the last passages in the conducting division of the respiratory system, from which the airways of the respiratory division receive air.

Quick Check Questions

1. The right primary bronchus branches into two secondary bronchi, but the left primary bronchus branches into three secondary bronchi. *True or False*

2. Consider the different angles traversed by the left and right primary bronchi.
   A. right lung
   B. left lung

3. The part of the airway which can create the greatest resistance to air flow is the:
   A. nasal cavity
   B. trachea
   C. bronchi
   D. bronchioles

4. The bronchioles are held open by cartilage rings. *True or False*

5. The ________ bronchioles are the smallest and last part of the conducting division of the respiratory system.

6. The primary bronchi contain cartilage rings. *True or False*

7. The right primary bronchus enters the lung at a more vertical angle than does the left primary bronchus. *True or False*

8. The bronchioles have a thick smooth muscle layer which can contract or relax to dilate or constrict the airways. *True or False*

16.3.2 The Bronchial Tree: Respiratory Division

18 minutes

The respiratory division of the bronchial tree begins, appropriately, with the **respiratory bronchioles**. The respiratory bronchioles have some **cilia**, but no mucus is secreted in the respiratory division because these membranes are specialized for gas transport. Each respiratory bronchiole branches into several **alveolar ducts**. Alveolar ducts do not have tubular walls: they are open air passageways with many out-pocketings of **alveoli** around them. Each of the alveolar ducts terminates in an **alveolar sac**, composed of a group of alveoli clustered around a common air space.

The Respiratory Epithelia

In addition to being equipped with cilia, the respiratory **mucosa** have many mucus-secreting **goblet cells**. The concentration of cilia and goblet cells is greater in airways near the external opening of the respiratory tract (excluding the

external nares themselves, which have neither cilia nor mucus). Thus, mucus production decreases toward the lungs.

The respiratory mucosa is composed of various types of epithelia, varying with the level of the respiratory tree. The external nares are lined with **stratified squamous epithelium**. The nasal cavity, pharynx, trachea, and the primary, secondary, and tertiary bronchi are mostly lined with **pseudostratified columnar epithelium**. The bronchioles, terminal bronchioles, and respiratory bronchioles are mostly lined with **simple cuboidal epithelium**. The alveoli and alveolar ducts are lined with **simple squamous epithelium**, which is specialized for gas exchange.

Smooth Muscle in the Respiratory Tract

A layer of **smooth muscle tissue** appears underneath the mucosa, beginning at the bronchi and continuing to the alveoli. As the tubes of the airways get smaller, the muscle becomes more prominent. The terminal bronchioles have the greatest amount of smooth muscle. The alveoli have rings of smooth muscle around their openings, which function like purse strings to open or close them.

Cartilage in the Respiratory Tract

Cartilage plays a vital role in supporting the structures of the upper respiratory tract, especially the larynx, trachea, and bronchi. The amount of cartilage diminishes as the airways get narrower. Structures smaller than the tertiary bronchioles do not contain cartilage.

Quick Check Questions

1. The respiratory division of the bronchial tree begins with the ___________ bronchioles.

2. The external nares of the respiratory system are lined with stratified squamous epithelium. *True or False*

3. Some air passageways contain pseudostratified ciliated columnar epithelium with goblet cells. *True or False*

4. The cells of the respiratory tract which secrete mucus are called ______ cells.

5. The type of epithelium found lining the inside of the trachea is:
   A. pseudostratified columnar
   B. simple squamous
   C. simple cuboidal
   D. stratified squamous

6. The primary bronchi contain more cartilage than the tertiary bronchi. *True or False*

7. Walls of the terminal bronchioles contain a great deal of smooth muscle, thus these airways provide the greatest:
   A. control over air flow
   B. resistance to air flow
   C. both of the above
   D. none of the above

8. The following structure is a part of the respiratory division of the airway.
   A. alveolar ducts
   B. trachea
   C. terminal bronchioles
   D. nasopharynx

16.4.1 The Alveoli

10 minutes

The **alveoli** (singular = alveolus) are the functional units of the lungs, where gas exchange takes place. Alveoli are arranged in clusters, like grapes. Each alveolus is covered by an extensive network of capillaries for gas exchange between blood and air.

The alveoli are very small (about half a millimeter in diameter), but also very numerous (about 350 million per lung). Since they are so numerous, the alveoli provide an extremely large surface area for gas exchange. If all the alveoli were opened up and spread out, it is estimated that they would cover the area of a baseball diamond. Each alveolus is only one cell layer thick. Thus, the total distance traversed by gas molecules between air and blood is through one alveolar cell (with its **basement membrane**) and one capillary cell (with its basement membrane). This is a distance of only about 2 **micrometers**.

Alveolar cells are of two types. **Type I alveolar cells** are very thin and are responsible for gas exchange. **Type II alveolar cells** secrete **surfactant**, a lubricant which reduces the surface tension within the alveoli. Since alveoli are so small and thin, without surfactant, the surface tension of water coating the inner membrane would cause the structure to collapse upon exhalation.

Quick Check Questions

1. Type I alveolar cells:
   A. remove waste material from alveoli
   B. secrete surfactant
   C. are the site of gas exchange
   D. secrete mucus

2. Each alveolus is covered by a network of ___________ for gas exchange between blood and air.

3. Type II alveolar cells:
   A. remove waste material from alveoli
   B. secrete surfactant
   C. are the site of gas exchange
   D. secrete mucus

4. Before entering the blood, an oxygen molecule would encounter the following structures in this order:
   A. carina, trachea, alveolar ducts, alveolar sacs
   B. trachea, carina, alveolar sacs, alveolar ducts
   C. carina, trachea, alveolar ducts, alveolar sacs
   D. trachea, carina, alveolar ducts, alveolar sacs

5. The _______ are the functional units of the lungs, where gas exchange takes place.

6. The alveoli:
   A. are only about one-half of a millimeter in diameter
   B. number about 350 million per lung
   C. provide a large surface area for gas exchange
   D. all of the above

7. The total distance traversed by gas molecules between air and blood is:
   A. the thickness of two epithelial cells and their basement membranes
   B. through one alveolar cell with its basement membrane
   C. through the basement membrane of a capillary cell
   D. only about 200 micrometers

16.4.2 The Lungs

12 minutes

As mentioned, the lungs are located in the thoracic cavity, on either side of the **mediastinum** (the medial division of the thoracic cavity). The **apex**, or superior portion of each lung, sits just above the **clavicle**. The **base**, or inferior surface of each lung, rests on the **diaphragm**. The **hilum** on the medial surface of each lung is the point of attachment for the bronchi, pulmonary arteries, pulmonary veins, nerves, cartilage, and muscle structures. The right lung is divided into three **lobes**: the superior, middle, and inferior lobes. The left lung is divided into two lobes (superior and inferior) and contains a prominent indentation, called the **cardiac notch**, where the heart is located.

Each of the lungs is covered by a double layer of **serous membranes** called **pleura**. The **visceral pleura** adheres to the exterior surface of each lung, extending into the fissures between lobes. The **parietal pleura** is attached to the interior walls of the thoracic cavity. The space between these two membranes, called the **pleural cavity**, contains a small amount of lubricating fluid secreted by the two membranes.

When the lungs expand during respiration, the lubricant in the pleural cavity prevents friction between the membranes, allowing them to move easily against one another. The pleura also provide separated compartments for the lungs, so infections are frequently limited to one lung. The lungs have a dual blood supply.

The **pulmonary system** supplies **deoxygenated** blood from body tissues to be **oxygenated** in the lungs. The **bronchial system** supplies fresh, oxygenated blood to feed the lung tissue itself.

Quick Check Questions

1. The base, or inferior surface, of each lung rests on the _________.

2. The hilum is located on the medial surface of each lung. *True or False*

3. The bronchial system supplies deoxygenated blood from the body tissues to the lungs to be oxygenated in the lungs. *True or False*

4. The hilum, on the medial surface of each lung, is the point of attachment of the:
   A. bronchi
   B. pulmonary arteries
   C. pulmonary veins
   D. all of the above

5. The cardiac notch is located on the inferior, medial aspect of the:
   A. right lung
   B. left lung
   C. heart
   D. left primary bronchus

6. The right lung has ____ lobes, and the left lung has ____ lobes.
   A. two, four
   B. three, four
   C. four, two
   D. three, two

7. Each of the lungs is covered by a double layer of serous membranes called the visceral and parietal ______.

8. The pleural cavity contains a small amount of fluid which is secreted by the pleura. This fluid:
   A. prevents bacterial infection in the lungs
   B. prevents friction between the pleural membranes
   C. maintains pressure in the pleural cavity
   D. supplies blood to the lungs

16.5.1 Pulmonary Ventilation

15 minutes

Pulmonary ventilation is the movement of outside air into the air spaces of the lungs, or **inspiration**, followed by a release of that air, or **expiration**. Inspiration occurs when the volume of the thoracic cavity expands, and expiration occurs when its volume decreases. The movement of air into and out of the lungs occurs because **pressure gradients** are created. When the volume of the **thoracic cavity** increases, air pressure in the lungs drops below atmospheric pressure, and air rushes into the lungs. When the thoracic volume decreases, higher pressure is applied to air in the lungs, causing it to flow out to the atmosphere.

Inspiration

When the thoracic cavity expands, the parietal pleura stretch with it, and a vacuum is created inside the pleural cavity. (Note, the pleural cavity contains fluid, but not air.) To fill the vacuum between the parietal and visceral pleura, the lungs are pulled toward the thoracic walls during inspiration. If air enters the pleural cavity, its vacuum is destroyed: it is difficult to fill the lung with air when this occurs, and the lung may collapse.

Inspiration is an active process, requiring muscle contraction, but expiration is a passive process of muscle relaxation. The muscles normally used in inspiration are the **diaphragm** and the **external intercostals**. As the diaphragm contracts, it pulls the bottom of the thoracic cavity down, making the cavity larger. At the same time, the external intercostals contract, increasing the width and depth of the **thorax**. In deep or labored breathing (when one is out of breath), the **sternocleidomastoid** and **scalene** muscles also aid respiration. These muscles increase the volume of the thorax by elevating the **sternum** and **ribs**. In a **forced inspiration** the sternocleidomastoid and scalene muscles are used to inhale a maximum quantity of air.

Expiration

Expiration occurs when the diaphragm and external intercostals relax and the size of the thoracic cavity decreases. In labored breathing, coughing, or when there is an obstruction to air flow, active, forced expiration may occur. Expiration is then aided by contraction of abdominal muscles, which push the viscera upward against the diaphragm, and **internal intercostals**, which pull the ribs closer together, decreasing the thoracic volume.

Quick Check Questions

1. During inspiration, the pressure within the pleural cavities is ______ ______ atmospheric pressure.
   A. greater than
   B. less than
   C. equal to

2. When the diaphragm contracts, the thoracic cavity becomes ________.
   A. larger
   B. smaller
   C. collapsed

3. The external intercostals contract during:
   A. inspiration
   B. expiration
   C. forced expiration

4. The internal intercostals contract during:
   A. inspiration
   B. expiration
   C. forced expiration

5. The movement of air into and out of the lungs occurs because ________ gradients are created.

6. If a person has air in the pleural cavity:
   A. it will be easier to breathe
   B. it will be easier to inhale but not to exhale
   C. the person will sneeze
   D. inspiration will be difficult

7. When the thoracic cavity expands, a vacuum is created inside the fluid-filled _______ cavity.

16.6.1 Properties of the Lungs

20 minutes

Compliance refers to the ease with which the lungs can expand. High compliance means the lungs expand easily. Consider blowing up a balloon. If the balloon is not stretched first, it is more difficult to get air into it, but if stretched, it is easier. A stretched balloon has greater compliance. Two forces oppose compliance of the lungs: **elasticity** and **surface tension.**

Elasticity of the Lungs

Elasticity is a measure of the tendency of the lungs to recoil after **distension** (stretching). In the balloon example, if inflated and then deflated immediately, the balloon will return to its original size. However, if the balloon is left inflated for a week before being deflated, it will remain larger than its original size: it has lost its elasticity. Lung tissue is equipped with many elastic fibers that promote its elasticity.

Surface Tension in the Lungs

Surface tension of the fluid in the lungs also increases their tendency to recoil. **Hydrogen bonds** exist between polar water molecules lining the inner surface of the alveoli. This attractive force tends to collapse the walls of the alveoli inward. Over the enormous alveolar surface area, this creates a considerable force of resistance to lung expansion. An opposing force, **surfactant** (which is released by alveolar cells), disrupts hydrogen bonds. The initiation of this action reduces surface tension, and the lungs easily expand.

Airway Resistance

The wall of the airways create some **resistance** to air flow. Resistance is greater in smaller airways than in larger ones. The greatest potential resistance is in the bronchioles, because they are the smallest airways and they can easily constrict. **Parasympathetic** stimulation and **histamine** release both cause constriction of the bronchioles, increasing resistance. **Sympathetic** stimulation and **epinephrine** release cause dilation of the bronchioles, decreasing resistance.

Pulmonary Capacities

The **total lung capacity** of five to six liters (5000 to 6000 milliliters) can be broken down into components of various volumes. These components are: 1) **tidal volume**, 2) **minute volume**, 3) **inspiratory reserve volume**, 4) **expiratory reserve volume**, 5) **residual volume**, and 6) **vital capacity**.

Tidal Volume

Tidal volume, which is about 500 milliliters, is the volume of air that moves in and out of the airways in a normal breath (inspiration, followed by expiration). As mentioned earlier, anatomic dead space is about 150 milliliters, therefore, only 350 milliliters of each tidal volume is involved in gas exchange in the alveoli.

Minute Volume

Minute volume refers to the total volume of air taken in one minute. (Minute volume = Tidal volume x Respiratory rate) At a normal respiratory rate of 12 respirations per minute, minute volume is 500 milliliters x 12 respirations per minute, or 6000 milliliters per minute (or 6 liters per minute).

Inspiratory Reserve Volume

In addition to tidal volume, inspiratory reserve volume accounts for approximately 3100 milliliters. Inspiratory reserve volume reflects the maximum volume of air one can inhale in a **forced inspiration**.

Expiratory Reserve Volume

Expiratory reserve volume accounts for about 1200 milliliters. Expiratory reserve volume reflects the quantity of air one can push out of the airways after a normal exhalation of 500 milliliters.

Residual Volume

A good deal of air remains in the alveoli and airways, even after a forced expiration. This is called the **residual volume** and amounts to about 1200 milliliters.

Vital Capacity

The **vital capacity** is the total amount of air that can be moved in and out of the lungs and airways. Vital capacity is the sum of tidal volume, inspiratory reserve volume, and expiratory reserve volume, or approximately 4800 milliliters.

Quick Check Questions

1. Alveolar surface tension is increased:
   A. in the presence of surfactant
   B. in the absence of surfactant

2. __________ refers to the ease with which the lungs can expand.

3. If the bronchioles are maximally constricted, the lungs have high:
   A. compliance
   B. resistance
   C. surface tension
   D. elasticity

4. If there is difficulty expanding the lungs during inspiration, the lungs may have high:
   A. surface tension
   B. elasticity
   C. both of the above
   D. none of the above

5. The volume of air that moves in and out of the airways in a normal breath (inspiration, followed by expiration) is called the:
   A. tidal volume
   B. residual volume
   C. vital capacity
   D. expiratory reserve volume

6. The vital capacity = expiratory reserve volume + inspiratory reserve volume + _____ volume.

7. The _____ lung capacity of five to six liters can be broken down into components of various volumes.

8. The _____________ amounts to about 500 milliliters during normal breathing.
   A. tidal volume
   B. residual volume
   C. vital capacity
   D. expiratory reserve volume

16.6.2 Restriction of Air Flow

20 minutes

Conditions which restrict air availability in the lungs may be either: 1) **obstructive** or 2) **restrictive**.

Obstructive Lung Diseases

Obstructive problems entail increases in resistance. For example, excessive bronchiole constriction in cases of **asthma** impedes airflow. Obstructive respiratory disorders are evaluated by measuring the percentage of vital capacity a person can exhale in one minute. This is called the **forced expiratory volume (FEV)** per minute. When there is high resistance to air flow, as in asthma, more time is needed to expire, and the forced expiratory volume in one minute is less than normal.

Restrictive Lung Diseases

Restrictive lung problems result from decreased compliance: for example, an over-abundance of fibrous tissue in the lungs will reduce their ability to expand. With such a restrictive lung disease, the lungs cannot be expanded as far, nor can they be deflated as much, so the vital capacity is decreased. Examples of restrictive lung disease include: **asbestosis** and **silicosis**.

Gas Exchange

Gas exchange occurs between air and blood across the alveolar-capillary border. **Oxygen** (O2), required by all cells to sustain life, moves from the air to the blood. **Carbon dioxide** (CO2), a cellular waste product, moves from the blood into the alveolus to be removed from the body by expiration. These gasses (O2 and CO2) move by **diffusion**: no energy is expended to get them across the air-blood barrier. Diffusion of oxygen and carbon dioxide takes place because of their differing concentrations on either side of the membrane. Any gas will passively move from an area of higher pressure to one of lower pressure, whether it is in liquid (blood) or gaseous (air) solution.

Both the air and the blood contain a mixture of gasses, including oxygen and carbon dioxide. **Dalton's law** states that each gas in a mixture of gasses exerts pressure independently, as if none of the other gasses were present: each gas has its own **partial pressure**. This means that oxygen and carbon dioxide each diffuse to areas where their own partial pressure is lower.

Gas Exchange in the Lungs

Blood entering alveolar capillaries has first passed through the tissues. Since the body tissues use oxygen and produce carbon dioxide, the partial pressure of oxygen is low and the partial pressure of carbon dioxide is high. The partial pressure of oxygen is much higher in the alveolar air than in the blood, while that of carbon dioxide is higher in the blood. Thus, oxygen diffuses into the blood, and carbon dioxide diffuses out into the air.

Gas Exchange in the Body Tissues

When oxygenated blood from the lungs circulates to the tissues of the body, the same principle operates, but in reverse. Tissue cells have a low partial pressure of oxygen because most available oxygen is consumed. Tissues are high in carbon dioxide because they produce it as a waste product. Thus, tissue capillaries release oxygen and receive carbon dioxide.

Quick Check Questions

1. Problems which restrict air availability in the lungs may be obstructive or ____________.

2. A person with asthma has difficulty breathing because of:
   A. decreased compliance
   B. increased elasticity
   C. decreased surfactant
   D. increased airway resistance

3. Obstructive respiratory disorders are evaluated by measuring:
   A. tidal volume
   B. inspiratory reserve volume
   C. forced expiratory volume
   D. residual volume

4. A person who demonstrates a low forced expiratory volume is more likely to have:
   A. obstructive lung disease
   B. restrictive lung disease

5. Obstructive lung diseases are characterized by increases in __________ to airflow.

6. A person who has a restrictive lung disease:
   A. may have difficulty during inspiration
   B. has increased compliance
   C. will have no difficulty during expiration
   D. all of the above

7. In the tissues, _________ moves into the capillaries, but in the lungs, it moves out of the capillaries into the air.
   A. carbon dioxide
   B. oxygen
   C. nitrogen
   D. hemoglobin

8. A gas will diffuse from an area of higher partial pressure to one of lower partial pressure. *True or False*

9. In blood entering the pulmonary circulation, partial pressure of oxygen and carbon dioxide are as follows:
   A. oxygen is high, and carbon dioxide is low
   B. oxygen is high, and carbon dioxide is high
   C. oxygen is low, and carbon dioxide is high
   D. oxygen is low, and carbon dioxide is low

10. In blood entering the tissue capillaries, partial pressure of oxygen and carbon dioxide are as follows:
   A. oxygen is high, and carbon dioxide is low
   B. oxygen is high, and carbon dioxide is high
   C. oxygen is low, and carbon dioxide is high
   D. oxygen is low, and carbon dioxide is low

16.7.1 Transport of Gasses in the Blood

20 minutes

Oxygen (O2) and **carbon dioxide (CO2)** are transported in the blood. There are certain molecules and specific chemical reactions in blood which facilitate the transport of these gasses.

Transport of Oxygen

Since oxygen does not dissolve well in water, it is carried in the blood bound to **hemoglobin**. Hemoglobin is a large protein molecule found inside red blood cells (or **erythrocytes**). Each hemoglobin molecule can bind with four oxygen molecules. With four oxygen molecules bound, the hemoglobin is **saturated**. When fewer oxygen molecules are bound to it, the hemoglobin molecule is **partially saturated**. The **percent saturation** of hemoglobin is a good assessment of the amount of oxygen that is being carried in the blood.

The Oxygen-Hemoglobin Dissociation Curve

As the **partial pressure** of oxygen increases, so does the percent saturation of hemoglobin. In pulmonary blood leaving the lungs, where the partial pressure of oxygen is high, hemoglobin is almost 100 percent saturated. In the tissues, hemoglobin is typically about 75 percent saturated. During exercise, there is a greater demand for oxygen to supply the working muscles. Since the partial pressure of oxygen is very low in working muscle tissue, oxygen dissociates more easily from hemoglobin, and the percent of saturation of hemoglobin falls below 75 percent.

Transport of Carbon Dioxide

Although carbon dioxide is much more soluble in blood than oxygen, only about 7 percent of it is transported in dissolved form. Hemoglobin carries some carbon dioxide. Twenty-three percent (23%) of carbon dioxide is bound at a site separate from oxygen. Most of the carbon dioxide in the body (70%) is carried in the form of **bicarbonate ion (HCO3-)**.

Bicarbonate ion forms inside red blood cells when a molecule of carbon dioxide joins with a molecule of water as shown in the illustration to the right (in software). This reaction is **catalyzed** by a red blood cell enzyme called **carbonic anhydrase**. When there is a large amount of carbon dioxide in the blood, this reaction will produce a large quantity of hydrogen and bicarbonate ions. As the negatively charged bicarbonate ions leave the red blood cells, negatively charged chloride ions (Cl-) are exchanged, diffusing into the red blood cells from the plasma. This process is called the **chloride shift**.

Blood pH: Effects on Gas Transport and Respiration

When carbon dioxide dissolved in the blood is converted to bicarbonate ion, hydrogen ions are released, lowering the pH of blood. When blood pH decreases, oxygen dissociates from hemoglobin more easily. This causes a shift in the oxygen-hemoglobin dissociation curve to the right. Oxygen-hemoglobin dissociation means that oxygen leaves the blood and enters working muscle tissue more easily. This change is known as the **Bohr effect**. The Bohr effect is important during exercise: working muscle releases hydrogen ions, thereby decreasing pH, while both carbon dioxide production and oxygen requirements increase. Other factors, such as body temperature, also affect the oxygen-hemoglobin dissociation curve.

Quick Check Questions

1. Oxygen is carried in the blood bound to __________.

2. In blood exiting the tissue capillaries, partial pressure of oxygen and carbon dioxide are as follows:
   A. oxygen is high, and carbon dioxide is low
   B. oxygen is high, and carbon dioxide is high
   C. oxygen is low, and carbon dioxide is high
   D. oxygen is low, and carbon dioxide is low

3. In blood exiting the alveolar capillaries, partial pressure of oxygen and carbon dioxide are as follows:
   A. oxygen is high, and carbon dioxide is low
   B. oxygen is high, and carbon dioxide is high
   C. oxygen is low, and carbon dioxide is high
   D. oxygen is low, and carbon dioxide is low

4. Restrictive lung diseases are characterized by decreases in __________.

5. Each hemoglobin molecule can carry ______ oxygen molecules.
   A. two
   B. four
   C. eight
   D. sixteen

6. Carbon dioxide is carried in the blood in the following forms:
   A. 7% dissolved, 23% by hemoglobin, 70% as bicarbonate ion
   B. 23% dissolved, 7% by hemoglobin, 70% as bicarbonate ion
   C. 70% dissolved, 20% by hemoglobin, 10% as bicarbonate ion
   D. 23% dissolved, 70% by hemoglobin, 7% as bicarbonate ion

7. In pulmonary blood leaving the lungs, hemoglobin is ______% saturated, but in the tissues, hemoglobin is typically ______ % saturated.
   A. 100, less than 40
   B. always 100, less than 60
   C. about 75, 100
   D. almost 100, about 75

8. Carbon dioxide joins with water to form ________ acid, which dissociates into bicarbonate ion and hydrogen ion.

9. When blood pH decreases oxygen dissociates from hemoglobin more easily.
True or False

10. When the Bohr effect is functioning in gas transport:
A. carbon dioxide is exchanged for bicarbonate ion across the RBC membrane
B. oxygen dissociates more easily from hemoglobin in muscle tissue capillaries
C. pH is higher than normal
D. none of the above

11. Carbon dioxide joins with water to form bicarbonate ion in a reaction catalyzed by the red blood cell enzyme, carbonic ________.
A. acidic
B. basic
C. esterase
D. anhydrase
E. protease

12. When the bicarbonate ion concentration in blood decreases, the blood becomes more:
A. acidic
B. basic

16.8.1 Regulation of Respiration

15 minutes

Maintenance of the rate and depth of respiration is under **involuntary control**. However, **voluntary control** may override the **homeostatic** breathing mechanism.

Nervous System Control

Involuntary control of respiration is accomplished in the central nervous system's **respiratory center**. Located in the **reticular formation** of the **medulla oblongata** and **pons**, the respiratory center contains a **rhythmicity center** (itself located in the medulla oblongata). The rhythmicity center contains both **inspira-**

tory neurons and **expiratory neurons**. Activity in these neurons alternates, stimulating the normal pattern of breathing.

The respiratory center of the central nervous system also contains two other structures (in the pons) called the **apneustic** center and the **pneumotaxic** center. The apneustic center excites the inspiratory nerves of the medulla, where as the pneumotaxic center sends inhibitory impulses to inspiratory nerves.

Chemoreceptors for Control of Respiration

Chemoreceptors are located in the brain and on the interior surface of certain blood vessels. Chemoreceptors are able to detect levels of oxygen, hydrogen ion, and carbon dioxide in the body. **Central chemoreceptors**, located on the anterior surface of the medulla, are sensitive to changes in pH of cerebrospinal fluid. When pH is low and carbon dioxide concentration is high, **ventilation** is stimulated. Chemoreceptors located at the **bifurcation** of the **carotid arteries** and the **aortic arch** are sensitive to changes in oxygen concentration and to changes in the pH of **arterial** blood. When chemoreceptors are stimulated, they in turn, stimulate ventilation.

Nervous and Endocrine Control of Respiration

The nervous and endocrine systems also exert control over respiration at the level of the bronchioles. **Parasympathetic** stimulation and the release of **histamine** both constrict the bronchioles, increasing resistance to air flow. **Sympathetic** stimulation and the release of **epinephrine** both act to dilate the bronchioles, decreasing the resistance to air flow.

Quick Check Questions

1. The central chemoreceptors, located on the anterior surface of the medulla, are sensitive to changes in ___.

2. When a person with asthma is having difficulty breathing, it would help them to be given:
   A. epinephrine
   B. parasympathetic stimulation
   C. histamine
   D. none of the above

3. Involuntary control of respiration is accomplished in the central nervous system respiratory center, located in the ________ formation in the brain stem.

4. The bronchioles will constrict in response to:
   A. parasympathetic stimulation
   B. histamine
   C. epinephrine
   D. all of the above

5. The __________ center in the medulla contains both inspiratory neurons and expiratory neurons.

6. Chemoreceptors located at the bifurcation of the carotid arteries and the aortic arch are sensitive to changes in ______ concentration.

7. Most of the carbon dioxide in the blood is transported inside red blood cells in the form of bicarbonate ion. *True or False*

Chapter 17
The Digestive System

17.1.1 Digestive System - Overview

15 minutes

In order to carry out all its magnificent functions, the human body needs fuel to drive its engines. One fuel source is oxygen acquired through the respiratory system. Another is nutrition acquired through the **digestive system**. The building blocks for tissue synthesis and repair in the body are called **nutrients**. They are also the matter from which the body derives energy as they are taken in, broken down, and absorbed through the digestive system.

The structures of the digestive system are divided into two major groups: 1) those of the **gastrointestinal tract**, and 2) the **accessory structures**. Each structure variably contributes to the digestive process.

Gastrointestinal Tract

The gastrointestinal tract (or **alimentary canal**), is a passageway where food is taken in mechanically and then chemically broken down, finally being absorbed into the **lymphatic** and **circulatory** systems. The remains of undigested food are eliminated from the body at the end or last exit of this passage-way, the **anal canal**.

Accessory Structures

The accessory structures are: 1) the **pancreas**, 2) the **liver**, and 3) the **gallbladder**. The main contributions of the accessory structures are the production and release of **hormones** and **enzymes** important for the breakdown of food and absorption of necessary nutrients. All the components of the digestive system work in unison to carry out its five main activities: 1) ingestion of foods (or eating), 2) the movement of food along the gastrointestinal tract, 3) breakdown of food to form nutrients the body can use, 4) absorbing these nutrients for transportation through the body to cells needing them, and 5) finally directing unused components of food out of the body by the process of defecation.

In this chapter, we will walk through the gastrointestinal tract stopping at the main segments of function. Each stop will consider pertinent anatomical structures and physiological processes. Afterwards, the accessory structures are covered with the same considerations, including their contributions to the functions of the gastrointestinal tract.

Quick Check Questions

1. Nutrients are acquired for the body through the:
   A. respiratory system
   B. digestive system
   C. reproductive system
   D. cardiovascular system

2. Nutrients are synthesized by the body. *True or False*

3. After food is taken in the body, nutrients are broken down and absorbed through the digestive system. *True or False*

4. The ______intestinal tract defines the main category of structures in the digestive system.

5. The lymphatic and circulatory systems transport nutrients absorbed by the digestive system. *True or False*

6. The liver, pancreas, and urinary bladder are all accessory structures to the digestive system. *True or False*

7. Which of the following is NOT a main activity of the digestive system?
   A. ingestion of food
   B. breakdown of food
   C. conversion of food to ATP
   D. elimination of waste

17.2.1 The Gastrointestinal Tract

7 minutes

The **gastrointestinal tract** may be considered one long tube through which food travels and is processed for the removal of **nutrients**. The composing structures run in continuity with each other. These include the mouth, pharynx, esophagus, stomach, small intestine, large intestine, rectum, and anus.

As food passes through the digestive system its character is changed into forms more readily acceptable to the body systems which need fuel to carry on their functions. **Carbohydrates, proteins**, and **lipids** are broken down into their basic components for absorption from the gastrointestinal tract. By-products of the processing which cannot be absorbed are eliminated from the tract through the **anus**. The anatomical and physiological makeup of the tract facilitate the passage of food, absorption of nutrients, and disposal from wastes out of the tract.

Quick Check Questions

1. All of the following, EXCEPT _________, are segments of the gastrointestinal tract.
   A. gallbladder
   B. esophagus
   C. stomach
   D. small intestine

2. Carbohydrates, proteins, and lipids are broken down for absorption in the alimentary tract. *True or False*

17.2.2 The Mouth

7 minutes

The mouth, also called the **oral cavity**, marks the beginning of the gastrointestinal tract. It comprises the lips, teeth, tongue, **hard palate** and **soft palate** and the **salivary glands**. Food enters the oral cavity bound by the lips, tongue, cheeks, hard and soft palates. Food is sealed inside the mouth by closure of the lips, the

labia. These are fleshy folds surrounding the mouth's opening, with a covering of skin on the outside, and lined by **mucous membrane** on the inside. Once inside the mouth, the morsel of food ingested is manipulated by the **tongue**. The tongue is composed of muscle, and has a covering of mucous membrane. Extrinsic tongue muscles (not strictly contained within the body of the tongue) enable the tongue to move food around, allowing food to come in contact with **saliva** and teeth.

Quick Check Questions

1. The lips, cheeks, tongue, soft and hard palates provide boundaries for the oral cavity. *True or False*

2. The ______ manipulates food in the mouth.

17.2.3 Saliva

10 minutes

Saliva, composed of mostly water, also contains mucus for lubrication, digestive enzymes, buffering salts, and ionic enzyme cofactors such as sodium and potassium. Water functions to dissolve food in the mouth. The majority of saliva is produced outside the mouth. The salivary glands which produce it are the **parotid glands**, **submandibular glands**, and **sublingual glands**. Saliva is secreted after **parasympathetic** stimulation and directed through the ducts of the parotid, submandibular, and sublingual glands which are the Stenson's, Wharton's, and Rivinus' ducts, respectively. There are also a few minor saliva producing glands within the **oral cavity**.

Usually, the parasympathetic nervous system regulates saliva secretion to a continuous, moderate amount. Parasympathetic stimulation increases by chemical stimulation from taste buds, dryness or friction on the tongue, or the sight, smell, or memory of food by the cerebral cortex. The **facial** and **glossopharyngeal** cranial nerves carry stimuli from the brain to the salivary glands to control secretion. Saliva is also produced in response to nausea and irritation of the pharynx and esophagus.

Enzymes of importance in the oral cavity include salivary **amylase** and **lysozyme**. Lysozyme, as discussed in the lymphatic chapter, is integral to the destruction of bacteria. Amylase is essential to the breakdown of carbohydrates to mono-, di-, and tri- sacharrides. **Triglycerides** are partially digested in the mouth by **lingual lipase** produced by glands at the posterior of the tongue. Saliva pH is kept between 6.35 and 6.85 with the help of **bicarbonate** and **phosphate** buffers secreted in the saliva. **Urea** and **uric acid** are also found in saliva, and like the sweat glands located in the skin, these two substances are the form in which some waste products are eliminated from the body.

Quick Check Questions

1. All of the following are components of saliva, EXCEPT:
   A. mucus
   B. salts
   C. enzymes
   D. fat

2. The parotid, sublingual, and submandibular glands are the main "factories" for the production of saliva. *True or False*

3. Saliva secreted from the parotid gland passes into the mouth through Stenson's ____.

4. Secretion of saliva is stimulated by sympathetic neuronal control. *True or False*

5. Salivary amylase and lysozyme are the main enzymes found in saliva. *True or False*

17.2.4 Mastication

10 minutes

The breakdown of food begins with the process of **mastication** or chewing, which entails the mixing of food with saliva, and its manipulation amidst the tongue and teeth. The lips aid in this process by keeping food particles between the upper and lower teeth, where they are broken down. The teeth, 32 in number, break down food by cutting and grinding actions. Food particles ultimately become softened and small, and are further passed on to the back of the mouth by the **tongue**.

The tongue works to mix and shape broken down food particles into a ball called a **bolus**. The bolus is then worked toward the pharynx where it is swallowed and propelled into the **esophagus**. In addition to these mechanical maneuvers, the tongue is essential for the sensation of taste. Anteriorly, **taste buds** are amongst the **fungiform papillae**, whereas posteriorly they lie amongst the **circumvallate** or vallate papillae. **Filiform papillae** are also along the anterior two thirds of the tongue, but do not contain taste buds.

Swallowing or **deglutition** of the food bolus takes place in three stages. The voluntary stage occurs as a food bolus is manipulated to the back of the mouth into the **oropharynx**, by the tongue. From the oropharynx to the **laryngopharynx**, and into the esophagus, food is propelled onward during an involuntary or **pharyngeal** stage. During this phase, breathing temporarily stops. In the pharyngeal stage, stimulation of the oropharynx by the bolus stimulates centers in the **medulla oblongata** and the **pons**. Impulses from these centers cause an upward contraction of the **uvula** and the soft palate which, in turn, close off the **nasopharynx** and lift the **larynx** causing the upper **esophageal sphincter** (contractible circular muscle fibers) to relax.

The same effect on the esophageal sphincter occurs during the process of expiration. Also, the **vocal cords** pull together which further seals off respiration, and the opening between the laryngopharynx and esophagus becomes larger. This allows quick passage of food into the esophagus. Once food enters the esophagus, breathing resumes, and the third or esophageal stage starts.

Quick Check Questions

1. Mastication entails the release of lingual lipase for the digestion of fats.
   True or False

2. The tongue shapes food into a ball called a _____.

3. Teeth aid in the breakdown of food by grinding, cutting, and tearing actions.
   True or False

4. The following are functions of the tongue, EXCEPT:
   A. the mixing of food with saliva
   B. the propulsion of food to the back of the oral cavity
   C. the sensation of taste through taste buds
   D. the stabilization of the lower teeth

5. Deglutination or __________ takes place in three stages.

17.3.1 The Esophagus

7 minutes

Collapsible and approximately 10 inches long, the **esophagus** is a tube lying anterior to the **vertebral column** and posterior to the **trachea**. It acts almost exclusively as a passageway for food traveling to the stomach, through the **esophageal hiatus** (opening in the diaphragm through which the esophagus passes). Utilizing mucus produced by mucus glands (as lubrication) and by contractions of skeletal and smooth muscle, food passes without further breakdown or absorption.

A wavelike movement of muscle (**peristalsis**) occurs within the esophageal wall. Circular fibers above a food bolus contract and push down, while longitudinal fibers below the **bolus** contract and relax the walls so that the bolus may move down under the pressure of the upper contracting fibers. Peristaltic movement is **involuntary**, controlled by parasympathetic nerves via the **medulla oblongata**. As food makes its way through the esophagus, it passes through another sphincter: the lower esophageal or **gastroesophageal sphincter**. Anatomically, this is the opening into the stomach. When swallowing occurs, the fibers in the sphincter relax allowing food to pass. It recontracts after passage to prevent reflux from the stomach back into the esophagus.

Quick Check Questions

1. The esophageal stage of swallowing is characterized by the pushing of food through the _________.

2. Nutrients are absorbed in the esophagus as food passes. *True or False*

3. Esophageal muscle consists solely of skeletal muscle. *True or False*

4. The esophageal ______ is the opening in the diaphragm through which the esophagus passes.

5. ___________ is the wavelike muscular movement in the esophagus to push food along.

17.3.2 Gastric Acid

7 minutes

Malfunction of the **gastroesophageal sphincter** results in two clinical conditions: **heartburn** and **achalasia**. Heartburn is the sensation resulting from the reflux of acid gastric contents into the **esophagus**. Achalasia refers to the non-relaxation of the sphincter at the time of swallowing. The lower third of the esophagus is composed of smooth muscle with columnar epithelium at the junction of the esophagus and stomach. The greater the degree of **reflux**, the more prone the upper two thirds of the esophagus become to the corrosive effects of the acidic gastric contents. Scarring may result causing a stricture or narrowing of the tube, impeding movement of food.

Another effect may be the transformation of the **epithelial cells** from squamous to columnar cells. This is an attempt to convert to the cell type found lining the stomach (that is, those cells in contact with these gastric contents normally). This transformation is called **metaplasia**, causing what has been named **Barretts esophagus**. Barretts esophagus has been correlated with a predisposition for esophageal **carcinoma**. It is important to stress that though almost everyone experiences reflux or heartburn with certain foods, the concern for Barretts esophagus comes into play only with constant, intractable heartburn.

Clinical Note:
Achalasia is the result of the gastroesophageal sphincter's inability to relax. The underlying cause is often neurological. When the sphincter is unable to relax, food is kept from passing into the stomach. As the food builds up, the esophagus becomes distended (**megaesophagus**) and painful.

This pain is often confused with chest pain, and thus people with achalasia may think that they are suffering from a heart attack. In many cases, relief can only be gained by cutting the muscle fibers defining the sphincter. The sphincter will never be able to close completely again, predisposing the patient to reflux, though measures are taken to reduce this likelihood.

Quick Check Questions

1. Heartburn results when gastric contents back up into the esophagus.
   True or False

2. _________ develops when the gastroesophageal sphincter is unable to relax.

17.4.1 The Stomach

10 minute

A J-shaped, muscular, collecting sac passing contents from the esophagus, the **stomach** receives food **boluses** for further digestion. The stomach is designed to process food, preparing for the absorption of nutrients in the remaining portion of the digestive tract. The four main portions of the stomach include the: 1) **cardia**, 2) **fundus**, 3) **body**, and 4) **pylorus**. The cardia surrounds the opening from the esophagus, while the fundus extends upward and to the left.

The body is the main segment of the stomach, as it swoops down bounded by the greater (outer convex surface) and lesser (inner concave surface) curvatures. The body ultimately joins the pylorus as it divides into the **pyloric antrum**, and then the **pyloric canal**. Food moves pass the **pyloric sphincter** (circular muscular valve) leading into the **duodenum**. Food passing into the duodenum is in a liquid pulp form called **chyme**. To reach this phase, food undergoes extensive processing through the various chemical and mechanical mechanisms in the stomach.

Much like the esophagus, the stomach undergoes **peristaltic** muscular movements. Enabled by three layers of smooth muscle in the wall (longitudinal, circular, and oblique), food is not only passed into the duodenum, but mixed with **gastric juices** and churned for further mechanical breakdown. Of all the complex mechanisms in the stomach, chemical digestion is the most intricate. The layout for different chemical processes begins with the arrangement of the gastric **epithelium.** The **mucosa** (columnar epithelium in the stomach) bunches into folds called **rugae**. Amidst these folds, gastric pits form with gastric glands situated deep in the epithelium. The chemical processing of food in the stomach is dependent on these glands because of their specific and interegulatory secretions. Four cells types are responsible for these secretions. They include the **parietal cells**, **chief cells**, **mucous cells**, and **G cells**.

Quick Check Questions

1. All of the following are portions of the stomach, EXCEPT:
   A. the cardia
   B. the fundus
   C. the pelvis
   D. the pylorus

2. In the stomach, food is processed in a form called chyme. *True or False*

3. Rugae are mucosal folds in the esophagus. *True or False*

4. All of the following are cell types in the stomach, EXCEPT:
   A. parietal cells
   B. chief cells
   C. alveolar cells
   D. mucous cells

17.4.2 Zymogenic Cells

8 minutes

Chief or **zymogenic cells** secrete the precursor of **pepsin**, **pepsinogen**. Activated at an acidic pH of **gastric** contents, pepsinogen, now as pepsin, breaks down protein (including milk proteins). The by-products are absorbable small chains of amino acids called **peptides**.

In addition to facilitating protein breakdown, chief cells assist **lingual lipase** in the breakdown of **triglycerides** to absorbable fatty acids, through the production of **gastric lipase**. It is important to identify gastric lipase as not extremely effective while in the stomach. Due to its preference for working under less acidic conditions at a pH of 5 to 6, gastric lipase works better in the more basic environment of the **duodenum**. With the secretions of the chief cells dependent on the pH of gastric contents, it is timely to discuss one of the main determinants of the acid-base content of the stomach: **hydrochloric acid (HCl)**. Parietal or **oxyntic cells** produce HCl and **intrinsic factor**. Intrinsic factor is important for the absorption of Vitamin B 12 in the small intestine.

Clinical Note:
Since red blood production relies on Vitamin B12 as a **cofactor**, its shortage (secondary to lack of absorption with intrinsic factor) may result in a blood disorder known as **pernicious anemia**.

Quick Check Questions

1. Chief cells secrete lingual lipase. *True or False*

2. ______ secreted by the chief cells work best in an acidic environment.

17.4.3 Parietal Cells

8 minutes

Along with the chief cells, **parietal cells** receive **parasympathetic** stimuli via the **vagus nerve** from the **medulla oblongata** reacting to the sight, smell, taste, or memory of food. This reflex comprises the **cephalic** phase of stomach digestion. In the gastric phase (that is, occurring as a result of changes in the stomach), stretch and **chemoreceptors** come into play. As food enters and distends the stomach wall, stretch receptors send signals to the brain indicating a need for increased muscular activity for churning, as well as, increased **hydrochloric acid (HCl)** and **enzyme** production to further chemical breakdown. Further digestion of the food enables it to pass, relieving the stress placed on the stomach wall.

Additionally, as food enters the stomach, it acts as a buffer lowering pH. This change is picked up by chemoreceptors transmitting back to the brain. The medulla oblongata of the brain responds again through **parasympathetic fibers** of the vagus nerve stimulating secretion by chief and parietal cells. Recall, the parietal cells produce the HCl essential for lowering the gastric pH.

As discussed, HCl converts **pepsinogen**. It is also vital for the destruction of microorganisms and direct denaturing of protein structures. With HCl production, one would expect the acidic pH to have a destructive effect on the mucosa of the stomach. This is where the role of the mucous glands becomes most evident. Mucus production is stimulated through the same triggers and pathways as the chief and parietal cells. It lines the stomach walls and protects them.

Clinical Note:
Secreted mucus protects the **mucosa** from being eaten through by the acidic gastric juices. A person with poor gastric mucus production will be at risk for developing **peptic ulcers**. **Gastric ulcers** may also be the result of hypersecretion of HCl or use of anti-inflammatory drugs. Stress, smoking, caffeine, and certain medications may lead to hypersecretion of HCl. Within recent years, the presence of **Helicobacter pylori** has been associated with a large percentage of gastric ulcers around the **pylorus**.

Quick Check Questions

1. HCl and intrinsic factor are produced by parietal cells. *True or False*

2. Vitamin ___ is absorbed in the small intestine with the help of intrinsic factor.

3. All of the following are phases of gastric digestion, EXCEPT:
   A. zymogenic
   B. cephalic
   C. gastric
   D. intestinal

4. Mucus produced in the stomach is protective against acid corrosion of the stomach epithelium. *True or False*

17.4.4 Gastrin

15 minutes

Under normal hormonal control, **hydrochloric acid (HCl)** secretion increases with stimulation by a hormone, **gastrin**, secreted by the fourth cell type called **G cells**. Gastrin secretion is stimulated by caffeine, partially broken down proteins, and distention of the stomach wall. Considered a **hormone** because it first circulates through the bloodstream before reaching **parietal cells**, gastrin stimulates acid secretion at high pH. HCl will inhibit gastric secretion if the pH is already low. **Histamine**, as released by mast cells, also plays a role in acid secretion. Histamine receptors on the parietal cells (also called H2 receptors) intensify secretion of acid triggered by gastrin or nervous stimuli.

Clinical Note:
The association of histamine with acid secretion is the basis for H2 receptor blockade as treatment for peptic ulcers.

Typically 2 to 6 hours after a meal, food is mixed with **gastric juice** (2 to 3 liters/day) and churned for further digestion. Eventually in the form of **chyme**, food is passed into the **small intestine** for absorption of the **nutrients**. The **stomach** itself has very little absorbing capability, limited to water, **electrolytes**, and alcohol. **Carbohydrates** take the least time to pass within the intestine, whereas, fats (lipids) take the most. Gastric emptying is partially controlled by gastrin as mentioned above. In addition to its effect on parietal cells, gastrin triggers contraction of the lower **esophageal** sphincter, triggers relaxation of the **pyloric sphincter**, and increases gastric **motility**.

Inhibition of gastric emptying entails additional control factors. Based on the capacity of the intestine to handle the contents from the stomach, there are feedback hormones impeding gastric emptying. These controls fall under the category of the intestinal phase of gastric digestion.

The intestinal phase begins when fatty acids, peptides, and glucose digested in the stomach reach the small intestine. Their presence stimulates secretion of three hormones: **gastric inhibitory peptide (GIP)**, secretin, and **cholecystokinin (CCK)**. GIP and secretin inhibit the gastric secretions, with GIP additionally slowing gastric motility. CCK works mainly to impede gastric emptying. **Distention** of the small intestine from the presence of food also inhibits

parasympathetic stimuli for gastric emptying and triggers the **sympathetic** inhibition of emptying. It should be noted, the hormones GIP, secretin, and CCK have additional functions in the digestive process, aside from in the intestinal phase. These will be discussed further later in the chapter.

Quick Check Questions

1. _______ is produced by G cells.

2. Low pH inhibits gastrin secretion. *True or False*

3. Most of the absorption of water occurs in the stomach. *True or False*

4. Ulcers are treated by medication which block H1 receptors. *True or False*

17.5.1 Function of Small Intestine

10 minutes

After **chyme** empties from the stomach into the **small intestine**, approximately ninety percent of the nutrients undergo absorption. The rest occurs in the **stomach** and **large intestine**. Histologically, the small intestine is effectively designed to carry out this function. The small intestine is divided into three different functional segments: 1) the **duodenum**, 2) the **jejunum**, and 3) the **ileum**.

The small intestine's absorptive function is determined by the cells contained in the **mucosal epithelium**. Amidst simple columnar cells exist **goblet** (mucus secreting) **cells, absorptive cells, enteroendocrine cells** (cells producing GIP, secretin, and CCK), and **Paneth cells** (lysozyme producing cells in the small intestine). Within the mucosa are built-in cavities lined with **Lieberkuhn's glands** secreting intestinal juice. Another type of gland, **Brunner's glands**, secreting buffer also exists in the submucosa.

Goblet cells provide mucus to lubricate and help pass food particles along the intestinal tract. Enteroendocrine cells provide regulatory hormones for the digestion and movement of food. Paneth cells offer immunological protection to the body from ingested microorganisms. Absorptive cells fold into fingerlike projections called **microvilli**. Additionally, the mucosa folds into larger projections known as **villi**. **Plicae circulares** or circular folds also increase the surface area for absorption in the small intestine.

Quick Check Questions

1. All of the following, EXCEPT _______, are segments of the small intestine.
   A. duodenum
   B. rectum
   C. jejunum
   D. ileum

2. ______ cells secrete mucus in the small intestine.

3. Brunner's glands produce enzyme containing intestinal juice. *True or False*

4. All of the following, except _________, increase the surface area of the small intestine.
   A. villi
   B. microvilli
   C. paneth cells
   D. plicae circulares

17.5.2 Function of Small Intestine (Cont.)

12 minutes

The anatomy of the **small intestine** is vital for the absorption of nutrients, distinguishing it from the other segments of the **gastrointestinal tract**. In addition, as in the mouth and stomach, much of its function is based on the production of digestive **enzymes**. **Brush border enzymes** are produced by the epithelial cells of the villi for breakdown of carbohydrates, proteins, lipids, and nucleic acids. One well-known carbohydrate-digesting intestinal enzyme deficiency results in **lactose intolerance**. This shortage or lack of the enzyme, lactase makes the digestion of milk products difficult.

Intestinal juice is composed of the following enzymes plus mucus and water. **Alkaline** in pH, intestinal juice interacts with **gastric juice**, **pancreatic juice**, and **bile** for further digestion of **chyme** in the small intestine. Production of intestinal juice is regulated by local reflexes responding to entering chyme and a hormone known as **vasoactive intestinal peptide** (**VIP**). Local reflexes and **parasympathetic** stimulation also regulate intestinal **motility**. **Peristalsis**, under these stimuli, works to move the food along the intestinal tract. **Segmentation** works to move the food back and forth, mixing and churning it with all the juices, at one segment of the intestinal tract. Segmentation is the predominant muscular activity in the small intestine for both digestion and absorption.

Absorption in Small Intestine

Absorption in the small intestine is multifactorial. Carbohydrates, as **monosaccharides**, are absorbed through **facilitated diffusion** and **active transport**. Mainly in the duodenum and jejunum, amino acids are absorbed via active transport. **Monoglycerides** and fatty acids are absorbed by simple **diffusion**, after incorporation with bile salts into **micelles** (tiny spheres) which are water-soluble. The fat soluble vitamins A, D, E, and K often accompany lipid absorption. Recall, vitamin B12 utilizes **intrinsic factor** for absorption by active transport.

Quick Check Questions

1. Lactose intolerant patients have some degree of _______ deficiency.

2. All of the following are involved in digestion in the small intestine, EXCEPT:
   A. gastric juice
   B. intestinal juice
   C. bile
   D. saliva

3. Peristalsis and segmentation mean the same thing. *True or False*

4. VIP is a hormone produced to regulate the production of intestinal juice. *True or False*

17.5.3 The Large Intestine

7 minutes

Food is passed from the **small intestine** to the **large intestine**. Digestion and absorption continue in the large intestine which is divided into the following segments: 1) **ascending colon**, 2) **transverse colon**, 3) **descending colon**, 4) **sigmoid colon**, and 5) **rectum**.

Bacteria in the large intestine interact with remaining food products for the production of **feces**. No further **nutrients** are absorbed, but water, **electrolytes**, and some vitamins may still be taken up. As **chyme** sits in the large intestine, it **desiccates** and collects to form feces. **Haustral churning** (tonic contractions of large intestine **pockets**, haustrum) and **peristalsis** push the waste onward for elimination from the body. Eventually, it reaches the end of the **gastrointestinal tract** at the **anus**. From the anus, feces leaves the body in a semisolid form. **Diarrhea** and **constipation** result from imbalances in digestion and altered water absorption in the large intestine.

Quick Check Questions

1. All of the following, EXCEPT _______, are segments of the large intestine.
   A. anus
   B. ascending colon
   C. rectum
   D. transverse colon

2. _______ are pocket-like divisions of the large intestine.

3. Feces exit the body from the rectum. *True or False*

17.6.1 The Accessory Structures

8 minutes

Providing the additional substances for chemical digestion, **accessory structures** to the **gastrointestinal tract** are integral to the entire digestive system. These structures include the **pancreas**, **liver**, and **gallbladder**.

The Pancreas

A major accessory organ, the pancreas is a large gland lying posterior to the stomach. As a gland, it is composed of both endocrine (secreting into the bloodstream) and exocrine (secreting into a duct system) cells. The **endocrine** cells are approximately one percent of the glandular epithelial cells. These cells produce the following hormones (as discussed in the *Endocrine System* chapter): **insulin**, **glucagon**, **somatostatin**, and **pancreatic polypeptide**. The remaining ninety-nine percent of the cells are exocrine and secrete **pancreatic juice**. Pancreatic juice contains chemical substances essential for the further digestion of food in the small intestine. The components of pancreatic juice include water, **sodium bicarbonate**, enzymes, and salts.

The sodium bicarbonate facilitates maintenance of the juice at an **alkaline** pH. Functioning in the small intestine, basic pancreatic juice buffers the acidic **gastric juice** just passed from the stomach. Included in this effect is the deactivation of **pepsin** which prefers a more acidic pH. Digestive enzymes secreted in pancreatic juice work best in the more alkaline environment.

Quick Check Questions

1. The pancreas is mostly composed of endocrine cells. *True or False*

2. Pancreatic juice is composed of all of the following, EXCEPT:
   A. sodium bicarbonate
   B. enzymes
   C. insulin
   D. water

3. Pancreatic juice has a basic pH for the:
   A. activation of pepsin
   B. deactivation of pancreas produced enzymes
   C. impedance of bacterial growth
   D. buffering of acidic contents passed from the stomach

17.6.2 Pancreatic Juice

10 minutes

Remaining carbohydrates, proteins, and fats in **chyme** passed from the stomach are the targets of **pancreatic juice** digestive enzymes. Recall, **carbohydrates** are first exposed to chemical digestion in the mouth by salivary **amylase**. In the small intestine, pancreatic amylase works to digest carbohydrates into **monosaccharides**. **Proteins** are digested in the small intestine by **trypsin**, **chymotrypsin**, and **carboxypeptidase**. These enzymes are produced in inactive forms preventing self-digestion of the pancreas. Trypsinogen is converted to trypsin in the small intestine. Chyme interacts with **enterokinase** (enzyme produced by the small intestine) and together they activate trypsin.

The activation of trypsin is important for activation of the other protein digesting enzymes. Both chymotrypsin and carboxypeptidase are activated (from **chymotrypsinogen** and **procarboxypeptidase**, respectively) by trypsin in the small intestine. Much more effective than **lingual lipase**, **pancreatic lipase** functions as the main triglyceride digesting enzyme. Nucleic acid digesting enzymes are also secreted in pancreatic juice. They are **ribonuclease** and **deoxyribonuclease**. Ribonuclease causes the breakdown of RNA, while deoxyribonuclease causes the breakdown of DNA.

Neuronal and hormonal control regulate the production and secretion of pancreatic juice. Under normal conditions, digestion is mainly under control of the parasympathetic division of the autonomic nervous system (ANS). Digestive enzymes are stimulated by **parasympathetic** control through the **vagus nerve**, located in the thoracic area near the spinal cord. This is in conjunction with gastric stimulation during the cephalic and gastric stages of digestion in the stomach. Hormonally, **secretin** stimulates bicarbonate rich juice, whereas **cholecystokinin (CCK)** stimulates enzyme rich juice.

Pancreatic juice produced is secreted into small ducts which converge into the larger **pancreatic duct**. The pancreatic duct empties into the **common bile duct** which passes into the small intestine just below the **pyloric sphincter** at the **ampulla of Vater**. Occasionally, the juice will be passed directly from the pancreas to the small intestine via the **accessory duct** (duct of Santorini).

Quick Check Questions

1. The pancreatic enzyme ________ does not digest ________ in the small intestine.
   A. pancreatic amylase, carbohydrates
   B. chymotrypsin, proteins
   C. trypsin, lactose
   D. pancreatic lipase, triglycerides

2. Ribonuclease and deoxyribonuclease are nucleic acid digesting enzymes found in pancreatic juice. *True or False*

3. Secretin stimulates the secretion of ___________ rich pancreatic juice.

4. The accessory duct of Santorini is the predominant passageway through which pancreatic juice passes into the small intestine. *True or False*

17.6.3 The Liver

10 minutes

An additional gland and accessory organ of the digestive system, the **liver** is the second largest organ of the body (second to the skin). With size an indication of its many functions, the liver has an interesting anatomical make-up. Divided by the **falciform ligament** into the right and left lobes, the liver takes up most of the right upper quadrant of the abdomen beneath the rib cage. Within the right lobe are the **quadrate** and **caudate** lobes. Composing the lobes are lobules consisting of **hepatocytes** (liver cells).

Hepatocytes are centered around a central vein. As opposed to capillaries, the spaces through which blood circulates are called **sinusoids**. Sinusoids are lined by **endothelium** like any other blood vessel. They are also lined by phagocytic cells called **stellate reticuloendothelial** or **Kupffer cells.** Kupffer cells ingest **microbes** and bits of foreign matter from the blood circulating through the liver. **Oxygenated blood** brought in by **hepatic** arteries and nutrient filled (as absorbed from the digestive tract) blood mix in the sinusoids running throughout the liver. **Hepatocytes** extract the oxygen, nutrients, and toxins from the blood in the sinusoids. Nutrients are taken up for synthesis and the toxins are taken up to be **detoxified**.

Blood continues to flow out of the sinusoids into the central vein, ultimately to leave the liver by the hepatic vein. Remaining nutrients in the blood are continued to be transported to the other cells of the body after leaving the hepatic veins. Kupffer cells are important in the **phagocytosis** of **bacteria**, **toxins**, and old red and white cells while circulating through the sinusoids.

Quick Check Questions

1. The liver lies in the left upper quadrant. *True or False*

2. Kupffer cells are mucus secreting goblet cells in the liver. *True or False*

3. _________ are the pathways through which oxygenated and nutrient filled blood mix and flow through the liver.

4. Liver cells or ___________ are arranged around structures of central veins.

17.6.4 Liver Function

10 minutes

Overall, the **liver** performs many functions. These include carbohydrate, lipid, and protein **metabolism. Glucose** is converted to **glycogen (glycogenesis)** and vice versa (**glycogenolysis**) in maintenance of blood sugar level. Glucose is also synthesized in the liver (**gluconeogenesis**). **Triglycerides** are stored and fatty acids broken down through the liver's functions. **Ketones, lipoproteins**, and **cholesterol** synthesis are amongst additional features of lipid metabolism in the liver.

For protein metabolism, the liver is invaluable. It is vital in the conversion of one **amino acid** to another, the deamination of amino acids, and conversion of **ammonia** to **urea** for elimination from the body. The synthesis of certain proteins essential for life is also performed. These proteins would include **clotting** factors, **globulins**, and **albumin**. Vitamins A, D, E, K, and B12 find storage in the liver. Iron does, as well, in the form of **ferritin**. Vitamin D is also activated in the liver, as it is in the skin and kidneys.

As if the aforementioned were not enough for the liver to perform, it also produces and secretes bile essential in the digestive process. Composed of water, bile acids, bile salts, cholesterol, lecithin, bile pigments, and ions, about a quart of bile is secreted per day from neuronal and hormonal stimulation. **Vagal** stimulation, **secretin**, blood content of bile salts, and blood flow all enhance the production and release of bile from the liver. Bile flows through bile ducts known as the right and left hepatic ducts. These converge into the **common bile duct**. Recall, the common bile duct is where the **pancreatic duct** drains. From the common bile duct, bile may go into the small intestine through the **Ampulla of Vater** or into the **gallbladder**.

Quick Check Questions

1. Anabolism (synthesis) is the least performed function of the liver. *True or False*

2. All of the following, EXCEPT _______, are stored in the liver.
   A. vitamin A
   B. vitamin B12
   C. ferritin
   D. bile

3. All of the following, EXCEPT _______, are components of bile.
   A. amylase
   B. cholesterol
   C. water
   D. bile pigments

4. All of the following, EXCEPT _______, enhance the release of bile from the liver.
   A. vagal stimulation
   B. CCK
   C. secretin
   D. blood flow

17.6.5 The Gallbladder

7 minutes

Bile is stored and concentrated in the **gallbladder** until needed for digestion in the **small intestine**. **Cholecystokinin (CCK)** regulates the release and flow of bile into the small intestine from the gallbladder. The route traveled runs from the gallbladder through the **cystic duct** into the **common bile duct** and into the **duodenum**. In the small intestine, bile salts are used to breakdown fat globules for absorption. The decomposition of fat is known as **emulsification** or the forming of smaller fat droplets out of large fat droplets. The rest of the bile is used for excretion of toxins, drugs, and hormones. Even the breakdown products of blood **heme** are eliminated as **bilirubin**.

Clinical Note:
People get **gallstones** when pigments and/or cholesterol in bile precipitate forming stones. Gallstones often lie static within the gallbladder but they may be dislodged upon gallbladder contractions. The stones occasionally pass into the small intestine and out of the body in feces without difficulty. But they may also get stuck in the cystic duct, common bile duct, or at the **Ampulla of Vater**. If this occurs, a person usually experiences writhing, cyclic pain as the stone tries to pass. In some cases it will, where in other cases surgery is needed to remove the stones.

Quick Check Questions

1. The __________ stores bile produced by the liver until it is needed for digestion in the small intestine.

2. Bile salts break down proteins for absorption. *True or False*

3. Feces do NOT contain any bile. *True or False*

4. Gallstones occur when components of bile precipitate stones in the gallbladder. *True or False*

Chapter 18
The Urinary System

18.1.1 The Urinary System - Overview

10 minutes

The **urinary system** and the **reproductive system** both arise from the elevated portion of **mesodermal** tissue called the **urogenital ridge**. At birth, both systems are fully formed, however, they are not completely separated in males, as the **urethra** serves to transport both **semen** and **urine**. Both the reproductive and urinary systems start developing during the **embryonic** stage, but the urinary system finishes its development first. During the early stages of development, three **kidneys** develop: 1) the **pronephros**, 2) the **mesonephros**, and 3) the **metanephros**. Only the metanephros remain as the permanent kidneys.

The fully developed urinary system consists of two kidneys, two **ureters**, the **urinary bladder**, and the urethra. The primary function of the urinary system is to regulate the **extracellular fluid** environment in the body. As it passes through the kidney, blood is filtered by the **nephrons**. The resulting **ultrafiltrate**, urine, then drains through the **cortex** and **medulla** and flows through the ureters to the urinary bladder. From there, urine is eliminated through the urethra.

As the kidneys filter the blood and produce urine, they also regulate: 1) the actual volume of plasma, thereby playing a significant role in maintaining blood pressure, 2) the concentration of waste products within the bloodstream, 3) the levels of electrolytes (sodium, potassium, and bicarbonate for example) in the serum, and 4) the pH of blood.

Quick Check Questions

1. The reproductive system and the urinary system both arise from the urogenital ridge. *True or False*

2. The urethra in the male transports both _____ and urine.

3. Which of the following are regulated by the kidneys?
   A. pH of plasma
   B. the extracellular fluid in the body
   C. waste products in the blood stream
   D. blood pressure
   E. all of the above

4. Urine, which is an ultrafiltrate of blood, is modified by the ________ in the kidney.

18.2.1 Anatomy of the Urinary System

20 minutes

Kidneys

The **kidneys** are reddish-brown in color and bean-shaped. They are located in the upper portion of the abdominal cavity, and they are **retroperitoneal**, which means they are located behind the **peritoneum**. The kidneys lie on either side of the **vertebral column**, between the twelfth **thoracic** and third **lumbar vertebrae**. The right kidney is lower than the left (about 1.5 to 2.0 centimeters), mainly to allow space for the liver.

Each kidney consists of a **cortex**, a **medulla**, **calyces**, and a **pelvis**. The cortex and medulla contain the functional units known as **nephrons**. Each nephron consists of a: 1) **glomerular (Bowman's) capsule**, 2) **glomerulus**, 3) **proximal convoluted tubule**, 4) **nephron loop** or **loop of Henle**, 5) **distal convoluted tubule** , and 6) **collecting duct**. Toward the lateral side of the kidney is a deep depression called the **renal sinus**. The **renal artery** and the **renal vein** pass through an opening in the renal sinus called the **hilus**.

Three layers of fatty and fibrous tissue enclose the kidneys. The innermost layer is called the **renal capsule**. This strong, transparent, fibrous membrane protects the kidney from trauma and prevents the spread of infection. The middle **adipose capsule** serves to cushion the kidney and to hold it in place, and the outermost **renal fascia** attaches the kidney to the peritoneum and the abdominal wall.

The outer cortex of the kidney is reddish-brown and granular in appearance because it contains many capillaries. The medulla is striated in appearance because of the orientation of both blood vessels and microscopic tubules. The structure of the medulla consists of eight to eighteen **renal pyramids**, the apexes of which, known as the **renal papillae**, point toward the center of the kidney. Between the renal pyramids are portions of the cortex called **renal columns**.

The central cavity of the kidney collects urine and funnels it into the **ureter**, located at the bottom of each kidney. Papillae of the renal pyramids project into small crevices called the **minor calyces**, and several of these calyces join to form a **major calyx**. The major calyces join together to form the **renal pelvis**. This funnel-shaped structure collects the urine and finally carries it to the ureter.

The Ureter

The ureter is a structure which transports the urine from the renal pelvis of the kidney to the urinary bladder. It extends twenty-five to thirty centimeters from the kidneys and enters the bladder medially from behind. The ureters pass into the bladder, and as the bladder fills up with urine the pressure inside compresses their openings and prevents back flow of urine into the ureters. When this mechanism malfunctions, a bladder infection (**cystitis**) can travel up the ureters and cause a kidney infection (**nephritis**).

Three coats of tissue form the ureters. The innermost coat, called the **mucosa**, is a mucous membrane lined by transitional **epithelium**. The middle layer, called the **muscularis**, is composed of layers of smooth muscle: it moves the urine through waves of contraction called **peristalsis**. The third coat, called the **serosa**, is a layer of fibrous connective tissue. Extensions of the serosa hold the ureters in place.

The Urinary Bladder

The **urinary bladder** is a hollow muscular organ located retroperitoneally in the **pelvic cavity** behind the **pubic symphysis**. In the female the bladder lies directly anterior to the **vagina** and inferior to the **uterus**: in the male it lies anterior to the **rectum**. The shape of the urinary bladder changes as it fills with urine. When empty, the bladder is collapsed and nearly flat. As the volume of urine in the bladder increases, the organ becomes pear-shaped and rises into the abdominal cavity.

The Urethra

A small tube running from the base of the urinary bladder to the exterior of the body, the urethra is the termination of the urinary system. The male urethra is about 20 centimeter (8 inches) long. It passes immediately below the urinary bladder through the prostate gland (**prostatic urethra**), then through the urogenital diaphragm (**membranous urethra**), and finally through the **penis** (**spongy urethra**).

The male urethra is composed of two layers: an outer layer which connects it to the organs through which it passes, and a mucosal lining made up of different kinds of epithelial cells. The **prostatic urethra** is lined with **mucosa**, which is a continuation of the transitional epithelium of the bladder. The membranous urethra and the spongy urethra are lined by **pseudostratified epithelium**. Near the opening of the spongy urethra, there is a lining of stratified squamous epithelium. Also located here are the urethral glands, which produce mucus for lubrication during sexual intercourse.

The female urethra, which is about 6 millimeters in diameter and 4 centimeters long, lies behind the pubic symphysis and in front of the anterior wall of the vagina. The opening of the female urethra to the exterior is called the **external urethral orifice**, and is located between the **clitoris** and the vaginal opening.

The walls of the female urethra have three layers: 1) an inner mucous coat 2) a thin venous, spongy layer of tissue, and 3) an outer coat which is continuous with the smooth muscle fibers of the urinary bladder. Most of the urethra consists of stratified squamous epithelium, with interspersed areas of stratified columnar or pseudostratified epithelium. Transitional epithelium lines the mucosa near the bladder.

Quick Check Questions

1. The right kidney is lower than the left, which allows space for the _____.

2. Most of the urethra in the female consists of:
   A. stratified squamous epithelium
   B. stratified columnar epithelium
   C. transitional epithelium

3. The female urethra lies behind the _____ symphysis and in front of the vagina.

4. In the male, the ________ glands produce lubrication during sexual intercourse.

5. The _________ carries urine outside the body.
   A. urinary bladder
   B. ureter
   C. urethra

6. _______ feed into the renal sinus.
   A. corpuscles
   B. calyces
   C. papillae

7. The rhythmic contractions of the ureters which push urine toward the bladder are called ___________.

18.2.2 Microscopic Structure of the Kidney

12 minutes

The **nephron** is the functional unit of the kidney. There are over one million nephrons per kidney, and each nephron is a collection of **urinary tubules**. Fluid passes from the capillaries to the tubules by the process of **filtration**. Once inside the tubules, the fluid is modified. The resulting fluid is called **urine**. The tubular portion of the nephron includes the **glomerular capsule**, the **proximal**

convoluted tubule (**PCT**), the **nephron loop** or **loop of Henle**, and the **distal convoluted tubule** (**DCT**). The glomerular capsule is a spherical structure which almost completely surrounds the **glomerulus.**

Together the glomerulus and the glomerular capsule form the **renal corpuscle.** The inside of the glomerular capsule is a visceral layer surrounding the glomerular capillaries, and the outside is a parietal layer. In between these layers is the **capsular space**, which receives the **glomerular filtrate**. Upon leaving the glomerulus, the glomerular filtrate next passes through the PCT.

The PCT is lined by a layer of cuboidal cells which form millions of **microvilli.** Substances needed by the body are reabsorbed from the fluid in the PCT, which then enters the descending portion of the loop of Henle. The loop of Henle is the portion of the nephron which has a **counter-current** mechanism. The contents of its ascending limb flow in the opposite direction of the contents in the descending limb.

The **permeability** and the transport capabilities of the two limbs of the loop of Henle are different. The descending limb is thin-walled and allows for free diffusion of water and **urea** in or out of the tubule (depending on their **concentration gradients**). At the same time, the ascending limb limits diffusion of molecules and utilizes **active transport** to move molecules (especially sodium) from the tubule into the **interstitial fluid.**

The major functions of the loop of Henle are: 1) In the descending limb, water flows from the loop out into the interstitial fluid, and urea flows in the opposite direction. 2) In the ascending limb, sodium and chloride are reabsorbed through active transport. Reabsorption of sodium creates high **osmotic** pressure, which drives the passive diffusion of water from the descending limb to the interstitial fluid of the medulla. Na^+ moves from the lumen of the nephron into the cell (**apical membrane**) by facilitated diffusion, and then is pumped out the other side (**basolateral membrane**) of the cell by the Na^+/K^+ pump. After forming the loop of Henle, the tubule coils into the distal convoluted tubule (DCT), which is shorter than the proximal convoluted tubule (PCT) and contains fewer microvilli.

Quick Check Questions

1. There are over one million ________ in each kidney.

2. The renal corpuscle consists of:
   A. the PCT, the loop of Henle, and the DCT
   B. the glomerular (Bowman's) capsule and the glomerulus
   C. ascending and descending portions of the loop of Henle
   D. all of the above

3. The ascending limb of the loop of Henle allows for free diffusion of water and urea into and out of the tubules. *True or False*

4. The ascending limb of the loop of Henle contains a large number of ________.

18.3.1 Blood Supply to the Kidney

10 minutes

At the **hilum**, blood is delivered to the **kidney** through the **renal artery**. The renal artery divides into **interlobar arteries** and passes through the renal columns in the **medulla**. These further divide into **arcuate arteries** at the border of the medulla and the **cortex**. Branches of the arcuate arteries divide into **interlobular arteries** which empty into the cortex and then further divide into **afferent arterioles.**

The many interlobular arteries subdivide to form microscopic afferent arterioles which deliver blood to the capillary system of the **glomeruli**. Recall that glomeruli produce a filtrate from the blood which enters the urinary tubules. Any remaining blood in the glomerulus leaves through **efferent arterioles**, which are narrower than afferent arterioles and therefore help increase the pressure of filtration in the glomerulus.

Blood from the efferent arterioles enters the **peritubular capillaries** which surround the tubules. This blood drains into the interlobular, arcuate, and interlobar veins. They run parallel to the arteries and descend between the pyramids, leaving the kidney as one renal vein, emptying eventually into the **vena cava**.

Quick Check Questions

1. Blood is delivered to the kidney through the _____ artery.

2. Remaining blood in the glomerulus exits via the ________ arterioles.

3. Efferent arterioles are narrower than afferent arterioles. *True or False*

4. Filtrate from the blood enters the:
   A. vena cava
   B. urinary tubules
   C. peritubular capillaries
   D. all of the above

18.3.2 Filtration

20 minutes

The main structure responsible for **filtration** in the **urinary system** is the **nephron**. This filtration is the first step in **urine** production, and is typically called **glomerular filtration**. In the **renal corpuscle** of the kidney, across structures known as **endothelial-capsular membranes**, blood pressure forces fluids and other dissolved substances through pores in the capillaries of the kidney called **endothelial fenestrations**. The fluid then travels through small openings in the visceral wall of the **glomerular capsule**.

This fluid, or filtrate, contains all elements found in blood except for proteins or substances too large to pass through the capsular membranes. Filtrate equivalent to sixty times the body's entire blood volume production (about 180 liters) pass through the nephrons each day. Only one to two liters of this production is excreted as urine: the rest flows back into the bloodstream after reabsorption.

There are three main pressures which work on the glomerulus to affect filtration: 1) **Glomerular blood hydrostatic pressure (GBHP)**, 2) **Capsular hydrostatic pressure (CHP)**, and 3) **Blood colloid osmotic pressure (BCOP)**. Glomerular blood hydrostatic pressure (GBHP) represents the blood pressure within the capillaries of the glomerulus (about 60 mm Hg). Capsular hydrostatic pressure

(CHP) is one force which opposes GBHP. As the filtrate is forced into the space between the walls of the glomerular capsule, it meets with resistance from two sources: the wall of the capsule itself and the fluid already collected in the renal tubule. The result of this resistance is that some fluid pushes back into the capillary. CHP is about 15 mm Hg.

Blood colloid osmotic pressure (BCOP) is the second force that works against GBHP. The amount of solutes in blood and glomerular filtrate are the same, except for proteins, which are found in higher concentrations in the blood. If not for the fact that blood pressure in the glomerulus is greater than BCOP, water would flow out of the filtrate and back into the blood vessel. BCOP averages 27 mm Hg in glomerular capillaries. The net filtration pressure (NFP) can be determined by subtracting opposing forces (CHP + BCOP) from the pressure which causes filtration (GBHP), which is about 18 mm Hg in a healthy individual. The total amount of filtrate which forms in the corpuscles of each kidney per minute is called the **glomerular filtration rate** (**GFR**) and is about 125 milliliters per minute.

Clinical Note:
Anuria, a condition in which urine output is too low (less than 50 milliliters), can be the result of a drop in blood pressure and GBHP, which may be caused by severe blood loss. This condition is unhealthy because the entire filtrate may be reabsorbed and certain waste products may build up in the body. The opposite may be true if urine production is too high: certain essential substances needed by the body may be lost due to heavy excretion.

The rate of glomerular filtration relates directly to the rate of glomerular blood flow, which in turn depends upon systemic blood pressure and the diameter of arterioles, both afferent and efferent. The following mechanisms regulate glomerular filtration.

Mechanisms that Regulate Filtration: Renal Autoregulation

For a short period of time, the kidneys can compensate for a decrease in arterial pressure. When filtration pressure is low due to a drop in blood pressure, more fluid and salts are delivered to tubules and the loop of Henle. As this fluid passes over the **macula densa** in the **juxtaglomerular apparatus**, the release of vasoconstrictor substances is inhibited. This inhibition in turn causes the afferent arterioles to dilate. This **negative feedback** system increases blood flow to the capillaries, returning **homeostasis**.

Mechanisms that Regulate Filtration: Hormonal Autoregulation

Juxtaglomerular cells release an enzyme called **renin** in response to a decrease of fluid over the macula densa, a decreased stretch of the juxtaglomerular cells, or an increase in nerve impulses to the renal sympathetic nerve pathways. Once released into the blood, renin converts **angiotensinogen** to **angiotensin I**. Angiotensin I cycles through the lungs and becomes **angiotensin II**, an active hormone. Angiotensin II acts upon the kidneys by: 1) promoting **vasoconstriction** 2) stimulating the **hypothalamus** to signal thirst 3) stimulating the adrenal cortex to secrete **aldosterone**, which enhances reabsorption of Na+ in the collecting ducts. Water follows Na+ by **osmosis**.

Another hormone, **atrial natriuretic peptide (ANP)** is secreted by cells of the heart in reaction to an increase in blood pressure. ANP suppresses the secretions of ADH, aldosterone, and renin. ANP is effective in lowering blood pressure and reducing edema (water retention), and may increase filtration rate by making the filter more permeable or by dilating afferent arterioles. Studies are being conducted as to whether ANP can benefit patients with renal failure by increasing their glomerular filtration rate.

Mechanisms that Regulate Filtration: Neural Regulation

Strong sympathetic stimulation can cause afferent arterioles to vasoconstrict, causing a decrease in glomerular blood flow.

Quick Check Questions

1. The main structure responsible for filtration in the kidneys is the:
   A. nephron
   B. macula densa
   C. juxtaglomerular apparatus

2. Angiotensin II acts upon the kidneys in all of these ways, EXCEPT:
   A. stimulating the release of aldosterone by the adrenal cortex
   B. stimulating the production of atrial natriuretic peptide (ANP)
   C. promoting vasoconstriction
   D. stimulating the release of antidiuretic hormone (ADH)

3. The three mechanisms which regulate the rate of filtration are renal autoregulation, hormonal autoregulation, and ______ regulation.

4. Atrial natriuretic peptide (ANP) may increase filtration. *True or False*

5. Angiotensin II acts upon the kidneys by stimulating the adrenal cortex to release ___________.

18.4.1 Tubular Reabsorption

20 minutes

Reabsorption refers to the process by which substances are removed from the filtrate passing through the renal tubules and re-enter the bloodstream. Only about one percent of filtrate leaves the body as urine. The rest moves into the blood via peritubular capillaries or **vasa recta**. Solutes involved in the process of reabsorption include glucose, amino acids, and various ions.

Water is absorbed by **osmosis**. Small proteins or other large products which have passed through the filter are reabsorbed through **pinocytosis. Epithelial cells** are responsible for reabsorption. Epithelial cells contain **microvilli** which increase the surface area available for reabsorption in the convoluted tubules. Reabsorption ensures that essential nutrients are returned to the body, rather than excreted through the **urine**. Small amounts of waste products, such as urea, are also incidentally reabsorbed.

Reabsorption of sodium ions (Na+) is extremely important: more sodium passes through the **glomerular filter** than any other substance except water. The major mechanism for sodium reabsorption is **primary active transport**. Primary active transport occurs in the tubules as well as the **collecting ducts**. The concentration of sodium inside tubule cells is low and the interior of the cell is negatively charged in relation to the exterior.

Sodium ions diffuse through the filtrate into the tubule lumen through facilitated diffusion in the tubule cells. As sodium is diffusing into the tubule cells, it is also being expelled by sodium pumps (Na+/K+ ATPase) into the **interstitial fluid** through membranes at the base and sides of the cell. Sodium diffuses into peritubular capillaries from interstitial spaces in tubule cells.

The Na+ promotes reabsorption of water by osmosis, because it increases **osmotic pressure**, first in the tubule cell's **cytosol** and then in the blood in peritubular capillaries. Water flows into these capillaries from the filtrate in order to maintain osmotic balance. As the water leaves, the concentration of solutes increases, promoting passive diffusion of other substances. The **proximal convoluted tubule (PCT)** cells normally reabsorb all of the filtered glucose, amino acids, and lactic acid, by Na+ **symporters**, which carry out **secondary active transport**. A symporter attaches itself to the substance, and brings it into the cytosol along with a Na+ ion.

In order for secondary active transport to occur the sodium pump must keep the intracellular concentration of sodium low. Reabsorption of these nutrients also promotes reabsorption of water by osmosis. Each type of symporter has a limit on how fast it can work. This limit is called the **transport maximum**, and it can be exceeded when the blood concentration of a certain substance is unusually high. Then the molecules of the substance pass the **endothelial-capsular** membrane faster than the can be reabsorbed, and the substance spills over into the urine. The point at which this occurs is called the **renal threshold** for that substance. Urine output is increased, because for every solute ion that is not absorbed, one water molecule stays in the urine.

The PCTs reabsorb about one hundred percent of the filtered nutrients and eighty-five percent of the HCO3-, sixty-five percent of the sodium and water, and about 50 percent of the chloride and potassium. The loop of Henle reabsorbs about forty percent of the potassium, twenty-five percent of the sodium, and fifteen percent of the filtered water. The rest is reabsorbed from the **distal convoluted tubules (DCTs)** and collecting ducts. Water and solutes continue to be absorbed by the DCTs, until they are about ninety-five percent reabsorbed. The remaining five percent are absorbed by way of two hormones which help regulate the absorption process.

The hormone aldosterone, produced by the adrenal gland, increases absorption of water and sodium by the nephron. Antidiuretic hormone (ADH) increases the permeability of cells to water. Thus, water flows from the tubular lumen into the bloodstream, instead of out through the urine. The hypothalamus is stimulated to produce ADH when there is a low concentration of water in the blood. In the absence of ADH, large amounts of very dilute urine are excreted.

Quick Check Questions

1. __________ cells are responsible for reabsorption.

2. Aldosterone, produced by the adrenal gland, plays this role in reabsorption:
   A. increases permeability of cells to water
   B. decreases absorption of water and sodium by principle cells
   C. increases absorption of water and sodium by principle cells
   D. increases reabsorption of water in the PCT

3. The renal threshold is the point at which:
   A. 95% of the water has been reabsorbed into the DCT and collecting ducts
   B. transport maximum has been exceeded
   C. a substance passes over the endothelial membrane and spills into the urine
   D. both A and B
   E. both B and C

4. The loop of Henle reabsorbs about forty percent of the potassium from the filtered water. *True or False*

5. Virtually all the the nutrients are absorbed in the loop of Henle. *True or False*

6. Potassium brings about reabsorption of water by _______.

18.4.2 Tubular Secretion

20 minutes

Secretion of Potassium

Unlike tubular reabsorption, which channels substances back to the blood from the fluid filtrate, tubular secretion extracts materials from the blood and adds them to the filtrate. Tubular secretion has two main effects: 1) it rids the body of certain chemicals and 2) helps regulate pH. The latter function, regulation of pH, will be discussed later in the chapter. Tubular secretion involves substances which include K+, H+, NH4+, creatinine, and drugs such as penicillin and para-aminohippuric acid.

In the **proximal convoluted tubules (PCTs)**, the secretion of potassium occurs because of the action of sodium-potassium **antiporters**. Like the symporters, antiporters (sometimes called **counter-transporters**) rely on the sodium-potassium pumps to keep sodium concentrations low and are therefore **secondary active transport** processes.

Although most filtered potassium is reabsorbed, principal cells in the **collecting ducts** actually secrete potassium in exchange for reabsorbed sodium to compensate for varying amounts of potassium in the diet. Potassium secretion is sometimes necessary because the electrical gradient inside the tubule **lumen** (negative) and chemical gradient (high concentration inside tubule cells) both favor flow of potassium into the tubule lumen.

Regulation of the secretion of potassium is important as high concentrations of potassium in plasma may cause **cardiac arrhythmia**. Three factors are known to affect secretion of potassium: 1) **aldosterone** (the presence of which causes potassium secretion), 2) concentration of potassium in plasma (high concentrations of potassium lead to high potassium secretion), and 3) potassium concentration in **distal convoluted tubules (DCTs)** (high levels increase the rate of sodium absorption and potassium secretion).

Secretion of Hydrogen

When hydrogen is secreted by tubular epithelial cells and the PCTs and the collecting ducts, it causes reabsorption and creation of new bicarbonate ions (HCO3-). Carbon dioxide (CO2) diffuses into epithelial cells from peritubular blood or tubular fluid (filtrate), or is produced as a result of metabolic actions within these cells.

Then, carbon dioxide combines with water and forms carbonic acid because of the presence of an enzyme called **carbonic anhydrase** (CA). Carbonic acid then breaks apart to form hydrogen ions and bicarbonate ions (HCO3-). The hydrogen is secreted into the filtrate. Bicarbonate ions can diffuse from epithelial cells into peritubular blood. For every hydrogen ion secreted, a bicarbonate ion is returned to the blood.

In the collecting ducts, however, secretion of hydrogen occurs by primary active transport. The hydrogen pump uses ATP to transport hydrogen against a thousand-fold concentration gradient, which means that urine can be up to a thousand times more acidic than blood. Inside the **intercalated cells**, bicarbonate ions cross **basolateral membranes** using a HCO3- / Cl- antiporter. This HCO3- is new (unfiltered), so blood leaving the kidney may have a greater HCO3- content than blood entering the kidney.

Secretion of Ammonia

Ammonia is a poisonous waste product which can be converted by liver cells to a less toxic compound called **urea**. Urea and ammonia both become part of the filtrate, and are thus expelled from the body. PCT cells may also **deaminate** urea, producing ammonia. This reaction also produces a bicarbonate ion, and at pH 7.4 ammonia rapidly picks up an H+ and becomes an ammonium ion. Through the help of a transporter, it leaves its cell of origin and is secreted into filtrate by Na+ / NH4+ antiporters.

Ammonia production in the PCT depends upon shifts in pH. Ammonia increases in acidosis (pH below 7.35), and the increase in bicarbonate ions helps correct the acidic condition. On the other hand, ammonia production decreases at pH levels above 7.45.

Quick Check Questions

1. Carbonic acid breaks apart to form:
   A. hydrogen ions and bicarbonate ions
   B. hydrogen ions and potassium
   C. hydrogen ions and ammonium ions
   D. bicarbonate ions and ammonium ions

2. Secretion of potassium in the PCT occurs because of secondary active transport. *True or False*

3. Unlike symporters, antiporters rely on the action of sodium-potassium pumps. *True or False*

4. Potassium effects the concentration of bicarbonate in the filtrate because:
   A. bicarbonate ions follow potassium ions by electrical attraction
   B. for every potassium ion secreted a bicarbonate ion returns to the blood
   C. potassium antiporters carry bicarbonate back to the blood

5. Aldosterone decreases potassium secretion. *True or False*

6. The main functions of tubular secretion is to help regulate ___ and rid the body of certain chemicals.

7. _____ cells convert ammonia to urea.

18.5.1 Urine Volume and Composition

20 minutes

Antidiuretic hormone (ADH) plays a significant role in the regulation of urine volume. As mentioned earlier, if water is not reabsorbed by the distal and collecting tubules, the body loses too much water because of excess urine production. Without the presence of **aldosterone, collecting ducts** of the kidney have an unusually low permeability to water.

Due to the influence of ADH, water is reabsorbed from the tubules, reducing water loss from the body. Aldosterone works hand in hand with ADH to regulate urine output. **Atrial natriuretic peptide hormone (ANP)** works to oppose the ADH / aldosterone mechanism by reducing the sodium in plasma and the **interstitial fluid**. Thus, ANP has the opposite effect of aldosterone and decreases the reabsorption of water while increasing urine output.

Urine solute concentration also affects urine output. Generally, the greater the solutes, the greater the volume of urine. For example, in persons with diabetes mellitus excess glucose spills over into the urine, increasing urine output. **Micturition** or **urination** is the act of expelling urine from the urinary bladder. Voluntary control of micturition is usually possible by the age of 2 or 3 years, and is governed by the cerebral cortex and the second, third, and fourth sacral segments of the spinal cord.

Urine production in an adult varies from 600 to 2,500 milliliters per day. The average capacity of the urinary bladder is 700 to 800 milliliters. A urine volume of 200 milliliters stimulates the micturition reflex. Urine is approximately ninety-five percent water, in which several substances are dissolved. The illustration to the right (in software) lists the substances found in normal urine.

Quick Check Questions

1. Aldosterone and ADH work as opposing forces in the regulation of urine output. *True or False*

2. Urine mainly consists of _____.

3. All of these factors increase urine output, EXCEPT:
   A. the presence of aldosterone
   B. the presence of ANP
   C. high concentration of solutes in the blood
   D. all of the above

4. High concentration of glucose in the urine is normal. *True or False*

18.5.2 Fluid and Electrolyte Balance

20 minutes

Constancy of fluid and **electrolyte** levels in the body is essential for **homeostasis**. Fluid volume and electrolyte levels inside cells, interstitial spaces, and blood plasma are interdependent, that is, when fluid volume is off balance, electrolyte levels are off balance also. Thirst is a powerful regulator of fluid consumption. Since water is the largest component of the body (about 45 to 50 percent of total body weight), fluid consumption is an important factor in maintaining proper fluid balance. The sensation of thirst is generally triggered by dehydration. Dehydration results in decreased saliva production and dryness in the throat and mouth.

Dehydration also decreases blood volume and thus blood pressure, which then stimulates the **juxtaglomerular** cells of the kidneys. Recall that these cells release **renin**, which leads to the production of **angiotensin II**. Both of these events decrease saliva production and decrease blood pressure, resulting in stimulation of the **thirst center** in the **hypothalamus**. Many factors lead to fluid loss in the body. For example, hyperventilation leads to fluid loss in the form of water vapor from the lungs. Vomiting, diarrhea, fever, and perspiration lead to fluid loss through the intestinal tract and skin. Fluid levels in the body are regulated by the three hormones previously discussed: 1) antidiuretic hormone (ADH), 2) atrial natriuretic peptide (ANP), and 3) aldosterone. ADH and aldosterone slow fluid loss, whereas ANP acts as a diuretic.

Body fluid contains many dissolved substances, both electrolytes and nonelectrolytes. Nonelectrolytes include organic compounds such as urea, glucose, and creatinine: they do not form ions when they dissolve. When electrolytes dissolve in body fluid, however, they dissociate into cations (positively charges ions) and anions (negatively charged ions). Acids, bases and salts are electrolytes.

Electrolytes serve four main functions in the body: 1) many are essential minerals, 2) they control the transport of water between compartments via **osmosis**, 3) they help maintain the acid-base balance in the body essential to normal cellular functions, and 4) they carry electrical current, which is important both for development and for production of action potentials (they also control secretion of some chemicals and **neurotransmitters**). There are different concentrations of electrolytes in the interstitial fluid, blood plasma, and the intracellular fluid. The main difference between plasma and interstitial fluid is that plasma contains many proteins while interstitial fluid hardly has any.

Since most normal capillary membranes are impermeable to protein, protein does not flow out of the plasma into the interstitial fluid. In **extracellular fluid**, the most abundant cation is Na+ and the most abundant anion is Cl-. In the **intracellular fluid** the most abundant cation is K+, but proteins and phosphates form the most abundant anions.

The **sodium** level in the blood is controlled by aldosterone, and ANP. Along with its action on the kidneys, aldosterone is secreted in response to a decrease in the extracellular sodium concentration, increases in K+, and during physical stress. Sodium plays a primary role in fluid and electrolyte balance as it creates most of the osmotic pressure.

Chloride is able to diffuse easily between extracellular and intracellular compartments because there are many chloride leakage channels. For this reason, chloride is important in balancing osmotic pressure between compartments. Regulation of chloride is under the control of aldosterone. Aldosterone regulates sodium absorption, and chloride follows sodium by electrical attraction. **Potassium** plays a key role in establishing resting membrane potential and helps maintain fluid volume in cells. The regulation of potassium was discussed earlier in the section on tubular secretion.

Calcium is the most abundant ion in the body. Along with phosphate, it is a structural component of the bones and teeth. Calcium plays an important role in blood coagulation, neurotransmitter release, maintenance of muscle tone, and the excitability of nervous and muscle tissue. **Phosphate** plays an important role in buffering reactions. Plasma concentrations of both calcium and phosphate are regulated mainly by the **parathyroid hormone** and **calcitonin**.

Quick Check Questions

1. Concentration of electrolytes in intracellular and interstitial fluid is approximately the same. *True or False*

2. Sodium plays a primary role in fluid and electrolyte balance because it:
   A. creates most of the osmotic pressure
   B. diffuses easily between extracellular and intracellular compartments
   C. regulates potassium
   D. regulates fluid volume of cells

3. _______ plays a role in the excitability of nervous and muscle tissue.

4. ________ does most of the balancing of osmotic pressure between compartments.

5. Potassium is an important buffer in chemical reactions. *True or False*

18.5.3 Regulation of pH

12 minutes

In addition to controlling fluid movement, **electrolytes** also help regulate the body's acid-base balance. The body produces a much larger quantity of **acids** than **bases** as it carries out its **metabolic processes**, yet it is able to maintain a normal blood pH of about 7.35 to 7.45.

Acid-base balance is accomplished through cells in the renal tubule that can raise blood pH in three ways: 1) secreting hydrogen (H+) ions into the urine, making the urine more acidic while disposing of the acid in the blood, 2) by reabsorbing HCO_3^-, which is the most significant **buffer** of hydrogen in extracellular fluids, and 3) by increasing buffering of hydrogen in the blood, by producing new HCO_3^-.

Hydrogen secretion in the **collecting ducts** is buffered to prevent drastic changes in pH level. Some electrolytes act as buffering agents because they quickly bind to excess hydrogen in filtrate. Most of the bicarbonate ions have been reabsorbed by the time it reaches the collecting ducts. Two other substances, however, are present to serve as buffers: ammonia, which forms ammonium ions (NH_4^+), and phosphate, which forms dihydrogen phosphate ($H_2PO_4^-$). The buffers cannot diffuse back into cells, so they are eliminated through the urine. Excreting H+ in the urine is the body's only method of dumping its huge acid load. When these mechanisms fail, dramatic shifts in pH can occur.

Acidosis occurs when the blood pH level drops below 7.35. **Alkalosis** occurs when the blood pH rises above 7.45. If a pH change is due to metabolic causes, hyperventilation and hypoventilation can help compensate for the shift by affecting CO_2 levels. When the pH change is due to respiratory causes, kidney excretion can help to correct the condition.

Clinical Note:
Drastic changes in pH can have severe effects and should be clinically treated. If blood pH falls below 7.0, clinical depression of the nervous system can be severe enough to cause disorientation, coma, and even death. Severe alkalosis causes extreme excitation of the nervous system. Regardless of the stimuli, nerves conduct impulses repetitively. This results in extreme nervousness, muscle spasms, and sometimes convulsions and death.

Quick Check Questions

1. Normal blood pH is 7.35 to 7.45. *True or False*

2. Kidney excretion can compensate for shifts in pH brought about by respiratory causes. *True or False*

3. Ammonia and _________ bind with hydrogen in the collecting ducts.

4. Severe ________ causes clinical depression of the nervous system.

5. The renal tubule functions to raise blood pH by:
   A. secreting hydrogen into the urine, which makes the urine more acidic
   B. reabsorbing bicarbonate ions, a buffer of hydrogen in extracellular fluid
   C. to produce new HCO_3^-, which buffers hydrogen in the blood
   D. all of the above

Chapter 19
The Reproductive System

19.1.1 Reproductive Systems - Overview

12 minutes

Reproduction is the process by which new individuals are produced and continuation of the species is ensured. The **reproductive system** generates **gametes**: **ova** in the female and **spermatozoa** in the male. Gametes are **haploid** cells, which means they have half the normal (**diploid**) number of chromosomes. When an **ovum** and a spermatozoon unite, a **zygote** is formed which will develop into a **fetus**. The female body provides the site for development, nourishment and protection of the growing fetus until the time of birth or **parturition**. After birth, the female supplies nourishment for the infant through lactation.

Female Reproductive System

The female reproductive system consists of the ovaries and the **accessory organs**: the uterine tubes, uterus, vagina, vulva and breasts.

Ovaries

The **ovaries** are the primary sex organs of the female. They produce ova (eggs) and the sex hormones estrogen and progesterone. Ovaries are almond-shaped, paired glands that lie in the upper pelvic cavity, one on either side of the uterus. The ovaries are homologous to the testes in the male. (Homologous organs correspond in structure, position and origin, but not necessarily function). The ovaries are held in place by several membranous attachments. The **broad ligament**, a part of the parietal peritoneum, is the principle supporting membrane of the female reproductive tract. A specialized posterior extension of the broad ligament, called the **mesovarium**, attaches to each ovary. The **ovarian ligament** anchors the ovary to the uterus, and the **suspensory ligament** attaches the ovary to the pelvic wall.

Each ovary consists of four layers. The **germinal epithelium** is the thin, outermost layer that consists of cuboidal epithelial cells. The germinal epithelium layer is continuous with the mesothelium that covers the mesovarium. The next layer is the **tunica albuginea**, which consists of dense connective tissue. The **stroma** is further in and is composed of two layers: the outer, dense **cortex** and the inner **medulla**.

The cortex contains the **ovarian follicles**, which are the sites of oocyte development. In the cortex, there are many ovarian follicles at various stages of development. A **vesicular ovarian (Graafian) follicle** is a large, fluid-filled follicle which contains a maturing ovum and its surrounding epithelial tissue. There is a fixed number of ova present at birth. Throughout the period from puberty to menopause, these ova mature sequentially, but no new ova are generated. The cortex also secretes estrogens. A **corpus luteum** is a mature vesicular ovarian follicle which has ruptured and released its secondary oocyte. The corpus luteum produces progesterone, estrogen, relaxin, and inhibin. It will later degrade into fibrous tissue called the **corpus albicans**.

Quick Check Questions

1. What ligament attaches the ovary to the uterus?
   A. mesovarium
   B. ovarian ligament
   C. suspensory ligament

2. In which layer of the ovaries do the follicles develop?
   A. germinal epithelium
   B. tuncia albuginea
   C. stroma
   D. cortex
   E. medulla

3. The corpus luteum is a type of ________.

19.2.1 Oogenesis and the Ovarian Cycle

15 minutes

The follicles in the cortex of the ovary are the site of **oogenesis**. Oogenesis is the process of creating a mature ovum or egg. During oogenesis, a specialized cell division called **meiosis** produces cells with only one set of 23 chromosomes, the haploid number. All other cells in the human body contain 2 sets of chromosomes, for a total of 46, the diploid number. When the egg and sperm fuse, the resulting zygote has 2 copies of all chromosomes. Thus, a constant chromosome number is maintained throughout the generations.

During development of a female fetus, primordial germ cells migrate from the endoderm of the yolk sac to the ovaries. Here they differentiate into ova precursors called **oogonia**. By the end of 5 months of gestation, all the oogonia have been formed. Oogonia (which are diploid) divide **mitotically** to produce larger cells called **primary oocytes**. Near the end of gestation, the primary oocytes enter the first stage of meiosis, prophase 1, and their further maturation is arrested until puberty.

Surrounding each primary oocyte is a single layer of flattened epithelial cells. The oocyte and its epithelial layer comprise a **primordial follicle**. Once a female reaches puberty, she begins a monthly ovarian and uterine cycle called the female reproductive cycle. In the ovarian cycle, several primordial follicles respond each month to the rising levels of **follicle-stimulating hormone (FSH)** from the anterior pituitary gland and become **primary follicles**, which are covered by a single layer of cuboidal follicular cells. Most of the primary follicles degenerate. Usually only one primary follicle enters the phase where meiosis resumes and completes meiosis I, producing two cells each containing 23 chromosomes.

Most of the cytoplasm from the first meiotic division goes to only one of the two daughter cells. The smaller is called the **first polar body**, and the larger is called the **secondary oocyte**: the follicular cells that surround it divide numerous times to produce many small **granulosa cells**. The secondary oocyte and its surrounding epithelial granulosa cells comprise the secondary (growing) follicle. The secondary oocyte continues meiosis up to metaphase II, beyond which further maturation (meiosis II) is completed only if fertilization occurs.

By ten to fourteen days after the first day of menstruation, one follicle has matured enough to become a vesicular ovarian follicle. Other follicles that started to mature at the same time now degenerate. The vesicular ovarian follicle is so large it makes a bump on the surface of the ovary. Under hormonal stimulus the follicle ruptures in a process called **ovulation**, releasing the secondary oocyte.

The secondary oocyte is now surrounded by the **corona radiata**, which is composed of the **zona pellucida** and a covering of follicle cells. After the follicle has ruptured, the blood within it clots and the whole follicle then collapses to become the **corpus hemorrhagicum**. The clot is eventually absorbed, and the follicle undergoes structural and biochemical changes to become the corpus luteum, which secretes estrogen and progesterone until the end of the ovarian cycle. Then the corpus luteum degrades to a nonfunctional corpus albicans.

Quick Check Questions

1. Production of gametes involves a specialized type of cell division called ________.

2. During the female reproductive cycle, estrogen and progesterone are secreted by the:
   A. follicle
   B. germinal epithelium
   C. corpus luteum

3. Females have all the primordial follicles they will ever generate at birth. *True or False*

4. The corona radiata covers the:
   A. vesicular ovarian follicle
   B. zona pellucida
   C. corpus albicans
   D. secondary oocyte

19.2.2 Uterine (Fallopian) Tubes

12 minutes

There are two **uterine tubes** (also called **oviducts** or **fallopian** tubes), each about 10 centimeters long and 0.7 centimeters in diameter, which extend laterally and upward from the uterus to meet the ovaries. The uterine tubes receive the secondary oocyte from the ovary and transport it to the uterus: they also serve as the site of fertilization.

Each uterine tube has a funnel-shaped opening near the ovary called the **infundibulum**. The infundibulum, though close to the ovary, is not actually attached. Finger-like fringed projections called **fimbriae** extend from the infundibulum to the lateral surface of the ovary. Movement of the fimbriae during ovulation helps direct the secondary oocyte into the uterine tube. The other, narrower end of the uterine tube attaches to the uterus and is called the **isthmus**.

Three histological layers comprise the wall of the uterine tube. The inner layer is the **internal mucosa** The internal mucosa lines the lumen and is comprised of ciliated columnar epithelial cells, which facilitate movement of the secondary oocyte to the uterus. The mucosa also contains secretory cells with **microvilli** which may provide nutrients to the oocyte. The middle layer of the uterine tube is called the **muscularis** and is composed of smooth muscle. The outer layer of the uterine tube is the **serous layer** which is part of the **visceral peritoneum** (membrane that covers the tube).

Fertilization

The oocyte takes four or five days to move down the uterine tube. If the oocyte is fertilized by a sperm cell, the event usually occurs in the uterine tube. **Fertilization** can take place anytime during the first 24 hours after ovulation. Once the nuclear material of the egg and sperm unite, the ovum is called a **zygote**. Normally, the zygote migrates to the uterus where it implants and develops.

Clinical Note:
Occasionally, the zygote implants into the wall of the uterine tube causing an **ectopic** pregnancy, which is a dangerous condition. Since a uterine tube cannot expand enough to support the growth of the fetus, it will eventually rupture. This rupture causes pain and internal bleeding, and requires surgery. A pregnancy is

termed ectopic if the zygote implants anywhere other than the uterus. If fertilization does not occur, the secondary oocyte degenerates.

Quick Check Questions

1. The _________ of the uterine tubes sway during ovulation to direct the secondary oocyte.
   A. infundibulum
   B. fimbriae
   C. isthmus

2. The _______ of the uterine tubes is the site of attachment to the uterus.

3. The uterine tubes are attached to the ovaries. *True or False*

19.2.3 The Uterus

16 minutes

The **uterus**, or womb, is the place where the fetus develops during pregnancy. The uterus also serves as part of the pathway for sperm to reach the oocyte, and as the site of menstruation and labor. It is the shape of an inverted pear and is approximately 7.5 centimeters long, 5 centimeters wide, and 2.5 centimeters thick in a non-pregnant state. It is situated between the rectum and the urinary bladder, and is usually tilted anteriorly such that it meets the **vagina** at almost a right angle.

The thick-walled, muscular uterus has several anatomical regions. The **fundus** is the dome-shaped portion above the entrance of the uterine tubes. The central portion is called the body, and the narrow portion opening into the vagina is the **cervix**.

The cervical mucosa secretes a mixture of glycoprotein, serum-type proteins, lipids, enzymes, inorganic salts, and water. Around the time of ovulation, this substance, called **cervical mucus**, is more receptive to spermatozoa because it is more alkaline (pH 8.5) and less viscous. At other times of the female reproductive cycle, the cervical mucus forms a plug that hinders sperm penetration.

The isthmus of the uterus is the narrow region, about 1 centimeters long, between the body and the cervix. The internal portion of the body is the uterine cavity, and that of the cervix is the cervical canal. Between the uterine cavity and the isthmus is a junction called the internal os. The cervix opens to the vagina at the external os.

The position of the uterus is maintained by muscular supports and ligaments that extend from the body wall. The paired **broad ligaments** are double folds of parietal peritoneum which attach the uterus to either side of the pelvic cavity. The ovaries and uterine tubes are also supported by the broad ligaments. The uterus is connected to the sacrum by the paired **uterosacral ligaments**, also part of the peritoneum.

The **cardinal ligaments** (lateral cervical ligaments) are sheets of peritoneum that extend laterally from the cervix and vagina across the pelvic floor where they attach to the wall of the pelvis. The **round ligaments**, which are continuous with the **ovarian ligaments**, extend laterally from the uterus below the uterine tubes to a portion of the **labia majora** of the external **genitalia**. These four pairs of ligaments maintain the **anteflexed** position of the uterus, but allow for some movement. Thus it is possible for the uterus to become posteriorly tilted, a condition called **retroflexion**.

The wall of the uterus is composed of three histological layers: 1) the **endometrium**, 2) the **myometrium**, and 3) the **perimetrium**. The inner endometrium has two distinct layers. The superficial **stratum functionale** is composed of columnar epithelium and contains secretory glands. The superficial stratum functionale is the layer that is shed during menstruation. The deeper **stratum basalis** is permanent and highly vascularized. It serves to regenerate the stratum functionale after each menstruation.

The myometrium is the middle layer of the uterus wall and consists of three layers of smooth muscle. The myometrium is thickest at the fundus and thinnest at the cervix. These muscle layers contract forcibly to help expel the fetus during childbirth. The thin outer perimetrium is part of the visceral peritoneum. Laterally it merges with the broad ligament and anteriorly it covers the urinary bladder and forms the shallow **vesicouterine pouch**. Posteriorly the outer perimetrium covers the rectum and forms the deep **rectouterine pouch** (pouch of Douglas), the lowest point in the pelvic cavity.

The uterus receives its blood supply from branches of the internal iliac artery called the **uterine arteries** and by **uterine branches** of the ovarian arteries. Branches from the uterine arteries penetrate the perimetrium to form the **arcuate artery**, along the outside of the myometrium. Numerous **radial arteries** arise from the arcuate artery to supply the myometrium. **Spiral arterioles** arise from the radial arteries to supply the endometrium. Uterine, ovarian and vaginal veins return venous blood from the uterus to the internal iliac veins.

Quick Check Questions

1. The internal os is below the:
   A. external os
   B. cervical canal
   C. uterine cavity
   D. vagina
   E. isthmus

2. Which ligaments support both the uterus and the ovaries?
   A. broad ligaments
   B. uterosacral ligaments
   C. cardinal ligaments
   D. round ligaments

3. The normal position of the uterus is ____flexed.

4. The ________ layer of the uterus is shed at menstruation.
   A. myometrium
   B. perimetrium
   C. stratum functionale
   D. stratum basalis

19.2.4 The Vagina

8 minutes

The **vagina** is a tubular, fibromuscular organ situated between the urinary bladder and the rectum, lined with mucous membrane arranged in ridges called **rugae**. It extends approximately 10 centimeters upward and backward from its external opening, the **vaginal orifice**. The vagina serves as the birth canal, receives sperm from the male during sexual intercourse, and allows exit of the stratum functionale endometrium during **menstruation**.

The mucous membrane of the vagina is continuous with that of the uterus and consists of stratified squamous epithelium and connective tissue. The rugae and the smooth muscle can stretch, either to accommodate an erect **penis** during **coitus** or to allow for the birth of a baby. The vaginal orifice is sometimes partially blocked at birth by a fold of mucous membrane called the **hymen**. The hymen is usually broken before or during the first sexual intercourse. Occasionally the hymen completely covers the vaginal orifice. This condition is called **imperforate hymen** and requires perforation before puberty to permit the discharge of the menstrual flow.

The mucous membrane of the vagina contains few glands. Most of the acidic mucus in the vagina comes from glands in the uterus. This acidic environment retards microbial growth, and is also harmful to sperm. The **semen** contains alkaline components which temporarily neutralize the acidity of the vagina and permit survival of sperm.

Quick Check Questions

1. The vagina is part of the exterior female genitalia. *True or False*

2. The _____ partially covers the vaginal orifice.

3. The _______ are ridges of mucous membranes on the vaginal wall.
   A. hymen
   B. imperforate
   C. rugae

19.2.5 The Vulva

12 minutes

The female external genitalia are referred to collectively as the **vulva**. The vulva includes: 1) the **mons pubis**, 2) the **labia majora**, 3) the **labia minora**, 4) the **prepuce of clitoris** and clitoris, 5) the **urethral orifice**, 6) the **vaginal orifice**, and 7) the **vestibule**. The mons pubis is an area anterior to the vaginal and urethral orifice delineated by the subcutaneous adipose layer and covered with coarse pubic hair. It cushions the **pubic symphysis** during sexual intercourse.

The labia majora (labium = lip) are two thickened folds of skin which extend inferiorly and posteriorly from the mons pubis. They contain adipose tissue, are covered with pubic hair, and have many sebaceous (oil) and sudoriferous (sweat) glands. The labia majora are homologous to the male scrotum, and function to protect the other parts of the vulva. The labia minora are two smaller folds positioned close together within the labia majora. They are devoid of pubic hair, and contain only a few sudoriferous (sweat) glands, but many sebaceous (oil) glands.

The clitoris is a small cylindrical organ composed of erectile tissue and richly innervated with sensory endings. Most of the clitoris is embedded: the exposed part is called the **glans**. The glans is located at the anterior junction of the labia minora and partially covered by the **prepuce** or foreskin. The clitoris enlarges upon tactile stimulation and is involved in sexual stimulation of the female. It is homologous to the penis of the male.

The vestibule is the cleft between the labia minora containing the vaginal and urethral orifices, and the opening of several ducts. A pair of **vestibular glands**, located in the vaginal wall just inside the orifice, provide lubrication to the vaginal orifice during sexual excitement. Two longitudinal masses of erectile tissue, the **vestibular bulbs**, are located just under the labia minora along both sides of the vaginal orifice. Upon sexual arousal, the bulbs engorge with blood and narrow the vaginal orifice. The bulb is homologous to the **corpus spongiosum** and **bulb of the penis**.

In a woman in the eighth to twelfth week of pregnancy, the vulva, especially the labia minora, becomes swollen and changes to a bluish color due to increased vascularity. This change in color becomes more apparent as pregnancy progresses, and is used as a diagnostic indicator of pregnancy.

Quick Check Questions

1. Which of the following are NOT part of the vulva?
   A. mons pubis
   B. vagina
   C. labia minora
   D. urethral orifice

2. Which part of the vulva is homologous to the male scrotum?
   A. mons pubis
   B. labia majora
   C. clitoris
   D. hymen
   E. labia minora

3. Which part of the vulva is homologous to the male penis?
   A. mons pubis
   B. labia majora
   C. clitoris
   D. hymen
   E. labia minora

4. Two areas of erectile tissue in the vulva are the clitoris and the mons pubis.
   True or False

19.2.6 The Perineum (Female)

10 minutes

The **perineum** is a muscular region between the vulva and the anus. During childbirth, the perineal region is stretched and can even be torn.

Clinical Note:
In preference to an uncontrolled tear in the perineum during childbirth, a surgical incision called an **episiotomy** may be performed. This incision is made from the vaginal orifice into the perineum, to increase the size of the orifice enough to accommodate the emerging infant. The cut is sutured after delivery.

The Breasts and Mammary Glands

The **breasts** lie over the pectoralis major muscle and are attached to them by a layer of connective tissue. The female breasts begin to develop at the onset of **puberty** under the influence of **estrogen** and **progesterone**. The size and shape of the breasts vary considerably from woman to woman due to percentage of body fat, genetic factors, pregnancy, and age. Breast size is mostly a function of the amount of fat in the breast, as the amount of glandular tissue does not much vary. Breast function (the ability to nurse) is not related to breast size.

Mammary Glands

The **mammary glands** are modified sudoriferous (sweat) glands located inside the breasts. Each mammary gland contains 15 to 20 **lobes** separated by adipose tissue. Each lobe is further subdivided into several **lobules**. Inside the lobules are the grape-like clusters of milk-secreting glands called **alveoli**.

When a woman is nursing, milk is conveyed from the alveoli into a series of **secondary tubules**, then into the **mammary ducts**. Close to the nipple, the mammary ducts expand into **lactiferous sinuses**, where milk can be stored. From these sinuses, the milk flows through **lactiferous ducts** which end at the **nipple**. The nipple is a cylindrical, pigmented projection which contains some erectile tissue. The pigmented area around the nipple is called the **areola**. The areola contains **sebaceous areolar glands**, which make the areola appear rough and which provide secretions to keep the nipple pliable. In women of light complexion, the nipple turns color from pink to brown early in pregnancy.

Lactation

Lactation is the synthesis and expression of milk which occurs while nursing an infant. The hormone **prolactin**, together with progesterone and estrogen, stimulates the production of milk. When the infant sucks on a nipple, the mother's posterior pituitary gland releases oxytocin, which in turn stimulates expression of milk into the ducts. The infant then extracts it by continued sucking. Milk is a rich source of nutrients, protein, and fat for a developing infant. Human milk also provides maternal antibodies which give the infant passive immunity.

Clinical Note:
In America, **breast cancer** affects one out of every nine women. Some forms of breast cancer have a hereditary component. Other forms of breast cancer are thought to result from external sources such as radiation, cigarette smoking, or excessive fat or alcohol intake.

Quick Check Questions

1. The perineum is the diamond-shaped muscular area between the vulva and the urinary bladder. *True or False*

2. Mammary gland and breast refer to the same thing. *True or False*

3. The pigmented area around the nipple is called the ______.

4. Breast size is determined mostly by:
   A. genetic factors
   B. adipose tissue in the breast
   C. complexion
   D. the number of alveoli

5. The secondary tubules empty into the:
   A. mammary ducts
   B. lactiferous sinuses
   C. lactiferous ducts
   D. nipple

19.2.7 The Female Reproductive Cycle

16 minutes

During the approximately 30 years between the onset of menses (**menarche**) and their cessation (**menopause**), women normally experience a monthly cycle of changes, the most obvious of which is **menstruation**.

Ovarian Cycle

The **ovarian cycle** describes the cycle of **oogenesis** and release of the secondary oocyte from the ovary. The uterine or **menstrual cycle** is the buildup and release of the **stratum functionale** endometrium (that is, about 100 milliliters of blood, tissue fluid, mucus, and epithelial cells from the endometrium). Together these cycles comprise the **female reproductive cycle**. The female reproductive cycle ranges from 24 to 35 days. We will assume a cycle of 28 days.

The major hormonal control of the ovarian and uterine cycle is accomplished by **gonadotropin-releasing hormone (GnRH)** from the **hypothalamus**. GnRH stimulates release of **follicle-stimulating hormone (FSH)**, and **luteinizing hormone (LH)** from the **anterior pituitary gland**. As its name implies, FSH stimulates development of and estrogen production by the follicle in the ovary. LH stimulates release of the secondary oocyte from the follicle and the production of estrogen, progesterone, inhibin and relaxin by the **corpus luteum**.

The reproductive cycle can be divided into three phases. The **menstrual phase** is characterized by the sloughing off of the stratum functionalis layer of the uterine endometrium and its release through the vagina. The first day of menstruation is designated the first day of the reproductive cycle. **Primary follicles** begin to develop at this time in preparation for the next ovulation.

The **preovulatory phase** is the time between menstruation and ovulation. The preovulatory phase lasts from about day 6 to day 13 in a 28 day cycle, although the length of time is more variable than that of the other phases. In this phase, a **vesicular ovarian follicle** develops from a primary follicle. Although about 20 primary follicles start development in each cycle, only one will develop into a vesicular ovarian follicle.

The dominant developing follicle produces moderate amounts of estrogen which inhibits secretion of FSH from the anterior pituitary. The reduced level of FSH prevents development of the other follicles. This degenerative process is called **atresia**. If two follicles happen to develop to ovulation and are both fertilized, fraternal twins may result. As levels of FSH decrease, levels of LH increase. A few days before ovulation, the follicles begin to secret small amounts of progesterone.

During the preovulatory phase, the estrogen secreted from the follicle stimulates regeneration of the stratum functionalis from the stratum basalis in the endometrium. This preovulatory phase is also called the **proliferative phase** (referring to the regrowth of the endometrium) or the **estrogenic** or **follicular phase** (referring to the development of follicles).

Ovulation

The level of estrogen is high right before **ovulation**. This stimulates release of LH from the anterior pituitary and GnRH from the hypothalamus, which stimulates even more LH secretion. The high levels of LH trigger ovulation. Ovulation occurs when the follicle ruptures the surface of the ovary and releases the **secondary oocyte** into the **fallopian tube** (or uterine tube). This occurs around day 14 of a 28 day cycle. The secondary oocyte is in **metaphase** of **meiosis II**, and is surrounded by an outer layer called the **corona radiata**. The **fimbriae** of the uterine tubes begin to sway before and during ovulation, helping to direct the oocyte into the uterine tubes.

The **postovulatory phase** lasts from ovulation to menstruation, about 14 days. The length of this phase is fixed, as compared to the length of the preovulatory phase. During the postovulatory phase, the remains of the vesicular ovarian follicle become the corpus luteum under the influence of LH. The corpus luteum secretes increasing amounts of estrogen and progesterone. Progesterone stimulates further development of the endometrium, preparing it to receive a fertilized **ovum**. The postovulatory phase is also called the **premenstrual** or **secretory phase**.

Quick Check Questions

1. The major hormonal control of the female reproductive cycle is accomplished by:
   A. FSH
   B. LH
   C. GnRH
   D. estrogens
   E. progesterone

2. The first day of the reproductive cycle is the first day of the ________ phase?

3. During the preovulatory phase, which of the following occur?
   A. development of the follicle
   B. shedding of endometrium
   C. ovulation
   D. development of the corpus luteum

4. During the postovulatory phase, which of the following occur?
   A. development of the follicle
   B. shedding of endometrium
   C. build up of endometrium
   D. ovulation

5. During the menstrual phase, which of the following occur?
   A. development of the follicle
   B. shedding of endometrium
   C. build up of endometrium
   D. ovulation
   E. development of the corpus luteum

19.3.1 The Male Reproductive System

6 minutes

The male reproductive system generates and transfers mature **spermatozoa** (male sex cells or **gametes**) to the female reproductive tract. The male and female reproductive systems work together to produce offspring, essential for the survival and propagation of the human race. Just as **puberty** marks the beginning of sexual maturity in females, this stage is also essential to male development.

Puberty

Puberty is characterized by high levels of hormones which stimulate the final stages of development of secondary sexual characteristics. Although females lose reproductive function at menopause, the male reproductive system enables most men to fertilize an egg at any time until death, provided they are healthy. The organs of the male reproductive system fall into two general categories: 1) the **essential** organs, and 2) the **accessory** organs. The former are the **testes**, the male gonads which produce sperm. **Genital ducts**, glands and supporting structures comprise the accessory organs: these each play an important supportive role.

Quick Check Questions

1. Male gametes are called testes. *True or False*

2. Puberty marks the beginning of sexual development in both males and females. *True or False*

3. Spermatozoa are the male sex cells which are produced in the genital ducts. *True or False*

19.3.2 The Perineum (Male)

6 minutes

Extending from the **symphysis pubis** anteriorly to the **coccyx** posteriorly, and between the two **ischial tuberosities** (recall Skeletal System chapter) males have an anatomically defined diamond-shaped area called the **perineum**. This area can be further divided into two triangular regions: 1) the larger **urogenital triangle**, containing the **penis** and 2) the **scrotum**, and the anal triangle, surrounding the **anus**.

Testes

Measuring about 4 to 5 centimeters in length, these small **ovoid glands** are suspended asymmetrically in the **scrotal sac** with the left testis hanging about 1 centimeter lower than the right.

When the **testes** descend from the abdominal cavity late in fetal development, they drag along with them **mesothelium** (epithelial tissue from the posterior abdominal wall) which becomes the **tunica albuginea**. This dense white fibrous capsule not only encases each testis, but also partitions the gland into more the 200 cone shaped lobules by means of **septa**. Each lobule contains 1 to 3 structures called the **seminiferous tubules** (each measuring about 75 centimeters in length) which produce sperm. These lobules are separated by specialized **interstitial** cells called **Leydig cells**, which secrete testosterone, the male sex hormone. The wall of each tubule may contain 5 or more cells in cross section.

Quick Check Questions

1. Anatomically normal testes hang symmetrically within the scrotal sac. *True or False*

2. The dense white fibrous capsule which encases each testis is called the:
   A. scrotal sac
   B. tuncia albuginea
   C. septa
   D. spermatozoa

3. The anatomic perineum can be divided into an anal triangle and a(n) __________ triangle.

19.3.3 The Function of Testes

10 minutes

The generation and development of sperm is referred to as **spermatogenesis** and begins at the periphery of each **seminiferous tubule** and moves towards the **lumen** of the seminiferous tubule, where the mature sperm are eventually released. In addition to providing mechanical support and protection to developing sperm cells, supportive cells called **Sertoli cells** also play an active role in the final release of mature sperm.

The testes are responsible for spermatogenesis (discussed further in the chapter on Inheritance) and for secretion of **hormones**. **Testosterone**, the principal hormone of the male system, secreted by the Leydig cells, is also a hormone **precur-**

sor which is converted to **dihydroxytestoterone (DHT)** in order to produce an effect in **target cells**. DHT serves the following general functions:

1) To promote and maintain the development of male secondary sexual characteristics (facial and pubic hair, voice deepening, etc.), **prostate gland, seminal vesicles** and adult male sexual behavior.

2) To stimulate protein **anabolism** which consequently promotes both muscular and skeletal strength, including the final closure of **epiphyses** (which marks the end of longitudinal bone growth - see chapter on the *Skeletal System*).

3) To decrease the growth of hair on top of the head. Men who become bald have both a genetic predisposition and large quantities of circulating testosterone.

4) To increase the thickness of skin and to increase the strength of **subcutaneous** tissue over the entire body.

5) To increase the rate of secretion of **sebaceous glands**. Excessive secretion can result in **acne**. It can sometimes take several years after the onset of puberty for the skin to sufficiently adapt itself to the high levels of hormones and overcome the acne.

6) It inhibits **follicle-stimulating hormone (FSH)** and **luteinizing hormone** (LH) release from the anterior pituitary in the brain in a negative **feedback system** which functions to prevent its over production.

Quick Check Questions

1. The structures within the testes which produce sperm are called:
   A. Leydig cells
   B. epididymis
   C. seminiferous tubules
   D. Sertoli cells

2. The following structures produce testosterone.
   A. Leydig cells
   B. spermatozoa
   C. seminiferous tubules
   D. Sertoli cells

3. DHT is a hormone precursor of testosterone. *True or False*

19.3.4 Puberty

6 minutes

At the onset of **puberty**, the anterior pituitary releases the **gonadotropic** hormones [**follicle-stimulating hormone** (**FSH**) and **luteinizing hormone** (**LH**)] into the circulation. Alterations in patterns of **gonadotropic-releasing hormone** (**GnRH**) secretions from the **hypothalamus** control their release. FSH stimulates **Sertoli cells** (spermatogenesis) and LH in the **Leydig cells** (testosterone production). Another hormone called **inhibin** is also secreted from the Sertoli cells.

When levels of circulating testosterone are sufficient, this hormone directly inhibits the secretion of FSH from the **anterior pituitary** and GnRH from the hypothalamus. A **spermatozoon** is a highly specialized cell which contains a head, a midpiece and a long tail. The head is packed with genetic chromatin and covered by a special acrosomal cap loaded with **hydrolytic** (splitting) enzymes which are able to penetrate both the cervical mucus and the outer covering of the egg to initiate fertilization.

Capacitation

Capacitation describes the complex process through which a sperm cell must go, once introduced into the female reproductive tract, in order to successfully fertilize an **ovum**. The midpiece contains a lot of mitochondria which provide energy for motility of the tail, which ultimately propels the sperm toward the ovum.

Quick Check Questions

1. Inhibin inhibits the release of FSH and LH from the hypothalamus.
   True or False

2. The release of hydrolytic enzymes from the acrosomal cap is a part of the complex process known as ____________.

19.4.1 Reproductive (Genital) Ducts

8 minutes

Though continuous with one another, the **epididymis**, the **vas (ductus) deferens,** the **ejaculatory duct** and the **urethra** are conventionally and functionally discrete reproductive **genital ducts** in the male.

Consisting of a fine tube (approximately 20 feet in length), each epididymis is coiled tightly into the shape of a comma. Packaged in fibrous casing atop each testes, this structure is continuous with the seminiferous tubules at one end and the vas deferens at the other. However, this duct serves as more than just a passageway through which sperm pass to get to the outside. It contributes both to sperm maturation, by allowing storage for up to 3 weeks, and secretes a small portion of the **seminal fluid (semen)**.

An extension of the epididymis, the vas (ductus) deferens is a somewhat thicker tube, made up of three concentric muscle layers, which functions both to store sperm and to propel sperm through the ductal system. Each tube ascends from the scrotum, passes through the **inguinal canal** up into the abdominal cavity, over the top and down the posterior surface of the bladder, where it finally meets the ejaculatory duct from the seminal vesicle at an enlarged structure called the **ampulla**. Formed by the union of the vas deferens and the **seminal vesicles,** each ejaculatory duct is a short tube that passes through the **prostate gland** to end in the urethra, which serves as a passageway to the exterior for both urine and semen.

Clinical Note:
Since it interrupts the route of the sperm to the exterior, a **vasectomy** is a highly effective contraceptive method. It can be performed with local anesthetics through a tiny incision in the scrotal sac which allows access to the vas deferens, each of which must then be completely severed and ligated for the operation to be successful.

Quick Check Questions

1. Sperm can be stored for up to 3 weeks in the:
   A. ampulla
   B. epididymis
   C. ejaculatory duct
   D. urethra

2. A vasectomy involves the severing of the:
   A. ejaculatory duct
   B. epididymis
   C. ductus (vas) deferens

19.4.2 The Reproductive Glands

10 minutes

The **seminal vesicles**, the **prostate gland**, and the **bulbourethral (Cowper's) glands** constitute the **reproductive glands** of the male system. The seminal vesicles are glands that lie in pouches tucked behind the bladder and in front of the rectum. Dependent upon normal levels of testosterone for normal activity, these paired structures contribute about 60 percent of the fluid component, of a thick yellowish alkaline fluid called **semen**. Semen secretion is rich in fructose, a simple sugar, which is used a a source of energy by the sperm for its **motility**.

The thin fluid from the prostate gland is responsible for about 30 percent of the **seminal fluid** volume and its **alkalinity**. Seminal fluid protects the sperm from the **acidity** in the male urethra and the female vagina and ensures a greater chance for survival and successful fertilization. Lying just below the bladder, the prostate gland is donut-shaped, with the urethra passing through the small hole in the center.

Clinical Note:
Enlargement of the prostate is clinically significant (fairly common in older men) because it can squeeze the urethra so much that it impedes the passage of urine. The bulbourethral or Cowper's glands, smaller pea-shaped glands connected by a duct to the **penile urethra**, contribute less than 5 percent of the seminal fluid secretion. The alkaline fluid not only protects against acidity, but also contains mucus which serves to lubricate the urethra.

Quick Check Questions

1. Most of the seminal fluid is produced by the seminiferous tubules.
   True or False

2. The prostate gland is a small pea shaped gland which is connected to the penile urethra. *True or False*

3. Cowper's glands are also known as ______________ glands.

19.4.3 The Scrotum and Penis

11 minutes

The **scrotum** and the **penis** together constitute the external genitals of the male and are considered **supportive structures**. Containing the **testes** and an **epididymi**, the scrotum is a skin-covered pouch split into two compartments by a septum, suspended from the **perineum**. So why are these organs hanging so vulnerably outside of the male body? The answer lies in the fact that the temperature required for sperm formation is about 3 degrees C below body temperature. However, when the environment is too cold, contraction of the **Dartos muscle** and **cremaster muscles** elevates the testes, bringing them closer to the warmth of the body.

The **corpus cavernosa** and the **corpus spongiosum** are the three cylindrical masses of **erectile tissue** which constitute the penis. The former are larger paired structures, dorsal to the single corpus spongiosum through which the urethra runs. (Note: The anatomic position of the penis is its erect state). The bulging distal end of the spongiosum is called the glans penis and is covered by loose fitting retractable skin called the foreskin or the **prepuce**. During sexual arousal the penis becomes erect, filling with blood and becoming rigid and larger in both diameter and length. In this way, the penis can perform as a **copulatory organ**, anatomically able to penetrate and inseminate.

Male Fertility

Although male **fertility** relates to many factors, the production of fertile sperm is probably the most critical. Semen analysis can be used to evaluate male fertility and provides the following information:

Volume

A low volume (2.5 to 5 milliliters is the average volume of semen in an ejaculation) could signify an anatomical or functional defect, inflammation, or infection.

Motility

Less than 60 percent of sperm showing good forward motility collected within the first three hours after ejaculation could indicate an abnormality in spermatozoa.

Count

Sperm counts under 20 million per milliliter are abnormal.

Liquefaction

Delayed liquefaction of more than two hours suggests a glandular problem.

Morphology

If more than 30 to 35 percent of sperm cells are deformed, this could contribute to decreased fertility.

pH

A higher pH than normal (too alkaline) could indicate inflammation of the prostate.

Fructose

Absence of fructose is always abnormal, indicating an obstruction or congenital nonexistence of seminal vesicles or ejaculatory ducts.

Quick Check Questions

1. There are two scrotal sacs, each containing a testis and an epididymis. *True or False*

2. The single mass of erectile tissue through which the urethra runs is the:
   A. corpus spongiosum
   B. corpus cavernosa
   C. prostate gland
   D. prepuce

3. _____ analysis is a technique used to evaluate male fertility by analyzing factors such as volume, motility and count.

4. The average ejaculate contains roughly:
   A. 1 to 2 milliliters of fluid
   B. 2.5 to 5 milliliters of fluid
   C. 10 to 12 milliliters of fluid
   D. 12 to 15 milliliters of fluid

5. Sperm counts under ___ million per milliliter are abnormal.

Chapter 20
Inheritance

20.1.1 Inheritance - Overview

12 minutes

Genetics is the study of inheritance, or the transmission of characteristics from parents to offspring. Every cell, with few exceptions, contains a nucleus. Inside the nucleus are **chromosomes**, long filaments of **deoxyribonucleic acid (DNA)**, which carry the genetic code. Genetic information is coded in units called **genes**. Each gene consists of a specific section of a filament of DNA, and may be identified by its location on a particular chromosome.

On each chromosome there are thousands of genes arranged in a distinct order. Each gene controls the formation of a specific protein. Proteins carry out many cellular functions: some act as **enzymes**, some function as part of the machinery of the cell, and some become structural components of the cell. By controlling **protein synthesis**, genes are able to affect all cellular functions, and therefore to determine the structure and function of the entire body.

Humans have 23 pairs of chromosomes in each of their **somatic** cells (that is, all cells except the reproductive cells). The two chromosomes which make up a pair are similar, but each of the 23 pairs has a distinctive appearance or **morphology** which can be distinguished by an expert. A **karyotype** is a picture of all the chromosomes in a single cell, arranged in a standard order. Karyotypes are made after the chromosomes have replicated and condensed in preparation for cell division. Thus, each chromosome in the pair appears doubled, attached by a **centromere** (a central connection between chromosome copies).

Of the 23 pairs of chromosomes present in all somatic cells, 22 are called **autosomes**. The 23rd pair contains the **sex chromosomes**, which determine the sex and **sex-linked traits** of the offspring. Every cell in the normal female body contains two X chromosomes, while in the normal male each cell has one X and one Y chromosome. Each chromosome pair consists of two **homologous chromosomes**. One chromosome originates with the mother and one with the father. Each **homologue** in a pair carries its genes in the same distinct order. Thus, there are two copies of each gene (two **alleles**) contained in each cell's nucleus, one from the mother and one from the father.

Although alleles are genes that code for the same trait and are found at the same location on homologous chromosomes, they may be slightly different. For example, if one chromosome carries a gene for eye color, its homologue will also carry a gene for eye color. But one of the alleles may code for blue eyes, while its homologue codes for brown eyes. The collection of all the genes in a cell, including the two alleles of each gene, is referred to as the **genome**.

Quick Check Questions

1. How many pairs of chromosomes are there in each white blood cell?
   A. 2
   B. 22
   C. 23
   D. 46

2. How many chromosomes are there in each white blood cell?
   A. 2
   B. 22
   C. 23
   D. 46

3. The mother and father each provide ______ chromosomes to a white blood cell.

4. In human somatic cells, all genes found on the autosomal chromosomes have two alleles. *True or False*

5. There are thousands of _____ on each chromosome.

20.2.1 Meiosis

12 minutes

Meiosis is a specialized kind of cell division which takes place only in the reproductive cells. In the male testes meiosis occurs during **spermatogenesis**, and in the female ovaries it occurs during **oogenesis**. Let us refer to "**n**" as the number of unique chromosomes in a cell. Every cell (except those undergoing meiosis) has 23 pairs of chromosomes. So, since n = 23, cells have 2n = 46 chromosomes. Meiosis includes two successive cell divisions: a reductive division (meiosis 1), followed by an equatorial division (meiosis 2). These two divisions result in a single 2n cell giving birth to four "n" cells. A cell with a chromosome number of "n" contains one copy of each chromosome. This type of cell is called a **gamete**.

The number of chromosomes contained in the gamete (n) is called the **haploid** number. Ova and sperm cells are gametes. The process of fertilization involves the fusion of the egg and sperm cells. The joining of n chromosomes from the egg with n chromosomes from the sperm leads to 2n chromosomes in the fertilized egg. The fertilized egg is called a **zygote**. The 2n chromosomes contained in the zygote is the **diploid** number. The process of meiosis reduces the number of chromosomes in the gametes to the haploid number, that is, one copy of each chromosome (n = 23). Therefore, when the egg and sperm fuse, the resulting zygote has two copies of each chromosome (2n = 46, the diploid number). Thus, a constant chromosome number is maintained from generation to generation.

The first meiotic division, meiosis 1, is a reductive division. Initially, the 2n cell contains "n" maternal and "n" paternal chromosomes, arranged in homologous pairs. As in mitosis, the **DNA** replicates so that each of the 2n chromosomes consists of a pair of **chromatids**. The homologous pairs line up at the center of the cell, and a chromosome from each pair migrates to opposite poles of the cell, then the cell divides. So the result of meiosis 1 is two haploid daughter cells, each containing one replicated chromosome from a pair. But these cells are not identical copies of the parent cell. There are two ways in which daughter chromosomes become differentiated from the parental chromosomes. These mechanisms (called **independent assortment** and **crossing over**) are described in more detail in the next tutorial.

Both mechanisms occur during meiosis 1, due to a structure formed during middle prophase. At this stage, each chromosome contains four chromatids (a homologous pair with replicated DNA). The chromatids line up exactly with each other to form a structure called a **bivalent** (or **tetrad**). The way in which the bivalents separate during metaphase and anaphase accounts for the production of **nonidentical daughter cells**. The second stage of meiosis (meiosis 2) involves equatorial cell division of the two daughter cells from meiosis 1. At this point, each of the haploid cells divides without further DNA replication, so that each of the sister chromatids from a chromosome goes to an individual cell. The final result is four haploid daughter cells, each containing a single set of the n chromosomes.

Quick Check Questions

1. Meiosis can occur in white blood cells. *True or False*

2. Does a white blood cell contain the diploid or the haploid chromosome number?
   A. diploid
   B. haploid

3. Does an ovum contain the diploid or the haploid chromosome number?
   A. diploid
   B. haploid

20.2.2 Independent Assortment

8 minutes

Genetic diversity is a result of the differentiation of daughter chromosomes from those of the parental cell. One mechanism of differentiation occurs by mixed distribution of chromosomes during cell division. Of the two sets of chromosomes in an individual, half come from the mother and half from the father. Recall that during **mitosis** (somatic cell division), a dividing cell contains one set of paternal chromosomes and one set of maternal chromosomes. These replicate, and a copy of each chromosome goes to each pole of the cell. Then the cell divides. In this way, the **daughter cells** of mitosis always contain one maternal set and one paternal set, so they are identical to the parent cell.

When an individual produces sperm or egg cells, each of the 23 pairs of chromosomes is independently divided such that each **gamete** will contain a different mixture of its maternal and paternal chromosomes. The **bivalent** structures which form during **prophase** 1 consist of one replicated maternal chromosome and one paternal **chromatid** pair. When the cell splits into daughter cells, the maternal and paternal chromosomes go to different cells. Each bivalent is independent of the others in terms of which pair goes to which daughter cell, so there are many possible combinations (think of the millions of ways to randomly split up 23 pairs). This way of creating genetic diversity, first described by Mendel, is called **independent assortment**.

The other mechanism which creates genetic diversity is called **crossing over**. Crossing over also occurs during meiosis 1, when the replicated chromosome pairs are lined up in bivalents. With the strands so close together, exactly aligned parts of **homologous chromosomes** are able to physically exchange pieces of DNA by breaking and rejoining. This results in chromosomes that are mosaics of maternal and paternal chromosomes. These two processes, independent assortment and crossing over, are responsible for the diversity of offspring that can be produced by a single male and female.

Quick Check Questions

1. Independent assortment and crossing over explain why children of a single pair of parents have different physical characteristics. *True or False*

2. Identical twins look the same because they have identical sets of chromosomes. *True or False*

3. ______ (last name) was the person who first discovered independent assortment.

20.2.3 Genotype and Phenotype

8 minutes

Although **homologous chromosomes** contain the same **genes** in the same location, each gene can exist in two or more alternative forms. A variant of a particular gene is called an **allele.** **Genotype** is the set of all alleles in a person's chromosome set. **Phenotype** refers to the physical expression of a particular genotype.

The relationship between genes on a chromosome and heredity can be illustrated with the inherited metabolic disease **phenylketonuria (PKU**). A certain genotype can cause PKU, a condition characterized by an inability to metabolize the amino acid phenylalanine. If high levels of phenylalanine build up in the blood, they inhibit proper brain development. If PKU is not detected early so that an infant can be fed a restricted diet, mental retardation will result. The development of PKU and its consequences is an example of a phenotype.

Let us look more closely at the process which produces PKU. The gene that codes for the enzyme **phenylalanine hydroxylase** is located on chromosome 12. The normal allele, symbolized "**P**", can make functional phenylalanine hydroxylase. There is an abnormal allele of this gene, symbolized "**p**", that cannot direct the synthesis of phenylalanine hydroxylase. Each chromosome 12 in the homologous pair can contain either allele. Thus, an individual can have one of three gene combinations or genotypes: PP, Pp, or pp. Only when both homologues carry the p allele will that individual have PKU (genotype pp). People with one normal allele and one abnormal allele (Pp) are normal, as are people with two normal alleles (PP). However, note that Pp individuals can pass on the abnormal allele to their offspring. Such individuals are called **carriers**.

An individual with the same allele on both homologues is said to be **homozygous** for that gene. When an individual has two different alleles of a gene, the person is **heterozygous** for that gene. Thus, individuals that are PP or pp are homozygotes, while individuals that are Pp are heterozygotes. In the case of PKU, the P allele dominates or masks the expression of the p allele. We say the P allele is **dominant** and the p allele is **recessive**. By convention, dominant alleles are written in capital letters and recessive alleles are lower case. As noted earlier, phenotype refers to the physical consequences produced by a particular genotype. So people with the pp genotype express a phenotype of PKU.

Consider a second example: **albinism.** The phenotype seen in albinism is a lack of melanin pigment in the skin, hair, and eyes. Albinism is caused by the defective allele of a gene on chromosome 11, designated **a.** Only individuals homozygous for the defective allele (genotype aa) are albino. Those with genotypes AA or Aa have normal pigmentation. Those with the Aa genotype are carriers.

Quick Check Questions

1. An individual can have the genotype PPp. True or False

2. Children of a Pp mother and a PP father will have PKU. True or False

3. Children of an Aa mother and an Aa father can be albino. True or False

4. Individuals who are heterozygous for the phenylalanine hydroxylase gene are carriers of PKU. *True or False*

20.3.1 Dominant Genetic Disorder

5 minutes

Sometimes the defective **allele** which causes a genetic disease is **dominant** over the normal allele. This is rare for severe genetic diseases, because a dominant lethal trait cannot be propagated in the population. However, severe dominant genetic diseases can be inherited if symptoms of the disease appear only after reproduction has occurred. For example, **Huntington's disease** (also called **Huntington's chorea**) is a degenerative neurological disorder which strikes adults in their early 40's. It usually results in death by age 55. Since symptoms of Huntington's disease appear years after reproductive maturity, this dominant disease can be propagated in the population.

Quick Check Questions

1. Severe dominant genetic disorders occur _______ severe recessive genetic disorders.
   A. more frequently than
   B. less frequently than
   C. about as often as

2. Sometimes the defective allele causing a genetic disease is ________ over the normal allele.

20.3.2 Codominance

10 minutes

Most human genes do not have simple dominant and recessive **alleles**. Sometimes the two alleles have a mixed effect on the **phenotype** of a heterozygous individual, so neither allele can be considered dominant. For instance, an allele for dark hair R and an allele for light hair r can be paired to produce an individual who has medium colored hair Rr. This phenomenon is called incomplete dominance. When the alleles have an equal effect on phenotype, it is called **codominance**. Another example is **sickle-cell anemia**, a condition which causes severe **anemia** due to defective **hemoglobin** molecules.

Hemoglobin is the protein component of red blood cells which carries oxygen throughout the body. The molecule contains two alpha subunits and two beta subunits. The gene encoding the beta subunit has a normal A and a defective a allele. Sickle-cell anemia occurs in individuals who are homozygous for the defective allele (genotype: aa). All hemoglobin molecules in aa individuals are composed of two normal alpha subunits and two defective beta subunits. Unlike normal hemoglobin, defective hemoglobin molecules tend to stick together, causing the red blood cells to form sickle-shaped cells. Besides carrying oxygen poorly, these cells also get stuck in places where normal cells would easily pass (such as the small capillaries in the brain). These capillary blockages cause many of the problems associated with sickle-cell anemia.

As we expect, heterozygous individuals (genotype: Aa) are carriers of sickle-cell anemia. However, such individuals also have a condition called **sickle-cell trait**, which is due to incomplete dominance. Some of their hemoglobin molecules are normal, while some contain the defective beta subunit. The result is mild anemia. Interestingly, sickle-cell trait also confers some resistance to the parasite which causes malaria. The incidence of sickle-cell anemia and sickle-cell trait is highest in regions of the world where malaria is prevalent. Thus, this genetic disorder which is harmful to homozygous individuals may persist in the population because it confers a genetic advantage to heterozygotes who are exposed to malaria.

Quick Check Questions

1. Individuals who have sickle-cell trait are carriers of sickle-cell anemia. *True or False*

2. A man and a woman who both have sickle-cell trait can produce children with sickle-cell trait. *True or False*

3. A man and a woman who both have sickle-cell trait can produce children with sickle-cell anemia. *True or False*

4. Codominance causes the heterozygote to have an intermediate phenotype. *True or False*

20.3.3 Polygenic Inheritances

5 minutes

Many inherited traits are not controlled by one gene, but are influenced by the combined effects of many genes. Such traits are referred to as **polygenic** or multifactorial.

Polygenic traits include blood pressure, eye color, height, body build, and even susceptibility to cancer. These traits generally show gradual variation within a population. Discovering which genes are responsible for a polygenic disease is a difficult task. In addition, the particular expression of a polygenic trait is influenced by environmental factors. For example, skin color is a polygenic trait controlled by three separate genes. Each gene has two alleles. An offspring of one dark-skinned person (genotype AABBCC) and one light-skinned person (aabbcc) will have genotype AaBbCc and skin color between the two. The offspring of two intermediate genotypes can have any of 64 genotypes, and each will be expressed as a different phenotypic gradation. Furthermore, exposure to the sun is one obvious environmental factor which will influence the final phenotypic expression.

Quick Check Questions

1. Multiple genes can be responsible for the expression of a single trait. *True or False*

2. Traits determined by many genes are called _________.

20.4.1 Inheritance of Sex

10 minutes

The **sex chromosomes** are the pair of chromosomes which determine gender differentiation in the offspring. This pair can contain two different types of chromosome: the larger X and the smaller Y. The cells of a normal female have two X chromosomes, while normal males have one X and one Y. Recall that meiosis results in separation of the chromosome pairs. In the case of the sex chromosomes, each ovum produced by a female must contain an X chromosome, but meiosis in the male will produce one sperm cell containing an X and another with a Y.

When an egg and sperm fuse (fertilization), the sex chromosome combination which results determines the genetic sex of the zygote. This causes development of testes (in the presence of a Y chromosome) or ovaries (in its absence). Later in development, these gonads secrete either male or female hormones that influence further processes leading to sexual differentiation. A group of genes on the Y chromosome called the **SRY** (sex determining region of the Y chromosome) is responsible for initiating male development. Without the proteins produced by this gene, the offspring will develop into a female.

Many of the genes located on the sex chromosomes do not contribute directly to sexual characteristics. Instead, they determine **sex-linked traits**. Most sex-linked traits are associated with the X chromosome, which has many more genes than the Y. Thus, sex-linked traits are often called **X-linked traits**. Like autosomal traits, the alleles of X-linked traits may be either **dominant** or **recessive**: recessive is more common. The phenotypic expression of sex-linked traits is more often seen in male offspring than in female.

One example of an X-linked trait is red-green color blindness. The genes for the red and green retinal photopigments are located on the X chromosome. There are no corresponding genes on the Y chromosome. A deficiency in one of these genes results in an inability to distinguish between the colors. The deficient alleles (r) are recessive to the normal alleles (R), so the presence of a normal allele will prevent color blindness. Males are color-blind if they inherit the defective allele from a heterozygous (Rr) or homozygous recessive (rr) mother, since they have no gene on the Y chromosome which might dominate. A female can inherit this form of color blindness only if her father is color-blind (r,Y) and her mother is a carrier (Rr) or is color-blind (rr).

Quick Check Questions

1. Which parent contributes the X chromosome to a female off-spring?
   A. mother
   B. father
   C. both
   D. neither

2. The gene with a defective allele which causes red-green color blindness is located on chromosome 3. *True or False*

3. The son of a color-blind father and a phenotypically normal mother may inherit color blindness. *True or False*

4. Males contribute an X chromosome to their male offspring. *True or False*

10.4.2 Mutations

10 minutes

A **mutation** is any change which occurs in the genetic information of the cell (that is, in the DNA sequence). Most mutations are minor and have no observable phenotypic effect. Mutations occur spontaneously (for instance, by mistakes made during DNA replication), or are induced by exposure to mutagenic agents. Such **mutagens** include X-ray and UV radiation, some types of chemicals, alcohol, cigarette smoking, and certain viruses.

Mutations can cause genetic changes ranging from a simple base-pair substitution in a single gene to massive rearrangement of an entire chromosome. A mutation can be beneficial to an organism if it results in better adaptation to the environment. Such changes allow species to evolve. Other mutations result in harmful traits that inhibit survival of the organism. The only mutations which can be inherited (propagated in the population) are those which occur in the DNA of reproductive cells. Many such hereditary diseases arise from mutations in a single gene. These include cystic fibrosis, Huntington's chorea, sickle-cell anemia, PKU, and Tay-Sachs disease. Another type of genetic disorder results from gross chromosome abnormalities which occur during spermatogenesis and oogenesis. These will be described in the next tutorial.

The major non-hereditary disease to result from somatic cell mutations is **cancer**. Cancers are produced by the unregulated growth and division of abnormal cells which form masses called **tumors**. Tumors originate with a single normal cell which has been converted into a cancer cell by mutation. The mutation must affect genes involved in regulating cell reproduction. Defective enzymes are produced, and the normal chemical signals which regulate the cell's growth are no longer recognized.

Quick Check Questions

1. Some types of skin cancer are thought to be caused by mutations in skin cells caused by the sun. Skin cancer caused by UV damage can be inherited. *True or False*

2. Mutations in DNA may be caused by any of the following, EXCEPT:
   A. alcohol
   B. cigarette smoking
   C. sunlight
   D. artic-cold temperatures
   E. X-rays

3. All mutations result from exposure of DNA to a mutagenic agent in the environment. *True or False*

4. Sickle-cell anemia may have arisen in the population when a _______ occurred in an individual.

20.4.3 Nondisjunction

10 minutes

One class of hereditary diseases is based on chromosomal abnormalities, rather than alteration of the DNA sequence. These conditions result from "nondisjunction" of a chromosome pair during meiosis. Occasionally, a homologous pair fails to segregate (disjoin) at anaphase 1. Similarly, sister chromatids may not disjoin during anaphase 2. In either case, one gamete receives both copies of the chromosome, and another gamete does not receive a copy.

When fertilization occurs following nondisjunction, the zygote either contains three copies of the chromosome (called **trisomy**), or only one copy (**monosomy**). One common condition resulting from nondisjunction is **Down's syndrome**, also called **trisomy 21**. Affected individuals have a triplet of chromosomes 21. Down's syndrome is characterized by multiple traits including mild to severe mental retardation, a distinctive facial appearance, short hands and feet, congenital heart disease, and a life expectancy shorter than average.

Nondisjunction of the sex chromosomes can occur during the formation of egg or sperm cells. Subsequent fertilization results in genotypes such as XO (a single X chromosome), XXX, XYY, or XXY. (YO can also occur, but is a lethal trait). Such infants often exhibit normal phenotypes, and some people with abnormal sex chromosomes will continue to experience little noticeable effect. However, certain of these genotypes prevent (or do not initiate) development of normal reproductive organs. This condition may not be recognized until later in life, for instance when the person tries to conceive a child.

For example, **Turner's syndrome** is caused by an XO genotype. Women with Turner's syndrome are sterile due to failure of the reproductive organs to mature. They may also be shorter than average, exhibit cardiovascular defects, and experience premature aging. These symptoms can be reduced by hormone therapy. Similarly, **Klinefelter's syndrome** is seen in males with the genotype XXY. It is also characterized by sterility resulting from undeveloped testes. Other symptoms can include chronic pulmonary disease, enlarged breasts, and subnormal mental capabilities.

Nondisjunction is relatively rare, but it can occur with any chromosome. Trisomy 13 (Patau's syndrome) and trisomy 18 (Edward's syndrome), are seen sometimes. Both cause severe mental and physical abnormalities, with survival on the order of a few months. However, most occurrences of trisomy and monosomy are lethal, causing spontaneous abortion of the fetus early in development.

Quick Check Questions

1. Turner's syndrome results from an XO sex chromosome constitution. *True or False*

2. People with Down's syndrome have _____ chromosomes in each somatic cell.
   A. 45
   B. 46
   C. 47
   D. 48

3. Nondisjunction only occurs in the female. *True or False*

4. The XXY genotype can result from a nondisjunction in the mother or father. *True or False*

5. All of these are trisomy syndromes seen in humans, EXCEPT:
   A. trisomy 13
   B. trisomy 16
   C. trisomy 18
   D. trisomy 21

6. Like all genetic conditions, Down's syndrome can be passed down through many generations. *True or False*

20.4.4 Mitochondrial Inheritance

5 minutes

Mitochondria are the energy-producing organelles present in all cells of the body. Mitochondria contain their own DNA. About 13 genes code for a number of important enzymes. This DNA controls self-replication of the mitochondria, usually at times when a cell has greater need for ATP production, or when it is dividing.

All the mitochondria in the body are inherited from the mother. The ovum or egg cell contains the maternal gene complement as well as all the organelles and components that will be required for early development of the zygote. A sperm cell is compact and mobile, carrying only the paternal DNA and proteins for recognition and penetration of the egg. Its mitochondria are clustered on its tail, providing the energy required for swimming. Upon fertilization, when the nuclear materials fuse, the sperm's tail disintegrates, leaving the zygote with only maternal mitochondria.

Clinical Note:
Mutations in mitochondrial DNA can cause several degenerative muscle and nerve diseases. **Leber's hereditary optic neuropathy** is a condition where the optic nerve degenerates, causing progressive loss of sight and total blindness by age 30. Leber's disease is caused by a mutation in mitochondrial DNA, and therefore, must be inherited from the mother.

Quick Check Questions

1. Mitochondria contain their own ______, which codes for a number of important enzymes.

2. All of the following disease types could be inherited solely due to a maternal gene, EXCEPT:
   A. autosomal recessive
   B. autosomal dominant
   C. X-linked recessive
   D. X-linked dominant
   E. mitochondrial

20.5.1 Genetic Counseling

12 minutes

Genetic counseling may be recommended for couples with higher than average risk for producing children with genetic diseases. A professional can help determine the probability of a healthy offspring, and can guide parents through the decision of whether or not to conceive. Genetic counselors can also give advice on treatment and care of children born with genetic disorders. One tool of the genetic counselor is a chart called a **pedigree** that illustrates the genetic pattern of a disease among people who are related. The medical history of each family member is diagrammed. Accurate information over several generations is needed for a fully useful pedigree.

The pedigree can help predict whether a genetic disorder may appear in the next generation. It can also indicate whether any family members have a disease for which symptoms will arise later in life, such as **Huntington's chorea**.

The **Punnett square** is another tool used to predict the probability of genetic traits being passed along. The genotype of interest is indicated along the top for the mother's gametes, with the father's shown along the side. All possible outcomes of fertilization are then written in the squares of the grid. The frequency of each possibility determines its probability of occurrence. Let us say that a couple who both have sickle-cell trait want to know their chances of producing a child with sickle-cell anemia. The Punnett square indicates that a child of these two carriers will have a 25 percent chance of having sickle-cell anemia, a 50 percent chance of being a carrier, and a 25 percent chance of having normal hemoglobin.

After conception, the genetic constitution of the fetus can be determined by acquiring a sample of cells from the uterus and analyzing their DNA and key enzyme levels. A fetal karyotype can indicate any serious chromosomal abnormalities. Such testing is recommended when there is evidence for a specific risk factor. Samples can be collected by **amniocentesis**, in which a small amount of amniotic fluid containing fetal cells is drawn into a syringe through the uterine wall.

Amniocentesis is performed at around 18 weeks gestation. The procedure is not without risks. One in every 200-500 cases may result in major complications, such as infection or induction of premature labor. **Chorionic villus sampling** is a newer technique for obtaining prenatal samples. A few cells from the chorion (the membrane surrounding the fetus) are collected through the cervix. This type of testing can be done during the first trimester, around week 10, which is a safer time to terminate a pregnancy if that decision is made. However, the rate of complications is higher than for amniocentesis.

Quick Check Questions

1. The inheritance of sickle-cell anemia can be predicted by a karyotype.
   True or False

2. The probability of Down's syndrome can be determined using a pedigree.
   True or False

3. The inheritance of sickle-cell anemia can be predicted using a pedigree.
   True or False

4. Using a Punnett square, what is the probability of a PKU offspring from a carrier mother and an affected father?
   A. 25%
   B. 50%
   C. 75%
   D. 100%

5. Using a Punnett square, what is the probability of a child with Huntington's disease from a mother with the disease and an unaffected father?
   A. 25%
   B. 50%
   C. 75%
   D. 100%

20.5.2 Treating Genetic Diseases

8 minutes

Today, genetic diseases cannot be cured. Their symptoms can be corrected or reduced using drugs or hormones, or by supplying the missing gene product or removing a defective gene product. The ideal cure for a genetic disorder would be elimination of its cause by altering the defective gene in every cell of the body. This would require overcoming monumental technical problems. But efforts are underway to accomplish this goal through **gene therapy**.

In one technique called **gene replacement**, a normal gene would be inserted into the chromosome containing the defective gene. **Viruses** survive by inserting their genes into a host chromosome. By replacing the virulent genes with a human gene for the disorder, scientists could use the virus to introduce the normal gene into the body's cells. This therapy does not remove the defective gene from the genome, but if the normal gene behaved as expected, a cure might result.

A second type of therapy, called **gene augmentation**, has shown some promise in treatment of certain disorders of the blood cells. Cells which have been altered to contain the normal gene are injected into the patient's blood, bone marrow, or under the skin. It is hoped that production of protein from the normal gene will overcome the effects of the genetic disorder. However, gene augmentation does not alter existing chromosomes in the body.

The first trials of gene augmentation were done in 1990 on young children with adenosine deaminase deficiency. In this rare recessive genetic disorder, the adenosine deaminase gene, **ADA**, is completely defective. Children suffering from this deficiency have **severe combined immune deficiency (SCID)** and are highly susceptible to infection. (Remember the boy in the plastic bubble)? The therapy involved collection of white blood cells (WBCs) from the patients. These WBCs were infected with a virus carrying the normal ADA gene, then reproduced 1000-fold in culture and injected back into the patient. The cells were able to supply normal ADA to the body for some time, which reduced the immunity-inhibiting effects of SCID. The experiment was partially successful, but fresh WBCs carrying the normal ADA gene were periodically needed. Undoubtedly, further research will improve this therapy.

Quick Check Questions

1. Today, most genetic disorders are treated by gene augmentation therapy.
   True or False

2. A gene therapy in which the defective gene is removed and a normal gene inserted is called:
   A. gene therapy
   B. gene augmentation
   C. gene replacement
   D. all of the above
   E. none of the above

3. Insertion of a gene into a chromosome is done using a _______.